FIFTY
THINGS

YOU NEED TO KNOW ABOUT

WORLD
HISTORY

ALSO BY HUGH WILLIAMS

Fifty Things You Need to Know About British History

FIFTY THINGS

YOU NEED TO KNOW ABOUT

WORLD HISTORY

HUGH WILLIAMS

Collins

First published in 2010 by Collins
an imprint of HarperCollins*Publishers*
77–85 Fulham Palace Road
London W6 8JB

www.harpercollins.co.uk

13 12 11 10 09
9 8 7 6 5 4 3 2 1

Text © Hugh Williams 2010

Hugh Williams asserts his moral right to
be identified as the author of this work

A catalogue record for this book
is available from the British Library

ISBN: 978-0-00-732650-1

Printed and bound in Great Britain by
Clays Ltd, St Ives plc

Contents

PART 3 Religion

Acknowledgements

This book follows the pattern of its predecessor, *50 Things You Need To Know About British History*, and has been written in the main using secondary sources. Any mistakes or infelicities are entirely mine: so are all its opinions. I would like to thank Denise Bates, the editor at HarperCollins who had faith enough in my abilities to commission the book in the first place, and her successors, Hannah Macdonald, Helena Nicholls and Iain MacGregor, who nursed it through to completion. I would also like to thank Antony Topping, my agent at Greene and Heaton, for his continued support of my efforts and Lucy Herbert who helped me with research in the early stages.

I owe a special debt to Jane McMullen, who researched a great deal of this book, checked all of it and offered advice throughout. Her knowledge and understanding of the subject matter have been invaluable. Finally I would like to thank my wife, Sue, whose patience with, and support for, her husband have been, as always, a precious source of strength.

Introduction

The world in which we live is growing smaller, and shrinking. There is hardly a corner of it that has not at some time or another appeared on television in our homes. The activities of African, Asian and Middle Eastern politicians are often as familiar to us as those in our own country. The world is a bubble into which, thanks to the internet and other forms of mass communication, we peer at will. But where do we fit into the seething mass we see? What do we have in common with other people, places, cultures and ideas? What do they share with us?

One book cannot possibly answer all those questions but, with the help of history, it can provide a guide. History is one of the most important things that we possess: knowing about the past helps us manage the present and plan the future. And today we need a knowledge of history more than we have ever done before. Our world may be smaller but it is also more complex. We have become participants in even its most extreme activities. We watch the progress of wars on CNN or the BBC and, if we want, travel to its most dangerous places. I read a newspaper report recently about an elderly British pensioner who spends his time visiting Afghanistan, Iraq and North Pakistan. 'You don't think about roadside bombs, or being kidnapped,' he said. 'You know it happens, but you're just too busy taking it all in.' Exactly what he was taking in, the newspaper did not go on to say – presumably it was the experience of being there, of doing something unusual and rather dangerous. While we might admire the pluck and energy of someone taking his holidays in war zones, the fact that it happens at all is rather mystifying and confusing. Man was once an explorer: now he is just a tourist.

These extraordinary developments have helped create a world that is easy to see but difficult to understand. Discussions about world problems and their possible solutions are commonplace. People of influence think globally, in politics and economics, the environment and entertainment. At the same time we sometimes feel that our national identity is slipping away from us to be replaced by forces that are unfamiliar and uncertain. We would probably quite like to become citizens of the world, if only we knew what that meant. How should we balance national interests against global requirements? Where does our country end and the world begin?

The upheavals that surround us become inexplicable unless we can put them into some sort of context. That is one of the uses of history: to create a shape that helps make sense of the confusion in which we live. In 1919, H. G. Wells published *The Outline of History* in which he used his skill as a novelist to trace the history of mankind from prehistoric times to the present day. It was hugely popular. 'The need for a common knowledge of the general facts of human history throughout the world,' he wrote in the Introduction to a later edition, 'has become very evident during the tragic happenings of the last few years.' He might well have written exactly the same sentence were he to publish his book today. The world moves on and its glories and disasters move with it. We will always need help in understanding its history.

But, people will say, the history of the world is so big and so long that to take fifty things from it is impossible. It cannot be reduced to such a formula without becoming ridiculously over-simplified. That is always a danger. In history it is always easier to complicate than simplify. The fifty things described in this book are not the only fifty things you need to know about world history, to make that claim would be absurd, but they are fifty very important things each of which provides a vantage point from which to survey large historical trends. Some of them are huge, others comparatively small. Each is unique and made an important contribution to the way in which world civilisations changed and grew. Taken together they provide a structure, a framework, on which to hang the great events of history.

There is another obvious and fundamental question relating to the selection of events from world history. Where do you begin? And once you have decided on your starting place, where do you end? I am writing this in a house on the East Devon coast in Britain, which is now a World Heritage Site because its cliffs and rocks are millions of years old. Today this beautiful part of the country has a temperamental climate – wind, rain and sun in almost equal measure. Once, however, it was almost tropical and dinosaurs, whose fossilised footprints can still be found along its beaches, plodded around in burning heat. I used to spend a lot of holidays in the Dordogne area of south-west France where, in the caves around Les Eyzies, some of the earliest signs of primitive man were discovered in the latter half of the nineteenth century. As I paddled with my children down the gentle summer waters of one of France's grandest rivers I could look up to the caves and hollows where Cro-Magnon once lived. He hunted with primitive spears and drew crude pictures of the world around him on the walls of his subterranean home. In September 1940, a few months after their country had fallen to German occupation in the Second World War, four teenagers stumbled on the wall paintings in the Lascaux Cave near Montignac, vivid pictures of horses, bulls and stags drawn by people who lived in the area 15,000 years ago.

Examples of 'pre-history', excitingly close to our everyday lives, are important in establishing how the world as a whole began to evolve. But in terms of explaining how mankind organised itself to create the world we recognise today, our starting point should be much later, at a time when man was beginning to organise himself into some sort of social structure, building places to live in rather than simply using the natural resources around him, and communicating in a language that was capable of being written down. This brings us forward to a time nearly 6,000 years ago, to the civilisation that existed in the Middle East in an area that today makes up Iraq and parts of Syria and Turkey.

The finishing point is more arbitrary. We can define a beginning, but we cannot predict the end. I can remember my wife, a journalist and broadcaster, asking me once what I thought she might say to a group of sixth-formers that she had been asked to address. The head teacher wanted her to come up with something that her pupils would find valuable and remember in later life. This was more than twenty years ago. The Berlin Wall had been torn down and we all felt optimistic and confident about the future. I suggested that she talk to them about a world that might at last be changing into a place of peace and prosperity. How wrong I was. Today world peace seems as distant as it ever was. As for prosperity, that too seems to have taken a battering thanks to the ceaseless turbulence in the financial markets. At the moment conflict and debt are the world's stopping points, and it is with these that this history will end.

Though this book looks at events about 6,000 years ago, much of it is concerned with the events of the past few hundred years. That is a sobering thought. Mankind seems to have accelerated the pace of change as he has grown older. We know from our own lives how rapidly things develop from one generation to another. For most of us today, life without email would be unthinkable. It is actually quite difficult to buy a flight ticket unless you have a computer. But these inventions did not exist in any form whatsoever until I was a grown man, and are completely beyond the grasp of many people in the generation before mine. In the history of the world such rapid transformations are unusual. I would speculate that someone from 1700 would not have been as bewildered had he found himself living in 1800 as a person from 1900 transported to the year 2000. But just because transforming change seems to pick up speed with time, we should not make the mistake of putting more emphasis on events that have taken place more recently in any particular cycle. That would simply unbalance the narrative of the world's historical development.

The other factor to take into account is the role of European civilisation. European people have been remarkably successful in spreading their practices and ideas around the world ever since mankind formed himself into discernible social groups. Their civilisation has tended to triumph where others have been lost. But the history of the world is not the history of Europe. It did not begin that way and, who knows, may not end that way either.

Throughout his life on earth, man has been driven by certain principal aspirations and I have taken some of these as the five themes of this book:

The first engine of man's development has revolved around Wealth – the story of his ambition to be rich, and to buy and sell and make money through barter and exchange. This section is mainly about man as a trader and entrepreneur.

The second theme is Freedom – the story of the explosive ideas and inspiring people that have led man on his journey to become master of his individual fate, and to be free. This part of the book is about rebellion and revolution and the bravery of those who spoke or acted against oppression.

The third of man's aspirations has been for Religion – the story of his continuing hope that his life has more lasting value than the one he spends on earth. This theme is used to describe the spread of the world's religions and their heritage.

The fourth part of the book is about Conquest – the story of man's appetite for expansion and territorial gain. This is all about the rise and fall of great empires, from the ancient world to the present day.

The fifth aspiration is Discovery – the story of man's hunger to find and invent new things in the world around him in science and the arts. Here, some of the great inventions that have changed the nature of the world sit side by side with the achievements in exploration that improved our knowledge and understanding of it.

Inevitably there are times when these themes overlap, as the paths through our past crisscross one another. Religion was sometimes man's motive for conquest; conquest was often carried out in search of wealth and so on. The Spanish conquest of South America in the sixteenth century is a good example. The conquistadors were motivated by both religious conviction and a desire for riches and their story might have been included in more than one place.

A good history book should be a companion as well as a teacher. It should help people understand as well as simply learn. From understanding comes confidence and hope, two feelings that sometimes seem in rather short supply in the world today. So if history can help us understand perhaps it can also help to inspire. And why not? After all, the world is ours: we owe it to ourselves to enjoy it.

1 Wealth

Introduction

Most of the children described in Hilaire Belloc's *Cautionary Verses* come to a sticky end. Matilda, who lies, is burned to death; Henry King, who chews string, dies from knots in his stomach; and Godolphin Horne, who is excruciatingly superior, becomes a bootblack at the Savoy. Only one child is saved from misfortune – the obsequiously good, horribly nice Charles Augustus Fortescue.

> *In eating Bread he made no Crumbs,*
> *He was extremely fond of sums,*
>
> *To which, however, he preferred*
> *The Parsing of a Latin Word –*

Such assiduous, good behaviour brings its just reward:

> *He rose at once in his Career,*
> *And long before his Fortieth Year*
>
> *Had wedded Fifi, Only Child*
> *Of Bunyan, First Lord Aberfylde.*
> *He thus became immensely Rich,*
> *And built the Splendid Mansion which*
>
> *Is called 'The Cedars, Muswell Hill'.*
> *Where he resides in Affluence still,*
> *To show what Everybody might*
> *Become by SIMPLY DOING RIGHT.*

The gentle satire of Belloc's comic verse, written at the very beginning of the twentieth century, has some relevance to life in Britain today. Men like Charles Augustus Fortescue still exist, their apparently effortless success a source of bewilderment and envy. How did they do it? Why have they been blessed with so much money? The way in which people set about acquiring wealth, and how they use it once they have got it, has preoccupied mankind for centuries.

Most human beings want to be richer than they are. In the English language there is a difference of meaning, or at least of usage, in the words 'wealth' and 'riches'. Wealth implies a sense of prosperity shared for the common good. Adam Smith's *The Wealth of Nations*, published in 1776, the same year as the American Declaration of Independence, has come to be seen as the great rational defence of capitalism, just as the United States has become its most controversial exponent. In this context 'wealth' means the collective output of a free market whose different functions reinforce one another to the benefit of all. We tend to use the word 'riches' rather differently. Riches can be envied as much as enjoyed. To be rich you need to have done better, or been luckier, than your fellow men. It denotes individual good fortune rather than social wellbeing. Man works to be wealthy, but gambles to be rich.

The fact remains, however, that a society cannot be wealthy unless at least some of its members are rich. And wealth cannot be created unless individuals are motivated to acquire riches. How people become rich – in other words, whether or not they can be said to have earned their wealth – lies at the heart of our attitude towards this whole subject. As I write, Britain is engulfed in a scandal about MPs' expenses. Many of them have been exposed for making extravagant and dishonest claims for the maintenance of their second homes. People are angry because they believe those they elected to be the guardians of the nation's money have behaved like cheats, trying to become richer without earning the privilege. Unearned wealth is not to be tolerated.

But what do we mean by 'unearned' wealth? Less than a hundred years after Adam Smith explained the advantages of a free market, Karl Marx described its dangers. Where Smith saw benevolent prosperity, Marx found exploitation and inequality. The huge process of industrialisation, which was beginning to rumble into action when *The Wealth of Nations* was published, had, in Marx's view, resulted in social and economic divisions that could only end in tension and conflict. How man has coped with wealth and defined both its benefits and drawbacks is an essential part of world history.

This chapter is about man's acquisition, and sometimes loss, of wealth and its consequences. It begins with the building of the Via Egnatia that carried the traffic of the Romans across the Balkans from the Adriatic to Constantinople. The Roman road system supported the wealth of the greatest of the empires in world history, helping to maintain a centralised grip on the huge territory it controlled. The chapter then explores the city of Chang'an in China, the first great city of the world – richer and larger than anything Europe would see for hundreds of years afterwards. Marco Polo and his family risked their lives in search of wealth, travelling from Venice to China towards the end of the thirteenth century. But in the middle of the fourteenth century the wealth that Europe had begun to enjoy from its expanding trade was nearly destroyed by the arrival of the Black Death. At the beginning of the seventeenth century the foundation of the Dutch East India Company demonstrated how easily merchants could become princes, and how money could rule the world. The invention of the Flying Shuttle in the early eighteenth century was a simple improvement to the business of weaving that, though small in itself, was the first step along a process of industrialisation that led to the biggest revolution in wealth-creation the world had ever seen. The discovery of oil in America accelerated that process and made some individuals fabulously rich. After the First World War, a failure to understand the economic interests of different countries lay at the heart of the Treaty of Versailles which, in trying to put Europe back together again, only succeeded in preparing it for another terrible war. Meanwhile the invention of the Model T Ford ushered in an age of consumerism: many more people could now at least feel rich if they wanted to. Finally, in our own time, the Credit Crunch brought to an end a period of continuous wealth expansion as people discovered that good times are never forever. From the tramp of Roman legions across the packed sand of a Balkan highway to the hideous devastation of the plague and the calculated ruthlessness of sober Amsterdam businessmen, from the belching ferocity of the Industrial Revolution to the economic failures of the Treaty of Versailles and the remorseless spread of the motor car, the history of mankind is a history of trying to get rich and stay rich.

CHAPTER 1

The Building of the Via Egnatia

146 BC

The Via Egnatia was a Roman road that stretched from the Albanian port of Durres on the Adriatic coast to Istanbul. It carried commercial and military traffic across the Balkans and through Greece and Turkey, sustaining the wealth of a great empire.

For nearly a thousand years, the Romans ruled an empire the like of which the world had never seen before, and has not seen since. Their rise to power began at the beginning of the fifth century BC when, as a republic, they elected their first ruling consuls. It ended with the sack of Rome, by then just another city in only half the empire, by the Goths in 410 AD. At its height, after the conquest of Britain in the first century AD, the empire covered all of North Africa, the Middle East, Asia Minor, the Balkans and most of Western Europe including Spain, France, the German lands and Italy. But its size, though vast, was not the most impressive thing about it. Its extraordinary achievement – one that has never been equalled in the history of the world – was the degree of organisation and control that it brought and then maintained to the disparate territories under its authority. When St Paul, a converted Jew from the town of Tarsus in Anatolia (in what is now eastern Turkey), fell foul of the law for his preaching about Christianity, he could claim that he was a Roman citizen – 'civis Romanus sum' – and therefore be sent to Rome for trial. Whether patrolling the bleak landscape on the border between occupied Britain and Pictish Scotland, or marching through the desert in the conquered provinces of North Africa, a Roman lived under the same laws and was entitled to the same treatment.

Legal and administrative systems were not the only things that bound together the peoples whom the Romans ruled. They were also connected by a great road network that ran throughout the empire. Aristides of Smyrna, an orator living in the second century AD, enjoyed flattering his Roman masters by proclaiming: 'You have merged all nations into one family.' He went on: 'You have measured the earth, bridged the rivers and made roads through the mountains.' For a man like Aristides, an educated Greek who travelled all over the empire, roads were one of the most obvious manifestations of Roman power and wealth. Journeys across huge territories were comparatively easy and helped to create a secure, prosperous environment.

The Roman Empire's extraordinary achievement was the degree of control it brought to territories under its authority.

The Roman road system began with the Via Appia which was built in the fourth century BC, when Rome was still a republic. It was named, as were most roads, after the official who ordered its construction and, by the middle of the second century BC, had reached what is now the port of Brindisi on Italy's Adriatic coast. At this point in time Roman expansion was confined to land within the Italian peninsula, although the republic subsequently grew into an international power following the defeat of the Greek king, Pyrrhus, whose armies invaded southern Italy in 280 BC. In the years that followed, the Romans pushed out beyond the boundaries of Italy itself, conquering all of Greece, the Balkans and North Africa. With these victories came the need for new roads.

The Via Egnatia picked up on the other side of the Adriatic from where the Via Appia ended. Starting on the Albanian coast it followed the line of the River Shkumbin and went over the mountains of Candava towards Lake Ohrid. It then dropped south, going through several mountain passes until it reached the Aegean Sea at Thessalonica in Greece. From there it went through the port of Kavala, today the second largest city in northern Greece, crossed into Turkey at Ipsala before travelling the last 160 miles into Istanbul, then called Byzantium and later Constantinople. It was a great Balkan highway 700 miles long, designed when it was built to help bring control to Rome's new conquests across the sea from its eastern shore, but eventually becoming the essential link between its western and eastern capitals. It was about twenty feet wide and paved with big stone slabs or packed hard sand. From the time when the Romans first gained power over the peoples of the Balkans and Asia Minor, to the moment, 500 years later, when their empire began to collapse, the Via Egnatia was one of the principal methods by which control was maintained and wealth distributed throughout this huge region.

The Roman road network not only carried troops and supplies but imperial messengers as well. The centre of the empire kept in touch with its provinces through the *cursus publicus*, the postal system, which could travel at very high speeds thanks to the frequent resting places where riders could change horses or repair their vehicles. The poet Ovid, who lived in Rome for about sixty years just after the assassination of Julius Caesar in 44 BC, said he received a letter from Brindisi in nine days – presuming that the post did not travel at night, an impressive average speed of thirty-six and a half miles per day. At the end of the eighteenth century, before mail coaches were introduced into Britain, the post from London to Bath could take nearly forty hours or more to reach its destination. Even with an improved road system a coach and horses could only manage an average speed of ten miles an hour by the time Queen Victoria came to the throne in 1837.

The Roman world was immensely rich in resources. Tin from Britain, silver from Spain, wheat from North Africa, and fruit from the Middle East, all found their way into Roman homes. Craftsmen who made clothes out of silk imported from China or glass objects created from the high-quality sand of the eastern Mediterranean could find markets for their goods in places far away from where they worked. Trade moved easily between one place and the next – and sometimes the merchants went with it, moving their places of business from one city, or one region, to another. A Roman altar discovered in Bordeaux in 1921 was found to contain an inscription from a wealthy merchant with positions in the cities of both York and Lincoln who thanked the 'protecting goddess of Bordeaux' for allowing him to complete his journey to her city. He might have been a trader selling French wine to the Roman legions stationed in Britain: the Romans were as familiar as we are with the free movement of goods across provincial boundaries. Today in Britain, we have grown used to enjoying the fruits of the world, but the generation that lived during and immediately after the Second World War did not drink much wine and rarely ate exotic fruits or other food from Europe and beyond. Now these things are part of the nation's everyday diet: we have become used to peace and plenty. In this we are not unlike the people who lived in the Roman Empire as it reached the height of its power. Its extraordinary cohesion was reinforced by language and law and oiled by the benefits of trade. The Roman road – straight, ruthless and capable of cutting through any obstacle in its path – was the physical embodiment of the empire's wealth and success.

The Via Egnatia survived the collapse of the Roman Empire in the West to remain an important highway for centuries afterwards. Inevitably it fell into disrepair. It is remarkable how the great buildings of Rome were allowed to decay: succeeding generations preferred to destroy or ignore what had been built, rather than make use of their remarkable architectural inheritance. The Romans were enthusiastic builders. Great cities as far apart as York, Lyon or Carthage (today part of Tunis), became the provincial capitals of the empire, each demonstrating the Roman taste for fortification and domestic architecture. The same types of buildings were reproduced everywhere, a coherent manifestation of the imperial presence. We can still see ruined examples of them all over Europe, beautifully constructed aqueducts, gates, theatres and villas that remind us of the extent of Roman power. The modern world has been brought up to believe in the concept of the nation state. We tend to talk about architectural style in terms of its country of origin – French, German, English and so on. When the Romans were the rulers of Europe it was not like that at all. Whoever you were, Berber, Celt or Slav, you were the citizen of a Roman province and subject to the tastes and disciplines of your Roman masters. Perhaps it was this that ensured their eventual destruction. Their beauty and usefulness was not enough to assuage the brutal forces of revenge. The historian Procopius, writing during the reign of the Byzantine Emperor Justinian in the sixth century AD, reported that: 'The barbarians ... destroyed all the cities which they captured so completely that nothing has been left to my time to know them by – unless it might be one tower or one gate or some such thing that chanced to remain.' The glories of Rome were extinguished with remarkable speed.

It was Justinian who undertook repairs to the Via Egnatia. He had ambitions to restore the power of the old empire and, with his general Belisarius, succeeded in briefly recapturing Rome itself. His was a remarkable period of power. He was from peasant stock and his wife, Theodora, one of history's more colourful consorts, was described famously in *The History of the Decline and Fall of the Roman Empire* by Edward Gibbon as: 'The prostitute who, in the presence of innumerable spectators, had polluted the theatre of Constantinople was adored as a Queen in the same city, by grave magistrates, orthodox bishops, victorious generals, and captive monarchs.' In the end, Justinian's legacy was not a new Roman empire, but a codification of Roman law that set out the basis for civil law still in use in many places today. He also rebuilt Constantinople, which he hoped to restore to the glory it had enjoyed under its founder, the Emperor Constantine, 200 years earlier. Beyond this, however, the architecture of ancient Rome continued to decay.

The Via Egnatia was the physical embodiment of the empire's wealth and success.

Despite the collapse of its infrastructure, the route of the Via Egnatia maintained its importance. At the end of the eleventh century, in 1081, the Byzantine Empire nearly collapsed after Norman invaders, having conquered southern Italy and Sicily, landed at Durres intent on breaking into Byzantium through its western gateway. The Emperor gathered an army and came down the Via Egnatia to confront the Normans who appeared to

Timeline of Roman History

c.753 BC	Foundation of Rome according to the legend of Romulus and Remus: a series of hill-top settlements established near the Tiber become the city of Rome.
616–510 BC	REGAL PERIOD: Rome ruled by the Etruscans, who dominated northern city-states. Tarquinius Priscinus was the first King of Rome.
510 BC	Expulsion of the last Etruscan King, 'Tarquin the Proud', from Rome.
510–31 BC	REPUBLICAN PERIOD.
451 BC	Rome ruled by a council of ten citizens chosen from the Senate. *Duodecim Tabulae*, the Twelve Tables, is the earliest code of Roman law outlining patrician and plebeian rights.
340–338 BC	Final Latin War, fought by Latin league. Rome emerged victorious with control of the Latium region.
264–241 BC	First Punic War against the Carthaginians. Sicily became Rome's first overseas province.
218–202 BC	Second Punic War; Scipio Africanus 'the Roman Hannibal' defeated Hannibal who had invaded Italy. He reintroduced 'decimation' – the killing of every tenth soldier – to enforce discipline.
214–148 BC	First, Second, Third and Fourth Macedonian Wars.
174 BC	Building of the Circus Maximus, the venue for lavish games.
149 BC	Publication of Marcus Porcius Cato's *Origines*, the first prose history to be written in Latin.
149–146 BC	Third Punic War. Carthage was destroyed and Rome emerged as the dominant Mediterranean power.
73–71 BC	Revolt of Spartacus.
60 BC	First Triumvirate: Julius Caesar, Pompeius Magnus and Licinius Crassus.
55 BC	Julius Caesar's first expeditions to Britain.
49–30 BC	Nineteen years of civil war and division lead to the destruction of the Republic.

44 BC	Caesar declared dictator for life and assassinated. '*Kai su, o teknon?*' (translated as 'Even you lad?') are the famous final words Caesar is supposed to have spoken to his assassin Brutus.
30 BC	Antony and Cleopatra committed suicide after their defeat by Octavian at the Battle of Actium.
27 BC	Beginning of the Roman Empire. Octavian was given the title of Augustus, First Emperor of Rome; a period of peace and stability followed. Literary figures such as Virgil, Horace, Ovid and the historian Livy, rose to prominence.
41–54 AD	Reign of Emperor Claudius; parts of Britain were conquered.
60–61 AD	Revolt of Boudicca, Queen of Iceni.
64 AD	Fire of Rome; first persecution of Christians.
98–117 AD	Reign of Emperor Trajan, marking the Empire's high point of territorial expansion and Roman prosperity.
117–138 AD	Reign of Emperor Hadrian. Building of seventy-three-mile long defensive 'Hadrian's Wall' in Britain.
212 AD	Citizenship granted to all free inhabitants of the Roman Empire.
235–284 AD	Empire weakened by a series of crises brought about by weak Emperors, religious conflict and barbarian invasion.
293 AD	Tetrarchy established. Empire divided into Eastern and Western halves. Milan replaced Rome as capital of the Western Empire.
313 AD	Constantine, the first Christian Roman Emperor, issued the Edict of Milan granting religious toleration throughout the Empire.
324 AD	Constantine became sole Emperor and Constantinople the Empire's new capital city; St Sophia became its first church in 360 AD.
325 AD	First Council of Nicaea. The first assembly of the Christian Church to define Christian doctrine.
410 AD	Rome sacked by Alaric and the Visigoths.

be isolated and disheartened after their invasion fleet had been defeated by the Empire's allies, the Venetians. But the Norman commander, Robert Guiscard, was a resourceful and brilliant soldier. Displaying the same sort military bravado that had seen the island of Britain fall to Norman control at Hastings less than twenty years earlier, he routed the imperial army. Its defeat did not bring about the fall of the Byzantine Empire, but the Via Egnatia had now become a much more open road than before. Overland trade between Constantinople and the rest of the Byzantine Empire had always travelled along it. Following the battle of Durres, or Durrazzo to give it its Italian name, it also became the chosen route for the armies of the Crusades as they made their way out of Europe into Asia Minor. The first Crusade was launched fifteen years after the battle, in 1095.

The Roman road was straight, ruthless and capable of cutting through any obstacle in its path.

The Via Egnatia retains its allure as a symbol of prosperity and hope even today. The Via Egnatia Foundation was set up recently with the mission 'to inspire this old road with new life' and to stimulate cultural and economic interest in the region by bringing together the different communities through which the road passes. The road, that was once used by 'by soldiers and later by crusaders, preachers, bandits, merchants and peasant caravans loaded with skins, wines, wood and sulphur', served 'economic and social functions for more than two millennia'.

So this great road is still with us. In the middle of the busy Greek city of Thessalonica the ruined Arch of Galerius, built at the end of the third century AD, stands across its route. Surrounded by cars, shops and the rest of the paraphernalia of modern city life it is a permanent reminder of an ancient empire and one of the great highways that carried its wealth.

CHAPTER 2

The City of Chang'an

750 AD

In the middle of the seventh century AD, the largest city in the world was Chang'an on the Guanzhong Plain in central China. Standing at the end of the Silk Route that brought traders from all over Asia, it was rich, civilised, and home to a population of about a million people.

China has the oldest surviving civilisation in the world. Its modern population can trace its ancestry back to the Shang dynasty that ruled from about 1700 BC. An earlier dynasty, the Xia, seems to have existed from about 1900 BC, but evidence of its activities remains slight. There were other civilisations living in other parts of the world before this date but they have since died out. China has enjoyed a continuous development, growing from a fragmented rural culture into a great, united world power.

In the West, our knowledge of this process has been remarkably limited, not least because China has often preferred to shield itself from foreign intrusion and investigation. Until the early part of the nineteenth century it was, to most Western eyes, an enormous secret world, whose wealth and attainments were glimpsed only sporadically. In the seventeenth and eighteenth centuries, imports of Chinese ceramics as a by-product of the tea trade promoted a fad for 'chinoiserie' as Western artists imitated what they believed to be Chinese styles in art and design. In 1793 a British diplomat, Earl Macartney, paid a visit to the Chinese Emperor on behalf of George III to try to win concessions for British trade in Chinese ports. Having agonised over the protocol of how to kneel in front of the imperial presence – his lordship would not 'kowtow' and prostrate himself, but agreed to go down on one knee as he would before his own king – Macartney presented a list of requests. But the Chinese were not interested. 'I set no value on objects strange and ingenious and have no use for your country's manufactures,' was the Emperor's haughty response. 'Our Celestial Empire possesses all things in prolific abundance ... there is no need to import the manufactures of outside barbarians in exchange for our own produce.' The British came home empty-handed.

The Emperor who dismissed the British expedition with such disdain was Qianlong. He was a member of the Manchu or Qing dynasty that ruled China from the middle of the seventeenth century until the end of imperial rule in 1911. China was first united under a dynasty that existed nearly 2,000 years earlier, the Qin (pronounced 'Chin') from whom the name 'China' originally derives. The last emperor in this line went to his grave in 210 BC surrounded by the famous terracotta army, one of the world's most exciting archaeological finds of the twentieth century. Although the Qin emperors only held power for fifteen years, the unification of the country under one government was an enormous, if bloody and ruthless, achievement. China did not enjoy the same measure of centralisation again until the second century AD, when first the Sui and then the Tang dynasties came to power. The Sui used the same repressive techniques as the Qin to gain control of all China's lands. When they fell, their successors, the Tang, ruled for nearly 300 years, ushering in a period of growth and civilised development. It was during this period, from the beginning of the sixth century to the start of the ninth century AD, that the city of Chang'an became the greatest in the world.

From the fall of the Roman Empire to the beginning of the Renaissance, the centre of the world lay in the East.

The history of mankind from the Middle Ages to the present day has been in the main the history of a European civilisation. But before then, in the time between the fall of the Roman Empire to the beginnings of the Renaissance, the centre of the world lay in the East. When the city of Rome was at its height its population stood at around a million people. By 800 AD, when Chang'an was thriving, it had been reduced to no more than 50,000. The biggest city in Europe at this time was Córdoba in southern Spain, with a population of something in excess of 150,000. It was not really 'European' at all, but the capital of an Arab dominion, a caliphate that controlled most of the lower part of the Iberian peninsula. That part of Europe had fallen to a foreign power as the Moors, inspired by the world's newest religion of Islam, pushed out from their original homelands in North Africa. Other European cities were tiny by comparison. London probably had a population of no more than 10,000.

Chang'an was a teeming, cosmopolitan city. High walls protected the inhabitants and no one except imperial messengers could enter or leave during the night when the city gates were locked and a strict curfew was enforced. The town was constructed on a grid with broad roads running either north to south or east to west. Speed restrictions applied to coachmen and riders on horseback. There were five canals that carried merchandise all over the town and delivered water to its parks and fed the lakes in the gardens of the nobility. Within this framework, Chang'an was divided into sections, each with its own walled boundary and housing its own complement of homes, offices, temples and workshops. The curfew applied here too: once its drumbeat sounded at the end of the day, the gates dividing the different areas were closed and movement between them was forbidden. A night patrol called the Gold Bird Guard enforced the law, capturing and beating those who disobeyed. There was a government office, a walled compound from which the Emperor's representative read imperial decrees to the city's seniors who stood before him in carefully designated ranks. There were many monasteries – fabulously wealthy places endowed by rich aristocrats or the Emperor himself – whose splendid pagodas dominated the

It was a teeming, cosmopolitan city.

city skyline. The pagoda was a form of architecture developed by the Chinese from an Indian design. Today the Giant Wild Goose Pagoda and the Small Wild Goose Pagoda – one 210 feet high, the other 141 feet – still stand in the modern Chinese city, renamed

X'ian ('Western Peace'), memorials to an age 1,300 years ago when the landscape they survey was the most prosperous in the world. The ancient city had beautiful parks, generally off limits to ordinary citizens, but places where the rich and well connected could go to enjoy the countryside or feast in tents that protected them from the spring rain. It also boasted a 'red-light district' where madams offered girls as young as eleven or twelve to their customers and courtesans entertained members of the imperial court and well-heeled merchants.

The wealth of the city was based on its markets. Chang'an had two, both of which were strictly controlled by a government agency that registered merchants, inspected the currency for counterfeit coins and imposed regulations relating to weights and measures. Some sold goods imported from all over the world – precious stones, silks and sacred relics. Others had more everyday produce on sale such as meat, vegetables, fish and herbs.

It became the greatest city in the world.

There were restaurants where customers could enjoy pastries and other delicacies and moneylenders were available to advance cash to those who needed it. There was also a primitive banking system. For a fee, certain traders would take charge of citizens' valuables giving them pieces of paper as proof of their deposits. The owners could then use these as a method of financing other purchases, in effect using a sort of paper currency. Many of the traders came from Central Asia – from the lands that now encompass countries such as Kazakhstan and Uzbekistan – and from Persia. It is also probable that the city had a number of night markets, today a normal feature of life in many large Asian cities, even though the authorities, who liked to impose restrictions on the movement of city dwellers after dark, disapproved of them. The Han dynasty poet Ban Gu described the busy scene as follows:

> *In the nine markets they set up bazaars,*
> *Their wares separated by type, their shop rows*
>   *distinctly divided.*
> *There was no room for people to turn their heads,*

Or for chariots to wheel about.
People crammed into the city, spilled into the
  suburbs,
Everywhere streaming into the hundreds of shops.

The blossoming of Chang'an coincided with another important feature in Chinese history – a shift of population from north to south. China's geography is dominated by its two great rivers: the Yellow River in the north and the Yangzi in the south. The Yellow River is prone to disastrous flooding and could wash

Merchants sold precious stones, silks and sacred relics.

away agricultural farmland devastating the livelihoods of peasants farming in the region. The area around the Yangzi is much drier and naturally less suitable for growing staple crops such as rice. But by the time of the Tang dynasty the techniques for irrigating paddy fields had become established (the Chinese imported them from Southeast Asia) and the population began to drift southwards. Today the majority of the country still lives in its southern part. In this way the nature of Chinese society for hundreds of years to come began to take shape, an enormous peasant population controlled as tightly as possible by a highly efficient and cultured bureaucracy.

Inevitably it sometimes broke down. The dynasties that ruled this great land did not succeed one another effortlessly, and the country succumbed to rebellion and disruption on many occasions. But it always grew, a growth that seemed to take it more into itself as it became stronger and bigger. Bureaucracy tends to dislike change – its very purpose is to preserve continuity – and this dependence on maintaining the status quo became typical of the way China chose to govern itself. Traders and travellers still managed to penetrate its heart, but their journeys were long and dangerous and the traffic always went in one direction. As Earl Macartney found to his cost a thousand years after the boom years of Chang'an, the Chinese did not feel the need to look much beyond their own immediate frontiers. No wonder he chose to describe the country as an 'old, crazy first-rate Man of War', over-awing its neighbours merely by its 'bulk and appearance'.

The name Chang'an means 'long-lasting peace'. No doubt the Turks, Persians and Arabs who thronged its bazaars, ate in its restaurants and visited its brothels, thought that this pulsating hub of commerce would last forever. By the start of the ninth century, however, the great city was no more. The last Tang emperor was deposed by a warlord who moved his capital (physically – by dismantling many of the wooden buildings and floating them on barges down the river), to Luoyang 250 miles away. The dynasty that later came to power, the Sung, lost control of the Silk Route and turned to maritime expeditions for commercial gain.

It is extraordinary to think that when George Macartney visited China at the end of the eighteenth century, London, the stinking city and burgeoning hub of a great world empire, home to his king, George III, was still not as big, and perhaps not as well ordered, as the ancient city of Chang'an. China had shut its doors by then. Foreigners could no longer enjoy places like the great cosmopolitan crossroads where the Tang poet Lu Zhaolin had once described the progress of an imperial procession: 'Chang'an's broad avenues link up with narrow lanes, where one sees black oxen and white horses, coaches made of seven fragrant woods … the dragon biting the jewelled canopy catches the morning sun, the phoenix disgorging dangling fringes is draped with evening clouds.'

As Chang'an died, so China's wealth became all its own. In the centuries that followed, the empires of the west – Portuguese, Spanish, French, Dutch and British – would grow rich from unashamed mercantilism. But China stayed behind its chosen boundaries, secure in its own customs and traditions, a parallel place of riches protected from the prying activities of the world beyond.

CHAPTER 3

The Travels of Marco Polo

1271–95

At the age of seventeen, Marco Polo left Venice with his father and uncle and travelled along the Silk Route to China. He did not return for seventeen years. His account of his experiences became one of the most influential books published in Europe during the Middle Ages.

The poet James Elroy Flecker had a very English vision of the Orient. He did not like the East very much, even though he served as a diplomat in both Constantinople and Beirut. He preferred his own country and the manners and habits of the Edwardian age in which he lived. But when he died, at the age of thirty from tuberculosis, he left behind some of the most beautiful verses ever written about the world beyond the Eastern Mediterranean and the ancient silk routes that took traders on their long and dangerous journeys:

> What shall we tell you? Tales, marvellous tales
> Of ships and stars and isles where good men rest,
> Where never more the rose of sunset pales
> And winds and shadows fall towards the West …
> … And how beguile you? Death has no repose
> Warmer and deeper than the Orient sand
> Which hides the beauty and bright faith of those
> Who made the Golden Journey to Samarkand.

Flecker's poem, 'The Golden Journey to Samarkand', written just before the First World War, created an image of the exotic that Europeans had enjoyed for centuries: hot sand, warm breezes, and the ceaseless chink of animal bells as caravans loaded with cloths, spices and precious stones picked their way along valleys and through mountain passes. The city of Samarkand, one of the oldest inhabited cities in the world, stood in a fertile river valley where travellers stopped before the last difficult climb across the mountain ranges into China. 'It is,' said a tenth-century Iranian writer, 'the most fruitful of all the countries of Allah.' This was the world that Marco Polo wrote about at the end of the thirteenth century. No wonder his account of his travels was one of the bestselling books of the Middle Ages.

The use of the term 'Silk Road' came into existence in the nineteenth century just before Flecker was writing. It was used to describe the many different overland trading routes that linked the Mediterranean with China from the days of the ancient classical world until the medieval period. Some ran through central Asia, Afghanistan, Kashmir and northern India; others went through Iran and the Caucasus, sometimes passing north of the Caspian and Black Seas. A third journey started in India after the traders had reached it by sea. Silk was not the only merchandise that travelled along these trading channels, but because it was light, beautiful and easy to carry, it was always one of the most highly prized imports from the east into Europe. The Romans are believed to have first seen the splendour of silk in the banners of the Parthians who defeated them at the battle of Carrhae in Turkey in 53 BC. Pliny the Elder, who composed his observations on natural history more than a hundred years later, believed that it came from the leaves of trees that had been soaked in water.

An image of the exotic: hot sands, warm breezes and the ceaseless chink of animal bells as caravans picked their way along valleys and through mountain passes.

The existence of these long commercial highways had a profound effect on the people who passed through them: ideas, technology, fashion and disease also travelled along their path. Empires grew on their back as warlords decided to exploit their commercial potential. The Khazar Empire, which became a great power in the ninth and tenth centuries, developed from the farming communities on the western shore of the Caspian Sea in what is the modern state of Dagesthan. Today it is still a place of enormous ethnic diversity whose people speak Caucasian, Turkish or Iranian languages. Religions, too, found the converts they wanted. Christianity, Islam and Judaism bred easily in this world of constant exchange, although following the death of Mohammed in 632 AD it was Islam that predominated. Inevitably there were times when trade fell away as wars and power struggles made the overland routes too dangerous. But there were also long periods of comparative peace and prosperity, the last of which coincided with the growth of the Mongol Empire of Genghis Khan and his successors. His army sacked and looted Samarkand in 1220 and he then went on to establish control over a huge area of China and Central Asia. It was just after this time that Marco Polo made his famous journey.

Marco Polo went much further and stayed for far longer than anyone before.

Marco Polo was not the first European to penetrate the heart of Asia but he went much further and stayed for far longer than anyone before. Two Franciscan priests, Giovanni di Piano Carpini and Guillaume de Rubrouck, had at separate times in the middle of the thirteenth century travelled to the capital of the Mongol Khan in Karakorum as emissaries from the Pope. Guillaume de Rubrouck described his journey in great detail, recalling at one point how he decided to walk barefoot as was the custom in his order, and how his feet froze as a result. 'The cold in these regions is most intense,' he said. In winter the frost never thawed, 'but with every wind it continued to freeze.'

Marco Polo came from a family of Venetian merchants. When he was six his father and uncle left Venice to set up a trading business on the Black Sea, eventually moving further north to a town on the River Volga. Here they became stranded as a war broke out between rival Mongol clans and they began a detour to the east in order to get home. They were then persuaded that the Great Khan, Kublai, who had never seen any Latin people, would like to meet them and so they went via Samarkand, Kashgar and the Gobi Desert to Kublai's new capital, in what is today Beijing, arriving there in 1266. This was an historic moment in the history of China. Kublai, grandson of Genghis, had conquered the whole country and founded the Yuan dynasty. Three years later, in 1269, the Polo brothers arrived back in Venice carrying messages from him for the Pope. They stayed for two years before setting off for China once more, this time taking Marco with them.

They decided against the route they had used before. They sailed to the port of Acre on the coast of modern Israel – a city that had already seen one siege in the Crusaders' attempts to gain control of the Holy Lands and would finally fall to the Saracens twenty years after the Polos were there – and then crossed Syria and Iraq, and went on through Central Asia to Balkh, in today's northern Afghanistan. From there they crossed the Pamir Mountains, 'the roof of the world', where the highest peak is more than 24,500 feet high, and made their way across the Gobi Desert. Marco reported that it was said to be so long 'that it would take a year to go across it from end to end … There is nothing at all to eat.' Finally they arrived once more at the court of Kublai Khan. The journey had taken them three and a half years. They had travelled 5,600 miles. Even today such an expedition would be a challenging undertaking, probably impossible for an ordinary family like the Polos, because it goes through so many areas of conflict. Nearly 750 years ago it must have been momentous. Most of it ran through territory completely uncharted by Europeans. Their desire to find things of unique value, to become the traders of treasure the like of which had never been seen before, drove them on.

Their determination yielded their reward. The Polos stayed for seventeen years at the court of Kublai Khan and built up a store of gold and precious stones. Marco's account of the time he spent there was dictated many years after he returned. Venice went to war with its rival city-state, Genoa, and Marco Polo seems to have been the captain of a galley that was captured by the Genoese. He told the story of his travels to a fellow prisoner who wrote them down and circulated them. They are the observations of a man with a keen eye for business. Describing the city of Kinsay – referring to Hangchow – he claimed that 'the number and wealth of the merchants, and the amount of wealth that passed through their hands was so enormous that no man could form a just estimate thereof'. With obvious envy he added that they 'live as nicely and as delicately as if they were kings and queens'. He described the produce in the markets – 'of duck and geese an infinite quantity; for so many are bred on the Lake that for a Venice groat of silver you can have a couple of geese and two couple of ducks' – and explained how Kublai Khan raised his revenues. Marco Polo obviously enjoyed the detail of commerce and 'heard it stated by one of the Great Khan's officers of customs that the quantity of pepper introduced daily for consumption into the city of Kinsay amounted to 43 loads, each load being equal to 223 pounds'.

It is not surprising that it fell to a Venetian to find and report all these things. The Venetians had gradually built up a maritime empire that extended all over the Adriatic. Their links with the Eastern Mediterranean meant that they also controlled most of Europe's trade in luxury goods such as spices, cloths and porcelain. During Marco Polo's lifetime his native city adopted a constitution that gave the adult males in about two hundred families the hereditary right to make and manage state policy. This limited the power of the Doge, the ruler of Venice, and reduced the chances of the inter-family squabbling that bedevilled many other places, like the imaginary Montagues and Capulets in Shakespeare's *Romeo and Juliet*. Stable government allowed the powerful group of ruling families to run things according to their own economic interests. Although the travels of Marco Polo were important as journeys of exploration, and greatly influenced Christopher Columbus when he was planning his voyage to the New World, they were prompted by a desire to improve and expand trade. Marco himself always argued that Europe could expand its trading links and grow richer through an economic relationship with China. 'Both in their commercial dealings and in their manufactures,' he said of the Chinese, 'they

The journey had taken three and a half years; they had travelled 5,600 miles.

are thoroughly honest and truthful … They treat foreigners who visit them with great politeness and entertain them in the most winning manner, offering them advice on their business.'

Marco Polo's stories of his journey to the court of the Great Khan and the time he spent in China were read eagerly and gained a wide circulation even though printing had not yet arrived in Europe. Not only were his descriptions of an unknown land exciting, they also hinted at the possibility of lucrative opportunities and, perhaps, at an alliance with the Mongols against the Islamic religion which had taken deep root in the countries of the East. This was the age of the Crusades, and Catholic warriors were always looking for allies in their holy war. In the end it was religion rather than commerce that flourished. In 1291 a Franciscan friar, Giovanni da Montecorvino, was sent by the Pope as a missionary to the Chinese capital and in 1307 made Archbishop of Peking. But this spate of activity did not last long. The Yuan dynasty created by the Mongols, although the first to rule over the whole of China, began to decline in the face of economic hardship and famine. By the middle of the fourteenth century it was facing revolt, and in 1368 was driven out to be replaced by the Ming dynasty. The Ming ruled China for nearly three hundred years, creating a highly centralised government that towards the end moved towards isolation from the rest of the world. It began by expelling all Christians from China. Opportunities for trade fell away. The road down which Marco Polo had wandered so successfully was blocked once more.

Many people chose not to believe Marco Polo's stories and some today are still inclined to think that he made up a lot of it, or took it from others that he met. In the end, however, the weight of evidence is on his side. He provided too much accurate description for his travels to have been pure invention. He died in about 1324 in Venice, a prosperous merchant and the father of three daughters. We have no contemporary picture of him, and his tomb, which was probably in the church of Sam Lorenzo, no longer exists. He has disappeared, as he did in his own lifetime, and we only have his stories as witness of what he did. Those tales tell us a great deal about the Silk Route and the life and adventures of those who journeyed along it.

In recent times, China has tried to resurrect the ancient trading routes that once linked it with the West. During the last thirty years of the twentieth century it began to open up to the markets of the world. When from 1991 onwards the old Soviet empire began to disintegrate into separate nations, China looked to the new neighbours that emerged on its western borders as opportunities for commercial expansion. The city of Horgos in the mountainous province of Xinjiang was identified as a place ripe for growth. The Chinese improved the road that links it with Shanghai in the east of the country, and built new gas and oil pipelines as well as a railway. Horgos lies about 750 miles north-east of Samarkand, on the other side of the forbidding mountains of the Kyrgyz republic. It is a landlocked world. The capital of Xinjing, Urumqi, is said to be farther from a seaport than any other large city in the world. The whole area is as large as Europe, and as ethnically diverse. In 2009, riots between Muslim Uighurs and Han Chinese, who form the majority population in the province, forced Chinese troops to intervene. The people are poor, and the struggle for survival a continuous battle. Border crossings, corrupt officials and impenetrable bureaucracy make everyday commerce difficult to pursue. It is a world that in many respects would have been familiar to Marco Polo and his family. They understood the value of the trade routes of the Silk Road, one of the main pathways to prosperity for the people who lived in the vast lands that separate China from Asia Minor and the beginnings of the European continent. Those routes have never completely died. As the modern world shrinks in pursuit of greater wealth, they may enjoy a full life again.

CHAPTER 4

The Black Death

1348–50

The Black Death was the name given to a pandemic of different types of plague that swept across Europe in the middle of the fourteenth century killing millions of people. Its social and economic consequences were devastating.

In October 1347 a Genoese ship entered the port of Messina in Sicily carrying a deadly cargo. Its crew was infected with the plague and within a short space of time the disease spread throughout the town. The ship was ordered to leave immediately, but it was too late: the damage had been done. 'Soon men hated each other so much,' said a contemporary account, 'that if a son was attacked by the disease his father would not tend him.' As more and more people died, 'many desired to confess their sins to the priests and draw up their last will and testament. But ecclesiastics, lawyers and notaries refused to enter the houses of the deceased.' The Black Death had arrived in Western Europe.

The ship had come from Caffa, a port belonging to Genoa on the Black Sea. The Genoese had bought the town from its Mongol owners at the end of the thirteenth century and built it into a prosperous commercial centre that dominated Black Sea trade. It was also the home of a big slave market. In 1347 the Mongols tried to capture it back, but their siege withered as their army was reduced by plague. In a last desperate attempt at victory they catapulted dead infected bodies over Caffa's walls and then withdrew. Their siege might have been a failure, but they left behind forces of destruction far greater than they ever imagined. By the beginning of 1348 the Black Death had reached Genoa itself. From there it crossed northern Italy into France.

In 1349 it entered Britain and a year later spread through Scandinavia and the Baltic. It is difficult to be precise about how many people it killed across Europe. Thirty million is not an unreasonable estimate.

This number, in a population the size of medieval Europe's, is a huge proportion – possibly a quarter of the total. The disease that brought such destruction had three variants. The most common was bubonic plague, carried by fleas hosted by black rats. The other two were septicaemic plague, which affects the blood, and pneumonic plague, which is a disease of the lungs. Other illnesses doubtless played their part as well – typhus and smallpox were both common – adding to the general feeling of overwhelming catastrophe. Bubonic plague is particularly horrifying. In medieval Europe black rats lived in houses and other inhabited areas, breeding profusely and never travelling far from their nests. Humans caught the disease from flea bites, or from bites from the rats themselves. Once a person had been bitten by a diseased creature the skin around the infected area grew dark and the body carried the germ to its nearest lymph node, the usual place for filtering foreign particles out of its system. The areas around the groin, armpit or behind the ear began to swell and became intolerably painful; this was followed by internal haemorrhaging. One of the clearest accounts of the plague was written by Gabriele de Mussis, a lawyer from Piacenza in Italy, who described how people died:

'Soon men hated each other so much that if a son was attacked by the disease his father would not tend him.'

> They felt a tingling sensation as if they were being pricked by the points of arrows. The next stage was a fearsome attack that took the form of an extremely hard, solid boil ... As it grew more solid, its burning heat caused its patients to fall into an acute and putrid fever with severe headaches. In some cases it gave rise to an intolerable stench ... In others it brought vomiting of blood ... The majority died between the third and fifth day.

With no medical knowledge to explain the causes of this rampant slaughter in their midst, the people of medieval Europe turned to heaven and hell for their answers. The clergy in fact were particularly badly hit because they inevitably became infected if they tried to minister to those who were ill. In England their numbers were reduced by nearly a half. Saint Sebastian was declared the patron of plague sufferers because his body full of arrows seemed to represent the onset of the disease. Many pictures of him began to decorate churches and cathedrals: one of the most famous was painted by Giovanni del Biondo for the cathedral in Florence just after the Black Death in the early 1350s. Charitable foundations sprang up as people looked for new ways to expiate the holy anger that had visited such death on the world. There were also scapegoats, particularly Jews. Thousands of them were massacred in Germany as people looked for someone to blame for the disaster. God had to be appeased, but as piety increased so did cruelty towards heretics. But the real effect of the Black Death was felt not in the bitter blows of flagellants as they tried to thrash evil spirits from their bodies, or in the exhortations of priests who claimed that the disease was part of 'God's command', but in the economic life of the people of Europe.

The people turned to heaven and hell for their answers.

The commercial activity of Europe in the middle of the fourteenth century was prosperous, conservative and confined. Its trading routes had reached a limit beyond which they would not significantly expand until Christopher Columbus sailed to America 150 years later. To the south, the Italian city-states controlled the Eastern Mediterranean and the Black Sea. To the north the German ports of the Hanseatic League, particularly Lubeck, dominated the Baltic. European towns tended to be run by powerful merchants' guilds that kept a tight rein on the activities of their craftsmen and artisans. The countryside was still in the grip of the nobility who expected service from their peasants in return for providing them with land to cultivate. It was a carefully protected, feudal world that had developed just enough to introduce the first fruits of capitalist enterprise into its system. But it was also an age of dreadful calamity, the worst of which was the Black Death, and it was this that brought about or accelerated a process of change. In the early part of the century there was a terrible famine. The European population had been growing steadily but a series of poor summers and hard winters destroyed crops and brought about mass starvation in the years 1315–17. The Hundred Years' War between England and France exhausted the energies and drained the resources of both countries. Edward III's victory over the French at the Battle of Crécy at which his son, the Black Prince, fought heroically and 'won his spurs', took place only two years before the Black Death carried all before it.

Thousands of Jews were massacred as people looked for someone to blame for the disaster.

Disease, war and famine began to corrode Europe's social structure. In the towns, craftsmen rebelled against the restrictions imposed on them. In Flanders between 1323 and 1328, city workers and peasants rose up and challenged the authority of their masters. In France the depredations of disbanded mercenaries from the French army who roamed around trying to live off the land contributed to a rebellion in the Ile de France in 1357. In England, the Peasants' Revolt of 1381 was the most serious challenge to the authority of the Crown and the ruling nobility throughout the whole of the Middle Ages. All these uprisings were crushed with rapid brutality. Europe in the fourteenth century did not succumb to revolution, but it did not escape from upheaval altogether. A catastrophe like the Black Death so reduced the total labour force that those who were left behind felt themselves to be in a stronger position than they had been before; a scarce labour force is always a valuable one.

Although manufacturing and trade were very important, land remained Europe's principal source of wealth. Land belonged to the Crown, the Church and the nobility. In this organisation the nobility furnished the monarch with military support in return for being given valuable estates which the peasants farmed in return for the service they gave to their lords and masters. By the middle of the fourteenth century, however, the nature of the relationship between landowner and peasant had begun to change. The old system of labourers being tied to the manor by bonds of duty and obligation had developed into one that was more similar to a straightforward relationship between landlord and tenant. With labour scarce the tenants had more bargaining power and in some cases were able to move from one manor to another in search of work. Some estates broke up as their owners decided to lease the land to peasant farmers rather than own and manage it all themselves. A nation's wealth, once the exclusive preserve of a small ennobled governing class, began to be shared more widely. This was a gradual but significant process. The Flemish, French and English peasants who marched in anger and desperation against those who ruled them won no immediate victories, but the underlying causes of their grievances began a slow transformation that would ultimately move Europe out of feudalism and into the modern world.

The plague remained a constant feature of European life after the Black Death of 1348–50 finally died out. It has been estimated that Europe suffered an outbreak somewhere every eleven years in the hundred years that followed. It continued after that: its last great manifestation was the Plague of London in 1665 which killed about twenty percent of the city's population. In the middle of the seventeenth century people were rather more organised about coping with an outbreak of disease than they had been three hundred years earlier, but they still had no idea what caused it. The author Daniel Defoe wrote an imaginary diary of the London Plague more than fifty years after it happened. It was based on parish records and the recollections of citizens who had been there at the time: 'So the Plague defied all medicines; the very physicians were seized with it, with their preservatives in their mouths; and men went about prescribing to others and telling them what to do till the tokens were upon them, and they dropped down dead, destroyed by that very enemy they directed others to oppose.'

Man cannot fight the things he does not understand. His greatest achievements can be destroyed by the unexpected. The Black Death terrified Europe, descending like a threatening cloud that brought it to a halt and left it groping for a new direction. Its effects were devastating. The population in many places declined by as much as thirty or forty percent – and stayed there, failing to recover even when the epidemic had long passed. The population of Toulouse, for instance, stood at 30,000 in the early fourteenth century: a hundred years later it was only 8,000. The Italian poet and author Boccaccio witnessed the effects of the disease in Florence and wrote about it in his book, *The Decameron*. He described the mass burials and claimed that some women developed loose morals because of the need to 'expose' their bodies as they investigated their illness. 'The authority of human and divine laws almost disappeared,' he wrote. 'Every man was able to do as he pleased.' The Black Death fundamentally changed people's attitudes towards wealth, and left behind a world very different from the one upon which it inflicted such horror.

CHAPTER 5

The Foundation of the Dutch East India Company

1602

For a hundred and fifty years, from the end of the sixteenth century to the middle of the eighteenth, world trade was dominated by the Dutch Republic. This achievement was largely due to the creation of a unique institution, the Dutch East India Company.

William the Silent is one of the great heroes of European history. His proper name was William of Orange, a Dutch nobleman who resented the injustice of the Spanish occupation of the Netherlands at the end of the sixteenth century, rebelled against it and led the seven Dutch United Provinces to independence as a republic. He was called 'the Silent' because he was careful about what he said in public, sometimes avoiding saying what he thought. Under his leadership in 1581, the United Provinces signed the Oath of Abjuration in which they renounced Spanish rule. Although they were not formally granted independence until nearly seventy years later, in 1648, they operated from this moment on as a nation in their own right. The Spanish King, Philip II, proclaimed William an outlaw and he was assassinated three years after the Oath. 'As long as he lived,' wrote the American historian, J. L. Motley, 'he was the guiding star of a whole great nation, and when he died the little children cried in the streets.'

At the time of his death the republic he had helped to create seemed an insignificant country compared to the magnificence of the Habsburg Empire from which it had seceded. Only the northern part of the Netherlands had secured its independence.

The south was still firmly under Spanish control: its Catholic nobility did not want to be part of William's little republic and remained allied to King Philip and his able commander in the Netherlands, the Duke of Parma. From these inauspicious beginnings the Dutch Republic grew with astonishing speed. At home, the work of its artists turned it one of the finest centres of painting Europe has ever seen, and the seventeenth century became known as the 'Golden Age' of Dutch art. Abroad it demonstrated rather more practical, and ruthless, skills as the commercial activities of the Dutch East India Company transformed it into a world power.

The Dutch East India Company changed the commercial history of the world. It was created after a period when it seemed as though William the Silent's dream of independence had died with him. Some of the Dutch provinces, disunited and unable to agree on a common ambition, were taken back into Spanish control by the Duke of Parma. But in 1590 he was despatched to France by Philip II to support Catholic opposition to the new French King, the Protestant Henry IV. With Parma out of the way, the Dutch rebels were at last able to consolidate their drive for independence and make the transition from a group of united provinces to a proper republic. But it was a still a nation made up of separate entities. Although it was governed by a 'States General' that represented all the country's different provinces, its constitution stated that this body 'had no overlord but the deputies of the Provincial Estates themselves'.

The Dutch East India Company changed the commercial history of the world.

The Dutch East India Company, the *Verenigde Oost-Indische Compagnie*, generally known then as the VOC, was the creation of rival merchants with one common interest – the pursuit of wealth. In 1598 all Spanish and Portuguese ports were closed to Dutch shipping, forcing the United Provinces to look beyond the Mediterranean for new trading opportunities. The obvious markets were South America, which was opening up steadily following the voyages of exploration of the sixteenth century,

William the Silent

William the Silent (1533–84) was a curious product of Habsburg Europe: a sixteenth-century German prince, he inherited the French princedom of Orange, spoke French and liberated the Dutch, who have called him ever since the 'Father of our Nation'.

William, whose full title was William I, Prince of Orange, Count of Nassau-Dillenburg, was introduced as a boy to the court of the Holy Roman Emperor, Charles V. Charles grew to trust William, charging him with important negotiations and military engagements in the Netherlands. But William, an important member of the Dutch political elite (he held the title of 'Stadtholder'), was far less enamoured with Charles's son, Philip II, who became King of Spain in 1556. William disliked Philip's religious intolerance towards Protestants and his encroachments on the Dutch nobility's tradition of autonomy.

William's upbringing as a Lutheran and then a Catholic (he would finally settle on Calvinism in 1573) taught him the importance of freedom of religion. 'I cannot approve of monarchs who want to rule over the conscience of the people,' he once said, 'and take away their freedom of choice and religion.' William's nickname 'Silent' is thought to have developed in this context. According to one story, while out hunting, the French king, Henry III, revealed a secret agreement to eradicate Protestant heretics, believing William, who was present but kept silent, to be a party to it.

William's combination of political reality and idealism prompted him to rebel against the Habsburgs in 1567. He led the Dutch to several military successes culminating in the Union of Utrecht in 1579 and a formal declaration of independence by the renegade Dutch provinces in 1581. But he declined the crown, hoping instead that the French Duke of Anjou would become the monarch. His support of the Frenchman, who left the Netherlands after a short and unhappy stay, made William unpopular with many of his fellow countrymen although he remained the Stadtholder of the two important provinces of Holland and Zeeland. Meanwhile Philip II offered 25,000 crowns for William's assassination. A French Catholic, Balthasar Gérard, took up the offer and, in a private audience with the prince, shot him in the chest. 'My God have pity on my soul,' he is supposed to have cried as he died. 'My God have pity on this poor people.'

and Asia. South America was a difficult destination for the Dutch because the Spanish and Portuguese had established firm control there. Asia seemed a better bet, but here the problem was that so many Dutch ships were chasing after the same things that the spoils were in danger of becoming dissipated. By 1599, nine different Dutch companies were in the business of trying to get their hands on spices, tea, cotton and other goods from the East Indies. Many voyages ended in disaster. About a tenth of the ships that set sail never returned and many Dutch crews were lost without trace. The man who came up with a rescue plan was Johan van Oldenbarneveldt.

Van Oldenbarneveldt was the *raadpensionaris* – the Secretary of State – of the province of Holland. By all accounts a rather imperious character with a stiff and difficult manner, he had a fine legal mind, great vision and indomitable determination. In his view, war brought 'little glory and great expense'. The provinces needed to be sure they could make money. The way to do that was to form their own company so that they could spread the cost of investment in ships and capital equipment. By pooling resources and sharing profits they would be able to build up the reserves necessary to fund the dangerous business of exploiting the East. They had not only the Spanish and Portuguese to contend with, but the English too. An English East India Company had been founded in 1600. Oldenbarneveldt set about trying to persuade the leaders of the different Dutch provinces to adopt his idea.

Many Dutch crews were lost without trace.

The desperate situation in which they found themselves speeded up their willingness to bury their differences and Oldenbarneveldt was able to devise a common plan for their commercial salvation. He then drew up the new company's statutes and charter, and the Dutch East India Company came into being in Amsterdam in January 1602. It had six chambers, one each in the main ports of the United Provinces. Each of these chambers elected delegates who sat as the company's directors. There were seventeen of them, the 'Heeren XVII' or Seventeen Gentlemen, who had the responsibility of guiding the fortunes of this semi-political, totally commercial and all-powerful corporation. Although the directors reported to the States General of the Dutch Republic, they were given enormous powers. In order to support their monopoly on trade in the Far East they were given the authority to raise armies, start wars, capture territory, build garrisons, negotiate with local chiefs and build their own ships. In the first instance their charter was to run for twenty-one years.

Nothing explains the success of the Dutch East India Company better than the exploits of Jan Pieterszoon Coen. An adventurer in the mould of Francis Drake or Robert Clive, Coen was harsh, clever and brave. Carefully controlled by the diligent burghers of the company for which he worked, he laid the foundations of the Dutch Empire in the East Indies and established its lucrative trading monopoly in Indonesia. He trained as a bookkeeper and sailed on his first voyage to Asia in 1607 where he experienced the rough and dangerous conditions in which the Dutch East India Company's employees worked. The merchants had nothing but contempt for the sailors who risked their lives to make them rich. They called them 'cats' and 'dogs' and forced them to sign contracts in which they agreed to reimburse their employers for their food and equipment, amounts that could take as much as a year's service to pay back. On his first journey, Coen's commander was killed on the Banda Islands in the Indian Ocean. Coen came to realise that nothing less than conquest would give the Dutch ownership of the valuable territory they wanted and in 1614 sent the Seventeen Gentlemen of the Dutch East India Company a paper setting out his views about how this could be achieved. What was required, he told them, was 'a grand resolution in our fatherland' to send ships and men to subdue the area and bring it into the ownership of the company. It is extraordinary to think that a group of merchants sitting in the coastal towns of the Netherlands could simply set about conquering a large part of the world. But that is what they did, and Jan Pieterszoon Coen was their agent in this task.

He captured Jakarta from the British, which the Seventeen renamed 'Batavia'. He subdued the Islands of Banda with great savagery – although he proposed the use of 'justice backed up by force', force tended to be the main method of achieving his aims – and established a thriving capitalist economy. This was to be the pattern of European colonial expansion for many years to come. Native peoples were coerced into conforming to the economic rules of their new masters. Coen called for higher quality settlers to emigrate to the East Indies rather than the 'scum' who normally travelled in Dutch ships. He encouraged Chinese workers to come and help the work of empire-building, and used slaves to swell their numbers. For all this he was rewarded with 23,000 guilders (a considerable amount, given that the daily wage for a skilled worker was about 1 guilder); each of his achievements was carefully itemised, valued and rewarded by the meticulous merchants for whom he worked. He died of dysentery in Batavia during his second tour of duty in 1629.

The Dutch East India Company provided much of the wealth of the Netherlands throughout the seventeenth century. At its height it had a presence in Persia, Bengal, Taiwan, Malaysia and Sri Lanka. It also expanded beyond Asia into South Africa when, in 1652, it sent a detachment of men to establish a base on the Cape. Its intention was to protect the passage of ships on their way east, rather than to colonise the area, but full settlement inevitably followed from this first expedition. By this time there were 1,700 Dutch ships involved in international trade, more than England and France combined. The accession of William of Orange to the English throne in 1688 began the long process of decline as, bit by bit, power and influence transferred from the Netherlands to Britain, and the Dutch became the junior partners in the alliance. The British East India Company became a serious competitor to the Dutch Company, as did the French *Compagnie des Indes* founded in 1664. The French were late entrants into the scramble for the riches of the Orient, but highly successful once they recognised the opportunity. Between 1780–84, the Anglo-Dutch alliance was over and the two countries went to war. The result was a disaster for the Netherlands which finally lost its monopoly over East Indies trade.

Native peoples were coerced into conforming to the economic rules of their new masters.

There is one other sad footnote to the history of the Dutch East India Company. The man who had been its chief architect, Johan van Oldenbarneveldt, became a victim of his country's religious struggles. The majority of the Dutch people were Calvinist, believing in John Calvin's stern from of Protestantism. This taught that God elected those he wanted to serve with him in heaven: man's fate was predestined. By following God's law he might hope to be elected, but there was no guarantee of this. We know from our own time how this sense of being entirely in God's hands adds strength to a political cause: in seventeenth-century Europe it helped fuel the Dutch revolt against their Spanish masters. Oldenbarneveldt and his followers came to believe in a more moderate approach than that which Calvin decreed, arguing for a greater degree of religious liberty. This brought them into conflict with powerful elements in Dutch society, and when Oldenbarneveldt decided to raise a militia to help protect the peace in his home province of Holland, his enemies pounced. He was already unpopular for supporting a truce with Spain and the Dutch Stadtholder, William the Silent's son, Prince Maurits, ordered his arrest. In a trial that was a mockery of justice he was found guilty, sentenced to death and executed at the age of seventy-one in 1619. 'Is this the wages,' he asked, 'of the thirty-three years' service I have given to the country?'

Today we can still look at him in the portrait by Michiel van Miereveld who, like his great contemporaries Rembrandt and Frans Hals, painted the men and women who led the Netherlands in its golden age. He looks towards us, serious, intelligent and sombrely dressed, a white ruff the only splash of brightness in a picture of unbending resolution. He showed his countrymen how the wealth of the world could be theirs for the taking. It was a lesson they learned with enthusiasm.

CHAPTER 6

The Invention of the Flying Shuttle

1733

In 1733 John Kay patented an invention called the Flying Shuttle. It transformed the cloth-weaving industry, the first of a train of events that came to be known as the Industrial Revolution.

In the early 1840s a young German called Friedrich Engels was despatched to Manchester to work in a family business. His father hoped that the experience would relieve him of his radical tendencies, but it had the opposite effect. In 1845, Engels published a book, *The Condition of the Working Class in England*, which has survived ever since as one of the great classic texts of socialist theory. In it he argued that the Industrial Revolution had transformed the lives of the English working classes. The workers' pre-industrial condition, he wrote, was 'not worthy of human beings': labourers could barely read or write and existed in a state of docile obedience to the so-called superior classes. 'Intellectually,' he said, 'they were dead; lived only for their petty, private interest; for their looms and gardens; and knew nothing of the mighty movement, which beyond their horizon, was sweeping through mankind.' They were woken from their submissive torpor, Engels argued, by the invention by James Hargreaves of the Spinning Jenny in 1764; this was the year that Engels took as the moment the Industrial Revolution began. Though it is true that large-scale industrialisation in Britain did not begin until the last quarter of the eighteenth century, the process really started much earlier – in 1733, when John Kay invented the Flying Shuttle.

Britain led the way in the Industrial Revolution and its history is essentially the history of Britain from the last years of the eighteenth century to the middle of the nineteenth. It was a revolution because it transformed everything. It changed people's lives – where they lived, how they worked and how they were organised. It changed the status of the nation, catapulting Britain into a great power that dominated world trade. Most importantly, it changed attitudes, ultimately creating a working class that demanded proper involvement in the affairs of the state in return for its role as an essential engine of prosperity. Britain today is a country that, aside from London, is built around its great industrial cities – Manchester, Birmingham, Leeds, Newcastle, Belfast and Glasgow. At the beginning of the eighteenth century this structure was very different. The main provincial centres were York, Exeter, Bristol (because of its importance as a port), Norwich and Newcastle. When the Industrial Revolution got under way, most of these places, all ancient cathedral cities and big market towns with a long history of being at the centre of their communities, began to lose their influence as factories and the jobs that went with them grew up elsewhere. Many new towns grew tenfold during the course of the eighteenth century. Manchester had a population of 10,000 in 1701 which grew to 84,000 by 1801; Liverpool increased from 6,000 to 78,000 in the same period; and Birmingham from 7,000 to 74,000. By the middle of the nineteenth century the population growth had accelerated even more: Liverpool's stood at 443,000, Manchester at 338,000 and Birmingham at 296,000. York had only 40,000 people, Exeter and Norwich less than that. Between 1750 and 1850 the axis of regional life in Britain swung and settled in a completely new position.

This great cycle of change was unique in Europe. In other countries, particularly France, the German states and Belgium, industrialisation followed the British lead and there was expansion and rapid growth. But it did not have the same effect of disrupting the influence of those countries' traditional urban centres. In Britain this experience was intensified by the realisation that steam power could be used for transport as well as manufacturing and the age of the railways began. From the 1840s new railway companies sprouted up all over the place. Like the emergence of the internet in our own time, the railway network became the epitome of achievement, a vital ingredient in a modern, aspiring society. The big difference was that railways, like the pulsating new towns they connected, required civil engineering on an enormous scale. Bridges, embankments, sidings and warehouses littered the countryside, while in the towns splendid new stations were built alongside other gothic monuments of civic self-confidence – town halls, libraries, museums and churches. The Industrial Revolution was like one long, relentless, burgeoning economic boom. But like all booms it eventually went into decline, leaving behind the people it had lured into its success and the buildings that accompanied its astonishing growth. It took barely two generations for a vision of the future to be seen, built, celebrated and lost. Today Britain's 'industrial heritage' is a central part of what the nation is. The memorials of the Industrial Revolution are a formidable reminder of lost wealth, almost as precious as the thing itself.

The Industrial Revolution was like one long, relentless, burgeoning economic boom.

One of the finest of those memorials is Manchester Town Hall. Designed by Alfred Waterhouse (whose other masterpiece is the Natural History Museum, London), the Town Hall is decorated with murals by Ford Madox Brown, a painter who enjoyed depicting moral and historical scenes. The Manchester murals tell the story of the city's history through some of its most-celebrated events. One of these is the occasion in 1753, legend has it, when machine-breakers raided John Kay's home to try to destroy his invention, forcing him to run for his life.

John Kay came from near Bury in Lancashire where he worked as a reed maker. Reeds are combs used to hold apart the crosswise threads (or 'weft') in a weaving loom. Until John Kay came up with his invention of the Flying Shuttle weavers used their hands to pass a shuttle containing the crosswise threads across the downward thread (or 'warp') on their looms. Building up pieces of cloth in this way was time-consuming. Weavers always had to change the position of their hands, and two or more of them were needed to make pieces of cloth bigger than the span of an individual's arms. There was also a lack of consistency. The quality of each piece of cloth depended entirely on the skill of its weaver. Kay simplified the whole process by automating the movement of the shuttle. He put it on wheels and mounted it on the edge of the loom's comb, allowing it to run quickly in a completely straight line between two spring-loaded boxes at either end. In this way a single weaver could make pieces of cloth to any size required by giving the shuttle a quick flick with a piece of string attached to a stick that sent the mechanism flying back and forth across the loom. Suddenly one weaver could make much more cloth than he could before and build it up on his own to any size required. The productivity of the weaving industry was dramatically increased.

Kay went on to invent several other pieces of equipment that were used to improve the efficiency of the textile industry, but he does not appear to have made any money out of any of them.

At the time Kay was viewed as just another clever man with expensive ideas.

He seems to have been a rather difficult and quarrelsome individual. He tried to charge hefty royalties for his Flying Shuttle, but manufacturers either refused to pay or simply copied his invention. Kay went to France to try his luck there, but ran up against the same problems as he had at home. His genius for invention does not seem to have transferred to the world of business and his death in France in about 1780 went unrecorded. Only time has given him his place in history. While he lived he was viewed as just another clever man with expensive ideas.

His ideas, and many of those that followed, such as Richard Arkwright's Spinning Jenny, helped create the Industrial Revolution – described by the historian E. J. Hobsbawm as 'the most important event in world history'. Britain was perfectly placed to lead it. During the second half of the eighteenth century, at the same time as industrialisation began to increase, large parts of its agricultural land fell into the hands of only a few landlords.

The Enclosure Acts created a system of large estates farmed by tenants or smallholders who no longer owned the land themselves. The peasant class, like the one in France that played an important part in the French Revolution of 1789, did not exist in Britain. Farming had succumbed to the power of the market. The country was a nation of traders – or 'shopkeepers' in Napoleon's famously dismissive phrase – where labour moved comparatively freely to support each new commercial opportunity. The textile industry provided many of these. The Industrial Revolution was built on the colossal expansion of the manufacture of cotton, as Britain became its biggest exporter throughout the world. The mill became a symbol of both prosperity and despair, the scene of many famous Victorian novels about life in Britain in the nineteenth century. Coketown in Charles Dickens's *Hard Times* is typical. It had, he tells us, 'a river that ran purple with ill-smelling dye', and in the mills where 'the hands' worked long, cramped and unhealthy hours, 'the piston of the steam-engine worked monotonously up and down, like the head of an elephant in a state of melancholy madness'. Dickens, writing ten years after Engels published his book about the working classes, echoed his concern for the state of Britain's labouring poor, although he probably would not have agreed with Engels's observation that the result of its exploitation had to be 'a revolution in comparison with which the French Revolution, and the year 1794 (the year of the Great Terror), will prove to have been child's play'.

That revolution eventually happened, but in Russia, not Britain. The country managed to absorb the surge in population and prosperity that the long cycle of industrialisation created. By the second half of the nineteenth century, many British writers and thinkers had come to realise that it had resulted in an unequal distribution of wealth that needed reform. The economic historian and passionate social reformer, Arnold Toynbee, whose book *The Industrial Revolution* was highly influential when it came out in 1884, set the tone when, talking about the working classes in a lecture in London, said, addressing them directly:

> We – the middle classes, I mean not merely the very rich – we
> have neglected you; instead of justice we have offered you
> charity, and instead of sympathy we have offered you hard
> and unreal advice ... You have – I say it clearly and advisedly
> – you have to forgive us, for we have wronged you; we have
> sinned against you grievously ... but if you will forgive us,
> nay whether you will or not, we will serve you, we will devote
> our lives to your service, and we cannot do more.

Such highly emotional and deeply felt calls for a change helped alleviate the social distress that accompanied the nation's riches. The Victorian Age was often harsh and hypocritical, but it was fuelled by a determination for improvement as well.

By the end of the nineteenth century, Britain's commercial supremacy around the world was beginning to face strong competition as other European countries began to catch up. After the end of the First World War in 1918, although Britain still called itself an empire, its problems were predominately national rather than global. But the Industrial Revolution continued, and is still continuing. New forms of energy – oil, gas and nuclear – have replaced steam. In our own time, the micro-chip has transformed our whole world of technology. If this sprawling, never-ending march of mechanisation can be said to have a beginning, it can be found as well as anywhere in John Kay's simple invention which, as the bulky memorial to him in his home town of Bury observes, 'quadrupled human power in weaving and placed England in the front rank as the best market in the world for textile manufactures'. Unveiled in 1908, the thirty-four-feet high monument is testament to the pride Bury feels for its famous son who died in France, though no one knows quite when, and is buried, though no one knows where.

CHAPTER 7

The Foundation of Oil City, Pennsylvania

1859

In 1859 the world's first commercially successful oil well was drilled in Titusville, Pennsylvania. The world discovered a commodity that would become one of the most valuable it had ever known.

In the late 1850s a former railway conductor called Edwin Drake turned up in the small community of Titusville, Pennsylvania in the United States. He had been sent there by a speculator who wanted him to see if oil could be extracted from the rocks in the area. Local farmers had complained for years that oil seepage polluted their wells. If its source could be located and extracted it could turn out to be a lucrative business opportunity. The speculator, James Townsend, had seen a report from a Yale University chemistry professor which said that oil, once refined, could be used for lighting, lubrication and other purposes. Townsend seems to have liked running his investments on a shoestring. The story goes that he only hired Drake because as a former employee he had a free pass on the railway.

Drake used his steam engine to drill for six days a week.

For the best part of a year Drake experimented with ways of trying to get to the oil, including using the money from his backer and his associates to buy a steam engine to bore down into the rock. They decided against giving him any more advances once he had spent the equivalent of $2,000 without any results – so Drake pressed on with funding the exploration from his own savings. Throughout the summer of 1859 he used his steam engine to drill for six days a week. When water flooded his borehole he drove down an iron pipe to protect his drill. On 27th August, at a depth of nearly seventy feet, he found what he had been looking for. Oil bubbled up to meet him: the world had discovered a new supply of fuel.

Oil bubbled up to meet him [Drake]: the world had discovered a new supply of fuel.

The Pennsylvania oil well was the first successful commercial enterprise, but drilling for oil had already begun on the other side of the world. Russian engineers had started sinking wells ten years earlier on the Aspheron Peninsula near Baku in Azerbaijan. In 1846 they reported to the Tsar that they had been successful, but development thereafter was rather slow. Imperial permission for drilling more wells was not given until more than twenty years later when Azerbaijan began to grow into a huge oil-producing area. By the end of the nineteenth century, Russia was competing with the United States as the world's biggest producer of oil: in 1900 it was producing 11.5 million tons a year compared to America's 9.1 million, but after the Bolshevik Revolution, oil production was diverted to domestic needs. The market, and the money that went with it, was left to America.

As is often the way with these things, no money found its way into Edwin Drake's pocket. He eventually retired with a pension of $1,500 a year. Others, however, became fabulously wealthy as they learned how to own and distribute the vast reserves of oil that lay beneath the American continent. In the same year that Drake found oil in Pennsylvania, two young ambitious business-men, John D. Rockefeller and an Englishman called Maurice Clark, opened a wholesale trading business a hundred miles away from Titusville in Cleveland, Ohio. Four years later, with the American Civil War still in full force, oil had turned the region into a fuming and disreputable place, thick with oil leaks, bars and brothels, known locally as 'Sodden Gomorrah'. Rock-efeller, a stern Baptist and anti-slavery campaigner, stayed out of the war for fear of losing his business. 'Those vast stores of oil were the gifts of the great Creator,' he said later, without adding that he was determined to turn the Lord's benevolence to his own advantage. He set up an oil-refining business with Clark and several other associates, and on 14th February 1865, exactly two months before Abraham Lincoln was assassinated following the defeat of the Confederate Army, bought out his partners for $72,500. 'It was,' he recalled, 'the day that determined my career.' Within four years, helped by an economy that had started to grow again in a country at peace at last, Rockefeller was running the world's biggest oil-refining business, producing ten percent of its output. At the age of thirty he changed his company's name to Standard Oil.

Rockefeller was not the only entrepreneur to recognise the value of oil. In 1864, a young Scotsman called Andrew Carnegie who had made money by building sleeping cars for first-class travel on the railways, invested $40,000 in a Pennsylvania oil well. The huge profits he made provided him with the foundation of a business empire on a similar scale to Rockefeller's. Carnegie eventually made most of his money from iron and steel, though it was oil that set him on the road to enormous wealth. Rockefeller always stuck with oil, first forming a cartel with the railroad companies to control distribution and, when public protest forced that to disband, simply buying out his rivals. By the end of the nineteenth century, Standard Oil was the biggest private business corporation the world had ever seen. In 1911, the United States Supreme Court ruled that its existence contravened anti-trust legislation and ordered that it be broken up. Standard Oil metamorphosed into household names such as Mobil, Exxon, Amoco and Chevron. John D. Rockefeller, no longer an active corporate executive but still a major shareholder with holdings in all of these new companies, became even richer.

Oil became a vital ingredient in national survival.

Oil was not the 'driving' energy of the world when Rockefeller's huge corporation was broken up. Its main use was for lighting and lubrication – Vaseline was one of Standard Oil's most successful products – and although valuable it was not seen as an essential part of a nation's strategic needs. Coal was the fuel that drove the steam engines that kept manufacturing and transport on the move. But as the First World War developed and the motor car and the diesel engine came into use, oil became not just a commodity that made money, but a vital ingredient in national survival. It was Britain, a country without any oil of its own, that first recognised the importance of securing and maintaining oil supplies.

In May 1908, a British engineer called George Reynolds was looking for oil in Iran. Rather like Edwin Drake in Pennsylvania nearly fifty years before, he had been sent there by an English millionaire, William Knox D'Arcy, who had bought the country's oil concession from the Shah. Armed with his pipe, pet dog and pith helmet, and sustaining his work force with supplies of cider and library books, Reynolds was one of those indefatigable Englishmen who never chooses to give up. Money was running out, conditions were becoming intolerable and he was about to be called home, when he found what he was looking for. His employers founded the Anglo-Persian Oil Company which, by 1912, had built the world's largest oil refinery at Abadan on the Persian Gulf.

In 1914 the British government, prompted by Winston Churchill, who as First Lord of the Admiralty was determined to modernise the Royal Navy by moving it into oil-fuelled technology, secretly took a majority share in the company. Oil now lubricated the national interest. In 1951 the republican government of Iran nationalised the country's oilfields, but fearing that it might align with the Communist East rather than the West, in 1953 the United States sanctioned the CIA to support a military coup that returned the Shah to the throne. Oil had also been discovered in Saudi Arabia, in 1938, and then in other parts of the Middle East. After the Second World War republican regimes that were hostile to Western interests came to power in countries such as Egypt and Libya. To defend their interests, America and Britain threw their support behind the old established kingdoms of Saudi Arabia and Jordan. The West's crucial dependence on oil has kept it closely involved in the politics of the Middle East ever since.

The enormous wealth created by the discovery of oil became an important issue for the two men who had first gained most profit from it. John D. Rockefeller and Andrew Carnegie were probably the two richest men the world has ever known. As businessmen they were ruthless, sometimes prepared to bribe or threaten to get their way: the expanding world of American commerce was a cruder place than it is today. At the same time a greater awareness of the responsibilities of wealth was beginning to appear. In 1894, the US journalist and progressive reformer Henry Demarest Lloyd, who attacked Standard Oil for its business practices, published a book called *Wealth Against Commonwealth* in which he observed: 'Liberty produces wealth, and wealth destroys liberty.' In an attempt to head off such stinging and potentially damaging criticism both Rockefeller and Carnegie poured hundreds of millions of dollars into public works. In Rockefeller's case the money went to Chicago University, the Rockefeller Institute for Medical Research (today Rockefeller University), and the General Education Board that announced it would teach children 'to do in a perfect way the things their fathers and mothers are doing in an imperfect way'. In 1913 he and his son established the Rockefeller Foundation that remains one of the richest charitable organisations in the world. Carnegie too used his money to encourage education. His grand scheme was to fund the opening of libraries, and between 1883 and 1929 more than 2,000 were founded all over the world. In many small towns in America and in Britain, the Carnegie Library is still one of their most imposing buildings, always specially designed and built in a wide variety of architectural styles. In 1889, Carnegie wrote his *Gospel of Wealth* first published in America and then, at the suggestion of Gladstone, in Britain. He said that that it was the duty of a man of wealth to set an example of 'modest, unostentatious living, shunning display or extravagance', and, once he had provided 'moderately' for his dependents, to set up trusts through which his money could be distributed to achieve in his judgement, 'the most beneficial result for the community'. Carnegie believed that the huge differences between rich and poor could be alleviated if the administration of wealth was judiciously and philanthropically managed by those who possessed it. Rich men should start giving away money while they lived, he said. 'By taxing estates heavily at death, the state marks its condemnation of the selfish millionaire's unworthy life.'

The names of Rockefeller and Carnegie live on through the philanthropic trusts their money endowed, permanent reminders of the wealth generated by oil and steel. In Azerbaijan, where the oilfields once competed with and might have overtaken their American counterparts, they remember another philanthropist. Zeynalabdin Taghiyev, the son of a shoemaker, went drilling for oil on rented land near Baku. In a repetition of what happened in other parts of the world, his partners gave up and sold him their shares. In 1873 he struck oil and became one of the richest men in Imperial Russia. He could neither read nor write, but used his money to build schools and theatres and to help pay for the pipeline that still brings water to the city of Baku from the Caucasus Mountains a hundred miles away. When the Red Army reached the city in 1920, Taghiyev's house was seized. He was allowed to live the last four years of his life in his summer cottage not far away, but his second wife was not so fortunate. She died in poverty on the streets of Baku in 1938. The Bolsheviks turned his splendid residence into the Azerbaijan National History Museum, which is what it still is today. The fortunes of the world's first oil tycoons were very different. In capitalist America their wealth was their greatest protector: in Bolshevik Russia it destroyed them.

CHAPTER 8

The Treaty of Versailles

1919

The Treaty of Versailles formally brought the First
World War of 1914–18 to an end. Its terms had the effect
of making a defeated Germany feel impoverished and
resentful. In trying to build a world of peace it laid
down foundations that would lead to another war.

In 1918, on the eleventh hour of the eleventh day of the eleventh
month, an armistice was signed that ended the fighting of the
First World War. Barely a month later, on 10th December, 75,000
soldiers of the German army marched back into Berlin. They
were greeted at the Brandenburg Gate by Friedrich Ebert, a
socialist politician who was the new Chancellor of the nation.
'Welcome to the German Republic,' he shouted. 'Welcome home.
You should march home with your heads held high. Never have
men achieved greater things.' Warming
to his theme, he continued: 'Your sacrifices have been unparalleled. No enemy
has conquered you.' With those words the
mood of the new Germany was born. It was
an undefeated country that had either been
sold out by conspirators in its own ranks or
was suffering from difficulties imposed by

*The Kaiser's
Fatherland still
existed ... it could
rise again.*

the punitive terms of an unfair treaty. The Kaiser's Fatherland
was not just a memory. It still existed. It could rise again.

Ebert was facing a situation that was in danger of running
out of control. He and the other moderate socialists that he led,
had supported the war as a necessary patriotic measure. He had
not wanted to see the end of the monarchy and felt that the
proclamation of Germany as a republic following the Kaiser's

abdication had been premature and needed to be ratified by a nationally elected assembly. But he was overtaken by events. By the time he addressed the first meeting of Germany's new national assembly the following year, 1919, the German Republic was a fact and the country's mood of resentment more entrenched. To maintain power he needed to respond to it. Germany's enemies, he told the assembly in his opening speech, were seeking 'to indemnify themselves at the cost of the German people ... These plans of revenge and oppression call for the sharpest protest. The German people cannot be made the wage slaves of other nations for twenty, forty or sixty years.' His remarks were met with loud applause. Ebert wanted above all to create a true democracy in his defeated homeland – but the task he faced proved hopeless. In the end the German people looked to the right-wing parties to redress their sense of grievance. Within fifteen years, the Nazis had assumed power, democracy died and Europe was on the road to war once more.

The victorious Allies who met in Paris at the end of the First World War wanted above all else to destroy German militarism. They also wanted to establish world peace, rearranging the fragments of disintegrated empires in a way that would ensure the future happiness and prosperity of their subjects. The task they faced was immense and probably impossible. The Habsburg Empire of Austria-Hungary had arisen out of the old Holy Roman Empire established by Charlemagne in 800 AD, and, in various forms, governed the whole of central and Eastern Europe for centuries. The Hohenzollern Empire of the German Kaiser, the Allies' main enemy, had used its Prussian base to unite the German states during the second half of the nineteenth century, creating a formidable military machine intent on expansion and conquest. These two great engines of state had collapsed and the people they had once governed were looking for new, democratic freedoms. The Allies recognised these ambitions, but they also wanted to punish the aggressor. Graciousness in victory is the greatest of all political virtues but it requires a degree of altruism unusual in human beings. At Versailles the Allies' understandable desire for punishment outweighed their careful consid-

Bismarck and the Creation of the German Empire

On 18th January 1871, German princes gathered in the Hall of Mirrors in the Palace of Versailles. They had come to witness the crowning of the Prussian King, Wilhelm I, as Emperor of a newly-formed nation – Germany. Before 1871, Germany was a patchwork of independent states over which Austria exerted the predominant influence. But German nationalism was growing. In 1848 revolutionaries demanded unification, offering the Prussian King the imperial throne. He refused, worried that it would lead to military intervention from Austria. But as Prussia's military, diplomatic and economic power grew, the whole idea of unifying Germany without Austria started to become a real possibility.

The principal architect of this extraordinary achievement was a skilful and loyal diplomat called Otto von Bismarck (1815–98). During the 1850s he became convinced that unification could be achieved in Prussia's interests. When in 1862 he was appointed Prime Minister and Foreign Minister of Prussia he began to employ astute diplomacy blended with timely military intervention to secure his ends. With the assistance of two Prussian soldiers, Albrecht von Roon and Helmuth von Moltke, the army was reorganised into an impressive fighting force. In 1866 it defeated the Austrian army at Königgrätz, east of Prague. This enabled Bismarck to annex the north German states including Hanover, Frankfurt and Saxony. France, frightened of being encircled by the growing power of Prussia, declared war in 1870. Prussia pounced. Having defeated France in the Franco-Prussian War, Bismarck wasted no time in negotiating with the leaders of the southern German states to complete unification.

Bismarck's political system ensured strong monarchical authority. As Imperial Chancellor, he pursued a policy of pragmatic, peace-oriented diplomacy that made the new German Empire a powerful country. But his approach met with criticism, not least from Wilhelm II, who became German Emperor in 1888. Wilhelm's politics were more expansionist and militarist than his Chancellor's and he forced Bismarck to resign in 1890. The man who more than any other built the modern German state lived in restless retirement until his death in 1898.

eration of the future and undermined the hopes of those who thought they had been liberated from imperial control.

The terms of the Treaty of Versailles were imposed upon Germany. The Germans took no part in any of the discussions prior to their being told what the Allies had agreed. Apart from being forced to reduce their army to 100,000 volunteers and to severely restrict their manufacture of weapons, the Treaty demanded that Germany accept sole responsibility for starting the war. It also insisted on severe economic penalties, forcing the country to make reparations – in the first instance settled at about $31.5 billion – stripped it of all its overseas colonies and reassigned a large part of its European territory to France, Belgium, Denmark, Czechoslovakia and Poland. France was also given all rights for fifteen years over the German coalfields in the Saar on the eastern border between the two countries. Some of these conditions were to be expected: Germany was bound, for instance, to have to hand back Alsace to France and to restore the land it had taken from Belgium. But the economic demands, combined with the requirement to accept all the guilt for causing the war in the first place, aroused the anger of the defeated nation. 'It was,' said the German writer, Ernst Troeltsch, 'reminiscent of the way Rome treated Carthage.' He was not the only person to feel that the Treaty was unfair. In Britain the economist John Maynard Keynes urged re-negotiation of the terms. In his book, *The Economic Consequences of the Peace*, published in 1919, he said that: 'Great privation and great risks to society have become unavoidable.' A new approach was needed to 'promote the re-establishment of prosperity and order, instead of leading us deeper into misfortune.' And he quoted the writer Thomas Hardy, whose long verse-drama, *The Dynasts*, is set in the Napoleonic war that had engulfed Europe a hundred years previously:

'It was,' said Troeltsch, 'reminiscent of the way Rome treated Carthage.'

... Nought remains
But vindictiveness here amid the strong,
And there amid the weak an impotent rage.

In fact France was treated rather more carefully in 1815 than Germany a hundred years later, not least because the French negotiator, Talleyrand, participated in the Congress of Vienna where the peace terms were agreed. Talleyrand was the great survivor of the European politics of his day, a famous prince who had played an important part in the early days of the French Revolution, served as Napoleon's Foreign Secretary, fallen out with him and then, after his defeat, planned the restoration of the Bourbon monarchy. The German representative at Versailles, Ulrich Graf von Brockdorff Rantzau had no such pedigree. Summoned to hear the terms of the peace the Allies had agreed, he and his delegation were kept waiting for several days before they were read out to them. They were shocked at what they heard. Brockdorff Rantzau wrote a letter to the President of the Peace Conference, the French Prime Minister, Georges Clemenceau, describing the attitude of the Allies as 'victorious violence'. He declared that the 'exactions of this treaty are more than the German people can bear'.

The economic demands aroused the anger of a defeated nation.

The whole approach to peace was also very different in Vienna in 1815 from that which existed in Paris in 1919. The monarchs and princes who set about rearranging Europe at the end of the Napoleonic Wars were trying to put things back to where they were before Napoleon's attempt to create a European continent in his own image. Talleyrand helped them by supporting the return of the Bourbons even though he knew, in his own phrase, that 'they had learned nothing and forgotten nothing'. After the First World War, the politicians making peace wanted to look forward, and to build a world in which war would not happen again. The American President, Woodrow Wilson, was intent on forming a 'League of Nations', a multinational body designed to discuss and debate grievances rather than allow them to slide inevitably into conflict. He got what he wanted, even though America did

The League of Nations

The carnage of the First World War generated widespread international agreement 'to develop cooperation among nations and to guarantee them peace and to avoid future bloodshed'. The League of Nations was established by the Treaty of Versailles to pursue this aim. It was the brainchild of the American President, Woodrow Wilson, who saw it as a mechanism for the promotion of diplomacy, the prevention of war through collective security, and a way of safeguarding human rights for minority groups. But he failed to persuade the American Senate of its value, and the United States never joined it. During its first ten years of operation, the League successfully resolved several disagreements and international diplomatic activity began to be conducted through it. It oversaw an international judiciary as well as a number of agencies dealing with pressing international issues such as refugees, health, disarmament, opium and slavery.

Structurally, though, the League was flawed; it was bureaucratic and unwieldy, and lacked teeth. In 1931 it declared the Japanese invasion of Manchuria in northern China to be wrong but was unable to enforce a withdrawal when Japan withdrew its membership from the organisation. Nor did it halt Hitler's militarism, which directly contravened its commitment to disarmament and failed to prevent the German invasion of Austria, Czechoslovakia and Poland. The outbreak of the Second World War was final proof of the League's ultimate powerlessness. It was eventually disbanded in 1946 following the foundation of the United Nations, which the Americans joined, and which inherited the League's ideals as well as many of its agencies.

not join the organisation because Congress refused to ratify its membership. The victors also created new countries out of the fragments of dismembered empires. Czechoslovakia and Yugoslavia came into existence as new independent states; Poland was given independent statehood for the first time in more than a hundred and twenty years; and two small and severely weakened countries, Austria and Hungary, came into being as separate entities. All this seemed fair and proper, responding to Woodrow

Wilson's 'fourteen points' for peace in which he explained how he believed Europe should be divided up to give autonomy and self-determination to its different ethnic groups.

Germany seethed with resentment. Stripped of much of its territory and saddled with the enormous cost of reparation it seemed to have been treated very harshly. In fact, however, its position was rather stronger than at first appeared, not least because the new countries that had been created were so weak. Furthermore it never repaid all the money that the Treaty of Versailles demanded. France and Britain put great pressure on Germany to pay its debts – they needed the money because they themselves owed $10 billion to the United States. When eventually Germany defaulted on the reparations, the country was leant $200 million in a loan floated on the American market by the banker, J. P. Morgan in 1924. It was quickly over-subscribed. The Great Depression of the 1930s brought further hardship to all the countries struggling with the aftermath of the war, and in 1932 the Allies agreed to cancel reparations altogether in return for one final payment. The German economy started to recover, the new, struggling countries surrounding it became victims of Hitler's demands for national *Lebensraum* – living space – and Europe was once again in conflict.

The destruction of empires, whether well-intentioned or not, is never easy. The Treaty of Versailles made two fundamental mistakes. First of all, it imposed economic terms on Germany that proved impossible to fulfil. Secondly, it created a patchwork of weak countries that ultimately fell prey to their aggressive neighbour, Germany. Czechoslovakia, Poland and Austria had all come under German control by the time the Second World War broke out in 1939. Implicit in both of these mistakes was a lack of economic common sense. In trying to repair a broken world, the Allies had thought hard about rewards and punishment, but had given little consideration to how any of it was to be paid for. They overlooked the fact that in the years leading up to the war, Germany, as the biggest industrial nation on the continent of Europe, was an important source of wealth for the countries that surrounded it. Their aims were almost entirely political – and in the case of Woodrow Wilson, almost religious. Of the Allies' approach to the post-war reconstruction, Keynes wrote that 'that the fundamental economic problems of a Europe starving and disintegrating before their eyes, was the one question in which it was impossible to arouse (their) interest'. The First World War destroyed the wealth of nineteenth-century imperial Europe. The Treaty of Versailles failed to provide a framework in which it could be replaced.

CHAPTER 9

The Model T Ford

1908

The Model T Ford turned America into a nation of motorists and put luxury within the reach of many. The sophisticated pleasures of life were no longer just for the wealthy.

An owner's manual is not an obvious place in which to look for lofty observations on life, but the one that the Ford Motor Company published at the end of the First World war was not shy about attempting such things. 'It is a significant fact,' it warbled, 'that nearly all Ford cars are driven by laymen – by owners, who in the great majority of cases have little or no practical experience with things mechanical.' They were, however, not to feel threatened by such ignorance. They had 'a singular freedom from mechanical annoyances' owing to the superior craftsmanship of their vehicle, but were still urged to indulge in a little gentle study of its working parts because 'it is a truism that the more one knows about a thing the more one enjoys it'. Homilies from a manufacturer to its customers reveal a lot. The Ford Motor Company seemed to know that it was in the process of changing the world.

'I will build a car for the great multitude' said Ford.

Henry Ford was a visionary in two ways. Firstly, and most importantly, he realised that it was possible to provide ordinary people with what seemed at that time to be an unobtainable luxury – a motor car. 'I will,' he declared, 'build a car for the great multitude.' Secondly, his manufacturing methods transformed industry by introducing an assembly line capable of mass production. His sturdy little car was a significant invention in its own right. What made it revolutionary was that Ford built a factory capable of distributing it to millions of people. In 1908, the year the first Model T Ford rolled off the production lines, the car cost $825. By 1927, when the last one was built, seventeen million of them had been sold and its price was just $275. The factory at Highland Park in Detroit had reduced the time taken to build each car from around thirteen hours to just over an hour and a half, and was capable of producing one every minute. One of every two cars in the world was a Model T. These are astonishing statistics. In 1927 the population of the whole of the United States was a little over 119 million: by selling seventeen million cars, Henry Ford had unquestionably realised his ambition of bringing the power of motoring to the multitude. The writer E. B. White looked back with wistful humour at the age of the Model T in an article for *New Yorker* magazine in 1936:

> The car is fading from the American scene – which is an understatement because to a few million people who grew up with it, the old Ford practically was the American scene. It was the miracle God had wrought. And it was patently the sort of thing that could only happen once. Mechanically uncanny, it was like nothing that had ever come to the world before.

For other writers the age of the Model T was not something to be celebrated, even teasingly. In Aldous Huxley's novel *Brave New World*, published in 1932, the characters live in an era known as 'AF' – after Ford – inhabiting a uniform world of drug use and recreational sex where everything is reduced to relentless monotony like the work on an assembly line. For some, Henry Ford's American dream was the beginning of a universal nightmare.

Henry Ford's own life provides a similar contrast between the bleak and the sunny. Born in Dearborn, Michigan, in 1863, he had little schooling and eventually set up a small business repairing farm machinery. He was a natural engineer and found a job with the Edison Illuminating Company where he was rapidly promoted. He and Thomas Edison became good friends, but Ford left to set up his own company building cars. To begin with his companies failed, even though he and a partner designed and built a racing car that set the world land speed record in 1902. A year later he was able to start a new company. His backers wanted to build luxury cars, but Ford was convinced that the opportunity lay at the other end of the market. He won the boardroom battle and after producing a series of small cars came up with the Model T. The car, and the way in which it was produced, became the epitome of industrial progress. Ford intro-duced a minimum wage for his workers of $5 a day, double the going rate at the time. His competitors thought he was mad, but he stuck to his principles and followed up his wages policy with, first, a sociology department, and then an education department to try and help his workers spend their new-found wealth wisely. Autocratic but benevolent, it was one of industry's first recognitions that the welfare of employees was an impor-tant component in commercial success. 'There can be no true prosperity,' Ford announced, 'until the worker upon an ordinary commodity can buy what he makes.'

Ford introduced a minimum wage of $5 a day, double the going rate at the time.

Like all autocrats, Henry Ford found change difficult and challenge impossible. He refused to respond to the need to manage his business in a more structured way, preferring to rely on the instinct and touch that had made it successful in the first place. Good managers left, and when after 1927 the production of his new car, the Model A, ran into difficulties, he hired thugs to terrorise union members and break up their meetings. At the same time he gave vent to his anti-semitic feelings by running a newspaper, *The Dearborn Independent,* that contained articles hostile to Jews. Hitler would be one of Henry Ford's strongest admirers. The brilliant mechanic who had put America – and the world – on a road from which it would never look back died in 1947 as a rather disagreeable example of a paranoid tycoon.

The life of Henry Ford provides a good description of the way in which the world changed during the twentieth century. It was a change that hinged on one thing above all others: the role of the individual as a consumer. Anyone was entitled to anything as long as he could pay for it. Wealth, even luxury, was within the grasp of all. The role of business, supported by new management techniques, was to ensure that consumers received the marketing messages that would encourage them to participate in this new opportunity.

At the same time as Henry Ford was beginning to manufacture his popular car, another mechanical engineer called Frederick Winslow Taylor published a short book called *Principles of Scientific Management*. Taylor was one of the world's first management consultants. A talented tennis player – he was a winning partner in the doubles competition for the first American National Championships in 1881 – he wanted to bring to industry the same precision and efficiency he applied to his sport. Good management, he argued, was the result of carefully designed rules and principles. Workers in America, he said, suffered from the delusion that improved efficiency reduced the amount of labour required; their methods of working encouraged 'soldiering' or taking as long as possible to complete each job; and they were organised on a 'rule-of-thumb' basis rather than by clear and precise systems. Taylor wanted to achieve the maximum amount of prosperity for both employer and employee and explained how properly defined tasks and responsibilities could achieve this. His ideas followed those of another pioneer in the field of management consultancy, Frank Gilbreth, who not only came up with ideas for improving efficiency but tried to organise his twelve children by the same principles (his efforts were turned into the film *Cheaper by the Dozen* based on a humorous book written by his son). But the effects of the ideas of men like Taylor and Gilbreth were serious and permanent. They brought to industry – particularly American industry – a belief in the idea of management as a science, even an art, deserving of recognition on the same level as other human activities hitherto regarded as more important or refined. Henry Ford remained very much his own man – an industrial dictator to the end of his working life –

but in creating the car plants based on mass production he used many of the principles of 'scientific management'.

With mass production went mass consumption. Henry Ford made sure that people bought his cars by setting up a system of dealer franchises across America: there were 7,000 of them by 1912. At the same time he campaigned for better roads and more petrol stations to ensure that his customers had all they needed to enjoy his products more. As his competitors – Chrysler, Packard, Dodge and others – entered the market, the motor car became the symbol of middle-class prosperity. The consumer boom stretched beyond tarmac and gas pumps to shops, cinema and home appliances. In the same year that Ford launched the Model T, Richard Sears was making $41 million a year in sales by offering the nation what it wanted to buy through his mail-order business. Later, as the suburbs sprawled out of the towns, he built department stores all over the country. In Britain, Marks and Spencer began a similar operation, but much more limited in size and with a smaller range of goods for sale. In 1927 the first talking movie, *The Jazz Singer*, appeared. Six years later, American families could watch a film from their cars as the first drive-in movie theatres were built. Meanwhile radios, refrigerators and sewing machines were selling in huge numbers – often bought on long-term credit plans. The liquid embodiment of American consumerism, Coca-Cola, was a worldwide brand by the end of the 1920s.

There were attempts to turn the relentless tide of acquisitive prosperity. The American temperance movement successfully lobbied for the introduction of Prohibition in 1919, which for fourteen years, until it was repealed in 1933, banned the manufacture, sale or transport of alcohol. This attempt at applied morality – its supporters called it 'The Noble Experiment' – was ultimately unsuccessful. Illegal bars, 'speakeasys', mushroomed in their thousands and, as with the modern drug trade, gangsters cashed in on the high profits to be made from illegal but much-wanted goods. In 1929 an economic theorist and writer called Ralph Borsodi inveighed against the way of life that America had adopted in a book called *This Ugly Civilisation*. 'America,' he wailed, 'is a respecter of things only, and time – why time is only something to be killed, or butchered into things which can be bought and sold.' Borsodi came from a family of Hungarian immigrants – one of millions that had been attracted to America because of its freedom, particularly its wide, open spaces. For men like him, the nation's founding fathers had been people who combined qualities of intellectual strength, physical vigour and a belief in the land – virtues that were being strangled in a jungle of greed.

America, happy and free in its new motor car, was not to be sidetracked. Even when its economy went into severe decline from 1929 as a result of the worldwide depression, the role of the new consumer was actually strengthened rather than weakened. President Roosevelt's 'New Deal', the economic legislation designed to resurrect the nation's fortunes, provided for consumers to participate in the new authorities he created in order to encourage industrial and financial reform.

The consumer – the spender – was to be the agent of renewal.

In the election campaign that first brought him to power he announced that: 'I believe we are at the threshold of a fundamental change in our popular economic thought, that in the future we are going to think less about the producer and more about the consumer.' The consumer – the spender – was to be the agent of renewal. The irony was that Henry Ford, who did more than anyone to create the acquisitive citizen whose willingness to spend lay at the heart of economic reconstruction, disliked the idea of government involvement in business and never supported Roosevelt's reforms.

The Model T Ford was by some accounts an exasperating car to own. Its popular name was the 'Tin Lizzie' and as E. B. White recalled in the *New Yorker* magazine: 'The lore and legend that governed the Ford were boundless. Owners had their own theories about everything; they discussed mutual problems in that wise, infinitely resourceful way old women discuss rheumatism.' Cantankerous, strange, cheap and constantly available, it became a fixture of the American way of life – a symbol of wealth that everyone could aspire to own.

CHAPTER 10

The Credit Crunch

2007

In 2007 the world's financial markets began to face serious problems as owners of houses in America began to default on their loans. It became clear that banks all over the world had extended credit unwisely and were about to collapse. This, combined with a general market recession, created the most serious global economic crisis for nearly a century. It became known as the Credit Crunch.

It is with some caution that I decided to include the Credit Crunch in this book. When in the future people look back at the first years of the twenty-first century, the world's economic problems that began in 2007 may not appear particularly significant. But for those who have lived and are living through them they represent a moment of reckoning. The Credit Crunch brought to a shuddering halt a cycle of prosperity and growth that had lasted, with one brief interlude, for more than thirty years. It seemed unstoppable and its sudden end sent waves of fear and panic round the world. As fear subsided it was replaced by sober reflection. Many people, particularly in the West, began to reassess their attitudes towards individual wealth. The chief executive of the Royal Bank of Scotland that lost more than £24 billion in 2008 – the biggest in Britain's corporate history – was urged to relinquish part of his pension as the public mood turned against the big salaries and bonuses earned by senior managers.

Waves of fear and panic went round the world.

In 2009, in a BBC Reith Lecture, an American political philosopher argued that it was time that the self-interest of the individual was replaced by what he called 'a new politics for the common good'. It is still too early to say whether these agonies of conscience have made a long-term difference to the way men and women behave. In part they are simply the result of the anxiety people always feel during a period of economic decline when wages and profits are falling, concerns that tend to evaporate once growth and prosperity return. That is why the Credit Crunch is important. Whether it was just another blip in the economic cycle, or something far more, only time will tell.

In 1873 the banker, journalist and author Walter Bagehot published a book about banking in Britain called *Lombard Street*. Britain was then the richest country in the world, its money markets a global hub for credit and exchange. Bagehot was a shrewd and lucid observer of British public life. 'Banking,' he said, 'is a watchful but not a laborious trade.' Watchfulness, however, had not been much in evidence in a recent banking scandal. In 1866 a private bank called Overend, Gurney & Company, collapsed. It had over-extended its lending and had invested heavily in the surging growth of the railways. When the market weakened it found itself unable to meet its liabilities. 'In a short time,' remarked Bagehot, its managers had 'substituted ruin for prosperity and changed opulence into insolvency.' Other banks followed Overend, Gurney & Co. into liquidation and a variety of companies also failed as the credit crisis took its toll on the country's economy. The directors of Overend, Gurney & Co. asked the Bank of England for help, but were refused. They were eventually tried for fraud at the Old Bailey, though the court found them guilty of 'a grave error' rather than a crime. Twenty-four years later, in 1890, the bank of Baring Brothers nearly collapsed because of unwise investments it made in Argentina. This time the Bank of England did step in, averting a crisis that might have brought the whole of the British banking system to its knees. Bagehot had proposed this course of action: he believed the Bank of England should be used as a central bank whose reserves could help other

> 'Banking,' said Walter Bagehot, 'is a watchful but not laborious trade.'

banks and businesses weather the difficulties of the economic cycle.

These dramatic events shook the confidence of Britain's powerful commercial interests, but they made few long-term differences to the way people behaved. Britain in 1900 was very similar to Britain in 1870 and its Prime Minister, the Marquess of Salisbury, a typical product of the grand Victorian world – aloof, patrician and suspicious of democratic change.

But by the time the next crisis arose, thirty years into the twentieth century, the situation had changed dramatically. As with the Credit Crunch, the Great Depression of the 1930s began in America when the country's stock market crashed in 1929. Although America had enjoyed a period of booming economic growth, there was still a wide division between rich and poor. The rich pumped their surplus cash into speculative stocks. When these failed not only they, but the poor they had left behind, suffered terribly. This suffering, which spread into Europe and the rest of the world, meant that the Great Depression had enormous political consequences. In America, President Roosevelt's New Deal introduced fierce banking regulations, farm subsidies and a more inclusive approach to many aspects of the economy. In Britain, Prime Minister Ramsay MacDonald formed a National Government to try to cope with the crisis. In Germany and Italy, Hitler and Mussolini used economic misfortune to strengthen their call for vigorous anti-democratic measures. The Great Depression did not create fascism, but it certainly helped.

Further afield the freedom movements that had begun to develop in the colonial territories of the great powers pointed to economic misery as the inevitable legacy of selfish, wealth-obsessed masters. The man who would become the first Prime Minister of an independent India, Jawaharlal Nehru, said in a speech in 1929: 'Our economic programme must ... be based on a human outlook and must not sacrifice man to money.' In Brazil, where growing prosperity suddenly began to decline, Getulio Vargas, one of the country's most influential leaders in the whole of the twentieth century, seized power in 1930 and became known as 'The Father of the Poor'. Economic turmoil had a global impact. At the end of the nineteenth century, capitalist economies were controlled by a few people and their mistakes could generally be contained without triggering revolutionary reverberations. By the middle of the twentieth century, the widening of the democratic process that accompanied the continuing march of industrialisation meant that 'the market' was everybody's concern. The whole world demanded answers when things went wrong.

Answers could no longer be heard above the noise of war by the end of the 1930s. But in the fifty years that followed peace the world economy was further transformed. To begin with reconstruction was slow and in many countries, including Britain, times were harsh and austere. Gradually, however, as the old Bolshevik Communist system in Russia collapsed, China began to open its doors, the European Community grew larger and communications improved through the growth of the internet and air travel, the privations of the past slipped away. 'The market' ran free. Capitalism was the great conqueror. In Britain and America emphasis on the power of individuals to control their economic destinies became the dominant feature of policy-making. This approach spawned attitudes that were satirised in the film *Wall Street* in 1987. One of the main characters is a ruthless corporate financier called Gordon Gekko. 'Greed,' he tells a shareholder meeting, 'for lack of a better word is good. Greed is right, greed works.'

'The market' ran free. Capitalism was the great conqueror.

Gordon Gekko is a caricature used to capture a prevailing mood. But when the Credit Crunch struck twenty years after he first appeared on the screen, his speech had something of a prophetic ring to it. In the film Gekko gets his come-uppance. In real life, too, the good times stopped as lifestyles financed by credit were no longer sustainable. In this atmosphere what people had once applauded as a healthy aspiration for wealth-creation was now condemned as nothing better than careless greed. The banks were blamed for over-extending themselves and lending money to creditors whose earnings could not support the debts they were encouraged to take on. The BBC

What Do We Mean By 'Financial Crisis?'

A financial crisis occurs when institutions or assets lose a great deal of value. Financial crises occurred more frequently from the seventeenth century onwards with the increasing circulation of money, the development of banking institutions, and globalisation.

Stock market crashes and financial bubbles occur when speculation drives up the price of an asset or stock above its true value. When participants begin to sell the stock, panic-selling often takes over, and the price declines dramatically, prompting a stock-market crash. 'Tulip Mania' in the 1630s is regarded as the first economic bubble. Prized as a luxury during the Dutch Golden Age, speculative trading saw tulip prices peak and collapse in 1636–37. In 1825 the stock market in London crashed partly as a result of highly speculative investments in Latin America, including the imaginary kingdom of Poyais, and nearly led to the collapse of the Bank of England. The best-known crash is that of Wall Street in 1929.

Bank runs occur when depositors rush to withdraw more money from the banks than the banks hold at the time with the result that depositors lose their assets. The Great Depression in America in 1931 saw a ferocious run on the Bank of the United States.

Currency crises and hyperinflation occur when the supply of paper money increases dramatically causing the value of the currency to decline. The Weimar Republic of Germany experienced this in 1923 when the Deutschmark fell to a value of DM 4,200,000,000,000 to the dollar. Between 1945 and 1946 Hungary experienced hyperinflation when prices rose by over nineteen percent per day.

Reith Lecturer Michael Sandel described the end of what he called three decades of 'market triumphalism'. It was time, he said, to think again about what 'the market' was for. Putting it all down to greed was too easy because greed, in the form of self-interest, was how markets functioned. What was wrong was allowing them to intrude into areas of public policy for which they were entirely inappropriate. Arguments like this are significant. If heeded, they mean that the Credit Crunch will result in a fundamentally different approach towards money and how it is made.

It is still too early to know whether the Western world will change its attitude towards markets and what they are for. But if they do, it is more than likely that those changes will be created, not by the application of a new philosophy, but by the impact of harsh economic reality. The principal difference between the Great Depression and the Credit Crunch is the effect upon the poorer people of the industrialised nations. In the Great Depression this was devastating, not least because to begin with banks did not know how to cope with it. In particular they made the fatal error of restricting money supply by raising interest rates. In America, the Federal Reserve, the country's central bank, did not intervene and lend to struggling banks in order to prevent their collapse. In the Credit Crunch the reverse happened. Interest rates fell and failing banks were bailed out by governments. This and the improvements in social welfare that have taken place since the end of the Second World War meant that the immediate consequences of the crisis were reduced. The sight of large crowds of homeless or unemployed people has not so far been a feature of the collapse in the markets.

In the longer term, however, that may change: the price of quick salvation is high. The cost of rescuing the financial systems of the West has plunged its governments into deep debt. In 2009 the International Monetary Fund reported that the world's ten richest economies had borrowed a total of more than $9 trillion in order to cope with the crisis. In a weak global economy, paying back these huge sums will prove a hard task. In Ireland the economic improvements of the previous twenty years have been all but extinguished by the financial turmoil. Everywhere countries face the prospect of introducing older retirement ages, higher taxes and deep spending cuts. In 1929 the sudden shock of the Wall Street Cash led to immediate devastation and despair. In 2010 the aftermath of shock may have been delayed, but not necessarily eradicated. The Credit Crunch could yet lead to the long term of erosion of wealth in the modern world.

2 Freedom

Introduction

Freedom is a much-abused concept. In English we use two words meaning the same thing – 'freedom' and 'liberty'. The first has a Teutonic root, the second comes from the Latin. Most other European languages have only one word, for example, *liberté* in French, *freiheit* in German or *libertad* in Spanish. The sad fact is that however many words are used to describe it, in the history of the world those promising liberty or freedom have often lied. Movements claiming to set people free have ended up imprisoning or suppressing them. True freedom is both hard to find and define. Like happiness, with which it is often associated, it is one of the most desired yet most elusive accompaniments to the progress of mankind.

In his book *On Liberty* published in 1859, the British political philosopher John Stuart Mill argued that 'the only purpose for which power can be rightfully exercised over any member of a civilised community, against his will, is to prevent harm to others ... Over himself, over his own body and mind, the individual is sovereign.' As with all philosophical pronouncements, it is a statement that begs some questions – most importantly in this case, what is the definition of preventing harm to others? But the broad principle of Mill's thought is one that many of us would agree with today. It remains a remarkably modern definition of liberty. For most of us our individual freedom is the most precious thing we possess. Furthermore, we take it for granted.

The journey to this state of affairs has been a long one, and it is not finished yet. It started in ancient Greece with philosophers like Socrates who argued that accepted truths should always be tested by rational argument and free discussion. From there it travelled into Roman thought where politicians like Cicero adopted the Socratic approach to open debate. The triumph of Christianity in Europe led eventually to the medieval age of suspicion and persecution. Argument became heresy in the mire of the Inquisition. By the fifteenth century, the ideas of the Renaissance, combined with the desire for greater religious freedom that inspired the Reformation, began to shake the foundations of the Church, although freedom of thought was still suppressed. Protestants could be just as ruthless as Catholics in exterminating opinions of which they did not approve. It was not until the end of the seventeenth century, when scientific discovery started to undermine the defences of a world built on religious foundations, that rational thought burst into the explosion of ideas we call the Enlightenment. From that time on concepts of freedom that we would recognise today came into being. Modern political thought has its beginnings in the philosophers of the late seventeenth and eighteenth centuries.

This section of the book picks its way through this process beginning with the slave rebellion against the Roman Republic led by Spartacus in 73 BC. Its bravery and brilliance have been an inspiration for many of those fighting for freedom ever since. Jan Hus, a Czech who was burned at the stake for his religious beliefs in Constance, Germany, in 1415 was one of the first great leaders of opposition to the Catholic Church in the Middle Ages, and is still regarded as a national hero in his own country. The American Declaration of Independence of 1776 and the French Revolution that began in 1789 were two of the greatest upheavals in world history. The first led to the creation of a great democracy while the other's high ideals were drowned in blood and resulted in Napoleonic dictatorship. The concept of individual freedom is arguably nowhere better expressed than in the works of Beethoven, whose music embodies the Romantic movement. The Zulu War of 1879 was an unsuccessful fight for liberty against the oppressive power of the British Empire; in Russia in 1917 the Bolshevik Revolution overthrew the monarchy of the Romanovs, promising liberation but building a terrifying Communist monolith instead; and in 1949 Mao Zedong became the Communist leader of China and began the ruthless control of his nation that would begin its transformation into a great world power. But in Europe the power of Communism fell into decline, its end signalled by the collapse of the Berlin Wall in 1989. A year later, the greatest African leader of the twentieth century, Nelson Mandela, was released from prison. The oppression of apartheid ended as he began the leadership of his country to black majority rule.

Each of these events can be seen as stepping stones to freedom. Together they provide a series of points from which we can look forward and back at man's attempts to make himself free. But a series of attempts is all they are. On the whole man's freedom remains something he desires rather than something he has found.

CHAPTER 1

Spartacus

73 BC

> Spartacus was a Roman slave and gladiator who led a
> rebellion against his Roman masters. He won a number
> of victories before being killed in battle. Since the
> eighteenth century his name has been used to evoke the
> idea of freedom.

In Paris in 1760 a five-act tragedy called *Spartacus* by the lawyer
and playwright Bernard-Joseph Saurin was a great popular
success when it appeared at the Comédie-Française. Exactly
two hundred years later, a Hollywood movie with the same title
starring Kirk Douglas brought the Spartacus story to the
worldwide cinema audience. The French philosopher Voltaire
described the Spartacus rebellion as 'the only just war in history'
and Karl Marx chose him as one of his heroes, calling him 'one of
the best characters in the whole of ancient
history'. Lenin also described him as 'one of   *Slavery is as old*
the most outstanding heroes of one of the
very greatest slave insurrections', while the   *as man.*
Communist revolutionaries in Germany
during and after the First World War took the name of Spartacus
as their inspiration and called themselves 'Spartacists'. From the
time of his death in battle in 71 BC until the eighteenth century,
Spartacus was little more than one of history's footnotes. But as
ideas of individual liberty took hold, the Western world looked
back to ancient Rome. In Spartacus it found the symbol of freedom it was looking for.

Slavery is as old as man. In the ancient world slaves were
valued in the same way as domestic animals and treated as
such. The Greek philosopher Aristotle said that both slaves

and animals were necessary for providing help in daily life. 'It is clear,' he said, 'that there are certain people who are free and certain who are slaves by nature, and it is both to their advantage, and just for them, to be slaves.' There are frequent references to slaves and slavery in the Old Testament; and many pre-colonial African countries operated systems of slavery, as did China, the countries of the Indian subcontinent and Southeast Asia. Different societies had different forms of slavery and different attitudes towards it as well. But all of them had one thing in common: slaves were human beings. They had a natural sense of freedom, and would always try to escape or rebel. Even though they might sometimes be well treated, the oppressive fact of their servitude was a constant burden. They knew that any freedoms and privileges they might enjoy could be taken away from them in an instant. They had no free will and no basic human rights.

The only way in which any such system can be maintained is through brutality. The achievements of classical antiquity may be inspiring but they were built upon a society that depended on the violence and human indignities of slavery. This acceptance of something that today we find abhorrent was regarded in the ancient world as perfectly appropriate, although in the early sixth century AD the legal code of the Eastern Roman Emperor, Justinian, recognised this conflict between the institution of slavery and its human effects. Slavery, it said, was contrary to the law of nature but was sanctioned as a legal activity.

Much later, when most European countries had in their own countries abandoned not only slavery, but its successor serfdom too, some of them adopted it again in order to support their colonial conquests. Once they had grown used to it, they found it almost impossible to relinquish it. Even the founding fathers of the American nation, some of the greatest apostles of liberty in the history of the modern world, could not face the issue of slavery when they devised the constitution of their new country. Their inability to do so contributed eventually to the American Civil War of the 1860s and the murderous battles that killed more than 600,000 people. In 1861, at the outset of the war, the State of Missouri gave its reasons for secession in a declaration. 'Our position,' it announced, 'is thoroughly identified with the institution of slavery – the greatest material interest in the world. Its labour supplies the product which constitutes by far the largest and most important portions of commerce of the earth ... These products have become necessities of the world, and a blow at slavery is a blow at commerce and civilisation.' No Greek philosopher, no Roman senator or emperor, could have put it better. In Brazil, where the Portuguese introduced slavery to maintain their sugar plantations, slavery was not banned altogether until 1888, even though the country had been independent for sixty-six years. Two years earlier, Thomas Hardy published one of his most famous novels, *The Mayor of Casterbridge*, in which, in the opening scene, a man auctions his wife and daughter at a country fair. His description of the event was met with horror and incredulity in late Victorian Britain but Hardy claimed that rural records showed that such activities still occurred in the English county of Dorset where his story was set. Not slavery perhaps, but not far off. Once men inure themselves against the obvious injustices of slavery and defend its use for the economic advantages they believe it brings, humanity deserts them.

In Spartacus, the Western world found the symbol of freedom it was looking for.

The economy of the Roman Republic and early Empire depended on slavery. We do not know exactly how many slaves there were, but estimates suggest that they made up a third of a total population of about six million. The main way in which people became slaves was through capture in war although traders and pirates also played their part. Natural reproduction helped maintain the numbers: a child born to a female slave was automatically enslaved, no matter who the father might have been. Slavery knew no racial or national boundaries. Anyone could become one. Slave markets flourished in towns throughout the Roman world as people went shopping for the human labour they needed to look after their homes or work their fields. Slaves involved in heavy labour were rarely set free – that was a privilege afforded to the better educated, who worked in clerical or educational jobs. At no time was this system of forced labour questioned or criticised. It did not change with the advent of Christianity. The Romans inherited slavery from the Greeks and used it as an essential part of their organisational structure until the last days of the Empire.

Spartacus came originally from Thrace, an area covering modern southern Bulgaria, northern Greece, and northern Turkey. According to the Greek historian Plutarch, writing long after the slave rebellion, Spartacus was brave and strong and also rather more intelligent than his fellow gladiators. He had seen service in the Roman army, was later sold as a prisoner and ended up in a school for gladiators in the prosperous southern town of Capua, not far from Naples. Gladiators were one of the sex symbols of ancient Rome. They were imprisoned in communal quarters, sometimes with their wives – Spartacus was married – and forced to take part in the violent spectacles that the Romans enjoyed. They lived in a world of constant uncertainty, thrust together with others they did not know and whose languages they may not have spoken. Their lives meant nothing, except to themselves. It is not surprising that there are recorded instances of gladiators committing suicide in order to escape from their life of bloody servitude. One man slit his throat in a lavatory before he was due to fight, another pretended to fall asleep as a cart carried him into the arena and broke his neck by thrusting his head between the spokes of its wheels.

In 73 BC Spartacus and about seventy other gladiators escaped from their school and set up a camp on the slopes of Mount Vesuvius about twenty miles away. From here they began to carry out raids on nearby properties. News of their activity spread and they began to be joined by other runaway slaves, building what seems to have been a quickly improvised dash for freedom into a significant insurrection. A military force of about 3,000 men was sent from Rome to suppress the rebellion, so we can assume the number of slaves under Spartacus's command must have grown to a considerable size. The Roman commander, Claudius Glaber, laid siege to the slaves' stronghold, but they escaped by climbing down the mountainside on ropes made from vines. Using what were presumably makeshift weapons they then attacked the Romans from behind and defeated them. More slaves now

Roman Slave Rebellions

There were two important rebellions by slaves before the one led by Spartacus in 70 AD. Both took place in Sicily where increasing numbers of slaves were brought from abroad to work on agricultural estates. The first started in Enna in 135 BC when Eunus, a Syrian fire-breathing entertainer who claimed to have prophetic powers, rebelled against an opulent landowner called Damophilus. His 400 men joined forces with 5,000 slaves led by Cleon, a horse-breeding slave. The rebellion engulfed half the island and became organised enough to resist several local governors until 132 BC, when the Roman army under the Consul Piso defeated it. In 104 BC a group of thirty slaves killed their wealthy landowning masters at the prosperous city of Halicyae near the modern town of Marsala. Their numbers spread spontaneously until they had a force of about 20,000 operating across a wide geographical area. Their leaders, Salvius and Athenion, became 'slave kings' and Salvius assumed the name 'Tryphon' after one of the rulers of the Seleucid Empire that succeeded Alexander the Great. The unplanned proliferation of their numbers sowed the seeds of the rebels' downfall. They found it too demanding and ultimately impossible to control such a large army. They were defeated when Rome committed adequate resources to defeat them in a full-scale battle under Consul Aquillus in 100 BC. Slaves were imported from many different countries and lacked common customs and attitudes. Their main purpose in rebellion was to take revenge against their owners and taste freedom. Beyond that they had little to sustain them.

joined Spartacus and his men. Many of them were agricultural workers and herdsmen who were used to living in open country and were fit and strong. The slaves acquired better weapons and horses, perhaps brought to them by the new recruits. Within a few months they had formed a powerful, well-managed army capable of challenging the might of Rome.

By the following year, 72 BC, the slaves were able to travel over large parts of southern Italy, carrying out raids and attracting recruits. New commanders were put into the field against them, but none was able to defeat the rebels. This persuaded the Roman authorities to take a very serious step. The two consuls for that year – Lucius Gellius Publicola and Gnaeus Cornelius Lentulus Clodianus – were despatched to quash the rebel forces once and for all. The consuls were the highest military and civilian authorities in the Roman Republic, elected on an annual basis by the Senate. The Romans obviously felt that Spartacus and his army represented a serious threat to the security of the state. This time the Roman army scored a quick victory. One of Spartacus's principal lieutenants, a Gaul called Crixus (the name means 'curly-headed' in Latin) with 3,000 slaves under his command, became separated from the main army. He was pursued, defeated and killed by the consul Gellius on a rocky promontory near Foggia on the Adriatic coast in Apulia.

Spartacus began to move north. Gellius came after him from the south while Lentulus tried to bar his way from the northern end. Spartacus defeated them both and then won another victory, this time over the commander of the Roman forces in Cisalpine Gaul, Gaius Cassius Longinus. This battle took place at Mutinae, near what is today Modena, nearly 400 miles north of the gladiator school from which Spartacus had originally escaped. The commanders of the Roman forces were recalled in disgrace, but Spartacus, instead of taking his army out of Rome and across the Alps, now turned south and began to make his way back to the area from which he had originally come. Another army, bigger than any of the others, was sent after him. Its commander was Marcus Licinius Crassus, one of the wealthiest men in the whole history of Rome and a politician and general of overwhelming influence and ambition. His army was paid for out of his personal fortune and when its first attack against Spartacus failed, Crassus decided to instil discipline by using 'decimation'. The army was divided into groups of ten and drew lots for one of them to be killed. The chosen victim was then clubbed or stoned by the nine others. In 71 BC, in far south-west Italy, Crassus succeeded in driving the rebel slaves into a

Spartacus's attempt to be liberated expressed a hope understood by all people who wanted to be free.

position where he could finally defeat them. Spartacus was killed. Six thousand recaptured slaves were crucified along the Via Appia into Rome – a warning to others about what would happen to those who defied the authority of the Republic. Crassus was awarded with an ovation.

Spartacus almost certainly knew that he could not destroy the institution of slavery. His rebellion was not an attempt to change the system. He just wanted to be free, probably to get home to the country from which he had originally come and lead a life where he did not belong to someone else. That is why his rebellion has become an enduring symbol of freedom. Spartacus could never have won, but in his attempt to be liberated, however briefly, from the bonds of slavery he expressed a hope understood by all people who want to be free.

Uncle Tom's Cabin by Harriet Beecher Stowe is probably the most famous novel about slavery ever written. It had an enormous impact when it was first published in America in 1852 because it explained the lives of slaves in human terms. Its style may now seem sentimental, but its message is still strong and clear. Reading it more than a hundred and fifty years after it was written awakens a spirit of anger and astonishment at how civilised men and women could rub along with a system of such iniquity. In one scene a trader, ferrying his slave cargo down river to the South, sells a baby to another man without the mother's knowledge. When she finds out she is distraught. 'The trader,' writes Harriet Beecher Stowe, 'had overcome every humane weakness and prejudice ... The wild look of anguish and utter despair that the woman cast on him might have disturbed one less practised; but he was used to it ...'. The passage ends with the words: 'You can get used to such things, too, my friend.' Written 2,000 years after the Spartacus rebellion it is a sobering reminder of how slavery has endured throughout the history of mankind.

CHAPTER 2

The Burning of Jan Hus

1415

Jan Hus was a priest and teacher from Bohemia, which today forms the Czech Republic and Slovakia. In 1415 the Catholic Church condemned him to be burned at the stake for his heretical views. He was one of the first Europeans to die in the struggle for liberty of thought.

When I was at school I was encouraged to view the world more widely through the debates and lectures organised by the Masaryk Society. It had been founded by a headmaster shortly after the Second World War in an effort to bring his traditional public school into the twentieth century. He named it after one of the most remarkable men in modern European history – Thomas Masaryk, the first President of Czechoslovakia. Masaryk was born in 1850, in a small town called Hodonin about 170 miles south-east of Prague. He began his working life as a teacher and philosopher, became the leader of his country in exile during the First World War and succeeded to its presidency when the Austro-Hungarian Empire collapsed in 1918. 'We can judge nations, including our own, quite impartially,' he once said. 'We need not worship the nation to which we belong.' This careful, rational approach to nationhood was founded on his deep love for his country and its history. He understood where his people had come from and how they had been shaped by events. They might have suffered as possessions of an empire but their desire to be free remained. It had been with them for 500 years, ever since Jan Hus had gone to his death rather than renounce his beliefs.

By the beginning of the fifteenth century, the administration of the Catholic Church in Europe had begun to enter the long, slow period of decline that would lead to the Reformation a hundred years later. To those who governed the Church the signs of decay were barely visible. The idea of any secession from its teachings was unthinkable. Christianity led from Rome had enjoyed triumphant progress ever since the first Christian Roman Emperor, Constantine, had, in 313 AD, ordered that persecution was to cease and Christianity tolerated. Having captured the Roman Empire, Christianity spread across Europe, its influence thwarted only in the Middle East where, after the death of Mohammed in 632, Islam became the preferred religion. At the end of the eleventh century, the papacy began a series of crusades against Islam in an attempt to take back control of places it believed were central to its religious authority. Ultimately they failed. By the time Jan Hus began to explain his interpretation of the Scriptures, Christian influence was largely contained within Western Europe, blocked from further expansion by the presence of Islam in North Africa, the Levant and Eastern Mediterranean and the Black Sea and the Balkans.

The European papacy saw itself as all-powerful.

The European papacy of the Middle Ages saw itself as all powerful. In 1208, Pope Innocent III issued an interdict against England's King John because the King had refused to accept his nomination for Archbishop of Canterbury. For a God-fearing people, an interdict was a serious imposition. It prevented them from observing everyday religious rites associated with such things as baptisms and funerals without which they were unprotected from salvation. In 1302, Pope Boniface VIII issued a bull entitled 'Unam sanctum' – a declaration of supreme Church power. It said that there was no salvation outside the Church and that those who resisted the Pope were resisting the law of God. Boniface felt the need to reassert the authority of his office because the French King, Philip IV, had begun to raid the Church for taxation and undermine the jurisdiction of ecclesiastical courts. The conflict between King and Pope resulted in

Power Corrupts

One of the most famous aphorisms in the whole of historical writing was composed directly as a result of a discussion about the medieval papacy. In the 1880s the cleric and scholar, Mandell Creighton, later a Bishop of London, published a *History of the Papacy during the Period of the Reformation.* Creighton was lenient in his judgements of the policies and actions of the medieval Catholic Church. Describing the trial of Jan Hus, for instance, he acknowledged that Hus 'had first deliberately asserted the rights of the individual conscience against ecclesiastical authority', but added that it was 'useless to criticise particular points in his trial. The Council was anxious for his submission and gave him every opportunity to make it.' This careful, temporising approach irritated another scholar of the age, Lord Acton. In a famous letter to Creighton he told him that he could not accept the idea that popes and kings should not be judged like other men. He went on: 'Power tends to corrupt and absolute power corrupts absolutely. Great men are almost always bad men, even when they exercise influence and not authority.' Acton believed that what he called 'the inflexible integrity of the moral code' was essential to the study of history. If debased history 'ceases to be a science, an arbiter of controversy, a guide of the wanderer, the upholder of that moral standard which the powers of the earth, and religion itself, tend constantly to depress'.

Boniface's capture and detention. Six years after he died, in 1303, the papacy moved from Rome to France, ending up in Avignon where it would remain for more than seventy years. Although housed in papal territory – Avignon was not part of France – the papacy inevitably fell under French influence. All the popes who took office during the period of the Avignon papacy were French.

Political instability began to undermine the papacy. The Avignon court lived well: to many people it appeared to prefer the luxurious trappings of an earthly life to the spiritual requirements of religious devotion. A splendid new palace was built, the number of wealthy officials needed to administer papal business grew and the Church became richer as it sought, not only to establish its presence in its new home, but to look after the territories and possessions it had left behind in Italy. One of the Avignon popes, Clement VI, believed that largesse increased papal prestige. 'No one ought to retire discontented from the presence of a prince,' he said. 'My predecessors did not know how to be popes.' Such comfortable grandeur might have reassured the papal hierarchy, but it worried many of its subjects. Franciscan friars compared Avignon to the captivity of the Israelites in Babylon. Matters worsened when in 1378 Pope Gregory XI decided to return to Rome. After his death, the French cardinals refused to accept his successor, the first Italian pope since the exodus to Avignon, and moved back to France where they elected an alternative pontiff, called the Antipope. For nearly forty years the Church was divided by the Western Schism. The rulers of Europe took sides, supporting either the popes elected by Rome, or those chosen by Avignon. It was against the background of this confused, highly political situation that Jan Hus began to question the behaviour of the Church.

Jan Hus was born in southern Bohemia. In 1398 he became a professor at the University of Prague where he was ordained and began to teach theology. His lectures and sermons in favour of clerical reform gathered widespread support, partly because many members of his audience were looking for release from the domination of Vienna and the German sovereignty of the Holy Roman Empire. Earlier in the fourteenth century, other Bohemian priests had begun to call for change. The Czech language and the individuality of the Czech people came together to form a nationalist movement that found expression in the language of its priests. Hus was influenced by the English cleric, John Wyclif, who had begun to identify a new approach to organised religion. Both men went back to the Scriptures, arguing that the Church should not own property or pursue wealth. The observation of religion should be founded on the teachings of its Christian founders, nothing else. The Church was a body of elected members predestined to enjoy salvation: Christ, not the Pope, was their leader. Hus's views alarmed the

Church authorities. In 1411 he was excommunicated and a year later forced to go into hiding where he wrote his most famous work, *De Ecclesia*. 'The opinion of no man,' he said, 'whatever his authority may be – and consequently the opinion of no pope – is to be held if it plainly contains falsehood or error.'

In 1414 the Holy Roman Emperor, Sigismund, called a council in the German city of Constance overlooking the Bodensee. His main concern was to heal the schism that had divided the Church since Gregory XI had returned to Rome from Avignon. Aware that the views of John Hus had found favour with many of his subjects in Bohemia, he invited Hus to attend the gathering in order to explain his views. He promised him safe passage and Hus, against the advice of some of his closest supporters, decided to accept. Instead of participating in the theological debate he had expected he was arrested and tried for heresy. His accusers urged him to recant but Hus refused, arguing that the charges against him were inaccurate. 'I stand at the judgement seat of Christ, to whom I have appealed,' he told them, 'knowing that He will judge every man, not according to false or erroneous witness, but according to the truth and each one's deserts.' In July 1415 he was removed from the priesthood and burned at the stake. He died singing hymns.

Hus's death stands as a uniquely important event in the whole history of man's desire to be free.

Hus, caught up in the political turmoil of the schism that had divided the papacy at the end of the fourteenth century, found that those who had supported him deserted him in his hour of greatest need. In England, John Wyclif was luckier. His strongest supporter was John of Gaunt, the most powerful prince in the land who, although not always agreeing with some of Wyclif's views, allowed him to die in peace in 1384 in the Leicestershire village of Lutterworth to which he had retired. It was not until after his death, at the Council of Constance more than thirty years later, that Wyclif's works were condemned as heretical.

While Wyclif was allowed to die quietly, his greatest apostle, Jan Hus, was burned. However the flames of change that Hus had set alight began a movement that was to change the Roman Catholic Church forever. In Bohemia his death was met with anger and rebellion. Between 1420 and 1436, the forces of the Hussites repelled the armies of the Pope and the Holy Roman Emperor that were sent to subdue them.

Inspired by Jan's teachings and united by a sense of Czech nationhood, the Hussites fought successfully against the crusades launched against them by an enraged Catholic Church. The lessons that Jan Hus had taught his people did not die. He – and Wyclif too – were the forerunners of the Reformation that in the century that followed would finally destroy the universal power of the papacy and set Europe and the world on a new course.

Hus's decision to die for his beliefs towers over the time in which it took place, a permanent reminder of man's desire for liberty.

The death of Jan Hus stands as a uniquely important event not only in Czech history but in the whole history of man's desire to be free. The Czech people have been some of the most oppressed in the history of Europe. Suppressed by the Habsburg monarchy of Austria-Hungary in what one writer called a 'truceless warfare against the soul of a people', they enjoyed a brief moment of independence under Thomas Masaryk after the First World War. This was crushed first by the Nazis and then by Stalinist Russia. In the fight for Czech freedom three men called Jan played important parts. Two of them were students who lived in the twentieth century. The first, Jan Opletal, was killed in Prague during demonstrations against the Nazi occupation of the country in 1939. The second, Jan Palach, burned himself to death thirty years later in 1969 after Russian troops destroyed the liberalising reforms of the Czech government. He died within walking distance of Prague's memorial to the third Jan – Jan Hus. In the Middle Ages, life and liberty revolved entirely around religion. By expressing a new approach to religious observation Jan Hus defined liberty for the time in which he lived. But his decision to die for his beliefs towers over the time in which it took place, and succeeding ages, unchanged by any historical context, a permanent reminder of man's desire for liberty.

CHAPTER 3

The American Declaration of Independence

1776

In 1776 the thirteen colonies on the continent of North America declared their independence from British rule. The reasons they gave, and the nation they created as a result, define many of the ideas of liberty in the modern world.

'Democracy starts here.' So proclaims the promotional material for America's National Archives in Washington DC. The Archives, it says, tell the story of the 'American journey to young and old, scholars and students, cynics and dreamers.' They are held in a grand neo-classical building on Pennsylvania Avenue, designed in 1935 by the same architect who created the city's Jefferson Memorial. Among their treasures is a 1297 copy of England's Magna Carta, as well as the 'Emancipation Proclamation' issued by Abraham Lincoln in 1863, freeing all slaves held in Confederate States. But pride of place goes to the so-called 'Charters of Freedom' kept in a splendid, echoing rotunda at the heart of the building. These are the American Constitution, the Bill of Rights and the Declaration of Independence. The Declaration is a faded document barely readable to the naked eye. To discover what it says, and who signed it, one needs to look at the facsimile displayed alongside it. But people do not come to read it: they simply come to look. This piece of dilapidated parchment, just over two feet wide and nearly two and a half feet long, is one of history's most important symbols of liberty.

The leaders of the thirteen colonies on the eastern seaboard of the American continent became the first people to give expression to modern ideas of democracy through the mismanagement and miscalculation of their imperial masters in Britain. During the last quarter of the eighteenth century, Britain enjoyed a system of government more open and more liberal than most other places in the world. Europe's other great world power, France, was in the sclerotic grip of the Bourbon monarchy and the *ancien régime*. Louis XV, who ruled for fifty-nine years, only thirteen less than his great-grandfather, Louis XIV, before him, died in 1774 having abandoned all attempts to reform his country's creaking administration. China was locked behind its wall of self-imposed isolation. In St Petersburg and Vienna, two powerful autocrats, Catherine the Great and Joseph II, attempted to modernise their vast lands, but never with a view to relinquishing any of their own enormous power. Catherine was the more impressive of the two. She was actually a minor German princess who deposed (and perhaps murdered) her weak-willed husband and seized the throne. In partnership with powerful Russian ministers, generally her lovers as well, she managed to get the wild country she governed to adopt some European ideas, but widespread reform eluded her. Her fellow emperor, Joseph of Austria, dismissed her as merely 'a woman who cares only for herself, and no more for Russia than I do'.

Britain was different. Ever since Henry VIII had broken away from the Roman church at the beginning of the sixteenth century and provided, though not intentionally, a form of royal licence for reformation, the nation had been involved in a long battle for religious liberty. This happened elsewhere in Europe too, but in Britain it resulted in the civil wars of the seventeenth century and, in 1649, the execution of the King and the creation of the brief republic of Oliver Cromwell. Over time, expressions of religious and political liberty came to mean similar things. The Bill of Rights that Parliament imposed on its new king, William III, in 1689, was both a religious and political settlement. It banned Roman Catholics from the monarchy – they were 'inconsistent with the safety and welfare of this Protestant kingdom' – but also restricted the powers of the sovereign. Freedom from royal interference in the law, freedom of speech in Parliament, and freedom from taxation by royal prerogative were all enshrined in the English constitution, an unwritten distillation of precedent and acts of Parliament. In the years that followed, these ideas were expanded and developed by eighteenth-century philosophers and writers, creating an age of freedom of thought – an 'enlightenment' – that was entirely new. But if the British felt that they enjoyed liberty, it existed in a form that fell far short of democracy. The aristocracy and landowners controlled Parliament because they owned its constituencies – sometimes so-called 'rotten boroughs' with no one living in them – and chose the members to represent them. These were people who had grown rich as Britain expanded her empire: caution and conservatism were the weapons they used to protect their wealth.

In the American colonies, English concepts of more open and more inclusive government began to find an opportunity for unfettered expansion. Self-reliance is a natural ally of democracy. The men and women who built new lives far from home developed a sense of fellowship and common identity. They viewed themselves very differently from the way they were regarded in London. But they were not revolutionaries. In 1760, Benjamin Franklin, one of the signatories of the Declaration of Independence, declared that he was not just a colonist but 'a Briton', and added: 'I have long been of Opinion that the Foundations of the future Grandeur and Stability of the British Empire lie in America.' In that statement can be found the seeds of the tension between the British government and its lands across the Atlantic. The colonists were loyal, but proud and independent too. They wanted to share in the growth of the British Empire on an equal footing, not as a subservient people. The British, meanwhile, grew increasingly irritated with the behaviour of the colonists who failed to act in unison, defied the King's instructions and, most importantly of all, baulked at paying the cost of the war that had protected them from French invasion. In Quebec in 1759, General James Wolfe defeated the French in a battle that gave Britain control of the whole of North America. It was one of the most significant victories of the Seven Years' War. The French,

Franklin declared that he was not just a colonist but 'a Briton'.

supported by native American Indians, had invaded areas west of British settlements planning to colonise them. George Washington, as a young major in the Virginia militia, saw action in an expedition against them.

By 1760, with the French removed, the British decided to force the colonists to help meet the cost of the war by imposing a Stamp Act on printed materials. The imposition of a tax without any right of representation was not something the Americans could accept. Tension turned to outright anger. In 1765, the year the tax became law, Patrick Henry, one of the great orators of the American Revolution, made a speech to the House of Burgesses, the Virginia colonial assembly, in which he compared the English King to two rulers who had suffered bloody deaths. 'Caesar had his Brutus,' he cried; 'and Charles I his Cromwell; and George III may profit by their example.' Though his inflammatory words were met with cries of 'Treason!' from some delegates, the situation was beginning to worsen. In 1766 Parliament passed the Declaratory Act that reinforced its supreme authority over the colonies by stating that it had the right to pass any laws it chose in the management of their government. In the years that followed, the colonies and the British government frequently clashed on issues of authority. In 1773 a Boston mob threw tea belonging to the British East India Company into the harbour because it carried an import tax imposed by the British government; in April 1775 the first military engagement took place between British troops and colonial militia men at Lexington and Concord in Massachusetts; and the following month the Continental Congress, the legislative body representing all thirteen colonies, met for a second time to raise an army and agree a strategy for war. Just over a year later, on 4th July 1776, the Congress adopted the Declaration of Independence.

The Declaration of Independence is probably the most famous statement about liberty ever made. Its first sentence states that any group of people with a reasonable claim that can be justified and explained is entitled under the Laws of Nature to assert its independence. The preamble that follows declares that all men are created equal and have the right to life, liberty and the pursuit of happiness. This is a truth that is self-evident, it says, and any government that denies men the expression of these liberties can be altered or abolished. The Declaration then explains the colonists' grievances against the British government, argues that it has tried to seek redress but has been rejected, and characterises George III as a tyrant for failing to listen to his people's needs. Independence, it goes on, is therefore the only route down which the injured people of the colonies can travel. It must treat Great Britain as it must treat all other nations – 'Enemies in War, in Peace Friends'. Finally comes the Declaration of Independence itself, to the protection of which the signatories 'mutually pledge to each other our Lives, our Fortunes, and our sacred Honor'.

'all men are created equal and have the right to life, liberty and the pursuit of happiness.'

The principal author of the Declaration was Thomas Jefferson who, with Benjamin Franklin and James Madison, gave the American Revolution its intellectual direction. The Declaration's arguments about natural law and natural rights, and the right of people to rebel when these are denied them, come largely from the writings of the English philosopher John Locke. His *Two Treatises of Government* were published in 1689 as a justification for the revolution of 1688 that drove James II off the English throne. But nearly a hundred years later, the ideas that Locke advanced found little favour in the country whose political actions had inspired them. Although the English politician, Charles James Fox, was of the opinion that the colonists 'had done no more than the English had done against James II', most of his contemporaries were of a very different view. The First Lord of the Admiralty, the Earl of Sandwich, wrote to an admiral to tell him that the 'nation are in a manner unanimous in their resolution to crush the unnatural rebellion that has broken out in America'. This hostility to the colonists' behaviour was rooted in the British idea of sovereignty. The King, ruling through Parliament, was the supreme authority and any attempt to destroy his power was a treasonable attack on the rule of law. Even the most eloquent critics of the British government's policy, such as William Pitt, Earl of

Chatham, did not support colonial independence, believing that a more conciliatory attitude towards the Americans would bring them back into the imperial fold. But the situation had moved beyond that, as the King realised. 'The die is now cast,' he told his Prime Minister, Lord North in 1774; 'the Colonies must either submit or triumph.'

The American victory that followed persuaded the newly independent colonies that they needed to revise their government. In 1787, representatives from Congress met in Philadelphia to adapt the colonies' constitution to their changed requirements. Rather than adapt, however, they came up with something entirely new. Under the guidance of Madison and the constitutional lawyer, Alexander Hamilton, they devised a federal system in which, as united states (they were no longer colonies), they could manage issues relating to foreign policy, common security and finance in the interests of all without undermining the independence of any of the separate entities. James Madison also drafted a Bill of Rights that sat alongside the Declaration of Independence and the Constitution itself as one of the three founding documents of the American nation. Together they echo Hamilton's words from a book he wrote in 1775: 'The sacred rights of mankind are not to be rummaged for, among old parchments, or musty records. They are written, as with a sun-beam, in the whole volume of human nature, by the hand of divinity itself; and can never be erased or obscured by mortal power.'

The American Revolution was the most successful political transformation in the history of the modern world, but its success obscured some if its inconsistencies. The idea of the natural rights of the individual, first espoused by John Locke and developed by the French philosophers of the eighteenth century, was not a basis for government. In the years that followed independence, America, and Europe too, defined liberty as the right of the individual to enjoy democratic privileges within an organised society. It sometimes had to be suborned to serve the interests of the nation as a whole. This goes some way to explaining why the American revolutionaries did not abolish slavery. In their huge dream of a new world, a true democracy, they allowed the continuation of one of the greatest of human evils. In 1789,

Monticello

Architect of the Declaration of Independence and later third President of the United States, Thomas Jefferson (1743–1826) was a man of the Enlightenment, a statesman, philosopher, architect, lawyer, horticulturalist and inventor. In 1768 he started building a house on a hill near Charlottesville in Virginia. He called it 'Monticello', a name derived from the Italian, meaning 'little mountain'. The house became more than his home: it was his intellectual laboratory. Another President, Franklin D. Roosevelt, said of it: 'More than any historic home in America, Monticello speaks to me as an expression of the personality of its builder … [At Monticello] there speaks ready capacity for detail and, above all, creative genius.'

Jefferson's designs were an 'essay in architecture', reworked and refined over forty years. At Monticello, he introduced for the first time to the United States the European neo-classical architecture of the Enlightenment, which complemented the civic values of his political outlook. Paradoxically, if his house symbolised Jefferson's vision for an enlightened America, it was built and staffed by slaves. Jefferson's mounting debt may have made them financially necessary.

A period in Paris as United States Minister to France in 1784–89 exposed him to the latest continental fashions, prompting him to modify and enlarge the house, and furnishing him with crates of art, artefacts and fruit trees which he shipped to Virginia. He also added an octagonal dome, the first in America. A radical departure from Virginia's architectural traditions, Jefferson acknowledged that his home counted 'among the curiosities of the neighbourhood', adding that: 'All my wishes end where I hope my days will end, at Monticello.' He is buried on the estate.

the year that George Washington, a slave owner, became the first President of the United States of America, William Wilberforce made his first speech to Parliament urging the abolition of the slave trade. By 1807, when Thomas Jefferson, who fathered children by one of his slaves, was halfway through his second term of presidential office, Britain had abolished it altogether. It had paid the price for obstinately spurning colonial ideas of liberty.

But as the colonies it had lost forever began their transformation into a democratic power, Britain demonstrated that in matters of human freedom it could still lead the world.

The independence of America was a huge achievement. Throughout a period of more than twenty years, the colonies remained on the whole united in their purpose. Although they had developed in areas that were far apart and had different traditions and outlooks, they were always steadfast both in their ambition to be free and in their opposition to British policy. The men who led it remained loyal to their principles. They were not without their rivalries, but having separated from the mother country and devised a constitution by which they were to be governed, they held to it and on the whole administered it with honesty and fairness. But the men who made America, sincere as they were, still had their blind spots. Slavery was one of them. Liberty is often in the eye of the beholder.

CHAPTER 4

The French Revolution
1789

The French Revolution was a momentous and bloody upheaval whose effects were felt all over Europe. It led to the execution of the King of France, the Terror and the rise of Napoleon.

Brilliant, shrewd, prescient and utterly corrupt, Charles Maurice de Talleyrand-Périgord is one of the most enigmatic figures in European history. His club foot proved no impediment to his talents as a seducer. His patriotism was always tempered by self-interest and he navigated frightening times with aplomb. He was a revolutionary, a servant of the Napoleonic Empire and a monarchist: he always behaved according to the requirements of the times in which he lived. When these changed quickly and unexpectedly he changed with them. He played an important part in the early days of the French Revolution; fled abroad when the Terror threatened to extinguish him, plotted to bring Napoleon to power and then plotted to get rid of him, and finally conspired with the victorious allies after the Emperor's defeat to bring the monarchy back to France. 'Regimes may fall and fail,' he said once, 'but I do not.' But, as one of his contemporaries later observed: 'Nothing remains that comes from him.' The life of this extraordinary man provides a useful insight to the French Revolution. It began with high hopes that France might be remade as a constitutional monarchy, but these aspirations died in the bloodletting and factionalism that ultimately overwhelmed it. What, like its greatest survivor Talleyrand, did it leave behind?

The causes of the French Revolution were deep and complex. Two long-lived Bourbon kings of France had, by the time Louis

XVI came to the throne in 1774, ruled their country for more than a hundred and thirty years. They bequeathed him a nation with enormous financial and administrative problems. France was a great world power. Although it had lost some its colonial territory in India and North America to Britain during the Seven Years' War, its size, unity and inherent wealth made it a formidable opponent. Within a few years of Louis XVI inheriting the throne, French forces fighting alongside George Washington's revolutionary army forced Britain to give America independence. Its political structure, however, was cumbersome and old-fashioned, dependent on a system of privileges and tax exemptions that caused social friction while at the same time failing to produce the revenue necessary to maintain the state. This creaking structure functioned in contrast to France's intellectual ideas. Its writers and philosophers were at the forefront of European thinking about economic and political liberty and the rights of man. The young king – Louis was nineteen when he came to the throne – turned to one of their followers, Jacques Turgot, to help reform the economy but Turgot's ideas proved too radical for the nobility and he was dismissed after less than two years. By 1787 the financial situation had got so bad that Louis reconstituted an ancient consultative body called the Assembly of Notables that had not met for a hundred and sixty years. When this failed to resolve the issue an even older institution, the Estates General – its last meeting had been in 1614 – was summoned to discuss the problems. The Estates General had three divisions. The First represented the Clergy; the Second, the Nobility; and the Third, the Commoners – mainly merchants and small landowners but also lesser members of the aristocracy and protestant clergy.

The Estates General met in Versailles in May 1789. The following month the Third Estate declared itself a National Assembly, representing the people of France in all aspects of government, and invited the other estates to join it. The King tried to shut it down, but the delegates moved to the royal tennis court where

The creaking structure functioned in contrast to France's intellectual ideas.

they swore an oath of solidarity until they had reformed their country's constitution. A large number of the clergy and some members of the nobility joined them. The debates and arguments of this new Assembly were circulated among the people of Paris and when in July the King dismissed his finance minister, Necker, who was perceived as being sympathetic to its objectives, violence erupted on the streets. A mob stormed the Bastille prison in Paris which, although it only housed seven prisoners, was regarded as a symbol of royal tyranny. From this moment on France was set on a course, not of reform, but of revolution.

The French Revolution developed through several phases. The National Assembly, later called the National Constituent Assembly, drew up a new constitution that it forced Louis XVI to accept. It also issued the Declaration of the Rights of Man and the Citizen, proclaiming ideas of individual liberty similar to those of the American Declaration of Independence, abolished the nobility; and passed legislation subordinating the clergy to the laws of the state. There were mob riots and violence on the streets of Paris, and in October 1789 a group of women, angered by bread shortages, marched on the Palace of Versailles. The King was eventually forced to abandon Versailles altogether and moved to the Tuileries Palace in the centre of Paris. Later the royal family tried to flee across the border to Austrian owned Belgium, but were stopped at the town of Varennes in Lorraine and brought back to the capital. The National Constituent Assembly dissolved itself in September 1791 to make way for a Legislative Assembly elected under the rules of the new French constitution.

The Legislative Assembly was dominated by the Jacobins, a political faction that took its name from the former monastery in which it met and the most radical of all the groups that sprang up in France during the Revolution. Within a year the assembly was dissolved and a National Convention, elected by all French males over the age of twenty-one, assumed power. The Convention abolished the monarchy and introduced a revolutionary calendar with twelve newly named months to replace the old ones. In January 1793, Louis XVI was executed and the Convention fell under the control of its Committee of Public Safety. This directed the course of the Revolution with zeal and ferocity. Under the leadership of its most determined member, Maximilien Robespierre, it pursued the Terror, removing all those who opposed the pure course of the Revolution by sending them to the guillotine. In La Vendee in western France, a royalist revolt against the revolutionary government was suppressed with a savagery that fell little short of genocide. The new government also adopted Robespierre's idea of the Cult of the Supreme Being, a state religion that worshipped a supreme rational force watching over France. In July 1794, Robespierre's enemies turned against him and he was executed without trial. Later that year the Convention was dissolved and a new constitution introduced a system of five executive directors nominated by an elected assembly. The directors were supposed to rotate, with one each retiring on an annual basis, but the system was unpopular and corrupt and survived mainly because France began to enjoy considerable success in wars abroad. The architect of these victories, Napoleon Bonaparte, became First Consul of France in November 1799, and proclaimed himself Emperor in December 1804.

A revolt was suppressed with a savagery that fell little short of genocide.

These tumultuous events threw up a succession of brilliant, exotic and strange figures. At the beginning the Estates General was dominated by the Comte de Mirabeau, an eloquent, raffish but brilliant politician who saw how the noble ideas of the revolution were likely to be drowned by political inexperience. He wanted to create a constitutional monarchy along British lines, but caught between an intransigent nobility and an excitable National Assembly, made little headway before he died in 1791. As the Revolution gathered steam, Georges Danton took centre stage, flamboyant, fiery and patriotic. He urged the Committee of Public Safety to take dictatorial powers and then stepped aside once it had assumed them. He became one of its first victims, riding to his death with the correct prediction that Robespierre would not be long behind him. The Marquis de Lafayette was a hero of the American War of Independence who threw himself into the early days of the Revolution with vigour

The French Revolutionary Calendar

Revolutionaries often try to abolish the past. In 1792 the French revolutionary government reorganised the calendar, getting rid of the old method of counting days, weeks and months and introducing an entirely new system. The years were numbered, with Year I (of Liberty) starting from the inauguration of the Republic on 22nd September 1792. They consisted of twelve thirty-day months each with three ten-day weeks (*décades*) that ended on a rest day (*décadi*) instead of a traditional Sunday. The five days left over were originally called *sans-culottides* but later redesignated as complementary days to be used for festivals and grand celebrations. The months were given names intended to evoke the seasonal rhythm of the agricultural cycle. The autumn months were called *Vendémiaire* 'grape harvest', *Brumaire* 'foggy' and *Frimaire* 'frosty'. The winter months were given the names *Nivôse* 'snowy', *Pluviôse* 'rainy,' and *Ventôse* 'windy'. The spring months became *Germinal* 'germination', *Floréal* 'flower,' and *Prairial* 'pasture' The summer months were *Messidor* 'harvest', *Thermidor* 'heat' and *Fructidor* 'fruit'. Each day of every *décade* was named after a fruit, a vegetable or a flower on weekdays, an animal on the fifth day. and a farm tool on the *décadi*. The whole calendar was meant to obliterate what the revolutionaries considered to be the superstitious religious practices of much of the population. It was abolished by Napoleon in 1805. The British enjoyed referring to the new months as Slippy, Nippy, Drippy; Freezy, Wheezy, Sneezy; Showery, Flowery, Bowery; Heaty, Wheaty and Sweety.

and panache, and drew up the first draft of the Declaration of the Rights of Man and the Citizen. He was forced to flee from the Jacobins, was imprisoned by the Austrians and rehabilitated by Napoleon. Camille Desmoulins was a failed lawyer who learned the art of oratory in front of the Paris mob and became through his writings and speeches the mouthpiece of violent revolutionary thinking. He went to the guillotine in the Terror. Jean-Paul Marat was a doctor turned journalist who waged an implacable war of words against conservative revolutionaries and was stabbed to death while soaking in a medicinal bath. The woman who murdered him, Charlotte Corday, was taking revenge for Marat's attacks on the Girondins, a political faction that she supported. Finally there was Robespierre himself. His jaw was shattered during a gunfight before his arrest and he travelled to the scaffold with a bandage tied around it. The executioner ripped it away and Robespierre let out a shriek as the guillotine extinguished pain and life forever. That was the human story of the French Revolution: vivid lives violently enacted.

Revolutions sweep away things that can never be replaced. Although the revolutionary process stopped when Napoleon took power as First Consul, its effects continued to be felt, and perhaps still are, in French politics. An announcement told the French people: 'Citizens, the Revolution is established upon its original principles. It is over.' The idea that the Revolution had succeeded and the future of France left in his safe hands was an idea that suited Napoleon perfectly.

Revolutions sweep away things that can never be replaced.

He always presented himself as its heir, claiming that he enshrined its ideals while restoring stability to France. This is hardly true. He did unify his country, and worked with different political elements to achieve this. He introduced important legislation. His civil code of 1804 that promulgated the principles of freedom of religion and promotion on merit, not privilege, remains a foundation of French law to this day. Its influence throughout Europe was enormous. But Napoleon was always an autocrat. He understood the importance of the revolutionary slogan '*Liberté, Egalité, Fraternité*' but his support for it never coalesced into a coherent political creed. He sustained himself in power, as he well knew himself, by giving France status and prestige through military success abroad. As one of the earliest French historians of the Revolution, Mignet, observed: 'He believed neither in the moral cravings which had stirred up the Revolution, nor in the convictions which had swayed it, and which sooner or later were bound to emerge again and bring about his downfall. He saw a revolt approaching its end, a weary people delivering himself up to him, and a crown which was his for the taking.'

After Napoleon's defeat and exile in 1815, the French were forced to accept a return to the Bourbon monarchy they had brutally despatched more than twenty years previously. The European powers, gathered in Vienna to pick up the pieces left behind by the long wars against Napoleon, chose to go back, not forward, and reinstate monarchical conservatism as a barrier to dangerous change. It could not and did not work. Revolutions in 1830, 1848 and 1870 sent French kings scurrying for safety to England. The quiet refinements of Dorset, Surrey and Kent became the preferred habitat of the men who thought they could rule France. In 1870, when France was invaded and defeated by the Prussians, radical elements in the capital established the Paris Commune, a system of government that harked back to the days of the Revolution and even briefly reinstated the revolutionary calendar. The Commune was crushed, but France would never be a monarchy again.

The revolutionaries of France in the eighteenth century described the period before they seized power as 'L'Ancien Régime' – the old system – and this is a description that has remained in use ever since. It is a telling phrase: the year 1789 marks the moment when a powerful European country broke with its past, never to return. The French Revolution was a political, cultural and intellectual volcano unlike any other in European history, spewing out hundreds of ideas about government and individual liberty, only some of which found their way into permanent constitutional form. It was, in some ways, a class conflict because it became subsumed by anti-aristocratic and anti-monarchical feeling. But the aristocracy survived and the institution of the monarchy took a long time to die. Its conflicting objectives and confused results make it feel, in retrospect, somehow troublesome and incomplete. It continues to be analysed, described and investigated by historians from every country in the world. Today one of France's leading universities, the Sorbonne in Paris, has a department entirely given over to its study.

A powerful European country had broken with its past, never to return.

'What,' someone once asked the Abbé Sieyès, 'did you do in the Revolution?' To which he replied: 'I survived.' The Abbé was an exact contemporary of Talleyrand. His pamphlet entitled 'What Is The Third Estate?' helped fuel the sense of national purpose during the Revolution's first excited days. He was on hand to administer the oath when the deputies swore never to disband until they had created a new constitution for their country. After the Terror, he served in the last days of the Directory and organised the coup d'état that brought Napoleon to power. He was amply rewarded for his efforts and died in Paris in 1836 after a brief period of exile under the Bourbon kings. There is a portrait of him by Jacques-Louis David, another revolutionary who survived the turbulence, in which he looks out at his onlookers in a quiet, contained and self-assured manner. He was a man of few words, something of an opportunist, not entirely trustworthy. But, like thousands of other Frenchmen, he was a revolutionary. As such he changed his country, and Europe, forever.

CHAPTER 5

Ludwig van Beethoven's Ninth Symphony

1824

Beethoven's Ninth Symphony – the choral – has been
used to evoke the idea of man's freedom ever since
it was first heard in public. Beethoven himself is
regarded as one of the principal representatives of the
Romantic Movement – artists whose belief in individual
expression became synonymous with ideas of liberty.

The English composer Ralph Vaughan Williams was not what he
called 'a loyal Beethovenite', but when he came to write down his
thoughts on Beethoven's Ninth Symphony he had to confess that
he was 'left dumb in the presence of its greatness'. Of the first
two movements he said they were 'like no other music before or
since. It seems sometimes to have come from the eternal source
of truth without human intervention.' When we think of eternity,
he went on, 'we turn to Beethoven'.

Vaughan Williams was writing 115 years after the Ninth
Symphony was first performed, in Vienna in 1824. His view
of it was not unlike that of the audience that heard it then. It
applauded tumultuously as Beethoven, completely deaf and
unable to hear anything at all, had to be turned to face the
rapturous reception his work received. Ever since the chorus in
the last movement first gave voice to the composer's setting of
Friedrich Schiller's poem 'Ode to Joy', many people have looked
on the Ninth Symphony as a symbol, not just of optimism and
hope, but of liberty and the free expression of the human spirit.
It represents a break from a classical, somewhat restrained, past
and looks forward to a vigorous and romantic future. It marks

the moment when the artist is no longer an employee of the wealthy patron, but someone in his own right, a hero and a seeker after truth. Freedom, it seems to say, is not just about equality and the natural rights of man, but about the unfettered ambition of the universal spirit.

> *Freedom is not just about equality and the rights of man, but the unfettered ambition of the universal spirit.*

Beethoven cut an extraordinary figure. He was rumpled, dirty and dishevelled. Some people thought that he was half mad. When he realised in 1802 that he was going deaf and would never be able to hear again, he wrote a letter to his brothers in which he seemed to suggest that he was going to kill himself. He never sent it, and it was discovered in his papers after his death twenty-five years later. By that time he was the most famous composer in the Western world. His music had swept all before it, overshadowing the reputations of his great predecessors such as Bach and Mozart. While staying within the broad boundaries of existing convention, he pushed musical composition to new limits and created new sounds. Later in the nineteenth century, some people came to realise that love of Beethoven and the Romantic School had been allowed to obscure the great music that just preceded it, and the works of the classical composers began to find their way back into the repertoire. But in the years after his death, Beethoven was the musical monument to which other musicians paid homage. The German composer, Richard Wagner, whose belief in his own musical genius tended to blind him to the talents of others, chose the Ninth Symphony to celebrate the opening of his opera house at Bayreuth.

It was not only Beethoven's music that earned him this reputation. There was something about him as a man, his roughness and uncertainties, that made him seem special. He had to strive for what he had achieved, overcoming the physical disability of his deafness as well as a certain lack of fluency as a composer. He was never a dazzling child prodigy like Mozart or Mendelssohn: Beethoven worked hard and constantly at everything he did.

Another great composer, Jean Sibelius, while living in Vienna as a young man wrote that Beethoven was 'the greatest composer of all'. He added that he 'did not have the greatest *natural* talent but he subjected everything he did to the most searching self-criticism and by doing so achieved greatness'. Beethoven was a hero, not just because he wrote good music, but because he believed completely in himself and the idea of the artist as a force in the world. He was a Romantic, part of a school that encouraged people in the West to look at themselves afresh.

Romanticism was never a philosophy. It was a name given to a movement that grew up through Europe during the last quarter of the eighteenth century and the first quarter of the nineteenth. Many of its ideas had their roots in the writings of Jean-Jacques Rousseau who published his most influential work, *The Social Contract*, in 1762. The book begins with the famous statement: 'Man is born free and everywhere he is in chains.' It goes on to explain how through a 'social contract' men can live together in a state of equality and freedom. They must give up their individual rights and make them available to something Rousseau calls the 'general will'–the common interest of society.

[on Beethoven]

He believed in the idea of the artist as a force in the world.

The general will is difficult to define. In Rousseau's thinking it is a kind of force made up of each individual's interest in the common good and is therefore always good, always right and will always act in the best interests of society as a whole. Rousseau also believed that associations within a state undermined the general will. There should either be none, or else so many that they cancelled the effects of one upon the others.

Rousseau's ideas were considered subversive by the authorities and were banned in his native city of Geneva. But they became the credo of France's revolutionaries. In the concept of the general will, men like Robespierre saw an almost metaphysical concept of the new, pure political condition in which they believed. Rousseau's lack of smooth and precise definitions made him attractive to people who wanted inspiration rather than instruction. His influence was enormous. He was different from the other philosophers whose ideas created the Enlightenment of the eighteenth century. They, too, believed in liberty and equality and their philosophical writings contributed greatly to the upheaval of the French Revolution. But they were concerned on the whole with legal and civil formulas that could be applied practically to the everyday workings of the state. Their work gave birth to the American Declaration of Independence and the American Constitution, which still exists today. Rousseau's ideas gave birth to Robespierre's Cult of the Supreme Being, a fantastic ideological notion that was swept away as the Revolution subsided.

Although Romanticism could never be described as a political movement, it had political effects. Rousseau's concept of the general will led European writers and philosophers to think how it could be applied to the situation facing their countries. Another eighteenth-century philosopher, Johann Gottfried von Herder, in Germany, believed like Rousseau in democratic ideas and the need for societies to organise themselves collectively. But he also promoted the value of national differences, believing that a society was strengthened if it fed from its own culture and history. This combination of democratic force and national identity fuelled nationalistic movements. Giuseppe Mazzini, who founded the 'Young Italy' movement, and whose writings and ideas were the cornerstones of the drive for Italian unification in the nineteenth century, took Rousseau and Herder as his inspiration. Having left England to escape from scandal, the English Romantic poet, Lord Byron, died while organising a military mission for Greek independence. Fierce ideas about individual freedoms found a natural outlet in the campaigns of countries looking to escape from the foreign domination of the empires that controlled their destinies.

The concept of Romanticism grew up in a Europe that was coming to terms with the scattered and confused effects of revolution. The political turmoil that engulfed France in the last twenty years of the eighteenth century started as a revolt against autocracy and a desire for human rights based on political ideas of equal representation, a fairer, more inclusive approach to government. But as it hurtled forwards it was overtaken with

Coleridge and the Writing of 'Kubla Khan'

Samuel Taylor Coleridge (1772–1834) was instrumental in
pioneering Romantic literary ideas in England. He is best
known for his poems 'The Rime of the Ancient Mariner' (1798)
and 'Kubla Khan' (c.1797, pub. 1816). 'Kubla Khan' was highly
influential in English Romantic poetry, celebrating creativity,
imagination and the unbridled beauty of nature. It begins
by evoking the Khan's magnificent and ordered empire ('In
Xanadu did Kubla Khan/ a stately pleasure dome decree'), which
is contrasted with the untamed, 'savage' landscape outside
its walls. For Coleridge the natural world is the true vision of
paradise, and he ends the poem by celebrating the poet's ability
to bring it to life.

Coleridge gave his poem a subtitle: 'A Vision in a Dream: A
Fragment'. He is supposed to have written it after an opium-
induced 'kind of reverie'. He suffered from depression and
took opium as treatment, becoming addicted to the drug. In
an introduction to the work he blamed its fragmented nature
on a man from the neighbouring town of Porlock who had
interrupted him, so that 'with the exception of some eight or
ten scattered lines and images, all the rest had passed away like
the images on the surface of a stream into which a stone has
been cast, but, alas! without the after restoration of the latter!'.
The veracity of this story has been disputed, but it at least
has the effect of intensifying the poem's Romantic enigmatic
qualities. 'Kubla Khan' remains one of the greatest poems in the
English language, while the expression 'a person from Porlock'
has become a popular phrase to describe the interruption of a
moment of inspiration.

other savage and strange ideas – the Terror for instance – that
once it had run its course were discarded because they were too
frightening and dangerous. But the feelings to which they had
given an outlet could not just be forgotten. The careful, classical world of the eighteenth century had gone forever. Before the
Revolution, men and women preferred 'sensibilities' to emotions.
They affected distress, but they avoided rage. Rage, however, was
the lifeblood of the Revolution and it gave to people's view of life
a deeper, more fervent feeling than they had experienced before.

Once it was over, while the world of politics settled back bit by bit to something approaching what it had been before, the vehement ideas of individuality and self-expression remained and found their outlet in the world of culture and the arts.

The Romantics preferred the aesthetic to the practical, the beautiful to the useful. They disliked what they considered to be the ugliness and depredation of the Industrial Revolution. They enjoyed the medieval world – many of their books were historical stories – where knights and maidens lived in castles and the mysterious and unknown were always on hand to play a part in the everyday. In Germany the movement was very strong, led not only by musicians such as Beethoven but also by writers and painters like Goethe, Schiller and Caspar David Friedrich. In England it gave birth to a school of poetry that has since come to be enjoyed as one of the glories of English literature. Wordsworth and Coleridge, Keats, Shelley and Byron all celebrated the beauty of the natural world and man's role within it. English watercolour painting, particularly the work of J. M. W. Turner, also promoted these ideas. In France, Romantic concepts expressed themselves in the music of Hector Berlioz and the writings of Victor Hugo. Géricault's painting of the *Raft of the Medusa* – a huge picture based on an actual incident – is one of the greatest works of art of the Romantic period, depicting the dead and dying victims of a shipwreck in heroic detail. A French historian, Jules Michelet, said of it: 'our whole society is aboard the raft of the Medusa'.

[on Beethoven]

His art represented a vision of hope that has sustained people ever since.

Ludwig van Beethoven was born in Bonn in 1770. His father was a drunk who hoped that his musical son might turn into a prodigy like Mozart and earn the family a bit of much-needed money. Beethoven never enjoyed such early stardom, but he was talented enough to be accepted by Haydn as a pupil and in 1792 moved to Vienna for lessons from the great master. For nearly thirty years, from 1761 until 1790, Haydn worked for the noble Esterházy family and spent a large part of his time at their splendid palace about sixty miles from Vienna in what is now Hungary. At last freed from his obligations he was able to start enjoying the fruits of the international reputation he had established despite working in aristocratic confinement. The relationship between the two men was difficult. Haydn, already an old man, was benevolent and probably somewhat set in his ways. Beethoven was young and excitable and rapidly made a reputation for himself, not least as a performer capable of astonishingly clever piano improvisations.

At the end of the eighteenth century, musical audiences in Vienna enjoyed piano duels between rival composers. These events had a gladiatorial ring to them. Each performer would play in turn, improvising and extending the music to demonstrate his keyboard skill. In 1793, Beethoven demolished a rival – a popular composer called Abbé Gelinek – in one such musical combat. 'He is no man,' said the defeated Abbé afterwards; 'he's a devil. He'll play me and the rest of us to death.' Vienna became Beethoven's home. In the city itself, or in the villages around it, he wrote the music that came to be associated with post-revolutionary ideas of liberty and the nobility of the human spirit. Vienna itself was under the control of the Austrian chancellor, Prince von Metternich, an arch-conservative anxious to suppress any revolutionary mutterings. His spies were everywhere. Beethoven became an admirer of Napoleon whom he regarded, as did many others, as the French Revolution's natural heir. He planned to dedicate his Third Symphony, the *Eroica*, to him but changed his mind when Napoleon gave himself an imperial title. His music came to represent the spirit of the age. The prisoners' chorus from his only opera, *Fidelio*, was a hymn to liberty; the opening drum notes at the beginning of his violin concerto sounded like the heartbeat of the whole Romantic movement; and the vigorous, contrasting

The Romantics preferred the aesthetic to the practical, the beautiful to the useful.

rhythms of his Seventh Symphony captured the swirling nature of the times in which he lived. His head, said one contemporary biographer, was the 'dwelling-place of mighty, sublime ideas'.

Beethoven had been working on the idea of setting Schiller's 'Ode to Joy' for several years before his Ninth Symphony was first performed. The poem itself was written in 1785 and was set to music by other composers before Beethoven used it. Its theme is the redemption of mankind. In universal brotherhood man will ultimately ascend to a joyful place where all enmities are forgotten and all tyrants vanquished. 'Be embraced, ye millions yonder!/ Take this kiss throughout the world!/ Brothers o'er the stars unfurled/ Must reside a loving father.' When writing about the Ninth Symphony, Ralph Vaughan Williams said that he had once been told that when Schiller wrote the 'Ode to Joy', he thought about replacing the word 'joy' (*Freude*) for 'freedom' (*Freiheit*) and that Beethoven knew of this when he composed the music. 'I have never been able to find any confirmation of this legend,' he said, 'but we may profitably keep it at the back of our minds when we play or sing or read, or hear this great Symphony.' Vaughan Williams wrote those words in 1939 as the Second World War was about to engulf Europe. Fifty years later one of the last relics of the Cold War that followed it, the Berlin Wall, was torn down. On Christmas Day 1989, Leonard Bernstein conducted a performance of the Ninth Symphony in Berlin to celebrate the reunification of the divided city. In the final choral movement he changed the word '*Freude*' for '*Freiheit*'.

We do not know if Schiller ever seriously thought about replacing the idea of joy with that of freedom but we feel as though he might have done because of the Ninth Symphony. Beethoven wrote music in a way that made it mean something: it responded to people's ideas of who they were and what they wanted to be. His art represented a vision of hope that has sustained people ever since. That was the achievement of the Romantics who, in music, painting and literature, began to fashion a world where people were urged to express themselves freely.

An Italian Hero

The Congress of Vienna in 1815 reduced the Italian peninsula to what it had been before Napoleon's wars of conquest – a scattering of small principalities. It became, in the words of the Austrian diplomat von Metternich, nothing more than 'a geographical expression'. But the experience of unity under Napoleon inspired a new generation of Italian nationalists to work towards unification. This movement was known as the 'Risorgimento'.

Two men were crucial to the success of this new nationalist force. Exiled in Marseille, Giuseppe Mazzini (1805–72) founded a movement called Young Italy in 1831 dedicated to securing the country's 'Unity, Independence, and Liberty' for Italy. Two years later, a soldier called Giuseppe Garibaldi (1807–82) joined the cause. Garibaldi, who was born in Nice, was sentenced to death for his part in an insurrection and fled to South America where for fourteen years he learned the art of war, fighting for the independence of both Brazil and Uruguay. By the time he returned to Italy revolutions had swept through Europe. In Rome in 1849 he and other patriots founded a republic but the European powers led by France soon overthrew it and Garibaldi was forced abroad once more.

Ten years later another and better opportunity arose. In 1859 the Second Italian War of Independence broke out. Garibaldi raised an army of volunteers – 'The Thousand' – and led them to victory in Sicily and then, after crossing the Straits of Messina, throughout the whole of southern Italy. His army was swelled by local people who thronged to his cause as he marched northwards. He became a national hero. Meanwhile Count Cavour, the Prime Minister of Piedmont-Sardinia, had been organising the unification of northern Italy on behalf of the House of Savoy. Although Garibaldi and Cavour mistrusted each other, Garibaldi recognised that the dream of Italian independence could only be achieved under the leadership of the Savoy monarchy. On 26th October 1860, in the town of Teano, about forty-five miles north of Naples, Garibaldi handed over his army and all his victories to Victor Emmanuel, shaking his hand and hailing him as the King of Italy. It is one of the famous scenes in modern Italian history and earned Garibaldi the undying devotion of his nation.

Garibaldi went on fighting after that. He led an expedition against the Papal States which were at first excluded from the Kingdom of Italy; fought against the Austrians in their war with Prussia; volunteered to fight for the Union in the American Civil War (he was offered the commission of major general); and raised an army to defend the new French Republic that emerged towards the end of the Franco-Prussian War. His cause was always liberty above all else. 'Let he who loves his country with his heart and not merely with his lips, follow me,' he said. He never allowed his natural bravery or skill as a soldier to get the better of his principles. With his red shirt, full beard and flashing sword, he was one of history's most adored men of action.

CHAPTER 6

The Zulu War
1879

In the late 1870s the British hoped to establish
complete control over all the different territories of
Southern Africa. As part of this plan, the British High
Commissioner decided he had to destroy the Zulu
army. The subsequent war had many parallels with the
campaign that the United States Army fought against
American Indians at almost exactly the same time.

At a meeting of the Zululand Mission held at Church House,
Westminster, in May 1894, one speaker was highly critical of the
'unjustifiable war' that England had waged against the Zulu a
few years earlier. The mission was discussing, in that earnest
Christian way in which the Victorians liked to approach such
matters, whether the Zulu could be dissuaded from their long-
practised habit of polygamy. The speaker was doubtful. One
might tell them it was wrong to have several wives, he told his
audience, but the Zulu were people of the keenest observation
and, if he had seen the slums or the gin shops of Cape Town,
would reply: 'Are you any better?'

The author of these remarks was Henry Rider Haggard, the
best-selling author of *King Solomon's Mines* and other adventure
stories. His tales of the exotic world of African kingdoms are
still in print today and have formed the basis of several successful films. Rider Haggard had first-hand experience of the Zulu
nation. He worked in the British colonial service and was posted
to Natal in South Africa during the time of the Zulu War. His very
first book, published in 1882, was an account of the British fight
against the Zulu chief, Cetshwayo. It is full of vivid descriptions
of colonial South Africa, its breathtakingly beautiful landscape,

the life and habits of the Boers and the rituals of native life. In one scene Rider Haggard describes a warrior in a Zulu wardance.

> As he stood before us with lifted weapon and outstretched shield, and his savage aspect made more savage still by the graceful, statuesque pose, the dilated eye and warlike mould of the set features, as he stood there, an emblem and a type of the times and the things which are passing away, his feet resting on ground which he held on sufferance, and his hands grasping weapons impotent as a child's toy against those of the white man – he who was the rightful lord of all – what reflections did he not induce, what a moral did he not teach!

Rider Haggard was a son of the British Empire, a friend of Rudyard Kipling, and a firm believer in the values of the age in which he lived. But, like Kipling, he understood and appreciated the beauty and mystery of cultures foreign to his own. He knew that the might of the country he loved had been used unfairly to crush the liberty of the Zulu nation.

The Zulu kingdom was born in blood. Before the beginning of the nineteenth century the Zulu were one of many tribes living in an area of South Africa sandwiched between Swaziland and Lesotho, bound on the west by the Drakensberg Mountains and to the east the Indian Ocean. They grew crops and grazed cattle, living in communities ruled by a headman and his family. In 1816, a Zulu warrior called Shaka, the illegitimate son of a chieftain called Senzangakhona, murdered his half brother and seized power on his father's death. Over the next ten years he defeated or absorbed neighbouring tribes to build a kingdom that controlled the whole area. Shaka was an astonishingly successful leader. He introduced rituals and ceremonies that helped create a sense of patriotism among his followers. He grouped the men under his command into regiments related to their age and taught them to fight using short, stabbing spears. In battle he deployed them by using a movement that first pinned down the enemy with a frontal assault and then encircled it from both sides. A large force was kept in reserve to support any areas where reinforcements were needed. He was cruel and bloodthirsty. According to some white observers, he ordered the massacre of thousands of mourners at his mother's funeral because they were not showing sufficient grief at her death. He ripped out the eyes of those whom he considered his enemies, leaving them to the jeers of their fellow tribesman as they staggered about. He died as he had lived. In 1828, in a plot devised by his two half-brothers, he was stabbed to death. One of them, Dingane, succeeded him as King of the Zulu.

These events took place against the background of the 'Mfecane' – an African word meaning disorder or upheaval – in which famine, tribal migration and violence created a period of disruption and deprivation among the people living along the eastern shores of South Africa. Shaka's activities probably contributed to this process, although in recent years some historians have decided that the Mfecane was a myth devised by white colonials to shift from themselves the blame for what happened to the Zulu. Whatever the truth, by the time of his death Shaka had built a powerful kingdom in which vassal chieftains paid homage to his rule. But he knew how vulnerable it was. According to a British colonial adventurer called Henry Fynn, Shaka prophesied that his kingdom would be overrun by the white man. This threat to Zulu independence became more serious during the reign of Dingane. Thousands of Boers left their homesteads in the southern Cape in the 'Great Trek' to look for better lands further north. Their journey was a landmark in the history of the Afrikaner people. It led directly to the foundation of the South African Republic in the Transvaal and eventually the establishment of an independent Boer nation within South Africa as a whole. It also brought the Boers into direct contact with the Zulu. In 1838, 10,000 Zulu attacked the Boer settlers in what became known as the Battle of Blood Rover. Dingane killed one of their leaders, Piet Retief, along with hundreds of other Afrikaner settlers. The Boers were not slow to take revenge. Dingane was ousted and killed and his brother, Mpande, became the new Zulu ruler, installed in office by the new leader of the South African Republic, Andries Pretorius, who demanded Zulu subservience to his new state. This was the moment when Shaka's legacy began to crumble.

Mpande ruled the Zulu people for thirty-two years, but for the last part of his reign real power lay with his son, Cetshwayo who, by the time he succeeded to the throne in 1872, governed lands threatened by European incursion. Mpande had successfully tried to appease his white neighbours, but their pressure on Zulu territory was unrelenting. The delicate nature of the situation was intensified during the 1870s by the British desire to unite all its lands in Southern Africa into one federation. In 1877, a new High Commissioner for South Africa, Sir Henry Bartle Frere, arrived in the country. Frere had no doubt that the Zulu needed to be put in their place. When dealing with a native population, he wrote, the 'two powers should settle from the outset which is to be superior, and which is to be subordinate'. He became convinced that Cetshwayo and his army was a serious obstacle to British ambitions. Meanwhile Cetshwayo had become suspicious of British motives after they changed sides and supported the Boers rather than him in a border dispute. Frere, ignoring concerns in London, decided to go to war and in 1879 invaded the Zulu kingdom.

The invasion was a disaster. At the Battle of Islandlwana on 22nd January 1879, Cetshwayo's Zulu army, carrying only spears and shields, utterly defeated a well-armed British force, killing 1,300 men. In the aftermath of the battle, a small force of less than 150 British soldiers held off an attack by nearly 4,000 Zulu at a fortified mission station called Rorke's Drift. The force's ability to withstand the onslaught of the might of a whole Zulu army was a brutal demonstration, if any were needed, of the advantage of firearms over native weapons. Cetshwayo was well aware of this. He wanted to avoid a full-scale war, and did not carry out an invasion into British territory following his victory at Islandlwana. But the British could not let their defeat go unpunished. Patriotic feelings in England ran high. The defenders of Rorke's Drift were given eleven Victoria Crosses and Sir Garnet Wolseley was despatched to suppress the

The British could not let their defeat go unpunished.

Zulu as he had the Ashantis of West Africa a few years earlier. Cetshwayo was arrested and imprisoned. After his release he was brought to London, where he met Queen Victoria, and was subsequently allowed to return to his former kingdom, which the British had partitioned into different tribal areas. It was a policy that was bound to lead to civil war. In 1883, Cetshwayo's forces were defeated by those of his rival, Zibhebu. Cetshwayo was driven into hiding and died in Eshowe, near where he was born, in 1884. The kingdom that Shaka had founded had risen and collapsed. By the end of the nineteenth century, the Zulu had lost all their traditional structure of leadership and organisation and were economically dependent on the European settlers controlling the territory in which they lived.

Cetshwayo was brought to London where he met Queen Victoria.

The Battle of Islandlwana was fought three years after another similar encounter on the other side of the world. In 1876, an American cavalry force of 600 was annihilated by an army of American Indians in an episode that became known as 'Custer's Last Stand'. Lieutenant Colonel George Armstrong Custer was a glamorous figure. During his lifetime he seemed to represent to many members of the American public the best human qualities their nation had to offer. He had seen distinguished service in the Civil War where he had risen to the temporary rank of major general of Volunteers in the Union Army. Once the war was over his rank had been reduced, but he steadily climbed his way up again and by 1874 was a lieutenant colonel. He was also a successful author. His book about his adventures fighting the American Indians, *My Life on the Plains* – an amalgamation of newspaper articles he had written regularly during his service – was a bestseller. His long, fair hair, luxurious moustache and colourful dress sense all combined to create the image of a great warrior. He was a frontiersman, an 'Indian fighter' and a sophisticated man about town, equally at home shooting game in the wild or watching a play at one of Washington's theatres. He was part of the new America – ambitious for opportunity as it expanded westwards towards the Pacific Ocean.

In July 1874, Custer led an expedition to explore the Black Hills of North Dakota. For sixty days he led his men through a wilderness that was still relatively unknown to most of his compatriots. He saw packs of wolves, found plentiful herds of deer and evidence of their fiercest predator, the mountain lion. He shot a grizzly bear. He also claimed to have found gold.

News that gold had been discovered in the Black Hills created furious excitement among the settlers in the region. Dakota had become part of the United States as a result of Thomas Jefferson's Louisiana Purchase in 1803, in which a vast swathe of land running through the mid-west to the south of the North American continent was bought from France. The northern part of the territory was joined to it as a result of a treaty with the British fifteen years later that defined the boundary between Canada and America. Settlers began to move west. There was good fur to be trapped along the waters of the Missouri River – the 'smoky river' according to the American Indians – and in 1863 and 1864 this booty was added to by the discovery of gold in Montana, further west. The Americans built forts to protect the settlers and to try to keep the Indians under control. There were a series of battles against Indian tribes in 1863 and 1864, but in 1868 the American government reached an agreement with the Sioux under the terms of which they agreed to dismantle two army forts. The Sioux were also guaranteed freedom across a wide area including the Black Hills, land that they regarded as sacred territory.

When Custer found gold, the government could no longer restrain its settlers. At first it tried to buy or lease the land from the American Indians, but when they refused it lifted all restrictions and allowed people in. It had broken its promise. War was inevitable. Custer and his men were part of a campaign designed to drive the Indians back onto their reserved land and free up the Black Hills for gold.

Custer's 'last stand', however, is a figment of marketing imagination. No one, apart from the Indians who killed him, saw him die. His whole troop, including his two brothers – fighting American Indians was a Custer family affair – was massacred. When his body was found it was discovered that he had been shot twice, once in the chest and again in the temple. *The Last Stand* was a fictional painting of the scene bought by an American brewing company and used as a marketing campaign for its beer.

In an echo of how the British behaved toward the Zulu of South Africa, the Americans took revenge on the Sioux after the Battle of Little Big Horn. The treaty of 1868 was revised, and the Indian lands were broken up into smaller reservations where the tribes were forced to live. The victor of the battle, Chief Sitting Bull, fled north to Canada, but cold and hunger drove him back a few years later. Like Cetshwayo, he became something of a celebrity and performed in 'Buffalo Bill's' famous Wild West show. In 1890 he was killed at Wounded Knee when a group of soldiers, frightened by the sight of Indians performing the ritual of the Ghost Dance, panicked and opened fire.

The ascendancy of the imperial white man was unstoppable.

The similarities between the battles of Little Big Horn and Islandlwana are striking. Both were examples of imperial ferocity; both were about the greed for land; both were unjustified attacks on native populations; and both gave birth to images of patriotic heroes defending themselves against violent savages. They both also took place at almost the same time in separate corners of the world, involving peoples and governments very different from one another. The ascendancy of the imperial white man, whether pushing out from his small island in northern Europe or striking westward from his settled territories on the eastern seaboard of the Atlantic, was unstoppable. The countries from which he came had been born out of carefully developed ideas of liberty; but it was a liberty of his own devising for his own uses. And one that was not averse to crushing the liberty of others.

CHAPTER 7

The Russian Revolution

1917

In March 1917, the Russian Tsar, Nicholas II, abdicated and a Provisional Government took power. The following October this was overthrown by the Bolsheviks who established the Soviet Union, the world's first Communist state.

Russia is part of Europe, yet stands outside it. Throughout the twentieth century it affected the way Europe was governed more than any country apart from Germany, but its history, culture and social development were very different from the rest of the continent. The history of Russia is the history of an autocracy. For 300 years, from the accession of Michael in 1613 to the abdication of Nicholas II in 1917, it was ruled by the Romanov dynasty or by members of the family who had married into it. Throughout that time the Tsar or Tsarina remained the supreme power in the land, accountable to the people only as far as he or she felt the need. Reform, when it came, was organised from above.

Repression, which often followed reform, came from the same place. The Tsar who did more than any other to modernise his country, Peter the Great – he became sole ruler in 1696 and died in 1725 – pursued his own policies with fierce dedication. He modernised his army and navy, transformed the country's civil government by restricting the power of the nobility, and strengthened its international position in a successful war against Sweden, then a great power. He did all this, not in response to internal pressure, but because he himself thought it was necessary. When Tsar Alexander II decided to emancipate Russia's serfs in 1861, freeing millions of peasants from a condition of medieval servitude, he took the view that it was 'better to abolish serfdom from above than to wait until the serfs begin to liberate themselves from below'.

In the nineteenth century, Russia waited to be governed: its people rarely tried to govern themselves. In 1825 a group of army intellectuals decided to seize power when Tsar Nicholas I came to the throne. They wanted to introduce democratic institutions modelled along American lines. Their rebellion failed because they were people acting on their own, motivated by their own perceptions of liberty and justice. Their ideas did not reach, or did not interest, the people they thought they wanted to help. But no nation suffers forever. When it finally arrived, revolution was driven by a population floundering in defeat during the First World War and ready at last to take control of its destiny. Its dream of liberty was short lived. The intellectual evangelism of professional revolutionaries ensured that once again change came from the top. The revolution of 1917 also metamorphosed into an autocracy. No wonder the twentieth-century Russian poet, Maximilian Voloshin, said of Peter the Great that he 'was the first Bolshevik'.

When the last Tsar, Nicholas II, came to the throne in 1894 Russia stood at the centre of a great empire. Its lands covered about a sixth of the world's surface, spreading out from the heartland of Muscovy to include central Asian states such as Kazakhstan and Uzbekistan, the Baltic countries of Estonia, Latvia and Lithuania, the Ukraine, a significant part of Poland and a large piece of eastern Turkey. Less than half of its subjects were actually Russian. The country still operated the Julian calendar that all other European countries had replaced with the Gregorian. It therefore operated eleven days behind most of the rest of the world. It also suffered from something of an identity crisis as its writers and intellectuals argued about where its roots lay. Some believed that the country's future was symbolised by St Petersburg, the great city laid out by Peter the Great as he dragged Russia into the European fold. Others, including the new Tsar, argued for Moscow, the ancient soul of Russia and the place where its historic identity could be found. Nicholas II complained that Peter the Great 'had too much admiration for European "culture" ... He stamped out Russian habits, the good customs of his sires, the usages bequeathed by the nation.' He saw himself as ruling in the manner of one of the earliest of the Romanovs, Alexei, who in the middle of the seventeenth century had presided over the affairs of his people like a father – strict but fair, deeply religious and unswervingly patriotic. Nicholas believed completely in his power as an autocrat: through him the nation lived and breathed and would be governed. This idea of monarchy as a semi-religious, mystical authority, had long disappeared from the rest of Europe (in Britain, Charles I was executed during the reign of Tsar Alexei) and struggled for acceptance in a country that, although still based on a peasant economy, was beginning to feel the effects of industrialisation.

Nicholas's image as protector of the Russian soul was dealt a severe blow by the events of 1905. The previous year Russia had drifted into war with Japan as both powers fought for control of Korea and the area of Manchuria on the Chinese mainland. The principal prize was Port Arthur (today called Lushun), at the southern end of the Liaodong Peninsula. A perfect natural harbour, it provided an excellent base from which to command the Yellow Sea and Korea. The Japanese captured it from the Russians in 1904, fuelling anger in an already discontented population. In January 1905 a group of workers, followed by a large but well-behaved crowd, decided to march to the Winter Palace in St Petersburg and present a petition to the Tsar. They wanted an end to the Russo-Japanese War, better factory working conditions, and constitutional reforms, including representational government and universal suffrage. As the

It was all too little too late. people assembled on the square in front of the palace, troops opened fire. More than a hundred were killed, and several hundred others wounded. The following month the Tsar's uncle, the Governor-General of Moscow, was assassinated and a series of workers' strikes and peasant revolts disrupted the country. The government continued to resist calls for reform, but by October decided that it had to yield. It promised a new constitution in which the Duma, the Russian parliament, would be able to approve all new legislation. Its representation was widened to include members from groups and classes hitherto excluded. New laws protecting the civil liberties of all Russian citizens would be introduced. It was a big step along the road to democracy, but it was all too little too late.

Russia had been identified as a country suitable for revolution. During the second half of the nineteenth century the ideas of Karl Marx took hold of many groups seeking to bring about change in the countries where they lived. His book, *Das Kapital*, the first volume of which appeared in 1867, explained why in his view European capitalism was doomed to failure. He set out the consequences of this in an earlier text, 'The Communist Manifesto', written with his collaborator Friedrich Engels in 1848. This proclaimed: 'Not only has the bourgeoisie forged the weapons that bring death to itself; it has also called into existence the men who are to wield these weapons – the modern working class – the proletarians.' The fall of capitalism 'and the victory of the proletariat' were 'equally inevitable'.

Russia had been identified as a country suitable for revolution.

As the century advanced, however, capitalism in Western Europe proved remarkably robust despite revolutionary attacks on its structure and Russia came to be seen as the place most vulnerable to radical change. An emerging industrial working class allied to a vast peasantry seemed to provide the right social mixture to overthrow the country's deeply entrenched autocracy. The Russian Revolution differed from its most important historical predecessor in France because of the existence of a political movement utterly dedicated to the destruction of the existing system. All it needed were the right conditions in order to succeed. The revolutionaries waited and watched, ready to spring as soon as they occurred.

Russian Marxists had begun to organise themselves since the 1880s. After 1906, the main leader of the movement was Vladimir Ilyich Lenin, a lawyer from a family of intellectuals steeped in the idea of political protest. His eldest brother, Alexander, was hanged when Lenin was seventeen for his part in a plot to assassinate Tsar Alexander III. Lenin hoped that the events of 1905 would 'light the lamp of revolution' throughout Europe. This did not happen, but what he saw strengthened his confidence in this ultimate objective. In *Das Kapital* Marx referred to, but did not fully explain, the concept of the 'dictatorship of the proletariat' as the transitional stage between the collapse of the bourgeois state and the implementation of communism. Lenin took this idea and developed it into a revolutionary tool. He argued that 'dictatorship' meant just that: the assumption of full power by proletarian forces to direct the course of the revolution until perfect communism could be introduced.

Karl Marx believed that the fall of capitalism 'and the victory of the proletariat' were 'equally inevitable'.

The outbreak of the First World War began to accelerate the social changes that Lenin sought. It went badly for Russia from the start. Like people in Britain, the Russians went to war in a high state of patriotic excitement, but their optimism turned to anger and fear as their army, huge in manpower but dangerously ill-equipped, blundered into defeat by the Germans at the Battle of Tannenberg. In his book, *August 1914*, part fiction, part fact, the Russian writer Alexander Solzhenitsyn took the battle as a symbol of Russian decline. The suicide of the Russian commander, Marshal Samsonov, seemed to spell the end of Russia itself:

> He began with the set prayers, then none at all, simply
> breathing on his knees and looking up into the sky. Then,
> casting aside restraint, he groaned aloud, like any dying
> creature of the forest: 'O, Lord, if Thou canst, forgive me and
> receive me. Thou seest – I could do no other, and can do no
> other now.'

The war dragged on but as it did so it brought new power and new political confidence to local groups forced to organise in order to survive hardship. In the nineteenth century, the reforming tsar Alexander II had set up 'zemstvos' – regional and local authorities made up of peasants and local dignitaries designed to bring a measure of self-government to Russia's lands. These, together with city councils and factory workers' representative bodies, took on responsibilities for looking after the sick and wounded and helping get supplies to the front. Food shortages hit the capital and workers went on strike. As the situation worsened, Tsar Nicholas decided to take command of the Russian army himself and disappeared to the front. He relied on his wife, Alexandra, for news of what was happening at home but she, heavily influenced by the Serbian guru, Grigori Rasputin, was not always a reliable source. In March 1917, the city of Petrograd (the name had been changed from St Petersburg during the war because it sounded too German) went on strike, and regiments from the army joined the disaffected workers. The Duma reached agreement with the soviets, the organisations representing the striking workers and soldiers, on a political programme. This did not include the Tsar. *This was their* The train carrying him back to Petrograd was stopped and he was promptly forced to *hour of destiny.* abdicate. The Romanov dynasty's 300 years of power had ended. Many Russian people believed that this was their hour of destiny – but the revolutionaries who had influenced these events but not yet taken power knew that it was not. The moment of greatest change was still to come.

On 3rd April 1917, Lenin arrived at the Finland Station in Petrograd to begin the revolution. 'The country,' he said, 'is passing from the first stage of the revolution to the second, which must place power in the hands of the proletariat and the poorest peasants.' He totally rejected any dealings with the Provisional Government that had taken office following the Tsar's abdication. Holding firm to his own vision of how the ideas of Marx could now be applied to begin the process of world revolution, he concentrated entirely on harnessing the support of the workers' soviets. To begin with he and his Bolshevik supporters were in a minority. They were condemned by the Provisional Government and Lenin was forced into hiding. In September, the commander in chief of the Russian army, General Kornilov, tried to seize power believing that Petrograd had fallen to the Bolsheviks. The leader of the government, Alexander Kerensky, armed the Red Guards, the workers' militia, in order to help defend the city. Kornilov's attempted coup collapsed but Kerensky and his supporters had been severely weakened. Lenin, still a fugitive, wrote a letter to his supporters quoting the French revolutionary leader, Danton: *'de l'audace, de l'audace, encore de l'audace'* ('daring, daring, yet more daring'). During October he visited meetings of the Petrograd Soviet in secret. On the 24th, following an attempt by some government troops to seize the Bolsheviks' printing press, the uprising began. Ten days later the revolutionaries were the masters of Russia.

The revolution did not bring liberty to Russia. To consolidate the revolution the Bolsheviks created the *Cheka*, an institution designed to enforce its principles. Surveillance and coercion became the methods by which Communist ideas achieved their objective. At the same time, a bitter civil war broke out between the revolutionaries and those opposed to their policies. The Cheka played its part in this too, rounding up and executing those it believed to be enemies of change. In the four years of the war the Bolsheviks killed more people in captivity than died under a century of tsarist rule. Lenin suffered a series of strokes and went into semi-retirement after the civil war ended in Bolshevik victory. He died in 1924. Within a few years of his death, Joseph Stalin, the General Secretary of the Central Committee of the Communist Party of the Soviet Union, became the country's dictator. He held power until 1953 – years during which he killed millions of his countrymen, removing individuals or groups that he felt represented a threat to his power.

Stalin's rule represents one of the most frightening and destructive periods of all European history. The countries he dominated are still only now beginning to recover from the effects. Stalin was not a revolutionary; he was simply someone who came to power through the process of revolution. But his success in achieving it, and holding on to it, stands as a warning: there are no revolutionary recipes for human happiness. The twentieth-century Russian poet, Anna Akhmatova, described in one of her most beautiful lyric pieces, how Russia, a country always loved by its people in a profound way, yearned for release from the sadness that overshadowed it.

Give me bitter years of sickness,
Suffocation, insomnia, fever,
Take my child and my lover,
And my mysterious gift of song –
This I pray at your liturgy
After so many tormented days,
So that the stormcloud over darkened Russia
Might become a cloud of glorious rays.

CHAPTER 8

Mao Zedong and the People's Republic of China

1949

On 1st October 1949, Mao Zedong announced the establishment of the People's Republic of China. China had been in turmoil since the collapse of its last imperial dynasty in 1911. It was now to embark on a long process of revolution from which it would emerge as a modern state and a great world power.

In August 1839, Lin Ze-xu, the Imperial Commissioner responsible for Guangzhou Province in China, wrote to Queen Victoria, complaining about British traders. Lin had been despatched to Guangzhou by his emperor who was concerned at the way illegally imported opium was taking hold of the population. The drug was not native to China. It was smuggled from India by mainly British traders who needed something they could sell to the Chinese. Trade with China was highly restricted: foreigners could buy the silk, tea and porcelain they wanted only if they complied with rules designed to keep them at arm's length. Commerce could be stopped at a moment's notice if the rules were broken.

In the early years of the nineteenth century, opium began to break down the trading barriers that the Chinese erected against the outside world. Chinese officials believed that addiction to the drug was growing alarmingly fast as chests full of it arrived from India's colonial ports. As they flowed in, so the silver earned from Chinese exports flowed out and, so the Chinese thought, the population became weaker both physically and economically as its dependence on opium increased. Lin Ze-xu was mercilessly efficient in carrying out his emperor's orders. He arrested Chinese dealers and smokers and confiscated their stocks. The British refused his order to surrender their supplies so he laid siege to their factories for six weeks. When they yielded he took all their opium, mixed it with lime and salt, and dumped it out at sea. In his letter he told the Queen that British traders 'are so obsessed with material gain that they have no concern whatever for the harm they can do to others. Have they no conscience? I have heard that you strictly prohibit opium in your own country, indicating unmistakably that you know how harmful opium is. You do not wish opium to harm your own country but you choose to bring that harm to other countries such as China. Why?'

Lin's eloquent appeal was typical of a man who was a scholar and a patriot but his words were not heard. It is doubtful that the young Queen ever received the letter. Although some of her subjects agonised about Britain's opium trade with China – Gladstone thought it 'infamous and atrocious' – most felt that Lin's actions were an assault on Britain's rights and liberties, to say nothing of the effect on its finances. The British Foreign Secretary, Lord Palmerston, while acknowledging that the Chinese had every right to ban opium, argued they should 'legalise, by a regular duty, a trade which they cannot prevent'. This logic served British interests perfectly. The Royal Navy was sent to protect British traders and their illegal merchandise, the Chinese were defeated and at the Treaty of Nanjing in 1842 forced to allow five of their biggest ports to accept free trade and cede Hong Kong to Britain. China's doors had been forced open. A country that had kept itself at arm's length from the rest of the world for centuries had been coerced into doing business.

The ancient traditions, customs and government of China began a long process of disintegration from the moment it admitted the Western powers into its ports. After a second trade war between 1856 and 1860, other cities joined Shanghai and Guangzhou (Canton) in falling under foreign influence. China was never colonised, but its sovereignty over these important places all but evaporated as Western merchants took control of their commercial affairs. These two wars were accompanied by rebellion from within. The defeat in the First Opium War led to hardship in areas of southern and central China. The old Silk Routes, employing a large number of tough, hardy people, dried up as the goods they carried could be handled by the new open ports that were closer to the sources of supply. Many Chinese came to believe that their country was being infiltrated by traitors and when a failed civil servant candidate called Hong Xiuquan announced that he was the younger brother of Jesus Christ and was ready to lead his people to a heavenly king-dom, supporters flocked to his cause. Preaching a mixture of Christian, Chinese and Buddhist ideas, Hong Xiuquan's rebellion against the rule of the Manchu Emperor spread rapidly through southern and central parts of China. His army captured the city of Nanjing and occupied it for eleven years. It is estimated that twenty million Chinese were killed during the rebellion. When it finally collapsed in 1864 it left behind large parts of the country devastated by war and famine.

Even more disastrous was the rebellion that broke out in northern China as the nineteenth century drew to a close. Groups of peasants – called 'Boxers' because of their belief in the magical power of the martial arts in which they liked to participate – began to rove around the countryside attacking foreigners and Christian missionaries. The Western powers demanded retaliation but the dowager Empress decided to support the Boxer cause. When in 1900 the Boxers laid siege to the foreign legation quarters in Beijing, an eight-nation force was sent to destroy what had come to be known as 'the Yellow Peril'. The Boxers fled, as did the Empress, and the victorious foreign troops took control of the whole area, invading local towns and looting property. The Chinese were also forced to shoulder an indemnity of more than £200 million, an impossibly large amount for them to be able to repay.

These catastrophic events coincided with the rise of China's aggressive neighbour, Japan. In 1894 the two countries went to war over the possession of Korea, a territory that China had long regarded as a tributary state. Its attitude to Japan was contemptu-ous – it too was a country heavily influenced by Chinese culture – but it discovered to its cost how much things had changed. China was totally defeated and forced to yield any claims to Korea as well as hand Taiwan over to the Japanese. The Japanese also laid claim to Manchuria on the Chinese mainland but intervention from the Western powers prevented them from getting hold of it. The Qing dynasty that had ruled China since the middle of the seventeenth century could no longer withstand the pressures it faced. Its emperors had held power since the first of them, Shunzhi, had been installed as the 'Son of Heaven' in 1644 and had begun the process of imposing order on the people of China. In its last struggle to retain its throne it abolished the civil service exams, the traditional method of advancement in the country's highly organised bureaucratic structure, and tried to devolve power to regional authorities. It was not enough. In October 1911, China became a republic. The following February, the Child Emperor, Puyi, announced his abdication, saying that 'the empire is seething like a boiling cauldron, and the people are plunged in misery'.

Mao Zedong rose slowly to power in a land struggling to come to terms with the collapse of its historical institutions. In the years following the abdication of the Emperor, warlords ran certain parts of the country, often controlling their fiefdoms with autocratic savagery. The central government, led by Sun Yat-sen, was founded on Marxist principles but also imbued with a sense of national purpose. When he died in 1925 the political organisation he had tried to put together split into two broad groups: Nationalists and Communists. The Nationalists united under the military commander Chiang Kai-shek, who took control of China in 1928. Mao Zedong and his Communist colleagues made their base in the provinces of Jiangxi and Fujian in southeast China, where they developed their strategy and decided to regroup. In 1933 they came under fierce attack from Chiang Kai-shek and in October 1934 decided they had no alternative but to retreat. Led eventually by Mao, they set off on the 'Long March' that took them to Yan'an, a remote and inaccessible corner of north-west China. It was a journey of nearly 6,000 miles that took them just over a year. Attacked by Nationalist troops and then by warlords who still controlled some of the country's outer areas, the Communist army toiled through appalling conditions of snow and swamp to reach its destination. A force of 87,000 men began the journey in October 1934. Fewer than 10,000 of them survived. It was, said Mao, 'a great historical punishment'. But it was also a symbolic achievement, a defeat with the trappings of victory, a moment of destiny that provided a foundation for the future. The Communists had shown that they could not be eradicated and would wait their turn to lead their vast country to salvation through revolution.

Mao Zedong proclaimed the foundation of the People's Republic of China before a vast crowd in Tiananmen Square, Beijing on 1st October 1949. He was the leader of a unified nation, its first for more than a century. By harnessing to his cause what he later called 'the tremendous energy of the masses' he achieved something that only the great emperors of China's history had managed before him. The long wait that followed the Long March was over. In the years in between, China had been occupied by the Japanese and torn apart by civil war. The Nationalist leader, Chiang Kai-shek, compared the Japanese to a skin disease while the Communists, he said, were a 'disease of the heart'. Ultimately, however, he was forced to combine with the Communists against the country's foreign invaders. The Japanese owned the railway in Manchuria and from the mid-1930s used this as a base to build up control. In 1937 the two countries went to war. The Japanese behaved with great cruelty, burning, raping, looting and killing indiscriminately, but their defeat at the hands of the Allies in 1945 only delayed the final battle for who ruled China. Nationalists and Communists fought another war which ended with Chiang Kai-shek's defeat and his exile to Taiwan, known in the West as Formosa, where he established his own Republic of China.

Mao rose to power in a land struggling to come to terms with the collapse of its historical institutions.

Mao's victory was not only due to his successful military strategy. He approached the battle for hearts and minds with the same vigour and discipline with which he tackled an enemy army. In 1942 he launched a 'rectification' programme in which groups of supporters were encouraged to discuss ideas and criticise one another. He purged the party of those who did not agree with him and sent them into the countryside to do menial work. But his main strength lay in his ability to wake the peasant population out of its passive approach to events. Party members infiltrated all parts of the countryside, supporting workers in their battles against landlords and organising village communities in a way that began to change the structure of traditional agrarian life. Resistance to these new ideas met with brutal repression. China's ancient world revolved to a large extent around the idea that man was subject to his fate. Mao Zedong taught his supporters that fate was not a prison: it was possible to escape to a world beyond.

Mao taught people that fate was not a prison.

Mao Zedong's ideas outlived the revolution which bred them and of which he was the principal architect. In the first years of the People's Republic he and his government, supported by Russian manpower and resources, embarked on wholesale reform. The policy of destroying the old agrarian structure continued. Landlords were forced to forfeit their property and peasant communes were established. Equality of the sexes was introduced, and even the rigidity of the party structure seemed to soften as Mao came to believe that the country's intellectuals should not continue to be intimidated and announced that 'a hundred flowers' should bloom. No sooner had the party licensed people to speak and write more freely than it came to regret its decision. Mao could not bear to be challenged and within weeks the policy was reversed. Mao then embarked on his 'Great Leap Forward' in which the production targets for agricultural collectives were racked up to impossibly high levels. He believed that if people had a stake in what they produced their productivity would increase and encouraged industry to be developed among the peasants' communes. Military trappings accompanied the whole process. Communes became brigades, factory production groups became platoons. But, as often happens in politics, the statistics failed to match the ambition. Bad weather and poor harvests made the situation worse. In 1960 China and Russia quarrelled and the Soviet Union's leader, Nikita Khruschev, withdrew all its scientists, engineers and advisors. China descended into famine. Tens of millions died.

The failure of the Great Leap Forward weakened Mao's authority and the Chinese leadership began to explore other ways of managing its economy. But Mao was by no means defeated. Determined to save what he believed were the ideals of the revolution, he launched in 1966 one of the most extraordinary political programmes in the recent history of the world: the Cultural Revolution. China was subjected to a vicious and destructive purge as Mao's 'Red Guards' set about destroying four things: old ideas, old habits, old customs and old culture. This was revolution in its purest form, Mao's version of Robespierre's or Lenin's terrors against the enemies of change. The Red Guards called for 'destruction before construction'. It is thought that about half a million Chinese died as a result of their campaigns: many intellectuals were driven to suicide by the harassment they received. This violent phase lasted for two years until the central Communist Party regained control of the nation's affairs in 1969. Mao remained leader until his death in 1976, pursuing his dreams of a cultural revolution through more careful methods as his colleagues jostled for power. His time was running out: China would begin to look in another direction once he was gone.

Mao rescued China from the selfish ambitions of warlords.

Mao Zedong is to many one of the great leaders of world history. To others he is China's Stalin. He gave his country structure and the foundations of power. He rescued it from the selfish ambitions of warlords. He gave it a sense of destiny and he imbued it with hope. But these achievements were partnered by something that cast a shadow across them, an intellectual idealism that often ran counter to natural humanity. Revolutions often make people free, but the ideas that fuel them turn out to be imprisoning. The Marxist-inspired Communist revolutions of the nineteenth and twentieth centuries took this route as their leaders discovered that people's behaviour does not always conform to philosophical notions of what a perfect society should be like. As one of Mao's old allies said of him: 'Had Chairman Mao died in 1956 there would have been no doubt that he was a great leader of the Chinese people ... Had he died in 1966 his meritorious achievements would have been somewhat tarnished, but his overall record would still have been very good ... Since he actually died in 1976 there is nothing we can do about it.'

To many Mao is one of the great leaders of world history; to others he is China's Stalin.

Nevertheless China today owes much to the work of Mao Zedong, even as it leaves his ideas behind and builds itself into a global economic power. The streets of Shanghai are once again awash with foreigners eager to make money in this extraordinary land. But this time they are there because they are invited, not because they have come to exploit. For that the Chinese have Mao Zedong to thank. He shaped much of modern China's attitude towards itself. Both its pride and paranoia owe much to him, just as the Chinese people's long journey to recovery owes much to his Long March.

CHAPTER 9

The Fall of the Berlin Wall
1989

In November 1989, the East German authorities opened the wall that encircled West Berlin, allowing people to pass freely from one side to the other. The moment marked the end of the Cold War and the domination of the countries of Eastern Europe by the Soviet Union.

In November 2009, the twentieth anniversary of the fall of the Berlin Wall, people across the world recalled what happened. The politicians who had to manage it remembered their fears that violence would erupt, and the people who experienced it described their euphoria. Some members of Eastern Europe's older generation looked back on it ruefully, acknowledging that their lives had been freer since the wall disappeared, but half-pining for the oppressive stability that its presence gave them.

All these memories had one thing in common: no one saw it coming. In a matter of days, even hours, the barriers that had separated Russia and Eastern Europe from America and the West collapsed. The Cold War, the name given to the political atmosphere in which both sides had stalked each other in fear of mutual destruction since the end of the Second World War, came to an end, not with some terrifying conflagration, but with a street party. The bubble burst and the self-delusion of a political system that had tyrannised millions of people for more than forty years evaporated like a passing cloud.

In March 1946, Winston Churchill was awarded an honorary degree by Westminster College in Fulton, Missouri, in the United States of America. His acceptance speech was one of his most famous:

From Stettin in the Baltic to Trieste in the Adriatic an iron
curtain has descended across the Continent. Behind that line
lie all the capitals of the ancient states of Central and Eastern
Europe. Warsaw, Berlin, Prague, Vienna, Budapest, Belgrade,
Bucharest and Sofia; all these famous cities and the populations around them lie in what I must call the Soviet sphere,
and all are subject in one form or another, not only to Soviet
influence but to a very high and in some cases increasing,
measure of control from Moscow.

Churchill was right. In the second half of the Second World
War, Russia, forced to fight against German aggression, had
seen its fortunes transformed from a comparatively weak
and vulnerable nation into a great conquering power. As the
Germans retreated, the Russians advanced.
The Allies, particularly the Americans, who
were preoccupied with the war against
Japan as well as the conflict in Europe,
welcomed the support they received from
this new and somewhat unexpected quarter.
Russia was a nation reborn, a victorious
power flushed with the spirit of patriotism.
To many people its Communist ideology
seemed for the moment to be subordinated
to the greater idea of European freedom. In
1943 its leader, Joseph Stalin, dissolved the
Comintern, the international organisation
founded by Lenin to promote revolution in other parts of the
world. In February 1945 he met Churchill and the American
president, Franklin D. Roosevelt, at the Yalta Conference to
discuss the shape of Europe after the war was over. He joined
with them in declaring that it was 'the right of all people to
choose the form of government under which they live' and
that nations should be allowed to solve their problems 'by
democratic means'. But America and Britain were misled. The
Soviet Union had troops in positions across half of Europe as
the Red Army occupied Bulgaria, Romania, Poland, Hungary
and parts of Yugoslavia. Britain and America would soon learn

The Cold War came to an end, not with some terrifying conflagration, but with a street party.

that Russia was no liberator and Stalin no friend to democratic nationhood.

Joseph Stalin had no respect for the lives of others. His smile was as lethal as his frown. Even his family was terrified of him. During his long tenure of power he became walled up behind his own tyranny, barely capable of a human relationship. He rose to the top of the Russian Communist Party in the wake of Lenin's death. Lenin, the revered leader of the Bolshevik Revolution of 1917, wrote a letter from his sick bed in 1923 in which he urged the party to sack Stalin from the post of General Secretary. It should, he said, appoint 'another man more tolerant, more loyal, more polite and more considerate of comrades'. The letter was revealed to the party after Lenin's death, but its advice was ignored. During the following four years Stalin proceeded to consolidate his position until he became the absolute ruler of Russia. When he realised that the Second World War had put the Soviet Union in a strong position, he proceeded to extend its authority into Eastern Europe. Exiles from countries occupied by the Germans who had spent the war in Moscow and were utterly loyal to Stalin's policies were sent back into their homelands to foment revolution and seize power. They used the tactics they had learned at the feet of their master – false accusations resulting in terrible imprisonment, coercion and murder. Supported and funded by Russia they were able to outwit other politicians struggling to repair their broken countries. Bit by bit, Communist governments emerged, claiming to represent the will of the people but in fact owned lock, stock and ideology by Stalin and his supporters in Moscow. Their leaders mimicked their benefactor. Men like Walter Ulbricht in East Germany, Enver Hoxha in Albania and Gheorghe Gheorghiu-Dej in Romania created dictatorships maintained through a network of informers and secret police where the will of the party, the ruling clique, ran everything.

Stalin's death in 1953 was met by overwhelming grief from his countrymen. He was implicated in the deaths of millions of them. Assisted by his head of state security, Lavrenti Beria, he had sent those he considered his enemies to die in labour camps, threatened them and their families or had them executed

The five Pandava brothers of the *Mahabharata* stand in line at the Somnath Temple in northern India. One of India's most holy places, the temple was destroyed six times before being rebuilt in 1947.

Rameses II faces the army of the Hittites at the Battle of Kadesh. Rameses used wall paintings to record his exploits. This one is in his temple at Abu Simbel.

Buddhist monks in Cambodia celebrate Buddha Day at a temple in the province of Siem Reap. Buddha Day falls on a full moon in either April or May each year when followers observe the birth, enlightenment and passing of their spiritual leader.

Alexander the Great was a favourite subject for painters of heroic scenes. In this painting, by Gasparo Diziani (1689–1767), he is seen entering Babylon, the city he captured from Persia and where he died in 323 BC.

Ecce Homo (*Behold the Man*). Pontius Pilate yields to pressure from the Pharisees and agrees to the crucifixion of Jesus Christ in this dramatic painting by Antonio Ciseri (1821–1891), now in the Gallery of Modern Art in Florence.

The coronation of Charlemagne illustrated in the *Grandes Chroniques de France*, a collection of beautifully illuminated manuscripts compiled between the thirteenth and fifteenth centuries.

Chinggis Khan addresses a congregation at a mosque in Bukhara, a great centre of Muslim art and culture in what is today Uzbekistan. It comes from the *Shahanshanama*, a fourteenth-century collection of Persian epic poems.

The plague continued to terrify people for centuries after The Black Death. This engraving was published in the first half of the seventeenth century. Britain experienced its last outbreak of the disease in 1665.

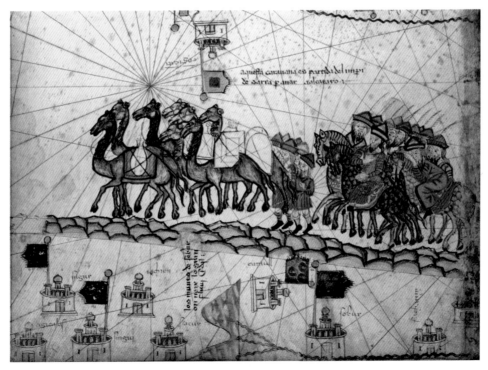

An illustration depicting the travels of Marco Polo from the *Catalan Atlas* of 1375, now in the Bibliothèque Nationale in Paris. The atlas was made in Majorca, whose inhabitants were great navigators and explorers.

A fresco painted on the outside of the Moldovita Convent in Romania in 1537 depicting the siege of Constantinople by the Turks. The people of Romania were forced to pay homage to their new Turkish masters with magnificent paintings like this one which, thanks to the artist's skilful use of his materials, has survived in the open air to this day.

The Virgin of the Rocks, one of two paintings of identical subjects by Leonardo da Vinci. This one is in the National Gallery in London, the other is in the Louvre in Paris. Leonardo was commissioned to paint the picture as an altarpiece for a church in Milan but, he was a notorious procrastinator and, as was often the case, failed to complete it in time.

Martin Luther in the Circle of Reformers, from the first half of the seventeenth century. Luther sits in the middle with John Wyclif sitting to his far right and Jan Hus sitting on his far left. Calvin sits to Luther's immediate right. Catholic clergy, keeping the devil for company, are ranged before them.

The disembarkation of the conquistadors at Vera Cruz in Mexico in 1519 is captured in one of the frescoes depicting Mexican history painted by Diego Rivera (1886–1957) on the walls of the National Palace in Mexico City.

after trials in which they faced trumped-up charges. But, like Mao in China, he had made his country powerful and important and for that his people were deeply grateful. A brutal dictator left the world revered and admired by the people he suppressed. He also left behind a world divided into two armed camps: East and West. The leader who eventually followed him, Nikita Khruschev, was a more approachable character and displayed attitudes that by the standards of his predecessor were almost liberal. He denounced Stalin and his policies, but his determination to maintain Russian control of Eastern Europe brought little respite for its people. The Warsaw Pact that was agreed in 1955 provided for each to come to the aid of the other if any one of them was attacked. Given that they were all under Russian control they probably would have done that anyway but the Pact reinforced their subservience to Moscow. In 1956 the Polish leader, Wladyslaw Gomulka, demanded greater independence for his country and warned Khruschev that the Polish army would fight if the Russians used force against it. He was allowed to introduce some economic reforms as long as he remained loyal to the Soviet Union: he agreed and Poland remained a Russian pawn. The Hungarians were not so fortunate. In October 1956 students in Budapest began to protest against the government. Russian troops entered the capital to impose martial law, but Khruschev decided, as he had in Poland, to restore order with a political rather than a military solution. The Hungarian leadership, however, did not prove as compliant as Poland's and the following month Russian tanks entered Budapest in force. The Western powers, frightened by the power of the Red Army, did nothing. Hungary's desperate grab for some form of self-determination was brutally extinguished and Russia remained in total control of its European satellites.

Perhaps emboldened by the failure of the West to interfere in the control of its European colonies, the Russian leadership took a step further. In 1962 Khruschev, observing that the Americans had nuclear missiles within striking range of Russian territory in Turkey, decided to retaliate by putting Russian weapons in America's back yard. In great secrecy he reached an agreement with the Communist leader of Cuba, Fidel Castro, to ship and install missiles on Cuban territory. 'Why not,' he asked, 'throw a hedgehog at Uncle Sam's pants?' As soon as the Americans discovered what the Russians were doing they ordered a naval blockade of Cuban waters. The world's two great nuclear powers were in direct confrontation with one another. A large and destructive war became a real possibility. Both sides were alive to the dangers of the situation. The American Secretary of State, Dean Rusk, told a meeting of ambassadors in Washington that 'we are in as grave a crisis as mankind has been in', while in Moscow, Khruschev said: 'This may end in a big war.' The rest of the world could do little but watch and wait: its destruction seemed to depend on whether two great powers could resolve their differences. I was a schoolboy in London at the time and I remember the events of that autumn very well. We were all frightened, but we behaved with stoic resignation. There was nothing else we could do. Luckily for us Russia and America drew back from the brink. The Soviet Union finally agreed to remove its missiles from Cuba on condition that the United States withdrew its military bases from Turkey. The Americans agreed, although not publicly. Neither Cuba nor Turkey was consulted. Fidel Castro flew into a rage when he realised the missiles were leaving and the following year the Americans quietly took their equipment out of Turkey claiming it was obsolete.

The Cuban Missile Crisis demonstrated the reluctance of the great powers to embark on a nuclear war, but it did not ultimately reduce the tensions between them. Hostility between Russia and America fuelled a nuclear arms race that dominated world affairs. Smaller nations either limped along behind their richer allies, or simply stood back and watched, potential victims of a hideous conflict between the titans of 'East' and 'West'. In Britain in 1981 a group of women camped outside the RAF base at Greenham Common in Berkshire in protest against the American cruise missiles that were being located there. They stayed in one form or another for nineteen years, a continuous reminder of the fear that ordinary people felt about the nuclear confrontation that threatened their daily lives. In Germany, fear of nuclear war led from public protest to political action. The Green Party won its first seats in the German Bundestag in 1983.

Change came from the country which had first drawn the 'iron curtain' across the European continent. As with many other great historic upheavals, its reasons were economic. By the middle of the 1980s the Russian economy was faltering. The highly controlled command economy of the Communist system was unable to compete with the growth and prosperity of capitalism. The standard of living in Western Europe was far higher than that in the East. America was richer than the Soviet Union and better able to afford expensive weapons. The US President, Ronald Reagan, proposed the construction of a defensive shield to protect his country from attack. A web of laser beams would intercept and destroy any hostile missile launched in its direction. The plan became known as 'Star Wars' after the popular Hollywood film, and it may well have been a similar fantasy. But it had the effect of persuading the Russians to subject their ailing economy to the further funding of expensive armaments. The country was stretched to the limit: a new approach was needed. In 1982, the man who had led Russia for the previous eighteen years, Leonid Brezhnev, died. He had held power longer than any Communist ruler other than Stalin and his fondness for medals and ceremony contributed to a cult of personality that grew up around him. But the grand old man of Politburo politics had presided over a period of economic stagnation, ignoring problems that festered beneath the surface. During his last years in office he was severely incapacitated by a stroke, barely able to make decisions of any kind. His two successors each died after little more than a year as heads of state, and in March 1985 a completely new kind of Russian leader, Mikhail Gorbachev, assumed the position of General Secretary of the Communist Party. Unlike all his predecessors he was born after the Revolution of 1917. He had grown up in a different world, and he took a different view of it.

Gorbachev stretched out his hand to Russia's traditional enemies in the West.

Gorbachev had two cardinal principles – *glasnost* meaning openness, and *perestroika* meaning reconstruction. These Russian

words became part of the world's vocabulary as the new Soviet
leader set about the invigoration of his country. He also stretched
out his hand to Russia's traditional enemies in the West,
encouraging them to participate in the reduction of nuclear arms.
He had little choice; he desperately needed to divert resources
away from military defence to the more pressing problem of
feeding and housing the Russian people. At
the same time he began to relax Moscow's
grip on its Eastern European satellites. He
urged the Communist leadership in Poland
to share power with the popular movement
'Solidarity'. He did not interfere when
the Hungarian government renounced
Leninism and embarked on a programme of
democratic capitalism. He was also aware of the profound changes
that were likely to follow when the Hungarian authorities flouted
their agreement with East Germany by allowing East Germans to
pass through Hungary in order to cross into the West through
its Austrian border. On a visit to East Berlin in October 1990, he
urged the East German leadership to consider reform. It refused.
After he left, the country was engulfed by a wave of protests and a
month later the government announced that it would issue visas
to anyone who wished to visit the West. A large crowd, excited
but suspicious, gathered near the Berlin Wall. When would the
visas be issued? No one seemed to know. Uncertain about the
best course of action to take the border guards decided to open
the crossings and the crowds flooded through. The fundamental
political divisions between the countries of East and West Europe
were over. The iron curtain had been lifted.

The Berlin Wall was a demonstration of the power of fear.

The immediate effects of the collapse of the Berlin Wall
were profound. The Communist regimes that had controlled
the nations of East Europe since the end of the Second World
War were driven from power. In Romania, the leader of one of
the most brutal of them, Nicolae Ceausescu, was captured while
trying to escape with his wife. They were brought before a hastily convened military tribunal, sentenced to death and shot as
they entered a courtyard to take up their positions before a firing
squad. Pictures of their ignominious execution caused great

delight when they were shown on Romanian television. They can still be seen on YouTube. Germany was reunified and took its place once again as the largest country in Western Europe. Meanwhile in Russia, the man who started the process lost his grip on power. Gorbachev always believed that Russia's systems of government could be maintained if they were reformed: he never intended that they should be completely swept away. But hardline opponents in his party tried to oust him from power in a failed coup in 1991. For those who wanted to see even greater change this was proof that the system itself was completely rotten. Gorbachev was forced to resign and a new leader, Boris Yeltsin, took charge. The old Soviet Union was dissolved into a commonwealth of independent republics. Within a matter of a few years one of the world's largest empires melted quietly away.

The Berlin Wall was a demonstration of the power of fear. To those who lived on either side of it, it was a physical embodiment of the world's divisions. To the east lay the exhausted spirit of revolution which used its convictions to justify tyranny. To the west lay the resurgent energy of capitalism which rebuilt itself after the ravages of war in a new partnership of trade and the freedom of movement of people, goods and ideas. One was far stronger but both were frightened of each other. The divisions ended, not when the stronger exerted its power, but when the weaker chose to change from within. Freedom can never be imposed.

CHAPTER 10

The Release of Nelson Mandela

1990

On 11th February 1990, the black South African leader, Nelson Mandela, was released from prison after twenty-seven years. His freedom marked the end of racial segregation in South Africa and set the country on the path to black majority rule.

On a hill overlooking the city of Pretoria in South Africa stands a great granite monument. Begun in 1937 and not inaugurated until 1949 it celebrates the achievements of the *Voortrekkers* – about 15,000 Boer men and women who emigrated from the Cape Colony in the 1830s and 1840s to settle in lands hundreds of miles away in the northeast. Their journeys became known as 'The Great Trek'. The monument contains huge statues of the Boers' leaders and a sculpture of a Voortrekker woman with her children, symbolising the people's enduring faith and hope. It also has a wall made up of sixty-four ox wagons, the main method of transport used by the Boers as they travelled to their new homes.

The number sixty-four is significant, for it was that many wagons that the Voortrekkers drew around themselves as protection in their victory over a Zulu army in the battle of Blood River in 1838. A hundred years later, just before work on the monument began, the Afrikaner descendants of the Voortrekkers held remembrance celebrations of the battle. One of their leaders, D. F. Malan, who was to become Prime Minister of South Africa ten years later, told them in a speech that the country faced a new Blood River, where 'black and white meet together in much closer contact and in a much more binding struggle'. The Voortrekkers' journey to freedom, he said, 'was also and above all the freedom to preserve themselves as a white race'. 'Today,' he went on, 'their task to make South Africa a white man's land is ten times more your task.'

The Boers who embarked on the Great Trek wanted to escape from British rule. Descended from the Dutch settlers who came to South Africa at the beginning of the seventeenth century, and sustained by strict Calvinist beliefs, they did not take kindly to the impositions that were being made on their traditional way of life. The abolition of slavery by the British in 1833 affected wealthier farmers and the activities of liberal missionaries created an impression that the government was siding with the black population against their better interests. They wanted their own land in which they could protect their customs and habits. They were descended from families who had always travelled in the pursuit of better grazing land and their journey north seemed a natural reaction to the situation in which they found themselves. By the middle of the 1850s their migration had resulted in the establishment of the Orange Free State and the Transvaal, or South African Republic, two independent republics that existed within the borders of South Africa until 1902. The Great Trek became the most important moment in their history, their exodus to a promised land, a flight from oppression into the arms of liberty.

The idea that Africans should become an integral part of the running of the country was never considered.

But their sense of history was infused with the issue of race. In 1893 at Pietermaritzburg Station in the British colony of Natal, a young Indian lawyer called Mohandas Gandhi was unceremoniously thrown out of his first-class seat onto the platform even though he was in possession of a legitimate ticket. He had refused to move to third-class compartment when he was told that where he was sitting was reserved for white people only. That incident became a turning point in Gandhi's life. As he sat, isolated, cold and alone, on the station platform he decided that he would devote his energies to fighting against racial discrimination.

South Africa became a self-governing dominion of the British Empire in 1910 when its four colonies were united under one administration. It was a very different land from the one that had inspired the Great Trek. The discovery of gold led to significant industrialisation. The exploitation of this new wealth exacerbated the constant tensions between the British and the independent Afrikaner republics, leading eventually to the Boer War of 1899 to 1902. The British, as victors, immediately set about trying to create a united federation. Once that was established they left the country to its new government with the vague hope that the black population would be decently treated under the recommendations of a native affairs commission that it had set up to investigate the issues surrounding African labour. But the idea that Africans should become an integral part of the running of the country was never considered by those who were leaving or by those who stayed behind to govern. The country divided itself automatically on lines of black and white. The blacks were treated less equally. They got the most menial jobs, were paid less in wages, were segregated from the white community and often forced to work far away from their families. In 1913, the Union of South Africa passed the Native Land Act which forced black people to live in designated

The South African native found himself a pariah in the land of his birth.

areas unless they were employed by whites and prevented the sale of land from white to black and vice versa. The South African Native National Congress (later the African National Congress, or ANC) that had been formed in 1912, spoke out against this repressive legislation. One of its founders, Solomon Plaatje, published a book in 1916 called *Native Life in South Africa* that summed up how the black population felt. Referring to the moment when the Land Act was passed Plaatje wrote: 'Awaking on Friday morning 20th June 1913, the South African Native found himself, not actually a slave, but a pariah in the land of his birth.' He went on: 'South Africa has by law ceased to be the home of any of her native children whose skins are dyed with a pigment that does not conform with the regulation hue.' The stage was set for the long and bitter battle between black and white that would nearly destroy the country completely.

Apartheid in Afrikaans means 'separateness'. It did not become the official policy of the South African State until the National Party came to power in 1948. Although segregation always existed, a legal definition of different racial types and the rights to which they were entitled did not become enshrined in South African law until after the Second World War. Throughout the 1930s, white Afrikaaners had strengthened their sense of purpose in the face of what they believed to be encroachment from blacks, 'coloureds' and Indians. The Afrikaner Broederbond, or brotherhood, became a powerful force encouraging the growth of Afrikaner literature and culture. In 1925, Afrikaans replaced Dutch as an official language in the country. When, in the immediate aftermath of the war, it was suggested that blacks should be allowed to reside permanently in urban areas in order to strengthen the workforce, frightened whites voted for the most extreme form of racial segregation instead. Apartheid divided the country into whites, Africans, 'coloureds' – meaning those of mixed race, and Indians.

The Boers' sense of history was infused with the issue of race.

Indians were classed as aliens. Only whites were deemed to be civilised and exercised total political and economic control over the rest of the population. In his book written decades earlier, Solomon Plaatje observed that if there existed someone whose objective was to prevent 'Natives' from ever rising above the position of servants to the whites, that person would be regarded 'as a fit subject for the lunatic asylum'. But those were the views of the people who governed South Africa at the end of the 1940s.

Nelson Mandela was born in the Transkei in the Eastern Cape of South Africa in 1918. He qualified as a lawyer and joined the ANC, where to begin with he supported a campaign of non-violence. In 1960, sixty-nine unarmed black protestors were killed by police who opened fire on a crowd outside a police station in the township of Sharpeville. Mandela became converted to armed insurrection and was a founder member of the ANC's military wing, '*Umkhonto we Sizwe*' or 'Spear of the

Nation'. In 1962 he was arrested and sent to prison for five years. A year later several of his associates were arrested for sabotage and treason and Mandela, who was implicated in their activities, was brought to trial again. He did not deny sabotage, but strongly denied treason or working to encourage an invasion of South Africa by a foreign power. He then said this: 'During my lifetime I have dedicated myself to the struggle of the African people. I have fought against white domination, and I have fought against black domination. I have cherished the ideal of a democratic and free society in which all persons live together in harmony and with equal opportunities. It is an ideal which I hope to live for and to achieve. But if needs be, it is an ideal for which I am prepared to die.' He was sentenced to life imprisonment.

[Mandela] 'If needs be, it is an ideal for which I am prepared to die'.

International pressure on South Africa to change its policy on apartheid came as early as 1960 when the British Prime Minister, Harold Macmillan, told the parliament in Cape Town that a 'wind of change' was blowing through Africa and independence for former black colonies was not far away. His remarks were met with frosty disdain. South Africa instead voted to become an entirely independent republic and severed all links with the British Crown and the Commonwealth in 1961. Led by its intransigent Prime Minister, Hendrik Verwoerd, it pursued its own narrow goals. Verwoerd believed he could preserve white supremacy in South Africa through the constant repression of anti-apartheid movements and the creation of so-called self-governing homelands for the native population. The homelands, however, were no more than South African puppets with no real authority of their own and the pressure to repeal apartheid began to be felt from abroad as much as within. South Africa was refused membership of international organisations such as UNESCO and the World Health Organisation; it faced opposition along its borders with countries such as Angola from where it was attacked by Marxist guerrilla movements; and television pictures of brutal police reaction to protests in townships such as Soweto fuelled a worldwide movement of condemnation. In 1977 the death of Steve Biko, a leader of the Black Consciousness Movement, led to further protests. Biko died in police custody. The police reported that it was due to a prolonged hunger strike, but it soon became clear that he had been brutally beaten and tortured and died as a result of a huge blow to his head. South Africa was becoming an outcast among the nations of the world.

In many respects it is extraordinary that apartheid and its consequences remained in operation for so long. It depended on the worst and most intolerant aspects of nineteenth-century European colonialism, and attitudes which even then many people found unacceptable. Its survival was a gruesome example of how a small and comparatively wealthy group of people can control and suppress a far greater number of the poor and poorly educated. But by pursuing a relentless policy of white supremacy, the supporters of apartheid planted the seeds of their own destruction. By the end of the 1980s various relaxations in South Africa's hierarchy of laws had already been introduced, but the National Party clung on as long as possible to its fundamental tenets. They knew that once they agreed to abolish apartheid and recognise the ANC, black majority rule would follow. Eventually, however, it became a policy impossible to maintain as world opinion, reinforced by economic sanctions, imposed increasing burdens on the state. In 1990 the President of South Africa, F. W. De Klerk, announced that the ban on the ANC was to be lifted and Nelson Mandela would be released from prison.

Mandela's release is perhaps one of the best-remembered events of modern times. At about a quarter past four in the afternoon of 11th February 1990, he appeared at the gates of his prison in Paarl where he had spent the last three years of his twenty-seven year confinement. Pictures of the occasion were watched on televisions all over the world. Like the assassination of President Kennedy in 1963, or the attacks on the World Trade Center in 2001, many of us can remember where we were and what we were doing when Nelson Mandela became a free man. With his release came hope, but also apprehension. Mandela had made no concessions in order to win his liberty. The ANC's armed struggle against political oppression was still in force.

Many were convinced that South Africa would become a blood-bath and violence erupted across the country from both black and white groups. But the reform process moved on and after elections in April 1994, Nelson Mandela became the first black President of South Africa.

He remained in office until 1999 when he retired at the age of eighty. His achievement is one of the most remarkable in the history of any country at any time. He never lost his strength of purpose and his vision of democracy for his country. When he was given power and the opportunity to implement the policies for which he had been incarcerated he did so without bitterness or revenge. The Truth and Reconciliation Commission which he established sought to relieve the country of the burden of guilt and animosity that many people felt after the long years of apart-heid. Witnesses who spoke truthfully about the wrong things that they did were given amnesty from prosecution. Although not entirely successful – measuring 'success' in matters of this kind is very difficult – it was generally regarded as a model of how to handle the difficult process of national reconciliation after a long period of hostility. South Africa faces considerable problems as it rebuilds after the long years of apartheid. Much of the black population is still desperately poor and its expectations have been encouraged by the transference of power from a small white elite to a government that represents its interests. Nelson Mandela's speech at his trial, in which he said he was opposed to both white and black domination, echo across the intervening years of his imprisonment. His words deserve attention today even more than they did when he first spoke them. It was largely because of him that South Africa re-entered the world in a state of confidence and calm. It was the triumph of Nelson Mandela as much as the triumph of the nation as a whole. He fought for his country to be different, but he preferred the liberty of victory to the heroism of war.

Mandela preferred the liberty of victory to the heroism of war.

3 Religion

Introduction

Mankind has grown more secular yet religion continues to exert its hold. Scientific enquiry has undermined religious belief but failed to demolish it. In the East, religious ideas such as Buddhism and Confucianism rely on man's ability to find his own fulfilment. In that sense they are intrinsically 'atheistic' although they do not reject all supernatural, mystical and spiritual beliefs. In the West, however, where since the invention of both Christianity and Islam, a belief in a single god has been the predominant form of religion, total atheism is comparatively rare. It requires an intellectual certainty that many people do not possess.

Most doubting people prefer the compromise of agnosticism, a position half way between belief and knowledge that is as old as philosophy itself. The ancient Hindu texts of the *Rigveda* asked the question: 'Who knows for certain? Who shall here declare it?/ Whence was it born, and whence came this creation?' The modern use of the word agnosticism was first used by the nineteenth-century British scientist, T. H. Huxley who, as a friend and supporter of Charles Darwin, wrestled with the problem of how to reconcile the discovery of evolution with religious observance. But long before Darwin's theories seemed to destroy the idea of a God-created universe, writers and thinkers had often questioned it. The Greek philosopher Protagoras who lived before Plato in the fifth century BC said: 'Concerning the gods, I have no means of knowing whether they exist or not.' In the eighteenth century the French writer Voltaire coined the famous aphorism: 'If God did not exist, it would be necessary to invent him.' From classical civilisation to the Enlightenment of the eighteenth century, man has preferred compromise to certainty. He finds it hard to believe that the world in which he lives, whose natural processes he constantly explores and better understands, frames his entire existence. There must be something more. But what?

On the whole the history of religious ideas is the history of the conflict between the spiritual and the temporal. In the middle of the ninth century the Tang Emperor of China, Wuzong, ordered the destruction of Buddhist monasteries and temples because he believed their religion threatened Chinese values. The Chinese have tended to prefer philosophical concepts, such as those devised by Confucius, to religious faith. For them religion has been the subordinate partner to civic law and order. One of the most important philosophers of the medieval world was a Muslim, Averroes, who lived towards the end of the twelfth century in the Arab emirate of Córdoba in southern Spain. Islam does not define a difference between 'Church' and 'State' in the same way as societies based on Christian thought. Islamic law governs all things. Averroes, however, believed that religion and philosophy could exist side by side. Religion, or faith, was certain and did not require to be tested. But philosophy, an intellectual pursuit reserved for the intelligent elite, provided another source of truth for those educated enough to understand it. Such views were highly controversial in a world constrained by the limits of medieval knowledge and brought Averroes into conflict with the authorities. He was briefly imprisoned before being allowed to live out his last years in freedom.

Nearly a hundred years later, in 1170, four knights murdered Thomas à Becket, England's Archbishop of Canterbury, on the choir steps of his cathedral. They believed they were doing the bidding of their king, Henry II, who had grown increasingly angry at Becket's attempts to assert the power of the Church over that of the monarch. These three unrelated events, scattered across the evolution of the world's beliefs, demonstrate how faith is always tested by reality. God may be beyond human comprehension, but the religion that worships Him is manmade.

It was through belief that man learned to think about the world around him. In the ancient world the multiplicity of gods provided people with a mosaic of functional disciplines that gave them a pattern for how to conduct their earthly lives. In Europe and the Middle East religious thought gradually coalesced into the idea of one God. How that God was to be obeyed became a matter of fierce intellectual debate: religious liberty developed naturally into political liberty. At the same time scientific discovery undermined belief in God's existence. The freedoms people won defending their right to worship in the way they wanted became the freedoms they needed to defend their civil liberties as their religious faith weakened. The atheist owes a lot to religion.

This chapter is about how man invented religion and how he has coped with his invention. It tells the story of the creation and dissemination of the world's most influential faiths and describes other powerful ideas and philosophies that existed alongside them. It begins at the point where the whole of this history begins in the city-states of Mesopotamia in about 2000 BC. In this part of the Middle East social and political groups began to emerge for the first time and with them the art of writing. The *Epic of Gilgamesh* is one of the world's oldest pieces of literature, a sprawling story of men, kings and gods written down on clay tablets. Its theme – the human hope for life eternal – sets the scene for everything that follows. From his earliest beginnings man has looked for life beyond the limits of his time on earth.

From Gilgamesh the story moves forward by more than a thousand years to another great epic, the longest in the world. The *Mahabharata* began life as a collection of religious and heroic stories later brought together as one sacred text setting out the fundamental principles of Indian culture and faith. By the time the *Mahabharata* had evolved into a single unified story the ideas of Confucius had arrived in China. His rules of behaviour, setting out the principles of morality that were needed to govern political, social and personal life, have had a fundamental influence on Chinese thought ever since.

The ideas that Confucius gave to the East were matched by the philosophy that Plato gave to the West. Writing in ancient Greece, Plato explained the difference between everyday perceptions of 'goodness' and real or true 'goodness', which is eternal and gives human life meaning and value. Immortality is the perpetuation of this search for true goodness, the higher truth. Only the ignorant need fear death.

Buddha, who lived and worked in the north-eastern part of India in about 400 BC, also provided his followers with a remedy for the pain of death and suffering. His name means 'Awakened

One', and he taught his disciples how selflessness in action and withdrawal from the worldly in thought would provide them with a state of perfect peace.

The teachings of Jesus Christ, executed as an irritating troublemaker in the Roman province of Judaea in 33 AD, gave the world a religion that became a cornerstone of Western civilisation. Those of Mohammed, who died in Medina in 632 AD, provided the whole of the Near East, Central Asia and ultimately the lands of the Indian Ocean and Northern Africa, with the values and ideas that still sustain them today.

This history of the world's religions ends with three great challenges. In 1517 Martin Luther nailed his criticisms of the activities of the Roman Catholic Church to the door of a church in Wittenberg in Germany. His defiant action accelerated a process of religious change that altered the shape of the western World. In 1859 Charles Darwin published *On the Origin of Species* and at one scientific stroke destroyed the concept of a world created entirely by the hand of God. Finally, on 11th September 2001, terrorists from the Muslim organisation Al-Qaeda attacked America, destroying the World Trade Center in New York and killing nearly 3,000 people. They were embarked on a 'holy war' against a country that they believed was trying to destroy their faith, and with it their political and cultural institutions.

From the mythological heroes of his ancient past to the bloodthirsty convictions of his modern world, man's quest for the eternal has been a central part of his development. Human beings crave order, and they look to religion and philosophy to provide it. Throughout history they have kept before them the concept of heaven as a place of escape to a higher truth. In pursuing and protecting these noble ideas they have often behaved with frightening savagery. Religion may promote peace, but it rarely protects it.

CHAPTER 1

The *Epic of Gilgamesh*

2000 BC

> The *Epic of Gilgamesh* is the oldest story in the world. It describes the struggle of a hero against his realisation that he cannot live forever. Man's destiny lies not with himself, but with the Gods.

The history of civilisation has to begin somewhere. There is no better place to start than in the land surrounding two great Asian rivers, the Tigris and the Euphrates. The Greeks gave it the name of Mesopotamia. Today we call a large part of it Iraq. As I write this, car bombs have exploded in Baghdad, the country's capital, killing more than a hundred people. Yesterday another explosion killed four children at one of the city's primary schools. It is an awful irony that this unhappy land is the place where man first learned the rules of civilised behaviour and wrote down his thoughts about his relationship both to the world around him and his life beyond.

Thousands of years ago, in a part of the world that is mainly hot and arid, the fertile ground fed by the Tigris and Euphrates rivers provided an attractive destination for the nomadic herdsmen who lived in the region. By 4200 BC the Sumer people had begun to build settled communities. They probably invented the wheel and used ploughs to help cultivate the land that they irrigated from river waters with a network of canals carrying their goods from one place to another. They also built the world's first cities.

The city of Uruk stood on a site near the Euphrates River about 170 miles south of Baghdad. First discovered and excavated in the middle of the nineteenth century, it represents one of the earliest examples of ancient Sumerian society. The people who lived here worshipped in temples. They were also property owners, identifying their possessions with seals made out of semi-precious stones. These city dwellers also began to develop a written language which they used entirely for keeping accounts or making lists. It was made up of signs or pictographs that were drawn, in a script known as cuneiform, using the end of a reed stick on a piece of wet clay shaped into a smooth pad several inches square. The clay was then baked or left to dry in the sun. These were important advances in the development of early human society and allowed the Sumerians to expand beyond the boundaries of the places where they had settled. Between 2900 and 2371 BC they established a number of independent city-states and these began to fight one another for control of the whole region. The cities had strong administrative centres, which, with their temples, provided organisation and government. Dynasties founded by powerful kings began to emerge. The first was led by Sargon of Akkadê who proclaimed himself 'King of the Four Quarters of the World'. His dynasty lasted for more than 150 years, ending with the reign of his grandson, Naram-Sin, between about 2191 and 2155 BC.

The collapse of the Sargon dynasty was followed by a period of anarchy. In about 2100 BC, twenty-one kings are recorded as having reigned during a period of ninety-one years. After that came another dynasty, this time from Ur, another of Mesopotamia's cities. King Ur-Nammu and his son, Shulgi, built the great temple of Ur, a 'ziggurat' tower, dedicated to the moon god Nanna. Shulgi ruled for forty-eight years, proclaiming himself a god and subjugating most of Mesopotamia to his rule. Excavations of the Ziggurat at Ur have revealed that Sumerian kings were buried with considerable ceremony, despatched to the afterlife surrounded by evidence of their earthly success: gold, jewels and other valuable possessions.

The temple lay at the heart of Sumerian government and provided both political and religious functions. It was the home of the city's particular deity that watched over its citizens and blessed their work. Both nobles and slaves belonged to it and carried out their responsibilities according to its instructions. This organisation provided the basis of the Sumerian city-state in which people began to take on increasingly specific tasks, dividing their labour according to the needs of the community as a whole, irrigating their land, trading with their neighbours and, as their ambitions grew, fighting for possession of more territory. It has been estimated that the imperial city of Ur was home to about 25,000 people; they were ruled by divine laws which they obeyed absolutely. The laws defined the Sumerian universe and everything it contained. According to one text, they were originally laid down by Enki, the god of water, and given to the city of Eridu. Inanna, the goddess of love, stole them from Enki after she had got him drunk and distributed their knowledge to others. 'Since that time,' the text goes on, 'nothing else has been invented.' The Sumerians seem to have believed that their world was unchanging: what they saw was what it was and what it always would be. Such certainties are inevitably fragile. In 2000 BC, the Sumerian civilisation disappeared, over-thrown by the Elamites, a people it had tried to conquer. By 1800 BC, Mesopotamia had fallen to the Kings of Babylon.

The *Epic of Gilgamesh* comes to us mainly from Babylon. Its story, however, is entirely Sumerian. The end of the Sumer civilisation did not mean the end of its language. The version we know today has been assembled from clay tablets that come from a period of history stretching over many centuries, from the earliest days of Sargon of Akkadê to a time long after his world had disappeared. It exists in Babylonian, Akkadan and Sumeran languages, but it tells the same story. It is the story of Gilgamesh, King of Uruk, who may have ruled in about 2750 BC. Gilgamesh is a tyrant who has rebuilt his city after a great flood and brought it back into prominence once again. 'Two-thirds god and one third human,' his energy and power is more than his exhausted subjects can bear. They ask the gods to divert him. The gods ensnare a wild man, Enkidu, luring him away from his life with the animals with the help of a prostitute. Enkidu and Gilgamesh become friends and set out on a journey to kill Humbaba, the monster who guards the timber in the Forest of Cedar. Having killed Humbaba the heroes return to Uruk where a goddess falls in love with Gilgamesh and tries to seduce him. He spurns her

It is the world's oldest piece of literature.

advances and she sends a raging bull to cause havoc in the city. Gilgamesh and Enkidu kill it. Enkidu then falls sick and dies.

In a state of grief Gilgamesh sets out to wander the earth in search of the secret of immortality. After several adventures he crosses the Waters of Death to meet the immortal Uta-napishti, who tells Gilgamesh that he was given immortality by the gods because he was the only person to survive the Great Flood. He was told to build a boat and fill it with all the beasts of the field and craftsmen of every skill. It survived seven days of a terrible storm before running aground on the side of a mountain. If Gilgamesh can survive without sleep for a week he too might discover the secret of immortality. Gilgamesh cannot, and prepares to return home. As he leaves, Uta-napishti tells him that there is a coral on the seabed that holds the secret of regeneration. Gilgamesh dives for it, but later, while he is resting, a snake steals it from him. He realises that he will never find it again and returns to Uruk with the recognition that his time on earth is limited and his memorials will always be human rather than divine.

> The abducted and the dead, how alike is their lot!
> But never was drawn the likeness of Death,
> Never in the land did the dead greet a man.
> The Anunnaki, the great gods, held an assembly,
> Mammitum, maker of destiny, fixed fates with them:
> both Death and Life they have established,
> but the day of Death they do not disclose.

A later version of the epic takes up the same theme:

> The life that you seek you never will find:
> when the gods created mankind,
> death they dispensed to mankind,
> life they kept for themselves.

The *Epic of Gilgamesh* is not in itself religious, but religion is an essential part of its story. The people who lived 4,000 years ago were as concerned as those of today with questions of immortality and the possibility of life after death. A belief in religion is the way in which mankind prepares itself for the certainty of death. How you behave on earth and how dutifully you obey the orders of your god or gods will determine the nature of your existence once you die. The Sumerians, like the later Greeks, had a number of gods in whom they believed. Each city-state belonged to a particular deity and each god served a particular function. The way in which these gods organised themselves reflected human behaviour. There was a hierarchy with a supreme master at its head, the 'Lord Air' from whom everything flowed. The other gods did their work within his jurisdiction. The god of water, a crucial resource in ancient Mesopotamia, was also the god of wisdom. There was a god of the plough. The goddess of love was also the goddess of war. The Sumerians protected with theology those aspects of their lives that could not be looked after entirely by their own efforts. In a harsh, unforgiving climate, where human attempts to tame the earth's natural resources and shape them into stable social structures could be swept away by flood, drought or other disasters, keeping peace with the gods was an obvious insurance policy.

The tale of the Great Flood is almost exactly the same as that of Noah in Genesis.

The story of Gilgamesh absorbs these ideas, weaving human impotence with heavenly mischief to build the world's first known picture of man's frailty in the face of the mighty universe. Like Hercules, Gilgamesh is superhuman in his strength and determination but this is not enough to outwit the gods. His friend Enkidu, seduced from the purity of a life of nature by the pleasures of the flesh, tells Gilgamesh as he dies that his god 'has taken against me'. For all his loyalty and sacrifice he will die an ordinary man. Many of these stories are forerunners to those that were incorporated into later religions. The tale of the Great Flood is almost exactly the same as that of Noah in Genesis, the opening chapter of the Hebrew Bible.

The exploits of Gilgamesh first reached the West in the middle of the nineteenth century. Excavations near the site of the biblical city of Nineveh revealed the existence of a library belonging to one of the last Assyrian kings, Ashurbanipal, who

Greek Mythology

Greek mythology is eternal. Zeus turning into a swan in order
to seduce Leda; Theseus slaying a minotaur; Perseus beheading
Medusa; and Oedipus killing his father to marry his mother are
tales of tragedy, treachery, love, jealousy and vengeance that not
only provided the Greeks with an essential way of understanding
their earthly existence but gave the world stories they have
enjoyed ever since. The Greek myths are a web where gods,
heroes and creatures are caught up in a series of complicated
adventures that combine to create a religious system. They were
originally passed along by word of mouth. Homer's epics, the
Odyssey and the *Iliad*, are the earliest known literary version,
dating from the end of the ninth century BC. His story of the
Trojan War, one of the most important of all the myths, was
reinterpreted in Roman times by Virgil. Virgil's long poem, the
Aeneid, was written over ten years between 29 and 19 BC and tells
the same tale, this time to glorify the foundation of Rome.

The myths infiltrated every aspect of Greek daily life and
were used to help manage social, religious and political issues.
They were also used as a moral and educational guide. At their
centre are the twelve Olympian gods (of a total of fourteen)
who can be compared to a gifted but argumentative and bad
tempered extended family. Zeus reigns supreme as god of the
sky. He is a serial adulterer. His behaviour arouses the jealousy
of his wife and sister Hera (ironically goddess of marriage) with
monumental repercussions. Poseidon, god of the sea, Hades,
god of the underworld and Demeter, goddess of fertility, are all
siblings. When Demeter's daughter, Persephone, is abducted by
Hades to the underworld for four months of the year, Demeter
is so full of sorrow that she lets the earth go barren. When
she is reunited with her daughter the earth blooms again for
eight months in a mythological explanation of the seasons.
The younger generation are mainly children of Zeus by several
mothers including Hermes, Ares, Apollo, Artemis, Athena,
Aphrodite, Hestia, Dionysus and even Hephaestus, the god of
metalwork. The Greeks had a god for everything and all of them
had the flaws, failings and petty jealousies of humans. These
made them easier to relate to: for instance, girls about to be
married gave sacrifices to Aphrodite in the hope of finding a
favourable first sexual experience.

ruled in the seventh century BC. Ashurbanipal was a scholar as well as a fighter and gathered a collection of clay tablets from all over Mesopotamia which he kept in a chamber in his palace. These were sent back to the British Museum in London but were not deciphered immediately. Mesopotamia's treasures included other finds such as statues and works of art that overshadowed the clay tablets covered with lines of cuneiform.

An amateur archaeologist called George Smith learned to read cuneiform and was given permission to study them. As he worked his way painstakingly through the tablets he realised that what he had discovered was the world's oldest piece of literature, one of whose stories, about the Great Flood, had existed centuries before it appeared in the Bible. In 1872 he announced his discovery in a lecture attended by the Prime Minister, William Gladstone. The *Daily Telegraph* paid for him to revisit the Nineveh site to see if he could recover a missing fragment from the Sumerian text. When he got there Smith discovered that the place had been used as a quarry. The clay fragments were piled in disorganised heaps. He began to assemble what he could. One evening as he began to sort through the jumbled remains he had managed to retrieve he realised he had

It is the first picture of man's frailty in the face of the mighty universe.

stumbled on the missing fragment. In fact what he had discovered was a piece from a later version of the story, but he could not have known that at the time. In any event his researches went no further. As far as the *Daily Telegraph* was concerned the story of Gilgamesh was complete and George Smith's expedition was summoned home. But the tales of the clay tablets of ancient Mesopotamia are not yet finished. New discoveries in the twentieth century have brought to light other aspects of the *Epic of Gilgamesh* and the beliefs of the people among whom he lived. Further finds are likely to extend our knowledge. But they are unlikely to change one of the things we know: that among the first organised communities in the history of the world, man's need for religion shaped his daily life and prepared him for the moment when it would inevitably come to an end.

CHAPTER 2

The *Mahabharata*

500–100 BC

The *Mahabharata* is a sacred text of India written over a period of several hundred years and handed down through generations. It has about 100,000 verses and 1.8 million words. The story it tells and the philosophy it explains provide many of the essential beliefs of the Hindu religion.

Hinduism is inseparable from the history of India, and much of the history of India is inseparable from that of Britain. In the last quarter of the eighteenth century, as the British strengthened their control of the Indian subcontinent, they began to take a deep interest in the ancient culture of their new possession.

Warren Hastings, who was Governor General of India between 1773 and 1785, encouraged his subordinates in Indian scholarship. In particular he was a great admirer of the *Mahabharata*, part of which was first translated into English by an employee of the East India Company, Charles Wilkins, in 1785. The sacred text, he said, 'will survive when the British dominion in India shall have long ceased to exist'. But it was another Englishman abroad, William Jones, who had the most profound influence on European perceptions of Asia. He arrived in Calcutta in 1783 to take up a position as a judge in the High Court of Bengal and a year later became the founding president of the Asiatick Society, an organisation devoted to the study of the continent in which he and his countrymen found themselves. It purpose was to encompass 'Man and Nature; whatever is performed by the one; or produced by the other.' Jones learnt Sanskrit, the language of the *Mahabharata*, and other Indian literature, declaring it to be 'of a wonderful structure'. In his view it was 'more perfect

than the Greek, more copious than the Latin, and more exquisitely refined than either'. He translated Indian religious poetry,
including a hymn to the god Camdeo, whom he saw as related to
the Greek Eros or Roman Cupid. Bubbling with excitement at his
discovery of a new deity described in, for him, a newly discovered
language, Jones felt that in his Hindu disguise this god 'has new
and peculiar beauties'.

> What potent God from Agra's orient bow'rs
> Floats thro' the lucid air, whilst living flow'rs
> With funny twine the vocal arbours wreathe,
> And gales enamour'd heav'nly fragrance breathe?
> Hail pow'r unknown! For at thy beck
> Vales and groves their blossoms deck
> And ev'ry laughing blossom dresses
> With gems of dew his musky tresses.
> I feel, I feel thy genial flame divine,
> And hallow thee and kiss thy shrine.

Translations like these, produced by amateur men of letters in
faraway corners of the emerging British Empire, began to teach
Europeans about the beauty and importance of Indian culture
and history. Their enthusiastic naivety adds to their charm. The
members of the Asiatick Society only skimmed the surface of a
deeply rooted culture. But their delight in what they found and
their intelligence in recognising its significance began to give
the West an understanding of how the history of Asia fitted into
the world as a whole. At the heart of it lay a set of beliefs with
universal appeal.

The *Mahabharata* is one of two Indian Sanskrit epics – the
other is the *Ramayana* – which combine historical stories with
philosophy and mythology. It is considered to be divinely
revealed, providing the reader with a code of conduct and
explaining the right path for individual behaviour. 'No story
is found on earth which does not depend on this tale,' it says.
'What is here is elsewhere, what is not here is nowhere.' The
work describes the lives and actions of two branches of the
same family who are rivals for a throne. Eventually they fight a

battle that lasts for eighteen days, involving huge armies from all over the Indian continent. Of around four million soldiers who fight, only a handful survives. The victors are the brothers of the Pandava family. They renounce everything and retire to the Himalayas where one by one they die and ascend into heaven. This central narrative comprises little more than a fifth of the total work. The rest of the epic is taken up with legends, folk tales, philosophy, information about places of pilgrimage, and romances.

The *Mahabharata* was written over a long period of time with the result that different groups exerted influence over its development. Its origins belong to the Aryan people who swept into north-eastern India around 1750 BC and gradually settled throughout the Punjab and the Upper Ganges. The Aryans – their name belongs to the language that they used – created the religious structure from which Indian beliefs, including Hinduism, are derived. They also constructed the primitive social order to which the Portuguese invaders of the early sixteenth century gave the name 'caste'. In this organisation the role of the priest, or Brahman, was very important.

It belongs to the land of India as much as to the Hindu religion.

In him resided knowledge of the path to the truth as laid out in the Sanskrit texts. The version of the *Mahabharata* that we know today probably dates from about 400 AD. It is a distillation of hundreds of years of story-telling and religious observance that survived the movements of peoples and the wars they fought. Some of the tribes mentioned in the *Mahabharata* fought against Alexander the Great when he invaded India in 326 BC. They only submitted after fierce fighting in which Alexander himself was wounded. Great events such as these provided the framework for religious invention: history and myth combined to create not only a system of beliefs, but a sense of purpose as well. The *Mahabharata* belongs to the land of India as much as to the Hindu religion.

In the middle of the epic, during the story of the battle, sits the 'Bhagavad Gita', a section of about 700 verses that is one of the guiding works of Hindu belief. 'Mahatma' Gandhi, one of the architects of Indian independence in the twentieth century, said that he turned to the 'Bhagavad Gita' when 'doubts haunt me, when disappointments stare me in the face, and when I see not one ray of light on the horizon'. The work, he said, had the capacity to make him smile 'in the midst of overwhelming sorrow'. It may seem curious that Gandhi, a believer in non-violence, should draw such comfort from a work that is a conversation between the god, Krishna, and the hero, Arjuna, in which Krishna explains the circumstances in which a war can be justified. Gandhi, like some other interpreters of the work, took the view that the battle in the *Mahabharata* is allegorical – a symbol for the fight of the soul against the forces of evil. This is a battle that can only be won through a process of enlightenment. By employing self-discipline and meditation, man can reach the serenity of mind necessary to eliminate selfishness and follow the path of righteousness, or 'dharma', which is what a Hindu should strive to achieve. Dharma is the moral law that governs all Hindus, teaching them how to relate to one another and how to manage their households and their society. The path towards a good life is not possible without pain and suffering but once reached bestows everlasting and happiness and enlightenment.

It could make Gandhi smile 'in the midst of overwhelming sorrow'.

The *Mahabharata*, like other Sanskrit writings, was passed to one generation from another through story-tellers who spoke to their audiences in local languages. By the time the British arrived to take control of India, a mass of beliefs and ideas were circulating throughout the continent. Hinduism is not a religion fuelled, like Christianity or Islam, with missionary zeal. Its spread was due to military and commercial expansion. In the ninth century, the Khmer Empire that ruled a large part of South-east Asia, including modern Laos, Cambodia, Vietnam and part of Malaysia, appropriated Hindu beliefs. The temple at Angkor Wat near Siem Reap in Cambodia, one of the most important religious foundations in the whole of Asia, was designed in the twelfth century to represent Mount Meru, home of the gods in Hindu mythology. Hinduism was adapted to customs: like many of the world's great religions, its ideas permeated its followers and were reshaped, or reinterpreted, according to their needs. The British, however, were influential in beginning to give it a structure that made it more comparable with their own religious notions. William Jones and his fellow orientalists of the Asiatick Society realised that Sanskrit, the language of the Hindu texts, was Indo-European and distantly related to Greek. 'Pythagoras and Plato,' said Jones, 'derived their sublime theories from the same fountain with the sages of India.' Such heady comparisons led naturally to a view that Western and Hindu ideas were somehow linked, an idea to which Indians themselves began to subscribe.

In the early nineteenth century, Ram Mohan Roy, an energetic writer and thinker, campaigned successfully to ban the Hindu practice of *sati* – in which a widow is burned on her husband's funeral pyre – claiming that it was a mistaken interpretation of Hindu scripture. He also condemned devotion to more than one god and the worshipping of idols. Roy was the first writer to use the word 'Hindu' in English and his assertion that 'superstitious practices which deform the Hindoo religion have nothing to do with the pure spirit of its dictates' made him celebrated in Britain, a country that he admired and in which he died. By speaking out against idolatry, Roy helped Hinduism to become a religion that assuaged India's colonial masters while still inspiring its subjects who were beginning to contemplate independence.

The battle in the Mahabharata is allegorical – a symbol for the fight of the soul against the forces of evil.

This process continued throughout the nineteenth century. The new leaders of Hinduism taught that all religions were true because each followed its own course of the truth. There was no need to convert people away from Hindu beliefs as Christian missionaries tried to do, and its guiding principles, appropriately reformed, should be left untouched. In Chicago in September 1893, one of the leaders of this new brand of Hinduism, Swami Vivekananda, addressed the first 'Parliament of Religions' that had been organised as part of a world trade fair. His opening words, 'Sisters and brothers of America', were met with rapturous applause, before continuing:

> To the Hindu, the whole world of religions is only a travel-
> ling, a coming up, of different men and women, through
> various conditions and circumstances, to the same goal.
> Every religion is only evolving a God out of the material
> man, and the same God is the inspirer of all of them. Why,
> then, are there so many contradictions? They are only
> apparent, says the Hindu. The contradictions come from the
> same truth adapting itself to the varying circumstances of
> different natures.

Vivekananda had been destined for a professional career in colonial India. His father was a successful lawyer and he himself went to university in Calcutta. As a young man he fell under the influence of the teachings of the new, reformed branch of Hinduism, abandoned any thought of formal work and took up the life of a religious teacher. Vivekananda taught that the Hindu concept of *Vedanta*, which argues that human nature is divine, transcending any form of self-realisation, was the central belief of this noble religion. India, he said, was a spiritual land: the materialistic West had much to learn from it. These ideas found great appeal. Hinduism was no longer the pagan belief of a benighted people. It had taken its place on the world stage where it could be adapted to all who wanted to partake in it. One of the greatest social reformers of twentieth-century India, Pandita Ramabai, although a Christian herself, argued both that Hinduism had many good characteristics that Christians should respect and that Hindi should be adopted as the country's national language. Through reform and adaptation Hinduism had achieved a cultural and religious significance far beyond the boundaries of India itself.

On one level the *Mahabharata* is a heroic epic, telling the story, like many other such works in world literature, of the struggle between good and evil. On another it is an ancient scripture providing communities with the means of teaching themselves the laws of behaviour and belief. While it contains many references to the meditative nature of the Hindu religion it also has passages that evoke the history of the Indian subcontinent. Like the country from which it grew, it has many faces and hidden depths. Since the beginning of the nineteenth century its religious ideas have belonged to the world but at its heart it is, and always will be, a work that belongs uniquely to India.

CHAPTER 3

Plato

429–347 BC

Plato is one of the most important philosophers in
the history of the world. We know very little about him
as a man, but his work, written nearly two and a half
thousand years ago, has had an enduring influence on
the history of mankind.

In the year 430 BC the leader of the Athenian people, Pericles,
delivered a famous funeral oration. His city and its allies were
fighting a war against its rival, Sparta. Pericles, one of the most
brilliant leaders of classical Greece, used the opportunity to
praise those who had fallen in battle and to remind his audience
of the strengths of the society they had died defending: 'We do
not copy our neighbours,' he said, 'but are an example to them.'

> It is true that we are called a democracy, for the administration
> is in the hands of the many and not of the few ... When a
> citizen is in any way distinguished, he is preferred to the
> public service, not as a matter of privilege, but as the reward of
> merit ... A spirit of reverence pervades our public acts ... We
> are prevented from doing wrong by respect for the authorities
> and for the laws ... For we are the lovers of the beautiful, yet
> simple in our tastes, and we cultivate the mind without loss
> of manliness ... An Athenian citizen does not neglect the state
> because he takes care of his own household; and even those of
> us engaged in business have a very fair idea of politics.

These words, recorded by the Greek historian Thucydides, have
come to be seen as a perfect expression of the ideals of Athenian
democracy. Pericles died not long after making his speech, a

victim of the plague that swept through the city. Plato was born a year later.

The Athens that Pericles described was undoubtedly glorious, but it was already in decline. Ancient Greece was never a unified country. Its people occupied city-states, each with different forms of government. In 480 BC, Athens and Sparta joined forces to repel the Persian king, Xerxes, who invaded the Greek mainland. First defeated at the battle of Thermopylae, where a small number of Spartans under their leader Leonidas held back the Persian army for two days before dying in a heroic last stand, the Greeks defeated Xerxes in a naval battle at Salamis. The architect of this victory was an Athenian, Themistocles, who drew the Persian fleet into a constricted area where it could not manoeuvre effectively. This triumph eventually forced Xerxes to withdraw, but the alliance that had stopped his invasion did not last for long. In the years that followed, Sparta and Athens separated and each took control of different leagues of city-states under their respective commands. In 431 BC they went to war against each other.

Sparta was militaristic and oppressive. From early in the sixth century BC it became the most powerful state in the Peloponnese peninsula, forcing the people from the territory that it conquered to become its slaves. A minority group of citizens, mainly people who could trace their ancestry back to the original city of Sparta, controlled everything. The people they had enslaved – called 'Helots' – outnumbered them and Sparta could only maintain control by exercising savage discipline. Each year Spartan magistrates declared war on the state's subjugated population so that killing them could be justified as an act of war rather than murder. The Spartans themselves were not expected to indulge in any economic activity (those duties were delegated to the Helots) and they were brought up in strict military atmosphere. Once boys reached the age of seven they were handed to government officers until they were twenty, when they were allowed to marry. But they still lived in barracks and visited their wives only occasionally. Sparta was a vast armed garrison maintained by slavery in which all individual rights were subsumed by the state. Athens, on the other hand, was a seafaring power. It was run on democratic lines where any person qualifying as a citizen had the right to participate directly in the government of the state. Its main legislative body was an assembly with a quorum of 6,000 that met ten times a year. In such a system it was inevitable that power was handed to men who were then left to act pretty much as they saw fit. It could not operate the same checks and balances that exist in modern democratic states. But the leader could be removed or appointed by popular will and inevitably the city became divided by different factions. Pericles himself was sacked as general of the Athenian army when the war against Sparta was going badly, although he was subsequently reinstated.

Plato was brought up in a city-sate that was struggling to maintain the supremacy it had enjoyed since its defeat of the Persian army more than fifty years previously. Pericles may have been an inspiring leader, but he was also an aggressive soldier. He believed that Athens needed to build on the achievements of its victory over Xerxes by breaking out of its maritime base to conquer mainland Greece, traditionally the preserve of the powerful Spartans. He wanted to carry Athenian democracy abroad as well as defend the Greek mainland from further Persian attacks. Athens stood at the head of a league of smaller cities upon which it had managed to impose its unique form of government, but it was the leader and most influential member of an alliance rather than an imperial power. It became overstretched, and in 445 BC Pericles negotiated a thirty-year peace with Sparta before their rivalries brought them to war once again, but by 404 BC, Athens's days of glory were over as Sparta became the military master of classical Greece.

Philosophy was Plato's way of bringing a sense of order to a fractured world.

Plato witnessed these things. As a young man he lived through the aftermath of the city's terrible defeat following its failed invasion of Syracuse in Sicily. Before he was thirty he saw it overwhelmed by a Spartan fleet under the command of Lysander, who installed an oligarchic government, the 'thirty tyrants', in Athens. This lasted less than a year before a democratic government was restored. The new government then did something

Aristotle

The Greek philosopher Aristotle (384–322 BC) is, alongside
Plato and Socrates, one of the founding fathers of Western
thought. His contributions to philosophy, politics, formal
logic and the scientific method were enormous. He famously
argued that politics was organic and that 'man is by nature a
political animal'. He was the first thinker to see philosophy
as a comprehensive system of morality, logic, science, politics
and metaphysics. He also made significant contributions on
an extraordinarily broad range of subjects, including anatomy,
astronomy, economics, zoology, meteorology, education and
literature. It is no wonder that the English writer Chaucer
noted that a student is never happier than having 'at his beddes
heed/ twenty bookes, clad in blak or reed,/ of Aristotle and his
philosophie'.

An aristocrat by birth, Aristotle was taught in Plato's Academy
as a young man, remaining there until Plato died in 347. Four
years later he was invited by Philip II of Macedon to tutor
his son, Alexander the Great. Aristotle encouraged Alexander
to undertake his Eastern conquest and to take a group of
zoologists, botanists and researchers on his campaign. He
returned to Athens in 335 BC to establish his own school, the
Lyceum, and it was during this period that he wrote many of
his best-known works, including *Physics*, *Metaphysics*, *Politics*, *De
Anima* (On the Soul) and *Poetics*.

that Plato could never forgive. In 399 BC it condemned his
friend, Socrates, to death for impiety and corrupting the young.
Plato was aghast. 'When I saw all this,' he wrote in a letter, 'and
other things as bad, I was disgusted and drew back from the
wickedness of the times.' After Socrates's death, Plato travelled
abroad before returning to Athens where in about 386 BC he
founded the Academy. He taught there for the rest of his life. 'I
was forced,' he said, 'to the belief that the only hope of finding
justice for society or for the individual lay in true philosophy,
and that mankind will have no respite from trouble until either
real philosophers gain political power or politicians become by
some miracle true philosophers.'

Plato lived in an age of uncertainty. Philosophy was his way of bringing a sense of order to a fractured world. We do not know much about him as a man. He speaks to us entirely through his works, but even in these he is disguised because most of them take the form of dialogues with Socrates, the lost friend he admired and tried to follow. Plato was one of the first people in the history of the world to recognise the importance of philosophy as a search for truth. He looked around him and saw that the way men organised themselves was unsatisfactory. He lifted his eyes to an intellectual horizon far beyond the immediate limitations of the society in which he lived and tried to establish principles upon which something better could be created. His importance rests above all on this achievement. The world we live in, he argued, is imperfect. There is another world beyond whose forms are eternal and provide us with the examples we need to improve our earthly existence. These forms are things like beauty, goodness and equality: they are abstract and unrelated to time or space. We may see around us objects that we find beautiful because they are good, or right, but their characteristics are derived from a further, and real, form of beauty. We need to make a distinction between these two forms, between the earthly and the eternal. Plato believed that the human soul is different from the body. It is immortal and remains unaffected by mortal contagion. The soul loves truth: it is 'capable of enduring all evil and all good' and faith in its eternal qualities will bring men 'peace with God and with ourselves, both in our life here and when, like the victors in the games collecting their prizes, we receive our reward'.

Plato expounded his ideas in a series of dialogues in most of which Socrates questions, or is questioned by, a group of friends and acquaintances. Plato tested his ideas thoroughly, subjecting them to intense scrutiny from the different characters in his books. This was the model for his Academy, where students would come to listen to lectures and get involved in robust debates. Plato did not leave behind a set of definitive pronouncements and sometimes his ideas seem to conflict with one another. In one of his most important works, *The Republic*, he displays his disillusionment with democracy by advocating government by 'guardians', a group of people rigorously assessed for their moral worth and then granted the supreme authority to rule. The traditional concept of the family is broken up, and women bear children during mating festivals organised by the guardians. In this Plato seems to be hankering after something rather like the Spartan model, except that throughout he emphasises the importance of education and the need to build a society capable of reaching truth in its pure form.

Plato's influence on the development of Western philosophy and religion derives from his belief that human existence and human values are derived from universal forms that lie beyond our immediate reach; that human souls understand these universal forms and are immortal; and that human knowledge is a process of recollection rather than perception. He was the first person to describe his view of a perfect state, the sort of place we call a Utopia. Sir Thomas More, who first used the name, did not publish his work until 1516, by which time Plato had been dead for nearly 2,000 years. Plato reached for perfection, offering a route towards it through the immortality of the human soul, and so began to formulate ideas that would become important in the development of religious ideas, particularly Christianity. The Greeks had no universal god. Their deities were the mythological interpretation of human emotions, functions and activities. In creating a rational basis for a belief in universal goodness, or truth, Plato gave his students an entirely new method of thinking about the world.

He was the first person to describe a perfect state, the sort of place we call a Utopia.

In one of his works, *Phaedo*, Plato described the death of Socrates. One of Plato's most admiring translators, the nineteenth-century academic, Benjamin Jowett, compared it implicitly to the Crucifixion: 'There is nothing in any tragedy, ancient or modern, nothing in any poetry or history (with one exception), like the last hours of Socrates in Plato.' His actual translation has something of a biblical ring to it. Socrates, forced to drink a poisonous cup of hemlock in the company of his friends, raises it to his lips with the words: 'I may and must ask

the gods to prosper my journey from this to the other world –
even so – and so be it according to my prayer.' His friends start
to weep once he has emptied the cup, but Socrates rebukes them.
'"What is this strange outcry? I sent away the women mainly in
order that they might not behave in this way, for I have been told
that a man should die in peace. Be quiet then, and have patience."
When we heard his words we were ashamed, and refrained our
tears.' Socrates, wise, kind, clever and much loved, leaves this
world for another, better place. That image, similar to the one
described later by the apostles of Jesus, is a picture of martyr-
dom familiar to religious belief.

Plato's reputation has suffered very different interpretations.
In the Middle Ages he was eclipsed by his pupil, Aristotle, but
his work began to be read extensively again during the Renaissance. Nineteenth-century translations of his work lifted him
to new heights. The English mathematician and philosopher,
Alfred North Whitehead, remarked that the European philosophical tradition consisted of 'a series of footnotes to Plato'.
More recently, however, his ideas about government have led
to his being accused of preferring a virtuous dictatorship to a
true democracy. But to take issue with Plato about his concepts
of government is hardly profitable. Confronted by the peculiar
barbarities of Sparta on one side, and the
disagreements and corruption of Athens on
the other, he looked for an organisational
solution based on his ideas of justice and
truth. In the years immediately before his
birth, Athens had enjoyed a brilliant age
that had built the Parthenon and encouraged arts and culture. The judicial murder
of his friend Socrates contributed to the
extinction of Athens's pre-eminence, which
had, in any case, suffered decades of decline. Plato tried to build
a new world, a world of the mind, which would ensure that the
greatness of ancient Greece was carried through subsequent
ages.

He looked for an organisational solution based on his ideas of justice and truth.

CHAPTER 4

Buddha

c.400 BC

> Buddha was a teacher who wandered across northern
> India explaining how he believed mankind could
> conquer its suffering and achieve liberation. The
> answer, he said, lay with man himself, not with god.

The atmosphere of India at the height of British imperial rule
was never better captured than in Rudyard Kipling's novel,
Kim. It tells the story of a quick-witted orphan boy living on the
streets of Lahore. His mother, a British military nursemaid, is
dead from cholera; his father, an Irish soldier, from drink. He is
taken under the wing of a British spymaster who employs him to
help track down foreign agents planning to make trouble on the
border with Afghanistan.

Kim's world is exotic and mysterious. When the book opens
he is being looked after by a 'half-caste' woman who runs an
opium den. He meets a Tibetan lama whose chela, or disciple,
he becomes. The lama is on a journey to discover the Holy River
that sprang from the arrow of Buddha and whose waters promise
enlightenment. The frail Buddhist needs the young boy to act as
his eyes and ears as he travels through India's teeming towns and
villages. In return he confers on Kim a degree of status because he
is a holy man, revered and respected wherever he goes. At the end
of the story, when the foreign agents' plans have been successfully scuppered, the lama tells Kim that he has come to the end of
his journey. 'Son of my Soul,' he says; 'I have wrenched my Soul
back from the Threshold of Freedom to free thee from all sin – as
I am free and sinless! ... Certain is our deliverance! Come!'

Kipling's novel first appeared in 1901 at a time of keen British
interest in the religions of the East. Like Hinduism, Buddhist

ideas reached Europe in the nineteenth century as orientalism, the study of Asian art and culture, became fashionable. Eight years before *Kim* was published, the philosopher and scientist, T. H. Huxley, explained in an Oxford lecture why Buddhism had become so attractive. Its 'ethical qualities,' he said, were the reason for its 'marvellous success'. A system that knows no God in the Western sense but asks men to 'look to nothing but their own efforts for salvation' had, Huxley explained, great appeal to people struggling to come to terms with religious ideas dented by the evolutionary discoveries of Charles Darwin. In *Kim*, Kipling evoked the attractions of Buddhism: it was ethical, pure, harmless and uplifting. It was also useful because it provided values, but made God redundant.

Buddha's birth name was Siddhārtha Gautama. He was born among the Sakya people in the Terai region of what is now Nepal. The exact dates of his life are not known but it is generally believed that he died about 400 BC. He was part of a social elite and may even have been the son of a king. The society he inhabited was defined by status with the Brahmans, the priests who administered religious rites, firmly established at the top. Their position was being challenged by travellers who followed an ascetic way of life. Like religious reformers in subsequent ages, they questioned whether virtue was confined to those who controlled the established forms of worship. The young Siddhārtha Gautama became attracted to their teachings.

He was part of a social elite and may even have been the son of a king.

The story goes that his father kept the sick and old hidden from public view. Gautama came across them: disturbed by what he saw he decided to leave his people and travel in secret to join the ascetics. He became a wanderer, set apart from the world: 'As a lotus flower is born in water, grows in water, and rises out of water to stand above it unsoiled, so I, born in the world, raised in the world, having overcome the world, live unsoiled by the world.' He practised under two ascetic teachers. Guided by the belief that self-mortification would expunge his sins he learned how to stop breathing for long periods and ate very little. 'My spine stood out like a corded rope,' he wrote, 'my ribs projected like the jutting rafters of an old roofless cowshed and the light of my eyes sunk down in their sockets looked like the gleam of water in a deep well.' But this extreme self-punishment failed to bring him enlightenment. He left his teachers behind and, on the banks of the Falgu River in what is today the Indian state of Bihar, meditated under a bodhi tree, some accounts say for forty-nine days. Whatever the length, he emerged at the end with an explanation of the truth. He had achieved enlightenment, nirvana, and was ready to offer his teaching to the world. He was the 'awakened one' – or *Buddha*.

He learned how to stop breathing for long periods and ate very little.

After he emerged from his meditation, Buddha preached a sermon in a deer park near the town of Benares (now known as Varanasi) in which he set out his 'Four Noble Truths'. They asserted that life is suffering; that suffering is caused by craving and the thirst for sensual pleasure; that suffering can have an end; and that there is a path that, if followed, will lead to this end. The first truth is the essence of Buddhist philosophy. Man suffers in birth, ageing and illness, not only because of his own condition, but also because of the condition of those dear to him. Suffering gives rise to grief, sorrow and despair. The path to release from this is to lead a life devoted to the development of virtue and knowledge – a cure somewhat similar to that suggested by Greek philosophers such as Plato. Buddha called this the 'Eightfold Path' because it required its followers to demonstrate eight things. These were the right view (an understanding and acceptance of Buddhist teachings); the right resolve (the determination to have the right approach); the right speech (telling the truth and speaking carefully); the right action (refraining from evil or purely sensual behaviour); the right livelihood (not doing things that will harm others); the right effort (developing a positive state of mind); the right mindfulness (being aware); and the right concentration (achieving a state of calm through such things as meditation). This simple list helps explain Buddhism's subsequent popularity. It is a tool-kit for a better life. It requires no faith other than a belief in oneself and one's ability to follow the

Buddhist code. 'Know for yourself' was the Buddha's creed. Only accept ideas which 'you have realised, seen, known for yourself'. Meditation was an important component in achieving this self-knowledge. It could not in itself provide a solution to life's problems, but it trained the mind and the body to develop the disciplines necessary for enlightenment.

It is a tool kit for a better life.

Buddha died when he was about eighty. His teachings were handed down orally and did not appear in writing until about the middle of the first century AD when they were collected in scriptures or 'canons' which included his sermons and his set of rules for leading a monastic life. By that time his philosophy had spread across India and beyond after being adopted by one of the greatest of Asia's ancient emperors, Asoka the Great, known as the Beloved of the Gods. Asoka was a ruler of the Maurya dynasty whose power extended across the whole of the Indian subcontinent, apart from its southernmost tip, during the second century BC. In 261 BC he conquered Kalinga, a kingdom on the north-east coast of India, in a battle so bloodthirsty that 100,000 men are said to have died. Asoka decided to renounce warfare and convert to Buddhism.

To demonstrate his faith he ordered inscriptions to be carved into pillars and rocks throughout his empire. Their different locations are evidence of its enormous size. One has been found in Kandahar in the heart of Afghanistan, another exists more than a thousand miles away on the monument that he built near Benares where Buddha first preached. These proclaimed Asoka's belief in the dignity of all people, religious toleration and non-violence. 'All men,' said one, 'are my children.' This was Asoka's *dhamma*, or 'universal law', and in his desire to see it promoted throughout the world, he sent Buddhist missionaries abroad. Asoka was a ruler as canny as he was profound. He recognised that to constantly try to expand his frontiers by warfare and conquest would be expensive, divisive and open to failure. He sought to unify what he had and Buddhism provided him with a set of principles with which to do it. 'Virtuous deeds are difficult to accomplish,' announced another edict chiselled into a rock. 'He who tries faces a hard task.' Asoka's efforts allowed Buddhism to become firmly established in India but from the first century AD it began to appear in different forms.

Buddha's failure to write anything down meant that his teachings were open to varying interpretations by his followers. One school of thought, the Theravada, adhered to the idea that he was human; another, the Mahayana, developed the theory that he was divine. In the twelfth century, Muslim Turks invaded northern India and destroyed Buddhist monasteries which they considered to be places of pagan worship. Eventually Buddhism was driven further south and east – to Ceylon (now Sri Lanka), Burma and Southeast Asia where the older, Theravada school held greater influence, and to Tibet, China and Japan where Mahayana beliefs predominated. These central ideas spawned further variations. Like any religion, Buddhism enjoys a richness of differences. The Dalai Lama, regarded by Westerners as the world leader of the Buddhist community, is from the Mahayana. His followers believe he is the rebirth of one of the earliest and greatest of the enlightened followers of Buddha.

Buddhism requires no faith other than a belief in oneself and one's ability to follow the Buddhist code.

The Western view of Buddhism has been influenced in recent years by events in Burma (Myanmar), where protests against the ruling military dictatorship have been organised by Buddhist monks. In September 2007 television news reports showed pictures of thousands of monks protesting against the Burmese government's decision to raise fuel prices. These protesters were dispersed by tear gas; many others were beaten or arrested and, it is believed, killed. The monks wield considerable influence in Burma where ninety percent of the population follow the teachings of Buddha. They have played an important part in the country's political development and led protests against British colonial rule before and after the Second World War. One monk, U Ottama, argued that as long as the Burmese people were slaves of another country, their religion would be a slave religion. Arrested by the British, he died in prison in 1939. He is a national hero in a land where monks have a long tradition of being politically active.

Buddha's teachings stress the need for good government. 'When the ruler of a country is just and good,' he said, 'the ministers become just and good.' In the eighteenth century, the kings of Burma appointed a senior monk to supervise the country's religious houses and maintain discipline, but this role disappeared under colonial rule and afterwards. The spiritual community of Buddhism, however, remains strong and is capable of rising in protest against authority of which it disapproves. The English writer, George Orwell, got a taste of this when he served as a British imperial policeman in Burma in the 1930s. His first novel, *Burmese Days,* was based on his experiences. He found himself hating his job and all its colonial trappings. But that did not stop him from hating the local people too: they liked to make his life difficult because of what he represented. 'With one part of my mind,' he wrote later, 'I thought of the British Raj as an unbreakable tyranny … with another part I thought that the greatest joy in the world would be to drive a bayonet into a Buddhist priest's guts.'

Buddhism, despite its emphasis on the virtuous life, is not passive. One of its most successful modern exponents, Thich Nhất Hanh, a monk who came to the West from Vietnam, takes teachings from different branches of Buddhism to advance the argument that people can be active in creating change and improving the societies in which they live. 'Monks and nuns,' he says, 'are revolutionaries … They cherish their freedom so they can be a source of happiness for many people.' Nowhere is that ability to spread happiness more needed than in Burma where an ancient religion keeps hopes of freedom alive.

CHAPTER 5

Confucius

551–479 BC

Confucius was a Chinese philosopher and teacher. His ideas about government, social structure and family life have had a profound effect on the development of China ever since he first proposed them. They still matter today.

For a young man eager to make his way in imperial China the teachings of Confucius were essential for success. They formed the basis of many of the questions in the civil service examinations held to decide who should enter the organisation. Run by rigorously trained bureaucrats, the Chinese civil service maintained imperial power, permanent and precise, a bulwark of continuity throughout centuries of change.

In 140 BC, *The Analects of Confucius*, a collection of his teachings compiled by his followers after his death, were made required reading for all those sitting the civil service exams. Although they changed in structure, they remained an almost unbroken part of the curriculum until 1905. The examination process was extremely gruelling and arranged in minute detail. Every three years, examiners were appointed by the Emperor from a list of recommended names. Once selected each was given a provincial centre in which to adjudicate, and an itinerary explaining how long it would take to reach it. Some journeys could last three months. On arrival at their destinations the examiners were greeted by a grand committee that included the provincial governor. Every provincial capital had an examination compound in which a maze of tiny, primitive cubicles, sometimes running into several thousand, housed the candidates. The cubicles were enclosed on three sides and open to the elements on the fourth.

They had no furniture apart from three planks of wood which were laid across them to form at the highest level a shelf, below that a desk and thirdly a seat. The candidates were not allowed to leave even though the exams could last for three nights and two days in succession. They began with a burst of gunfire at around midnight. The candidates gathered at the gate of the compound in groups lit by lanterns. Carrying food, water and bedding to last them through their ordeal they were thoroughly searched before going to their allotted cubicles. The gate was then locked and sealed. In the chill of the autumn air the candidates settled to the task of answering questions on the works of Confucius. Their chances of success were small: only between one and five percent of them would ever pass through the first round.

Very little is known about the man who had such an enduring influence on the country in which he was born. 'Confucius' is a Westernised version of the name Kong Fuzi and was first used by Jesuit missionaries to the Chinese court. The story of his life was recorded by a historian, Sima Qian, at the court of the Han dynasty about 100 BC. Confucius, he tells us, was brought up in poverty and resolved as a young man to restore the virtues of China's ancient past in order to build a harmonious society. He gathered a group of disciples around him and together they discussed political and philosophical matters. His activities were recognised by the King of Lu, the area of north-eastern China where he lived, and at the age of fifty Confucius was appointed Minister of Public Works and then Minister of Crime. But he seems to have fallen out with members of the court and was sent into exile. After looking for another ruler to employ him, he returned to Lu in 484 BC where he spent the rest of his life studying and teaching.

Sima Qian credits Confucius with the authorship of several Chinese classic texts although it is not proved that he wrote them. Our main source of information about him comes from *The Analects*, which set out his thoughts and describe what he was supposed to have been like. 'At home in his native village,' they say, 'he was simple and unassuming in manner, as though he did not trust himself to speak. But when in the ancestral temple or at Court he speaks readily, though always choosing his words with due caution.' This image of the careful, decorous scholar is an important part of Confucius's influence. He was not only a thinker but a role model: like Socrates in Greece, his ideas about behaviour turned the man himself into a symbol of moral perfection.

Confucius lived during a time of war and disruption. China was ruled by the Zhou dynasty, which originally came to power around 1100 BC, more than five hundred years before Confucius was born. The Zhou did not preside over a unified country but a collection of regional powers, only some of which were dependent on its patronage. In about 771 BC they were driven out of their capital by a barbarian invasion and relocated to the city of Luoyang further east. When the Zhou first took power they justified their conquest by adopting the doctrine of the 'Mandate of Heaven'. This stated that heaven wanted what was best for human beings and therefore granted the right to rule to the family that would govern with justice and fairness. If that family failed to govern in this way heaven transferred the right to rule to another family better equipped to meet these celestial requirements. This new family, having received heaven's blessing, could then rebel. Victory in the ensuing war would reveal whether the mandate had in fact been granted in the way the rebelling forces maintained.

By the time Confucius was born, the Zhou's territory in eastern China had succumbed to warfare between rival states. Confucius looked back to a time that he saw as more harmonious and better governed when the 'Mandate of Heaven' had provided for a country that was united and secure. He saw himself as a messenger from antiquity, a man 'who invented nothing' but simply looked back to examples from better times. The institutions of government, he believed, appeared to have broken down because the rulers lacked morality, and his philosophy explained how they could cultivate and maintain the virtue necessary for the proper application of their task. Although he turned to history for his examples, the remedies that Confucius proposed were radical and new.

Confucius placed great emphasis on 'ritual', by which he meant the form and manner of everyday behaviour. His own behaviour, described in *The Analects,* gives a clue to the sort of thing he had in mind. 'When sending a messenger to enquire after someone in another country,' it says, 'he himself bows twice before seeing the messenger off.' Or again: 'In bed he avoided lying in the posture of a corpse.' Behaving carefully, said Confucius, was all-important. It encouraged people to understand their place in society and to observe propriety in a way that promoted social harmony. Punishment did not achieve this. When people were punished they behaved well without understanding why they should: ritual on the other hand ingrained behaviour and led to a fairer and more just society. This was especially important for rulers. In setting out his theory of behaviour, Confucius took the Chinese word '*li*', which had hitherto had the connotation of religious sacrifice, and used it to describe his ideas about social functions, thereby investing them with an importance they had never previously enjoyed. 'Look at nothing in defiance of ritual,' he said, 'listen to nothing in defiance of ritual, speak of nothing in defiance of ritual, never stir hand or foot in defiance of ritual.' During the Song dynasty in the twelfth century, this emphasis on ritual became more pronounced as scholars influenced by other philosophies such as Buddhism formed ideas for purifying the human mind through careful observance and even meditation.

Confucius believed that codes of behaviour were important in preserving social structure. Knowing your place was an essential piece of his philosophy. The family was the basis for an ideal government and the relationships that grew from it a model for society as a whole. He believed in ancestor worship and the respect of elders by their children. Women and people of low birth were relegated to the bottom of the social ladder. In the family each individual had particular duties depending on his position within it. Junior members owed reverence to their seniors, but in return the seniors had a duty of compassion towards the young. Loving other members of the family was extended in the community to mean loving others in general. This was a calling, a mission, to which everyone must subscribe and set out in a 'Golden Rule': 'What you do not wish for yourself, do not do to others.'

These strict rules required self-discipline. It therefore followed that the self-discipline of the ruler was paramount. Rulers had to be moral and virtuous, devoted to the needs of their people. They would get people to follow them by setting an example, not through coercion. 'The moral character of the ruler is the wind,' he observed. 'The moral character of those beneath him is the grass. When the wind blows, the grass bends.' Confucius believed that although men lived their lives within confines dictated by heaven, they were still responsible for their actions and for how they treated others. Their ability to achieve success lay in their own hands. The society he described was rather like a grave and serious Victorian family where a well-meaning patriarch presided over a wife and children grateful in their dutiful obedience. In ancient China, where belief in family loyalty was very strong, his teachings found a receptive audience.

'What you do not wish for yourself, do not do to others.'

In the immediate aftermath of his death, the ideas of Confucius were taken up by other Chinese scholars in a period of the country's history recognised for its 'Hundred Schools of Thought'. The philosopher Mencius, who lived for about eighty years in the third century BC, said that: 'Ever since man came into this world, there has never been one greater than Confucius.' During the Han dynasty, which held power for more than 400 years between 206 BC and 220 AD, Confucianism became the official state philosophy. In 205 BC, the Emperor Gao offered sacrifices to the memory of Confucius in the town of Qufu where he was born. The process of transformation from sage to saint had begun.

Confucianism survived the tumultuous years after the end of imperial China with remarkable success. To begin with, as the country became disrupted by war in the years following the Emperor's abdication in 1912, there were many who felt it was time for the country to turn its back on Confucianism. The author Lu Xun, one of China's most prominent writers of the early twentieth century, who had a great influence on Mao Zedong even though he never joined the Communist Party, wrote a collection of stories in 1925, one of which described the deprivations of an ordinary woman suffering at the hands of Confucian morality. Lu Xun attacked Confucian beliefs for encouraging a subservient conformity that he felt promoted injustice. As the revolutionary trend grew stronger, Confucius became the enemy of many who wanted to rid China of what they thought was its backward mentality. He became a particular target during the Cultural Revolution. He was dismissed as a reactionary and in 1966 his temple at Qufu was badly damaged and more than 6,000 artefacts destroyed.

The society he described was like a grave and serious Victorian family.

Since then, however, the ancient philosopher has risen from his desecrated shrine to take his place once more at the centre of Chinese society. Confucian ideas are grounded in principles of loyalty and reverence that have always had a strong influence in China. The politician who established the modern, somewhat autocratic, state of Singapore, Lee Kuan Yew, argued that the Chinese are not naturally given to democracy because of their innate loyalty towards their superiors. Such opinions have the advantage of becoming a convenient truth. As China begins to build a flexible economy on the back of its post-war Communist past, the ideas of Confucius can be deployed as readily as those of Marx in the pursuit of success. Some of China's leaders have already invoked Confucianism as an appropriate antidote to the materialism accompanying the country's rapid economic growth. High ethical standards combined with a lack of belief in a god make it a useful creed for modern purposes. The great sites of Confucianism are being restored and Qufu is a place of pilgrimage heavily promoted by China's growing tourist industry. Confucius himself has become a symbol of his country's desire to spread its cultural influence abroad. There are now nearly 300 Confucius Institutes in cities all over the world teaching Chinese and organising events.

Confucius was wary of the supernatural. 'Pay your respects to the spirits and the gods,' he advised, 'but keep them at a distance.' Like Buddha, whose beliefs also took root in the Far East, he took

He became a particular target during the Cultural Revolution.

the view that mankind owned the answer to life's problems. This approach explains many of the differences between the civilisations of East and West: there is a wide gulf between respect for the wisdom of the ancients and reliance on the salvation provided by a beneficent god. But even if Confucius has endured China's history to find himself still admired today, governments that promote his teachings would do well to remember his words: 'Good government consists in the ruler being a ruler, the minister being a minister, the father being a father, and the son being a son.'

CHAPTER 6

The Crucifixion of Jesus

33 AD

> The crucifixion of Jesus was carried out by a Roman
> governor under pressure from leaders of the local
> Jewish community. His death gave birth to a religious
> movement that conquered the Western world.

The town of Iznik on the eastern edge of Lake Iznik in Turkey is
famous for its beautiful pottery. In the sixteenth and seventeenth
centuries its tiles in vibrant shades of blue were used to decorate
the mosques and palaces of the Ottoman Empire and its jugs,
vases and plates were much sought after by collectors abroad.
Iznik, however, has an even greater claim to fame. Before it was
captured by the Turks in the first half of the fourteenth century,
it was known as Nicaea and was an important centre in both the
Roman and Byzantine Empires. In 325 AD, the Roman Emperor,
Constantine, who rebuilt the city Constantinople 120 miles to
the north-west and made it the capital of his empire, convened
a conference of Christian bishops to establish the principal articles of faith of their Church. He was the first Christian Roman
Emperor and his Edict of Milan in 313 AD granted freedom of
worship to Christianity throughout the Empire. At Nicaea the
bishops devised a creed that, with some later modifications, is
still in use today.

> We believe in one God, the Father, the Almighty, maker of
> heaven and earth, of all that is seen and unseen ... For us
> men and for our salvation, he came down from heaven:
> by the power of the Holy Spirit he was born of the Virgin
> Mary, and became man. For our sake he was crucified under
> Pontius Pilate; he suffered, died and was buried. On the third

day he rose again in fulfilment of the Scriptures; he ascended into heaven and is seated at the right hand of the Father. He will come again in glory to judge the living and the dead, and his kingdom will have no end ...

Those words, recounting the circumstances of Jesus's execution and subsequent ascent into heaven, were written down and accepted as a universal truth by the most powerful ruler in the Western world 300 years after the Crucifixion. The teachings of Christ became the official religion of the Roman Empire and changed the course of history in Europe.

Jesus was born in the Roman province of Judaea, an area on the shores of the Eastern Mediterranean stretching from the country around the Dead Sea in the south to the port of Caesarea in the north. It fell under the jurisdiction of the Roman Governor of Syria and was administered by a prefect who reported to him. Local rulers were allowed to run parts of it as clients of their imperial masters: they only had as much authority as Rome was prepared to grant them. It was a land seething with discontent. The native population were Hebrews who had settled there in about 1200 BC. They called themselves Israelites after the name of one of their earliest tribal leaders, Jacob Israel. Around the year 1000 BC, under the leadership of one of their most celebrated kings, David, and his son, Solomon, they built an empire that stretched from Egypt to the territory of Mesopotamia north of the Persian Gulf. But by the time of Jesus's birth those days of expansion and success were a fading memory. The Israelites had fallen to a succession of invaders and in 36 BC became the subjects of the most successful and tenacious of them all – the Romans. They were sustained in their servitude by the stories of their religion that told them a messiah would come to lead them to freedom once more.

The Hebrews were unusual in one important respect. Unlike most other peoples in the Roman Empire they believed in one god, Yahweh, who would follow and protect them as long as they obeyed his code and observed the proper rituals for his worship. They had a covenant with this god and during their journey to the land in which they now lived had accepted his commandments as the ethical basis of their existence. They took this belief with them when they left to look for work, or peace, elsewhere. Communities of Jews, people from the land of Judah, or Judaea, existed all over Europe where they absorbed the cultures of their new homes with that of the place from which they originally came. The Roman world was one in which people were able to travel comparatively easily and when Jews from abroad returned to their native land their new ideas inevitably influenced some of the resident population. The Hebrew priesthood became suspicious. It wanted to maintain the continuity of ancient Israelite belief but this was often a difficult task in a country awash with the visitors and traders that a great empire encouraged. Some priests believed that only an armed uprising against the Romans could restore Hebrew customs; others simply awaited the arrival of a god-given leader who would restore history's glories to them. Wandering preachers predicted his arrival. One of them, John, fell foul of the local puppet king, Herod Antipas, by criticising him for a divorce he arranged so he could marry a new queen. Herod had him arrested and executed.

His all-embracing philosophy was supported by the concept of love.

Before his arrest John baptised Jesus in a ceremony in the running waters of the River Jordan. Baptism was an ancient Jewish ritual that signified a cleansing of the body and the spirit. Jesus became a preacher too, but his message was larger and more profound than that of the prophets who had gone before him. He said that the forgiveness of God was available to the whole world, not just to the Jewish community. If people repented of their sins they would be accepted into heaven whoever they were and wherever they lived. This all-embracing philosophy was supported by the concept of love. 'Love thy neighbour' was a central part of Jesus's teaching, by which he meant not only kindness and compassion, but greater equality and concern for the poorer sections of society as well. Like reformers who attacked the establishment of the Christian Church 1500 years later, he criticised the structure of the Jewish Church which he saw as corrupt and venal. He claimed descent from the great Israelite

The Jews

The history of the Jews alternates between periods of autonomy and exile. It began with a loose confederation of Israelite tribes who came together in around 1020 BC to form a united kingdom of Israel. In around 1006 BC, King David succeeded in creating a strong, unified monarchy with Jerusalem as its national capital. His military victories established secure borders for the nascent kingdom, and his successor, Solomon, built the 'First Temple' in Jerusalem. In about 930 BC, economic disputes under Solomon's successor left Israel divided into the kingdoms of Israel and Judah. In the 720s BC, Israel was conquered by the Assyrian Empire and the majority of its people were sent into exile. Judah, meanwhile, remained an independent state until around 586 BC, when it was conquered by the Babylonian Empire. The First Temple along with much of Jerusalem was destroyed and most of the population was expelled. This marked a crucial turning point for the Jews. From then until the creation of the modern state of Israel, they lived as a scattered people across the world, although the Maccabee revolt in 163 BC revived a short-lived Jewish kingdom.

Under Roman rule they were uprooted from their homelands and dispersed across the Empire, where they formed communities across Western and, later, Eastern Europe. During this period they also spread as far as southern Africa and China, developing new ethnic and cultural identities as well as new

king, David. To his excited followers he seemed to be the person-ification of the Messiah many of them had been expecting: he was royal but he belonged to and cared for the people; he had a message of importance for the whole world; and he performed miracles.

On the feast of the Passover, one of the most important days in the Jewish calendar, they followed him to Jerusalem, the reli-gious centre of Judaea. For the Sadducees and Pharisees, the elite who controlled the priesthood, Jesus's activities were getting too close for comfort. They complained to the Roman prefect who brought him to trial and in an act of political expediency rather languages and liturgical practices. One such group was the 'Ashkenazim' Jews of Western Europe, numerically the largest. The 'Sephardim' Jews of Iberia, who enjoyed contact with the 'Mizrahim' Jews of North Africa and the Middle East, developed their own unique traditions.

As a scattered minority, the Jews endured centuries of forced expulsion and persecution, interspersed with periods of tolerance when ruling authorities thought there might be financial or religious merit in it. The Holocaust is the world's most horrific incident of anti-Semitic brutality, but Jews were frequently persecuted and ostracised in the name of Christianity and at the instigation of Rome. During the Crusades, Jews were killed all over Germany and religious zeal led to massacres in York and London in 1189–90. After the Edict of Expulsion in 1290, 16,000 Jews were expelled from England, although other rulers like Henry II and Oliver Cromwell saw the merit of adopting a more tolerant attitude. In Spain and Portugal, 200,000 Jews were expelled in the 1490s during the Catholic wars of reconquest against the Moors. In the nineteenth century there were vicious pogroms against Russian Jews, prompting over two million to flee for the United States between 1881 and 1924. Today, roughly half of the world's 13.2 million Jews live in Israel, where they comprise seventy-five percent of the population. The majority of Israel's Jews are Ashkenazi, descended from European Jews.

than natural justice ordered that Jesus be flogged and then cruci-fied. For good measure he had the ironic inscription, 'King of the Jews', nailed to his cross. It was this brutal solution of a little local difficulty that gave birth to the Christian Church.

To begin with the followers of Jesus concentrated on trying to reform the Jewish Church but their movement spread gradu-ally to include non-Jewish believers, or Gentiles. Paul of Tarsus, a Roman citizen who began life as a strict Pharisee but became converted to the new beliefs, was an enthusiastic supporter of encouraging people outside the Jewish community to join the movement. These recruits were known as 'Christians' from the

Greek word *Christos* meaning 'the anointed one'. Paul began to shape traditional Jewish beliefs to make them more palatable to Christians, devising a religion that stood apart from that which had spawned it in the first place. He moved away from the ritual of the Hebrew faith: the old Jewish 'God' was still there but his divinity was given a new dimension through the activities of the person now accepted as the Messiah, Jesus Christ. Human salvation could only be achieved through the grace of God and belief in the truth of what Jesus had said.

A brutal solution to a little local difficulty gave birth to the Christian Church.

Paul's activities were helped by a Jewish revolt in 66 AD. At first the Jews were successful in expelling the Romans from Jerusalem, but four years later the general Titus, later Emperor of Rome, laid siege to the city. Having captured it he destroyed the Jewish temple. Those Jews who survived his attack fled by secret tunnels into the surrounding countryside. The Jewish historian Josephus acted as a mediator between the Roman army and the Jews and described what happened when the imperial legions finally entered the city: 'Those places which were adorned with trees and pleasant gardens were now become desolate country … The war had laid all signs of beauty quite waste.' The revolt against occupation had been led by the Zealots, a group who had always believed that Jewish salvation required the defeat and expulsion of the Romans. Their utter defeat left their Church and its supporters in disarray. Its new branch, busily at work throughout Asia Minor, had been offered an opening: the spread of Christianity was afoot.

The new religion faced many adversaries. The Romans were always concerned about movements that threatened the stability of the management of their empire. They were happy to tolerate harmless idiosyncrasies but took a more serious view of opinions that might threaten the established order. The need to maintain peace had led to the execution of Jesus in the first place: the same considerations led to the persecution of Christians. Pliny the Younger, who was Governor of Bithynia (now central Turkey) at the beginning of the first century AD, wrote to the Emperor Trajan for advice about how best to deal with Christians who were denounced to him. He was in charge of an area where Christianity was taking deep root as it spread out of Palestine towards the Black Sea and Western Europe. Pliny, an administrator with moderate attitudes, was intent on carrying out imperial orders forbidding illegal political associations. He told Trajan that he had cross-questioned Christians brought before him, and tortured a couple of women to see if he could extract useful information. 'I discovered,' he said, 'nothing else but depraved, excessive superstition.' He added: 'The contagion of this superstition has spread not only to the cities but also to the villages and farms.' He was confident, however, that it would be possible 'to check and cure it'.

Their Roman rulers were not the only opposition that Christians faced. They also had enemies within. In the second century AD, Christian beliefs were taken up by Gnostics, men and women who believed that the revelations of God were only available to those with special knowledge. Theirs was a cult of mystery and magic that deprived Christianity of its simple universal appeal. But Christianity survived. Its strength lay in its inclusiveness and its promises of a better life. In a world where people were strictly segregated by birth, rank, wealth and gender, a religion that opened its doors to all provided an attractive sense of community. St Paul was right to encourage non-Jews to swell the ranks of the new believers: Christian ideas naturally transcended the restrictions of existing systems of worship. Even Pliny seemed impressed by the simplicity of their customs. 'They asserted,' he wrote to the Emperor, 'that the sum and substance of their fault or error had been that they were accustomed to meet on a fixed day before dawn and sing responsively a hymn to Christ as to a God, and to bind themselves by oath, not to some crime, but not to commit fraud, theft or adultery, not to falsify their trust, nor to refuse to return a trust when called upon to do so.' Communion and Christianity went hand in hand and provided people with a social shape to their lives.

'Christian' from the Greek word Christos meaning 'the anointed one.'

Doctrine of Papal Infallibility

Promulgated at the First Vatican Council in July 1870, the doctrine of papal infallibility allows the Pope formally to declare universal and binding teachings to the Catholic Church with the understanding that his teachings are divinely sanctioned and free from error. Anyone who does not accept the teaching is considered to be outside the Catholic Church. Statements invoking papal infallibility are called 'solemn papal definitions' or *ex cathedra* teachings. Actions committed by the Pope in his private life or official capacity, other than when *ex cathedra* is declared, are not covered by papal infallibility.

The doctrine rests on acceptance of the divinely sanctioned supremacy of Rome over the Church. Roman Catholics believe that the papal succession can be traced back to St Peter and that the Pope has supreme, full and universal power over the Church. The doctrine had intellectual roots in the medieval period but was not formally defined until the nineteenth century. It divided the Church, prompting serious dissent in Germany, Austria and Switzerland, where many Catholics chose to form their own independent Churches.

Since 1870 the power has only been invoked once, in 1950, when Pope Pius XII's declaration '*Munificentissimus Deus*' defined the Assumption of Mary (Mary's ascension to heaven at the end of her life) as a binding article of faith. Pius declared: 'By the authority of our Lord Jesus Christ, of the Blessed Apostles Peter and Paul, and by our own authority, we pronounce, declare, and define it to be a divinely revealed dogma … Hence if anyone, which God forbid, should dare willfully to deny or to call into doubt that which We have defined, let him know that he has fallen away completely from the divine and Catholic Faith.'

Today, Catholics remain divided over papal infallibility, and a survey carried out between 1989 and 1992 found that only about a third of young people accept it.

The comfort derived from mutual support was not enough on its own to secure Christianity for the future. It needed intellectual and organisational backbone too. The early Church developed a system of bishoprics in which the faithful gathered in regional groups under a central authority, which made sure they followed the Scriptures and gave coherence to their faith. The main centres were cities like Alexandria in Egypt, Carthage in North Africa, Antioch in Syria and Rome itself – places with a strong Greco-Roman cultural tradition in which Christianity was sifted through some of the finest minds of the age. One of them, Irenaeus, travelled out of Asia Minor to become the Bishop of Lyon, in Roman Gaul, towards the end of the first century AD. He spoke out against the Gnostics, providing Christianity with the beginnings of an accepted doctrine. 'The church,' he wrote, 'although scattered throughout the whole world believes these points of doctrine just as if she had but one soul, and one and the same heart, and she proclaims them and teaches them, and hands them down with perfect harmony, as if she possessed only one mouth.'

Nothing, however, could give Christianity the authority it needed more than the conversion of a Roman Emperor. In the history of the world, the reign of Constantine is a watershed. He gave his empire unity, defeating his rivals to become its undisputed master; he gave it an Eastern capital, Constantinople, a city designed to rival Rome itself; and he gave it a new religion, Christianity. Of these three legacies, Christianity proved the most significant, surviving Rome's collapse less than a hundred years later and giving the Western world a set of beliefs that would sustain it for long afterwards. It marked the moment when the classical world began finally to melt away to be replaced by the litter of a fragmented empire in which Christianity was the indomitable force.

CHAPTER 7

The Death of Mohammed

632 AD

Mohammed's death gave birth to Islam. The religion
that he founded united the Arabic tribes of the Middle
East and spread with astonishing speed throughout
Europe, Asia and North Africa.

In 732 AD a battle took place near the town of Poitiers in west
central France. On one side was the army of Charles Martel,
leader of the Franks and a consummate general who had been
successful in reuniting an empire consisting of most of France,
Western Germany and the Low Countries, under Frankish rule.
On the other was Abdul Rahman al Ghafiqi, the Arab governor of
the Muslim caliphate of al-Andalus, based in Córdoba in southern Spain.

Having conquered the whole of the Iberian Peninsula the
Arabs were looking to invade and occupy territory north of
the Pyrenees. They captured Bordeaux, defeated an army under the
Duke of Aquitaine on the River Garonne and then pushed north.
It was October and the weather had turned cold. An account by
an Arab chronicler suggests that Abdul Rahman and his men had
extended their supply lines to a dangerous extent as they went in
search of loot. 'It was manifest that God's chastisement was sure
to follow such excesses,' he wrote, 'and fortune thereupon turned
her back upon the Moslems.' Charles Martel had no cavalry: his
main advantage was that he managed to marshal his army into
a position where it caught the invaders by surprise. The Arabs
were defeated and Abdul Rahman killed.

On the whole Arab historians have not paid much attention
to the encounter. In the West, however, it has been described
as an apocalyptic moment, a battle that saved Europe and

Christianity from 'militant Islam'. Poitiers after all is only about 200 miles from Paris and 450 miles from London. Edward Gibbon, the eighteenth-century historian of the Roman Empire, wrote that if Charles Martel had not been victorious 'perhaps the interpretation of the Koran would now be taught in the schools of Oxford, and her pulpits might demonstrate to a circumcised people the sanctity and truth of the revelation of Mahomet'. An exaggeration no doubt: but Gibbon was justified in reminding us that the history of peoples and civilisations often turns on comparatively small events. Other Western writers have agreed with his assessment. The German philosopher Friedrich von Schlegel – who believed that 'a historian was a prophet looking backwards' – said of the battle that it 'saved and delivered the Christian nations of the West from the deadly grasp of all-destroying Islam'.

Resounding verdicts such as these are questionable. The confrontation between Abdul Rahman and Charles Martel was nevertheless an extraordinary event. An Arab army steeped in the faith of Islam was fighting more than 2,500 miles north of where its religion had been born exactly a hundred years previously. In the period of the early Middle Ages, in a Europe still disrupted by the conflicts and uncertainties that followed the collapse of the Roman Empire, the Arabs' journey northwards represented expansion on an extraordinary scale. Christianity never enjoyed such rapid success. Islam, the youngest of the world's great religions, became a force almost as soon as it was bequeathed to the world by its prophet.

Many of the details of Mohammed's life are not known. The first biography of him was not written until the middle of the eighth century, a hundred years after he died. He was born around 570 AD in Mecca, a member of a branch of an influential Bedouin tribe. His parents died when he was young and he was brought up by an uncle. He married a wealthy widow who ran a business trading with Syria. Mecca was an important trading centre. Situated in the southern half of the Arabian peninsula, in a valley about forty-five miles from the sea, it was a busy junction for caravans travelling from Yemen in the south to the ports of the Eastern Mediterranean further north. The tribe to which

Mohammed belonged, the Quraysh, believed in all sorts of gods and demons, but the religious foundations of their society were beginning to feel the effects of Judaism and Christianity as their commercial links with the outside world strengthened.

As part of the custom of his tribe Mohammed was used to spending some time on a nearby mountain, where he would pray to his gods, be visited by his family and feed poor people who came to visit him. One night he had a vision. The Angel Gabriel (Jibraeel) came to him in his sleep and commanded him to:

> Recite, in the name of the Lord,
> Who created Man
> [created] from a clot of blood.

At first alarmed by what had happened Mohammed sought reassurance that he had not been ensnared by the devil. But a local Christian told him that his experience was similar to that of Moses. He was 'the prophet of the people'.

Mohammed gathered followers around him but his position in his hometown came under threat. Like another prophet, preaching in Palestine more than 500 years before, his views were regarded as unwelcome, even revolutionary, by those in control of the society in which he lived. Some of his followers left to live and work in Ethiopia, which had already begun to receive Christianity. In 622 AD, Mohammed ordered the rest of his followers to emigrate to the city of Yathrib, 250 miles further north, where his message would be better received. He then went after them. His journey, or pilgrimage, is known in Islam as the *Hijra* and is taken as the first year of the Muslim calendar, and Yathrib became Medina, the 'city of the Prophet'. Mohammed spent the last ten years of his life there. He consolidated his power base, subduing the city that had once rejected him, Mecca, and eventually bringing many different tribes of the Arabian Peninsula under his command. He also created a political system, or *umma*, in which different people and their religions were brought together in the concept of brotherhood. Many Arabs were Jews. They resented the fact that God's prophet had not risen from their ranks: Mohammed tried to provide them with a community structure that gave them religious freedom within the confines of his ultimate supremacy. Prophet, soldier and politician, Mohammed gave the Arab tribes a sense of unity. At the heart of this was his revelation of not only of a new religion, but of a framework of law as well.

Allah, all-seeing and invincible to whom all men and women on earth must submit.

The word Islam means submission or surrender. Mohammed saw himself as the servant of God, the prophet who would, through the revelations he received, deliver this God's final message to mankind. The messages of previous prophets had been corrupted by Christians and Jews; there was only one God: Allah, all-seeing and invincible, the creator of the whole universe and the being to whom all men and women on earth must submit. These beliefs were recited by Mohammed as the Angel Gabriel had ordered him to do and later written down by his disciples in the Koran. Many figures familiar to other religions were included – Adam, Noah, Abraham, even Jesus himself – but their roles were adapted to show that their calling was Islamic, rather than Jewish or Christian. Jesus, for instance, was certainly a prophet, but he was never the son of God. The Koran, therefore, is the centrepiece of Islamic belief, but it is also much more than that. It sets out the laws which Muslims should obey. Mohammed gave his followers not only faith in a new vision, but the practical methods for realising it as well. The rules he laid down, for diet, prayer, marriage and so on, were entwined in this vision. Islam is different from the other monotheist religions of the world because it goes beyond the purely religious in its approach.

After Mohammed's death in 632 AD his supporters devised the concept of the 'caliphate' in which they came together under a leader who represented their whole community. With this organisation they rapidly conquered the rest of the Arabian Peninsula and began to push out towards the empires that surrounded them. On one side lay the Empire of Byzantium, ruling the territory of the old Eastern Roman Empire from its capital in Constantinople. On the other was the Sassanid Empire of Persia that ruled the lands of Mesopotamia and Iran. United in their great purpose, the forces of Islam waged war against them. Within a year of the Prophet's death, Muslim armies invaded Syria and Iraq. Jerusalem fell to them in 637 AD. The ancient Sassanid Empire, already struggling from invasions from its Byzantine neighbour, was extinguished and its nobility fled into central Asia. By the early 660s AD, the caliphate-controlled territory extended from Yemen to the shores of the Caspian Sea and from Egypt to Kabul.

But the militant zeal of the new believers was not supported by perfect unity. The first Islamic caliphs were descended from Mohammed's family: his immediate successor was his father-in-law through his favourite wife. Before long they came under criticism. To their opponents they seemed to represent the corrupt continuation of power and privilege rather than the strict code of righteousness that the teachings of the Prophet required. The Arabs fought two ruthless civil wars, laying the foundations for the separate interpretations of Islamic belief that have existed ever since. The Umayyad dynasty that eventually emerged victorious was not led by people directly related to Mohammed himself: they murdered his grandson when he rebelled against them. His followers, called Shiites, continued to nurse grievances against his killers as the world of Islam steadily expanded. These divisions within the Arab community made this expansion even more remarkable. The Arabs faced enemies incapable of marshalling themselves against their ferocity and determination. As they broke out of their desert homelands, the prizes that they found intensified their desire for further gains and the ramshackle empires they invaded proved an easy target for their new and uncomplicated view of the world.

Death to the enemy on the battlefield brought a promise of paradise.

The Umayyad Arab faction that emerged victorious from the civil wars established its capital at Damascus in Syria. In 750 AD it was overthrown by the Abbasids who moved it eastwards to Baghdad. The Umayyads transferred their capital to Córdoba

The Islamic Emirate of Córdoba

The Muslims or 'Moors', began their conquest of much of modern-day Spain and Portugal in 711 AD, when a young general, Tariq bin Ziyad, was sent with an army of 7,000 troops to conquer Iberia. He landed at Gibraltar, which gets its name from the Arabic for 'Rock of Tariq'. Meeting with little opposition he conquered most of Spain and Portugal fairly easily but the government of the area remained fragmented until the arrival of Abd al-Rahman in 756 AD. His family, the Umayyads, had been deposed from the caliphate at Damascus and the prince was keen to gain a position of power in Iberia. He declared himself as 'emir', or prince, of a new Muslim principality: the emirate of Córdoba.

What followed was a golden age of great learning and artistic achievement. In the late eighth century Abd al-Rahman started building the Great Mosque at Córdoba and also created a civil service and a loyal standing army. Relative religious tolerance was permitted. Non-Muslims, who made up the overwhelming majority, were treated as second-class citizens, but were allowed to live in peace as long as they acknowledged the superiority of Islam.

Under Abd al-Rahman III (r.912–61 AD), Moorish Spain reached new heights. The new emir went one better than his predecessor, declaring himself Caliph (a ruler in his own right) and pushing militarily towards the Christian border to the north. Córdoba, unrivalled for its size, wealth and cultural achievements, was the epicentre of the kingdom – the largest city on the continent of Europe with perhaps more than a thousand mosques and over seventy libraries. It enjoyed philosophical interchanges between Hellenism, Christianity and Islam, and saw huge advances in science, history and geography. But the caliphate did not last. In the eleventh and twelfth centuries it broke up under increasing aggression from its Christian neighbours coupled with a civil war between its rulers. It disintegrated in 1031, although a Moorish kingdom remained in the south, until its reconquest in 1492 by the Catholic monarchs Ferdinand and Isabella.

in southern Spain. From this moment on, the Arabs established their power base throughout the Near East and in Southern Europe as the two rival dynasties consolidated their military victories with institutions that allowed them to manage the territories they conquered. The dominant force was the Abbasid dynasty who built a new and mighty empire between the years 700 and 950 AD. Baghdad, their capital, became a cosmopolitan city no longer dominated by the families from the Arab peninsula who had first established it. As it grew, Islam embraced all the nationalities within its extensive sphere of influence – Europeans from Iberia, Berbers from North Africa and Indians from Sindh fell under its control. The Abbasids ran their empire strictly, persecuting those who failed to conform and introducing the machinery of state. Taxes on land provided the revenue to maintain their imperial splendour; and they secured the continuation of their dynasty by ensuring that power remained within the hands of the family and its supporters.

At the same time, however, the influences of other civilisations – Greek, Christian, Jewish and Hindu – contributed to the development of a rich culture and the proliferation of the Arabic language as the primary means of communication throughout a large part of the world. It was a civilisation that produced some of the world's earliest and greatest mathematicians and astronomers and its architecture and works of art stand testament today to the glories of its achievement. The Persian mathematician, Al-Khwarizmi, introduced the word 'algebra' into the study of mathematics in the early ninth century. The word 'tariff' is also derived from Arabic, a reminder of the complex system of caravan routes that were the commercial arteries of Islam. But these are just odd examples of a civilisation rich in trade, immersed in scholarship and skilled in politics and war. By the middle of the tenth century, Europe and Asia was divided by a religious frontier. The Umayyads controlled Iberia; the Abbasids owned land that stretched across the Maghreb

Islam captured the world in which it was invented by providing it with rules as well as ideas.

area of North Africa, across the whole of the Arabian Peninsula, throughout Eastern and Central Asia and into north-western India. To the west of these boundaries stood Christendom, a multiplicity of disunited kingdoms. Eventually, encouraged by its religious leader, the Pope, it would try to rescue the birthplace of its religion, Jerusalem, from Islam in a series of Crusades. In this it failed. Islam was not to be dislodged from the lands that it had brought under its control. Its structure and the centre of its authority would change significantly as time passed. By the beginning of the sixteenth century, Spain became a Christian nation. But the central line of division did not move, and still exists today.

The religion that Mohammed created was astonishingly resilient; its message simple but profound. There was only one God, unlike Christianity where the concept of the Trinity smacked of polytheism. This God, if worshipped correctly, would satisfy all man's earthly cares in the afterlife. Death to the enemy on the battlefield brought a promise of paradise. There was no difference between the principles of this religion and the law of the state – again unlike Christianity, which assumed clear distinctions between the two. In the Islamic structure belief and community came together. Christianity had to fight for acceptance from the authorities in whose lands it was first preached. Not so Islam: it captured the world in which it was invented by providing it with rules as well as ideas. Having done that, it set out to conquer, not to convert. It possessed all the components that it needed because the Prophet's message was final, clear and gave to his followers an energy with which its rivals could not compete. Christianity was a religion born out of suffering that had to fight for its survival as soon as it came into the world; its victory came when it was given the Roman Empire by Constantine. Islam was born with a sword in its hand. It had no need of a Constantine: from the beginning it had Mohammed.

CHAPTER 8

Martin Luther's Ninety-Five Theses

1517

Martin Luther was a German monk who believed that the selling of indulgences by the Catholic Church was corrupt. In 1517 he published his arguments by posting them in Latin on the door of a church in Wittenberg, Germany. His ideas became the mainspring of the Protestant Reformation which transformed the history of modern Europe.

The 'pardoner' is a character who has long since disappeared into history. One of the best descriptions we have of one comes from Geoffrey Chaucer who poured scorn on the profession in his *Canterbury Tales*. Chaucer's pardoner is a fraud. With a bag stuffed full of pig's bones that he intends to pass off as holy relics and a satchel brimming with official pardons sent from Rome, he persuades gullible people to part with their hard-earned money in return for an undertaking that they will be forgiven for their sins. Medieval Europe was as superstitious as it was devout. Men and women were often terrified that they would be cast into hell for their misdemeanours. Any promise of salvation was attractive, whatever the cost. Today we buy lottery tickets in the hope that financial rewards will lift the clouds from life: 600 years ago we might have bought an indulgence, a promise from the Church that some or all of our sins had been forgiven, in order to save ourselves from the fear of eternal damnation.

The idea of indulgences had a perfectly respectable history. The early fathers of the Christian Church sometimes devised rituals – singing psalms, surviving on bread and water and so on – in which those who had sinned could display contrition and be forgiven. Over time rituals gave way to the giving of alms or going on pilgrimages. Pope Urban II, who launched the First Crusade at the Council of Clermont in France in 1095, announced that: 'Whoever out of pure devotion, and not for the purpose of gaining honour or money, shall go to Jerusalem to liberate the Church of God, let that journey be counted in lieu of all penance.' Fighting for God would bring reward in heaven. In 1215, Pope Innocent III summoned a Lateran Council – so called because it was held in the Lateran Palace in Rome – in which strict new rules of clerical behaviour were promulgated. The sale of false relics, it announced, caused 'great injury' to the Christian religion. Catholic doctrine was clear: the properly contrite could be forgiven their sins, but the sins themselves could never be simply obliterated. Nevertheless abuses continued and grew. Greedy clerics promised their customers that the purchase of an indulgence would wipe the slate clean, expunge all previous sins (and sometimes those yet to come as well) and prepare the purchaser for a safe passage heavenwards. Geoffrey Chaucer's pardoner was a familiar figure: criticised by the devout, sneered at by the sophisticated, and admired by the gullible, he was the personification of the problems facing the Church.

Any promise of salvation was attractive, whatever the cost.

Martin Luther was not always above the superstitions that typified the age in which he lived. Returning to his studies in the town of Erfurt in Germany one summer in 1505, he was caught in a violent thunderstorm. Terrified by a thunderbolt that struck the earth nearby he called out: 'Help me Saint Anna, and I will become a monk.' No doubt he was contemplating this course of action anyway, but his rescue led to his ordination as an Augustinian monk the following year. He became an avid reader of the Scriptures and a few years later moved to nearby Wittenberg where, in 1512, he became a doctor of theology at the university. His training as a monk provided him with the foundation of his beliefs. Long periods of solitary reading and praying drove him towards the pure, written source of the Christian religion – the

Bible. The more he read, the more he rejected intellectual additions and commentaries that had become fashionable in Catholic theology and condemned the use of Aristotelian philosophy to refine and interpret the Scriptures. He looked back to the founder of the order in which he served as a monk, St Augustine of Hippo, who taught that the faith by which men are Christians 'is the gift of God'. Luther took the view that human beings were powerless in the hands of God. All they could do was hope and pray that through God's mercy he would intervene to save them as he had when he sent Jesus into the world. He was terrified by the overwhelming, all-powerful 'righteousness of God' which, like the thunderbolt that had sent him hastening to the monastery in the first place, was poised to strike as God chose. In the first lectures he gave as a university teacher in Wittenberg he fashioned the basis of an approach to religion that would change the Western world.

In 1517 Luther decided to put his interpretation of Holy Scripture into the public domain. Pope Leo X had appointed a Dominican friar, Johann Tetzel, as commissioner of indulgences for the whole of Germany. The Pope was looking for money to help fund the rebuilding of St Peter's Basilica in Rome, a lengthy and expensive project in constant need of financial replenishment. Tetzel's activities fell under the jurisdiction of the Archbishop of Mainz, a member of the powerful Hohenzollern family and a son of the Elector of Brandenburg, who was also the Archbishop of Magdeburg and administrator of the diocese of Halberstadt. The holding of this many ecclesiastical offices was against Church law. It would only be excused in return for payments to Rome. Johann Tetzel would raise the money by selling indulgences and the Archbishop would give fifty percent to Rome and the rest to the bankers from whom he had borrowed in order placate the Church authorities in the first place. Luther was unaware of the intricacies of these arrangements at the time; what concerned him was the fraudulent theology implicit in the idea that people could buy their way out of sinfulness. As one of his theses stated: 'Any Christian whatsoever who is truly repentant has, as his due, plenary remission from penalty and guilt, even without letters of indulgence.' Luther categorically refuted the idea that indulgences had any spiritual or religious value. 'Preachers of indulgences are wrong to say that a man is absolved and saved from every penalty by the Pope's indulgence,' he said. The whole system was nothing better than 'a false assurance of peace'.

These ideas were set out in the document he nailed to the door of the castle church in Wittenberg, a recognised method of promoting intellectual debate that in this case reached far beyond the courteous refinements of theological scholarship. Luther's theses were the equivalent of a sixteenth-century Power-Point presentation – a series of crisp, closely argued headlines that expertly demolished the arguments in defence of a long-established Church practice. The document caught the public imagination. Versions in the original Latin and others translated into German were run off on printing presses and circulated all over Germany. A revolution had begun.

Luther was a brilliant writer and a skilful polemicist, a man born for the new age of printing that was beginning to change communications in Europe. He rose to the opportunity effortlessly. But he was lucky to find a protector in the ruler of the state where he lived, Frederick of Saxony, without whom he might have been burned as a heretic before achieving recognition. As well as posting his theses in public, Luther also sent a copy to the Archbishop of Mainz who thought they were probably heretical and promptly sent them on to the Pope. Luther was condemned as a Hussite, a supporter of the Czech priest Jan Hus who had been burned at the stake for heresy a hundred years before. But condemnation by the Church was not enough for Luther to lose support from many people in Germany, both lay and clergy, who felt that he was saying something of importance. Luther touched a chord and, as his following grew, his views became more extreme. He published a number of works criticising the Church, and in 1520 he produced his 'Address to the Christian Nobility'. 'All classes in Christendom, particularly in Germany,' he wrote, 'are now oppressed by distress and affliction.'

Luther's cause was not just religious, but national, a deliberate appeal to his serious-minded countrymen who disliked the flashy affluence of the Roman Church. In 1520 he was excommunicated and his books burned in public. Luther responded by burning a copy of the papal bull that condemned him. He was then summoned to appear before the Emperor of the Holy Roman Empire, Charles V, at a meeting of the estates of Germany in the ancient city of Worms on the River Rhine.

The meeting between Martin Luther and the great and good of the German nobility at the Diet of Worms in 1521 is one of the most dramatic in European history. Luther presented himself as 'a man at home in the cell of a monk not the courts of kings'. He was invited to retract and disown all his writings. He refused. 'I cannot, I will not, recant anything,' he said, 'for it is neither safe nor right to act against one's conscience.' He concluded his defence with a heroic cry of defiance: 'Here I stand! I can do no other! God help me. Amen.' The diet found him guilty – 'not a man but the devil himself' – but Luther had been promised safe conduct to and from Worms and was therefore allowed to leave the city. The Emperor's edict left no one in any doubt that his freedom was to be short-lived. He was to be 'apprehended and punished as a notorious heretic, as he deserves'. Anyone assisting in his arrest would be rewarded.

'Here I stand! I can do no other! God help me. Amen.'

Luther intended to make his way home to Wittenberg but he never got there. His journey was interrupted by a party of armed horsemen belonging to Frederick, Elector of Saxony. They snatched the heretic from his wagon, mounted him on a horse and rode at a furious speed to the castle of Wartburg near Eisenach, north-east of Worms. Here he was lodged in safety. Luther, and the future of the Protestant Reformation, were saved.

In his study at Wartburg, Luther wrote his German translation of the New Testament. It was a work aimed at ordinary people and it used language that he knew they would understand. Of all the extraordinary achievements of the Reformation the use of everyday language in order to deliver its message is perhaps the most important. Until the beginning of the sixteenth century, the texts of the Scriptures were only available in Latin and Greek, and attempts by reformers to translate them were ruthlessly

John Calvin

Martin Luther (1483–1546) may have sparked the Protestant
Reformation with his Ninety-Five Theses, but it was John Calvin
(1509–64) who helped its spread across Europe. Born in the
Picardy region of France, he was a pious and precocious boy
who studied Latin, Greek and philosophy and began a career in
law. In the early 1530s he seems to have experienced a sudden
religious conversion and he returned to Paris where he mixed
with humanist reformers in the Collège Royal. But when the
group's leader, Nicolas Cop, was denounced as a heretic, Cop
and Calvin were both forced into exile in Switzerland.

In 1536 Calvin published his *Institutes of the Christian Religion*,
setting out his beliefs. He said that the Church is inclusive and
accessible to all through study. 'For anyone to arrive at God
the Creator,' he argued, 'he needs Scripture as his Guide and
Teacher.' He attacked the primacy of the papacy. All Christians,
he said, were united by Christ at their head. He believed in
predestination, the idea that God determines the fate of the
world with the result that he 'adopts some to the hope of life
and adjudges others to eternal death'.

Calvin was also asked in the same year to participate in
reorganising the Genevan Church. He encountered bitter
opposition from powerful local families but supported by
religious refugees, including those fleeing from Mary I's rule
in England, he gained the upper hand. In the final years of
his life he undertook missionary work in France and
Switzerland and by the time of his death Calvinism was well
established across Europe in Switzerland, Scotland, France and
Hungary.

suppressed. Most people could not understand them and relied
on the clergy for their interpretation. The power of the Church
was to a large extent the power of the knowledgeable over the
ignorant. Luther – and those who followed him, such as William
Tyndale who translated the New Testament into English a few
years later – gave their countrymen a means of expression they
had been denied, lifting the lid on a sealed casket of precious
information that flooded into their minds. With this first-hand
appreciation of the religion that dominated their lives came

ideas about liberty, nationhood and the role of a human being in society. The assault on the Catholic Church had political as well as religious consequences that remained a cause of war and dissension for more than a hundred years after its inception. Luther himself, although still an outlaw, moved beyond the immediate jurisdiction of those who condemned him at the Diet of Worms. Following his period of seclusion at Wartburg he returned secretly to Wittenberg in 1522 where he continued to write and preach. In 1525 he got married, demonstrating that he did not subscribe to the idea of a celibate clergy.

Luther presented himself as 'a man at home in the cell of a monk not the courts of kings'.

In 1530, the Emperor Charles V called another diet, this time at Augsburg, in which he asked his princes to explain their religious beliefs in an attempt to impose religious unity on his German lands. Luther was asked by John, the Elector of Saxony, who had succeeded his brother Frederick, to prepare a summary of Lutheran beliefs. The Elector and several other German rulers presented this document to the Emperor at Augsburg. The ideas of Martin Luther had taken shape as a set of distinct beliefs. The Protestant Church had become an institution.

Luther died in 1546. By that time his ideas and others related to them were spreading across Europe. In England, Henry VIII, who had once earned the blessing of the Pope by publishing a rebuttal of Luther's views, broke from the papacy. His reasons for doing so were personal as much as ecclesiastical, but the result was that the Protestant Reformation swept through the country. In Zurich, Ulrich Zwingli persuaded several Swiss cantons to join the cause of reform. He was killed in a battle against rival cantons that had chosen to stay within the Catholic Church. In Geneva the Church reformer John Calvin developed his influential theories on predestination that became a cornerstone of Puritan belief. Translations of the Bible started to appear in many different languages. The first versions in Dutch appeared in 1526, in French in 1530. During the second half of the sixteenth century, translations also appeared in Slovenian and Polish.

A movement that began as a call for reform became, within the space of twenty years, a different way of looking at the world and a separate force in its own right. It developed during an age of enterprise when the people of Europe began to explore trading opportunities in newly discovered lands. The energy of religious fervour became partner to the energy of commerce and Christian divisions began to form into territorial enclaves with different beliefs and individual ambitions. Martin Luther's passion for reform broke the omnipotence of the Catholic Church. As a result the concept of 'Christendom' began to fade and a different continent, one divided by national rivalries, started to take shape.

CHAPTER 9

Charles Darwin's *On the Origin of Species*

1859

In 1859 Charles Darwin published *On the Origin of Species by Means of Natural Selection*, in which he proved the process of evolution. It was one of the most important books ever written and caused bitter religious controversy.

Charles Darwin trained to become a priest. Early nineteenth-century Britain, in which he grew up, had developed a contented relationship between religion and science. Many men became ordained as clergymen without pursuing full-time careers in the Church. They often entered academic life where, in the fashion of the times, they investigated the natural order of things by hunting for fossils on the beach. They tended to subscribe, as Darwin had done as a young man, to the idea of natural theology. The universe, and the world within it, had been designed by an unseen hand and the intricate processes of science, which they researched and understood, provided the machinery by which this great creation worked. The laws of science were framed within the laws of God.

This approach went back to the seventeenth century and the ideas of Britain's greatest scientist, Sir Isaac Newton. 'Gravity,' said Newton, 'explains the motion of the planets but it cannot explain who set the planets in motion. God governs all things and knows all that is or can be done.' Intellectuals of the eighteenth-century Enlightenment sometimes argued against this theory. The Scottish philosopher, David Hume, was a natural sceptic, branded an atheist by some, who cast doubt on the concept of an unseen hand. Nothing existed without a cause, he maintained, and anyone who promoted the notion of a universe designed by a supernatural power 'is left afterwards to fix every point of his theology, by the utmost licence of fancy and hypothesis'. Such doubts represented a minority view. In 1802, William Paley, a distinguished churchman and academic, published a book entitled *Natural Theology* in which he advanced the theory that just as we infer the existence of a watchmaker from finding and studying the design of a watch, so, from looking at the world and its complicated components, can we be sure of an intelligent creator. The work was enormously popular. It provided people with a scientific explanation for the existence of God; knowledge alone did not have the power to dislodge religion.

When the Earl of Bridgewater died in 1829 he left money in his will for the publication of a book to be called *On the Power, Wisdom and Goodness of God as Manifested in the Creation*, to be illustrated by examples drawn from the sciences, arts and literature. Eight distinguished academics recruited by the Royal Society in London, with the advice of the Archbishop of Canterbury, were invited to contribute and the result was published in 1834. At that moment, Charles Darwin was far away in Tierra del Fuego aboard HMS *Beagle* making the discoveries that would threaten to destroy the well-defended edifice of nineteenth-century Christianity.

Charles Darwin was born in Shrewsbury in 1809, the son of a wealthy doctor and financier. His paternal grandfather was Erasmus Darwin, a distinguished philosopher, inventor and poet; on his mother's side his grandfather was Josiah Wedgwood, the pottery manufacturer and social reformer. These two men had known each other when, as members of the Lunar Society in Birmingham, they had met to discuss the great ideas of the day. Charles Darwin went to Edinburgh University to study medicine, but the brutality of surgery was not to his taste and he found himself drawn towards natural history. Darwin's father, worried that his son was being too easily diverted, sent him to Cambridge University where

The laws of science were framed within the laws of God.

he became friends with the Professor of Botany, John Henslow. Botany was not held in particularly high regard at the university. The faculty possessed little more than its botanical garden and Henslow confessed that when he took the chair he knew little about the subject but 'probably as much of the subject as any other resident of Cambridge'. He was an energetic and sympathetic teacher and, recognising Darwin's interest in plants and fossils, suggested to the captain of HMS *Beagle* that Darwin would be the ideal naturalist to fill the position of unpaid gentleman's companion during a two-year voyage to chart the coastline of South America. Darwin overcame his father's opposition to the scheme and on 27th December 1831 set sail from Plymouth.

HMS *Beagle* took nearly five years to complete its voyage. By the time it finally returned to Britain in 1836, Charles Darwin was a scientific celebrity. He joined the ship, in his own words, as 'a collector of specimens'. He thought of himself at the beginning of the voyage merely as 'an errand boy sent out by the bona fide scientists back in England'. In a journey that took him across the Atlantic to South America, round Cape Horn and into the Galapagos Islands; then across the Pacific to Tahiti, New Zealand and Australia; and finally to Mauritius, Madagascar and South Africa, with a further stop on the coast of South America before returning home, Charles Darwin was transformed from a mere errand boy and carefree young graduate into a serious naturalist. All thoughts of a career in the Church, if they had ever seriously existed, were abandoned.

Darwin was transformed from a mere errand boy into a serious naturalist.

While he was away, Darwin spent most of his time on land, observing and collecting specimens and examples. His findings were published in 1839 as the *Journal and Remarks*, to accompany the captain of the *Beagle's* own account, but they soon developed a separate and popular life of their own. They contained some of his early thoughts about evolution and the natural world, which were then not completely formed. Darwin's family wealth meant that he did not need to find a job, and he spent the next few years lecturing, writing up his notebooks and developing the ideas he had come up with on his worldwide voyage. Before long these had taken the shape of certainty. Mankind had not been created by a single godly act. It had evolved.

Darwin moved to Downe in Kent where he lived happily with his family – he was a devoted husband and father, and was deeply distressed by the death of his eldest daughter, Annie, in 1851 – but did not publish his ideas about evolution. For nearly twenty years one of the most important scientific theories in the whole history of mankind remained locked in his home in Kent, the only written evidence of its existence contained in a manuscript nearly two hundred pages long, which Darwin had had carefully copied and kept in his study with instructions to his wife, Emma, to publish in case of his sudden death. On a purely domestic level, he did not want to upset his wife's religious beliefs. More widely, he knew that what he had discovered would shake Victorian Britain to its foundations.

All human beings, however noble and however kind, have egos, and Darwin was no exception. In 1858 he discovered that his was the better part of discretion when out of the blue he received a paper from a naturalist called Alfred Russel Wallace. It was entitled 'On the Tendency of Variations to Depart Indefinitely from the Original Type'. Darwin did not know Wallace, but he quickly recognised his ideas. Here, in an unsolicited manuscript sent from the Malay Archipelago, where Russel had been working, were some, although, not all, of Darwin's own theories. Darwin agonised, then sat down and wrote. In late November 1859 his book went on sale.

In *On the Origin of Species*, Darwin stated that all the species that have ever lived on earth may form a single tree of life. He had first drawn a sketch of an evolutionary tree after the end of the *Beagle* voyage, in 1837. He went on to say that any group of a similar species – such as a type of bird – was descended from a single, common ancestor and all birds, of all types, were also descended from a single ancestor from an earlier time. All animal and plant species could share a common ancestry if they were traced back far enough. Darwin then explained the process by which this ancestral development had been driven – natural selection. Species diverged as they evolved from their single ancestor; they adapted to their changing needs – flying, swimming, burrowing and so on; and they progressed in their development so that higher creatures had sophisticated mech-anisms – arms and legs, mouths and ears – while lower ones moved and reacted in a more cumbersome manner. In other words, Darwin said that all human beings and all animals evolved from common species which may themselves have evolved from one single root; and that in the process of evolving, natural selec-tion – the survival of the fittest – determined which species lived on and which did not. All of his subsequent works were to a large extent a further discussion of these fundamental ideas and built and expanded upon them.

Darwin's book inflicted severe damage on conservative thinking in Victorian Britain. The established Church was powerful. Six years before *On the Origin of Species* appeared, F. D. Maurice, a distinguished professor at King's College, London, had been forced to resign for publishing essays that in his colleagues' opinion demonstrated unsound theology. He had dared to ques-tion the idea that a refusal to acknowledge sin at one's death automatically led to the torments of hell. Not long after Darwin's book appeared the British Association for the Advancement of Science held a meeting to discuss its contents. The greatest scientific minds of the day gathered in the newly completed Museum of Natural History at Oxford, a neo-gothic masterpiece which brought under one roof the university collection of natural history and anatomical specimens. Darwin himself did not attend. Stress made him ill and brought on stomach pains and vomiting: he preferred the calmness of a clinic to the vigour of debate, particularly if his own work was at the centre of the argu-ment. Several of his supporters were there, but so were many of his opponents, including Samuel Wilberforce, Lord Bishop of Oxford. Wilberforce – known to his contemporaries as 'Soapy Sam' – was the third son of the anti-slavery campaigner, William Wilberforce, and, like his father, had a national reputation for eloquence. On the second day of the meeting, he got to his feet and began to attack the theory of natural selection. What he then said has become a matter of debate almost as intense as those surrounding Darwin's book.

Turning to Darwin's friend and champion, T. H. Huxley, Wilberforce is supposed to have asked him whether it was through his grandfather or grandmother that he claimed descent from a monkey. To which Huxley, small, slight and serious, is reported to have replied that he was not ashamed to have a monkey for an ancestor, but would be ashamed to be connected with a man who used his great gifts to obscure the truth. Wilberforce's sneering question vanquished by Huxley's poised response has become a legendary episode in the controversy generated by *On the Origin of Species* in Victorian Britain: the haughty intransigence of the Church defeated by the forensic skills of science. Almost certainly, it was not quite like that. Wilberforce was not so arrogant, although he probably overstepped the mark, and Huxley not so sharp, although he seems to have rebuffed the bishop very well. The episode is interesting not only for what was said, but also for how people realised that Darwin's book was revolutionary.

The fierce reaction to criticism of conventional thought was often simply defensive, the angry outburst of those who felt their influence was waning in a changing world. By 1860 many parts of Britain had become an industrial hotbed as an expanding urban population fed the machinery of the country's industrial revolution. Men and women read widely, and much of what they enjoyed was secular rather than religious. As well as clergymen who believed that Darwin was on the side of the devil, there were some, like the author and Christian socialist, Charles Kingsley, who recognised in his work ideas that they themselves had entertained. Four months after Darwin's book, seven senior members of the Church of England published a selection of essays in which they explored the path of contemporary Christianity. One of them, Baden Powell, the Oxford Professor of Geometry and father of the founder of the Scout Movement, declared that Darwin's work 'must soon bring about an entire revolution in favour of the grand principle of the self-evolving powers of nature'. Darwin knew that his theories represented a challenge to Anglican orthodox thinking. He himself came from a strong Nonconformist background and although he eventually stopped going to church, he never described himself as an atheist. He preferred the term 'agnostic', a word invented by T. H. Huxley in 1860 to describe the thinking of people like him whose faith had been tempered by science. This balanced scepticism found a home in the age in which he lived. In one sense, his ideas were like a new religion. The concept of the survival of the fittest was almost a parable for the grimy, competitive lives that many of his countrymen were suffering.

[Darwin] 'it is truly surprising that I should have influenced to a considerable extent the beliefs of scientific men on some important points.'

The man who discovered the actual truth stayed apart from the great debate, professing illness when it grew too close, preferring simply to deliver his conclusions than debate their consequences. Charles Darwin was modest about his achievements. In his autobiography he remarked that he thought he was 'superior to the common run of men in noticing things which easily escape attention, and observing them carefully', but added that 'with such moderate abilities as I possess, it is truly surprising that I should have influenced to a considerable extent the beliefs of scientific men on some important points'. History has taken a rather more forceful view. Darwin was one of the world's great messengers, as important and influential as any religious prophet. What he discovered and what he wrote changed forever man's view of his existence and his life on earth.

CHAPTER 10

9/11

2001

On 11th September 2001, Muslim terrorists carried out suicide attacks on two important American landmarks. They destroyed the World Trade Center in New York, killing nearly 3,000 people. The attacks, now referred to as '9/11', were the most serious incident in a 'holy war' carried out by some Islamic organisations against Western targets.

Terrorism seems to us to be a modern phenomenon. Murderous and arbitrary attacks on civilian populations in support of a cause from which the victims appear far removed are an affront to our reason and sense of justice. They test our morality and our belief in law to their utmost. They are incalculable. But they are not as recent as we may think. Terrorism – that is to say, the use of terror in pursuit of political or religious objectives – is as old as history itself. It has always been defended by those who commit it by the age-old comforter that the end justifies the means.

In 1095, Pope Urban II called for a crusade against the Arab occupation of Jerusalem with the words: 'Let this be your war cry in fighting, because the word is given to you by God. When an armed attack is made upon the enemy, let this one cry be raised by all God's soldiers. It is the will of God! It is the will of God!' The Christian Church has always known about holy war. In 1572, when thousands of French Protestants were massacred in Paris on St Bartholomew's Day, the Pope ordered a Te Deum to be offered in thanks and invited the artist Vasari to decorate the Vatican with a painting in honour of the occasion. Catholic militancy lay behind the Gunpowder Plot of 1605 which, had it succeeded, would have destroyed the English Houses of Parliament and killed the King. Protestant vengefulness was a characteristic of Oliver Cromwell's campaign in Ireland in 1649 when he ordered the killing of hundreds of innocent men, women and children at the siege of Drogheda. 'I am persuaded,' he wrote, 'that this is a righteous judgment of God upon these barbarous wretches.' Their deaths, he argued, 'will tend to prevent the effusion of blood in the future.' In the eighteenth century, terror became a partner to revolutionary politics. Maximilien Robespierre, the leader of the Jacobin faction in the French Revolution, called for terror to be used against those whom he believed were the enemies of change. In a speech in 1794 he said: 'The springs of popular government in revolution are at once virtue and terror; virtue without which terror is fatal; terror without which virtue is powerless. Terror is nothing other than justice, prompt, serene, inflexible ... Subdue by terror the enemies of liberty, and you will be right, as founders of the Republic.' The same theme was taken up by Lenin after the Russian Revolution of 1917. 'We stand for organised terror,' he said in a newspaper interview in 1918; 'this should be frankly admitted. Terror is an absolute necessity during times of revolution.'

On the morning of 11th September 2001, nineteen hijackers seized control of four commercial passenger planes travelling at about the same time in the morning from different cities in the United States to Los Angeles. They flew two of the planes into the towers of the World Trade Center in New York and one into the Pentagon building in Virginia, the centre of America's military planning operations. The fourth plane crashed in open country in Pennsylvania after its passengers fought a battle with the hijackers. The whole of the World Trade Center collapsed in a terrifying spectacle that sent a roaring cloud of lethal dust and debris through the streets of Manhattan. The destruction of the building accounted for most of the 3,000 people killed that day. There were no survivors from any of the plane crashes.

The names and identities of the hijackers were discovered very quickly.

The names and identities of the hijackers were discovered very quickly. They were all members of al-Qaeda, a militant Islamic organisation dedicated to carrying out attacks, particularly suicide missions, against Western targets. Its leader, Osama bin Laden, at first denied any involvement in the 11th September events, but later claimed full responsibility. Al-Qaeda recruits its members from countries all over the world. It pays allegiance to no individual country or state although some Islamic regimes are believed to have colluded at times in its activities.

In that sense it is similar to other revolutionary organisations in history such as the Bolsheviks in Russia, the IRA in Ireland or the ANC in South Africa. But unlike them, its ambitions are global, not national. It seeks to unite Islam in a war against Western countries, in particular America, whom it perceives to be the enemies of its beliefs and way of life.

The Christian Church has always known about holy war.

The atrocities that it carried out on 11th September 2001 amounted to the most serious terrorist incident in the history of the modern world. In the nineteenth and twentieth centuries, the world seemed to divide itself along political lines, first between fascism and democracy, and then between democracy and communism. The twenty-first century began with a terrifying statement about religious division: Islam and Christendom seemed to be at war once again.

The Commission of Enquiry into the '9/11' attacks, set up by the President of the United States, George W. Bush, said in its report published in 2004 said that al-Qaeda received support because 'the Muslim world has fallen behind the West politically, economically and militarily for the past three centuries, and because few tolerant or secular Muslim democracies provide alternative models for the future'. Such a large generalisation tends to reveal the gulf that separates some Western thinking from Islam, although it is true that the great Muslim empires of Europe and the Near East began to decline as a world force from the eighteenth century onwards. In 1453, Christian Byzantium fell to the Turks when they captured its capital, Constantinople. By the end of the seventeenth century, the Ottoman Empire that then rose to power ruled territory that stretched across the whole of Asia Minor, the Balkans, the Middle East, Egypt and North Africa. In 1683 its armies were repulsed from the gates of Vienna. To the east of the Ottoman lands lay the Persian Empire of the Safavid dynasty, the greatest of whose kings, Shah Abbas, built a magnificent capital in the city of Isfahan at the beginning of the seventeenth century and whose territory stretched from Iran to Afghanistan. Christendom and Islam both enjoyed power, prestige and a rich cultural heritage. The Muslim world was every bit as strong as its Christian neighbour: from the death of Mohammed in 632 AD it enjoyed a thousand years of conquest and growth.

The balance began to tilt in favour of the West during the eighteenth century as the Ottoman Empire was forced on the defensive by nationalist movements in the Balkans and the increasing strength of the Austro-Hungarian Empire. In 1797, Napoleon, still dreaming of becoming the leader of the French nation, wrote that the 'approaching death of the vast Ottoman Empire' meant that France should occupy and conquer Egypt in order to protect its trade with the Middle East. Driven more by dreams of glory than any practical considerations he set sail with a great armada. Despite losing a large part of his fleet to the British in the Battle of the Nile in 1798, he succeeded in capturing Cairo and establishing a new French colony. 'Peoples of Egypt!' he declared in a proclamation. 'You will be told that I have come to destroy your religion. Do not believe it!' With typical Napoleonic gusto he set about introducing Western institutions, including Egypt's first printing press, before returning to Europe. He even explored the possibility of building a canal at Suez, a project that did not come to fruition until 1869.

Napoleon's incursion into the heart of Islam was a significant turning point in Europe's relationship with the Muslim world. The Western powers expanded, gaining territory in the New World as, led by Britain and France, they pursued a programme of relentless colonisation in India, Africa and the Americas. In 1853, just before the outbreak of the Crimean War, Tsar Nicholas I of Russia was said to have called Turkey 'the sick man of Europe', as the lands under its control rebelled and it was forced into alliances with its European neighbours to protect its position. In the First World War, the Ottoman Empire fought on the side of the German and Austro-Hungarian Empires. Its defeat resulted in its collapse and the founding of a secular Turkish republic under the leadership of Mustafa Kemal Atatürk. 'The Turkish republic,' he said, 'cannot be a country of sheikhs, dervishes and disciples.' Its former territories in the Middle East were handed to the British and the French who introduced administrative structures designed on European lines. Large parts of Islam, it appeared, had been folded into a Western model and the strict theocracy that bound Church and state together in an indivisible union started to melt away in the face of these new influences.

These changes, however, though far-reaching in many respects, were in others superficial. New systems of government did not extend beyond the literate and well-heeled. The majority of people living in Middle Eastern countries remained poor and ill educated. After the Second World War, the European powers withdrew from the region, leaving behind an intractable problem: the partition of Palestine to create Israel, a new homeland for the Jewish people. The grievances that this loss of land created were exacerbated by nationalist revolutions in Egypt and Syria. Lebanon disintegrated into a civil war that lasted for fifteen years from 1975 to 1990. In 1979 the Shah of Iran was forced from his throne in a revolution that returned a strict Islamic government to power. The long, slow collapse of a great imperial organisation resulted in the weakening of states and the emergence of many different problems – religious, social, political and economic. At their core lay large numbers of people whose values and beliefs were comparatively untouched by change. They knew that Western ways had failed to solve their problems: far from it. They were naturally receptive to the ideas of intellectuals and revolutionaries. They were the perfect targets for Osama bin Laden and al-Qaeda.

It was the most serious terrorist incident in the history of the modern world.

In the aftermath of al-Qaeda's assault, America declared 'a war on terror'. The month after 9/11 it invaded Afghanistan to drive out the extremist Islamic government, the Taliban, which harboured al-Qaeda terrorists in training camps in the country. It also tried, but failed, to capture or kill Osama bin Laden who was hiding there. In 2003 it went further. With the aid of Britain and other international allies, it invaded Iraq because it said it believed the country owned weapons of mass destruction. Neither of these invasions was entirely successful. The new government of Afghanistan required constant military support to protect it and at the time of writing, 2010, a large allied force remains stationed there. The invasion of Iraq succeeded in toppling the regime of the dictator, Saddam Hussein, but a failure to plan properly for the consequences meant that parts of the country fell into anarchy. These Western incursions were designed to try to build those 'alternative models for the future', to which the Commission of Enquiry into 9/11 referred. The trouble was that many of the people for whom they were intended took a different view of what they should be like. To those already disillusioned by the failure of the West to improve conditions in the Islamic world, the wars in Afghanistan and Iraq seemed further evidence of an attempt to impose external machinery on a traditional way of life.

[Robespierre]

'Terror is nothing other than justice, prompt, serene, inflexible ...'

9/11 was a violent eruption by Islamic forces against an amorphous enemy loosely described as 'the West'. 'The West' was once the enemy of Islam, just as 'Islam' could be described as having once been the enemy of 'the West'. But not anymore. Some of Islam's problems may be due to historical Western influences, but just as many of them are self-made. The great danger of acts of terror such as the attacks on the United States in September 2001 is that they unbalance Western belief in its own judgments. At the time of writing, a Christian worker for British Airways has complained to the courts because her employers have forbidden her to wear a necklace with a cross for fear of offending non-Christian customers. Such behaviour by employers displays an alarming lack of confidence, the most dangerous consequence of acts of terrorism. We need to believe in ourselves and the religious beliefs of all members of our community. At the same time we are unlikely to be successful in overcoming terror by generalised acts of war. Human beings long for certainty. Sometimes they adopt final solutions in the hope of finding it. But one of the lessons of history is that nothing is certain: we know that from the past, and we should prepare for it in the future.

4 Conquest

Introduction

Modern science has taught mankind to treat the world carefully, but this is not a lesson he has always understood. Land was the source of all his treasure. It was there to be exploited. The German king, Ariovistus, told Julius Caesar in 58 BC that 'the right of war was that conquerors should govern those whom they had conquered in any manner they pleased'. Since the Romans acted in that way, he argued, he should be allowed to do the same and govern as he wished the tribes of Gaul he had subdued. Ariovistus overplayed his hand and Caesar subsequently defeated him, but his description of a conqueror's rights was typical of the age in which he lived. In early times man grouped himself in small communities, cultivating the land on which he lived to sustain his needs. As he grew more sophisticated, learned social organisation and how to use weapons, he looked to enrich himself through expansion. Communities became city-states, city-states formed alliances and alliances bred empires whose rise and fall form an undulating pattern throughout the history of the world. Empires depend on conquest – man's passion to acquire new territory.

One of the most frightening things about conquest is that it has survived. When we read about the astonishing empires of Alexander the Great, or of Rome, or of Asoka the Great in India and Chinggis Khan in China, we tend to admire them. We view them from a distance and accept that people behaved differently then. But that behaviour has travelled with us through time. Thomas Jefferson, the main author of America's Declaration of Independence and its third President, wrote in 1791: 'If there be one principle more deeply rooted than any other in the mind of every American it is that we should have nothing to do with conquest.' As a liberal figure of the eighteenth-century Enlightenment he knew that the prosperity of his new nation depended on its turning away from war and imperial ambition. He was also the President who agreed to the Louisiana Purchase in which the

United States bought nearly a million square miles of American territory from Napoleon and the French in 1803. That agreement began an expansion of America's frontiers that encouraged an insatiable appetite for land in the nineteenth century. The country's growth westwards required the subjugation of Native American tribes that often smacked of conquest. Napoleon's motives in agreeing to the sale were to help build a nation powerful enough to resist Britain's naval expansion so that he would not be threatened in his imperial ambitions in Europe. His conquests in Italy, Spain and Germany built the first new empire of the nineteenth century.

After Napoleon's defeat in 1815, the next piece of European empire-building fell to the Prussians who announced the creation of the German Empire after their victory in the Franco-Prussian war of 1870. Six years later, Queen Victoria was made Empress of India, the ruler of lands thousands of miles away that she had never seen and would never visit. The British Empire was, in territorial extent, the biggest the world has ever known. It learned the art of conquest through the power of commerce, but other empires since have been created out of historic ideas of simple physical expansion. In 1901 a German geographer called Friedrich Ratzel coined the term 'Lebensraum', or 'living space', by which he meant the geographical boundaries needed for human or animal development. The word was taken up by another influential academic, Karl Haushofer, who developed it into a concept of foreign policy for Adolf Hitler. Lebensraum became the justification for the German conquest of Europe in the middle of the twentieth century. In 1934, Japan took a similar position in the Far East, declaring that it was to be the nation responsible for East Asian security. This abandoned the 'open-door' policy that had given European powers access to Chinese trade since the end of the nineteenth century. Japan invented its version of Lebensraum in order to build an Asian empire.

The Second World War was a global catastrophe. Once it was over it seemed as though the old days of empire had died in its ashes. Britain gave India independence and began relinquishing its colonial ties with the countries it had governed in Africa and the Caribbean. Other European nations did the same. But empire-building continued elsewhere. America's role in the defeat of both Germany and Japan made it the unquestioned leader of the so-called 'free world' – in other words, non-Communist countries operating capitalist systems. Its enormous economic and cultural influence meant that many people felt that it represented in effect a great empire. Although it always refrained from conquest, as Thomas Jefferson had urged it to do, it was often prepared to intervene in the affairs of other countries if it felt its wider interests were threatened. Meanwhile the Soviet Union decided that it would control the fortunes of the countries of Eastern Europe. Russia today, following the collapse of the Soviet regime, remains determined to be the power of influence in the new nations on its borders, particularly Ukraine and Georgia. In 2008, Russian troops invaded South Ossetia, an area of Georgia that was seeking independence. Elsewhere the desire for land fuels dissent. The division of Palestine that resulted in the creation of Israel lies at the heart of the conflict that bedevils the Middle East. The ownership of Kashmir has led to wars between India and Pakistan. The Chinese conquest of Tibet is a cause of deep concern to many in the international community. In 2010, Argentina threatened the territorial integrity of the Falkland Islands in the South Atlantic from which it had been repulsed by British forces after invading the islands in 1982. The discovery of oilfields in the waters surrounding the islands reawakened its claim to their ownership.

Today we know that our planet is in danger because of our own depredations. We urge ourselves to act globally in order to repair it. But global action ignores territorial boundaries which have been one of man's greatest concerns since he first began to develop as a social animal. The ownership of land has always mattered more to him than almost anything else. While he retains his unsatisfied appetite for conquest he will probably ignore the lessons of history and continue to apply the solutions of the past to the problems of the present.

CHAPTER 1

Ozymandias (Rameses II)

1279–c.1213 BC

Ozymandias is the Greek name for the Egyptian Pharaoh, Rameses II. He conquered a large area of North Africa and the Middle East to become one of the most powerful rulers of ancient Egypt.

'Ozymandias' by Percy Bysshe Shelley is one of the finest sonnets in the English language. It was written in 1818, the year the colossal statue of Rameses II was discovered in Egypt and taken to the British Museum in London. Shelley enjoyed a romantic attachment to the idea of liberty. He was expelled from Oxford for publishing a pamphlet called 'The Necessity of Atheism'. His short, vivid life was a somewhat self-obsessed journey of personal freedom. In 'Ozymandias' he used the seven-and-a-half-ton statue as a symbol of the ephemeral nature of power and conquest. Its 'frown/ And wrinkled lip and sneer of cold command' reveal a contempt for the people the great Emperor rules. The inscription on the pedestal is a howl of domination: 'My name is Ozymandias, king of kings:/ Look on my works, ye Mighty, and despair!' But such arrogance is now no more than a futile echo from history. 'Nothing beside remains. Round the decay/ Of that colossal wreck, boundless and bare/ The lone and level sands stretch far away.' Shelley looks at a great conqueror through a poet's eyes. In eleven lines he builds an image of vast and cruel grandeur, only to blow it into oblivion in the last three. It is not an entirely fanciful vision of history.

The civilisation of ancient Egypt lasted for nearly 3,000 years, but our knowledge of it is remarkably scanty.

Although the civilisation of ancient Egypt lasted for nearly 3,000 years our knowledge of it is remarkably scanty. It was first unified as a kingdom in about 3100 BC, fell to the Macedonian Greeks under Alexander the Great in 332 BC, and was then ruled by the descendants of one of Alexander's generals, Ptolemy, until its absorption into the Roman Empire following the defeat of Anthony and Cleopatra at the Battle of Actium in 31 BC. A priest called Manetho who lived in Egypt shortly after Alexander's conquest compiled a list of kings and dynasties from records and anecdotes and this has survived as the main source of information about them. In about 3100 BC, Menes, king of the peoples from southern Egypt, conquered his neighbours in the north and established a unified state in which the first signs of an ordered community began to emerge. From its capital at Memphis, south of Cairo, the King ruled a land that stretched for 600 miles along the River Nile. As time passed he was elevated to a divine status, an all-powerful ruler upon whom the people depended for everything. He was a child of the sun god and would ascend to eternal life when he left earth. The afterlife of his subjects was held in his personal gift.

This highly controlled world, called the Old Kingdom, began to collapse in about 2100 BC and the country became divided before being reunited under another dynasty. This second period, known as the Middle Kingdom, lasted for nearly 1500 years during which Egypt enjoyed the position of a great power in the region, extending its rule over Nubia, modern Sudan, to the south and developing trading links with countries beyond its Mediterranean coast to the north. Osiris became the god of all the people, offering the opportunity of eternity to everyone who worshipped him properly. The capital moved south to Thebes near modern Luxor. The rulers were buried in pyramids as they always had been, but nobles also built tombs for themselves. The Middle Kingdom eventually broke down to be followed by a time of war and invasion. Egypt was ruled by foreigners, probably tribal leaders from territory in Mesopotamia and the borders with Asia. Egyptian rule was re-established under the New Kingdom, which came into existence in about 1550 BC. This was an age of empire. Egypt expanded across North

Africa, Mesopotamia and into the Middle East. It was the height of ancient Egypt's power and the period during which Rameses II became pharaoh.

Rameses was the King's birth name given to him in honour of his grandfather, Rameses I. His other title was 'Usermaatre-setepenre', meaning: 'The justice of Re [the Egyptian sun god] is powerful: Chosen of Re.' In Greek this translates as 'Ozymandias'. He was born in 1303 BC and, having served as co-regent with his father, succeeded to the throne in 1279 BC. He ruled for almost sixty-seven years and fathered more than a hundred children. As the pharaoh he represented his people's mortal link with the gods, with the responsibility of ensuring their good harvests and general wellbeing, as well as winning victories in battle. He had eight principal wives and other lesser ones, some of whom may have been his daughters. This form of incest was common practice in ancient Egypt where daughters of kings were not allowed to marry below their status, leaving them only princes and the King himself as possible partners. His mummy, discovered in 1881, revealed him to have been five feet seven inches tall – a greater than average height for the time in which he lived – with red hair and a thin, hooked nose set in a narrow face with a long jaw. His body showed signs of old battle scars. By the time he died he was suffering from crippling arthritis, hardened arteries and severe dental problems. Forensic science is frightened of nothing, not even the glory of a god.

He fathered more than a hundred children.

Rameses II had been trained in the art of war. During his reign he regained much of the territory that Egypt had lost during the previous dynasty and, commanding an army of 100,000 men, was successful in securing the borders of his empire. He had not been long on the throne before he defeated the Sherden, one of the groups of 'sea-people' who threatened Egypt's security by attacking its cargo vessels and forming alliances on land with other enemies. The Sherden seem to have been a tribe based in the Mediterranean who were driven towards the North African coast in search of food and somewhere to settle. His main campaign, however, was against the Hittites, whose empire lay to the east of Egypt (today Syria and eastern Turkey). The Hittites were a warlike race who, during the period before Rameses acceded to the throne, extended their borders towards the frontier with Egypt. Rameses conquered the Hittite territory of Amurru in northern Palestine, forcing a confrontation with the Hittite army at Kadesh near the River Orontes in western Syria. This was a great battle, the course of which was recorded in the temple of Abu Simbel and other monuments that Rameses built to honour the gods and remind posterity of his achievements. Like many successful emperors he always had an eye to history and indulged himself in building splendid memorials to his reign.

Every foreign country trembled before him.

The Battle of Kadesh, which was fought in about 1274 BC, is one of the best-recorded military encounters of the ancient world – although the accounts all come from the Egyptian side. 'His Majesty had prepared his infantry, his chariotry and his Sherden of his capturing,' reads one temple inscription. As with the Roman Empire much later, a people defeated in battle could be absorbed into the society that had conquered it: the defeated Sherden were now part of the Egyptian army, 'equipped with all their weapons to whom the orders of combat had been given'. The inscriptions go on to tell us that: 'His Majesty journeyed northward, his infantry and chariotry with him … every foreign country was trembling before him, their chiefs were presenting their tribute, and all the rebels were coming, bowing down through fear of the glory of His Majesty.' Some of this may be simple propaganda, a rewriting of history to project an image of the pharaoh. In fact Rameses seems to have nearly lost the battle. On his arrival at Kadesh scouts told him that the army of the Hittites was still some distance to the north and believing that he had gained a strategic advantage he moved his army forward. But the scouts were Hittite spies who had deceived him. The enemy army was hiding near the village settlement and ambushed the pharaoh's troops who were driven back towards the river. Apparently distracted by the prospect of loot from the Egyptian camp, the Hittites delayed pursuing their advantage and were routed by reinforcements from the pharaoh's army. The Hittites were forced to retreat and the pharaoh survived to regale history with his version of events. In verses that Rameses ordered to be inscribed on five temples, including one at Karnak, he described how he stood alone against the enemy and how the supreme god, Amun, protected him:

> Here I stand
> All alone
> There is no on at my side,
> My warriors and chariots afeared,
> Have deserted me, none heard
> My voice, when to the cravens, I, their king, for
>   succour cried.
> But I find that Ammon's grace
> Is better far to me
> Than a million fighting men and ten thousand
>   chariots be.

The Battle of Kadesh was certainly a huge encounter. The Hittites may have had as many as 3,500 chariots in their army. Rameses had an infantry of about 20,000 men as well as his force of noblemen charioteers. After further campaigning the Egyptians agreed peace terms with the Hittites. The details of the treaty and correspondence between the two opposing courts still survive as remarkable evidence of the diplomatic machinery of the ancient world.

Much of Egypt's history remained a secret for hundreds of years after its empire had disappeared. In Europe the country was regarded simply as the place that had enslaved the Hebrews before they were led to their promised land by Moses. The Renaissance generated new interest in antiquity and the Bible lands, while in the seventeenth and eighteenth centuries Egyptian ruins became attractive symbols for evoking man's distant past. The reverse of the Great Seal of the United States depicts a pyramid to signify, according to its designer Charles Thomson in 1782, 'strength and duration'. Napoleon's Egyptian invasion sixteen years later aroused Europe's imagination in the country's ancient history. French troops discovered the Rosetta Stone in 1799, a slab containing inscriptions in Egyptian hieroglyphics with a Greek translation. An Englishman, Thomas Young, realised that the hieroglyphics were phonetic as well as symbolic. They could be translated alphabetically: they were not just symbols, or picture stories, as had been previously assumed. In 1822 a Frenchman, Jean-François Champollion, used Young's theory to break this phonetic code and a hidden world emerged into modern view.

Rameses II, the great builder and propagandist, was a particular beneficiary of this discovery. He built many new magnificent temples and redecorated or rebuilt existing ones. He changed the method of carving inscriptions, making the reliefs deeper to give them more prominence and a better chance of survival. The greatest of his creations were the twin temples at Abu Simbel built as a monument to him and his principal wife, Nefertari. Carved out of the mountainside, they are engineered with extraordinary precision. Twice a year, on the spring and autumn equinox, the rays of the rising sun penetrate the innermost chamber more than sixty yards from the entrance to illuminate the statues of the gods on the back wall.

When Rameses died his people thought that without him the world might end.

Rameses II held such power over his people that when he died they thought that without him the world might end. In one sense they were right. The great days of the Egyptian empire were gone. The country came under increasing attack and found it difficult to maintain its borders. A later pharaoh, Rameses III, had some success in halting the decline, but he died as a result of an internal conspiracy. Dissension began to undermine the Egyptian state. The power of the pharaoh ebbed away to be transferred to priests and officials as its civilisation crumbled into the sand. In some ways its longevity is an extraordinary feature of world history. A peasant population dominated by despotic rulers and overshadowed by forbidding religious beliefs ploughed its way through 3,000 years of continuous existence in which many of the fundamental forms of its life seemed to change remarkably little. Its huge monuments along the path of one of the world's greatest rivers, the Nile, stand as testament to its 'strength and duration'. They are symbols of a fascinating history, but unlike those of Greece and Rome, a curiously remote one. The name of Rameses was never lost from this long, slow historical pageant: it is the epitome of power and conquest in Egypt's ancient lands. Beyond that, however, as Shelley observed: 'the lone and level sands stretch far away'.

CHAPTER 2

Alexander the Great

356–323 BC

Alexander the Great was one of the most successful conquerors the world has ever seen. He built a vast empire but remains a mysterious and captivating figure.

The Greek philosopher Diogenes was famous for his ascetic lifestyle. He was a Cynic, and believed in a school of thought that rejected everyday desires in order to live a life without any possessions. He ended his days in the city of Corinth where his home was a barrel. The story goes that Alexander the Great asked to visit him. As he approached the philosopher the great conqueror asked if there was anything he could do for him. 'Yes,' replied Diogenes, 'stand out of my sunlight.'

We do not know if this anecdote is true, but it provides an amusing historical vignette: one of history's most famous strongmen confounded by one of its most humble. The supposed meeting between the two men is almost a parable, a tale with a moral ending that says the sword is never mightier than the human mind. Nevertheless it was Alexander's heroic exploits that caught people's imagination once he was long dead. *The Alexander Romance,* a collection of legends about him, first appeared in Greek in the third century AD and continued to emerge in European, Persian and Arabic versions until the Middle Ages. It tells the story of how an Egyptian king and magician came to Alexander's country of Macedon where he fell in love with the wife of his father, King Philip, and seduced her by disguising himself as a god. Philip was complicit in this arrangement and believed that the child of the union, Alexander, was the son of a god. Alexander killed his father and the magician when he discovered the truth and then set out on a series of half-magical, half-historical exploits. Some scholars believe that the story of the 'Two-Horned One' in the Koran and mention of the 'King of the Macedonians' in the book of Daniel in the Bible may also be references to Alexander the Great. These fabulous stories demonstrate the spell that Alexander cast upon the people among whom he lived and many of those who came after him.

Alexander was born in the city of Pella, the capital of Macedon, in 356 BC. Macedon was a country on the north-eastern fringes of Greece, but it was different from its neighbour's city-states in its political structure. The people regarded themselves as Greek and competed in the Olympic Games, but many Greeks considered the Macedonians to be barbarians. Alexander's father, Philip II, was one of the hard-bitten noblemen who ran the country but he ended his life as its undisputed king by expanding its frontiers in a ruthlessly successful series of conquests. He was the role model for his son. He unified his country and gave it access to the sea. He then enlarged its territory by capturing land to the north and south with the help of a large army that employed new techniques of warfare. His infantry used longer spears than other Greek armies and learned the art of siege with battering rams, catapults and moving towers. Philip was assassinated in 336 BC, by which time he had become the undisputed master of all Greece. Only Sparta lay beyond his control. The other city-states were all part of the League of Corinth, an alliance formed to prepare for an attack against its long-standing enemy, the Persian Empire. They purported to be independent but in fact were subservient to Macedonian command. The ancient structure of classical Greece disintegrated, its variety and rivalries subsumed into a determined military empire.

One of the last great Athenian orators of that period, Demosthenes, railed in vain against the collapse of the old order. 'I observe,' he cried, 'that when a league is knitted together by goodwill and when all the allied states have the same interests, then the coalition stands firm; but when, like Philip's, it is based on treachery and greed and maintained by fraud and violence, then on some slight pretext or by some trifling slip it is instantly shattered and dissolved.' Demosthenes was right to point out the true motives behind Philip's plans, but he was protesting against the inevitable. The baton of power had passed to Macedon, firstly to Philip and then to his son, Alexander.

Alexander was already well versed in warfare when his father died. At the age of sixteen Philip left him in charge as regent when he went north to fight. A tribe from Thrace, the Maedi, took the opportunity to revolt and Alexander defeated them. He was a well-educated young man. His father had searched carefully to find him a tutor and had settled finally on the Greek philosopher Aristotle who instructed him in morals, art, science and logic. His classroom was a temple in the Macedonian village of Mieza where his companions were the children of other noblemen who would later accompany him on his campaigns. Alexander fought alongside his father in subsequent wars and joined him in the march south to subdue the rest of Greece. In 338 BC, the Mace-

His genius is still cloaked in mystery.

donians supported by troops from Greek states they had already conquered fought a battle at Chaeronea against the combined armies of Athens and Thebes. Philip commanded the right flank, his son the left. At their rear were their famous cavalry, the Companions, fast and deadly, an elite troop of noblemen with the best horses and the best armour that moved as one, turning and wheeling with disciplined precision. Chaeronea was Philip's greatest victory. It made him master of Greece. Some sources say Alexander was the first to break into the Theban lines after their allies, the Athenians, had been routed. Certainly he played a crucial part in the battle: by the age of eighteen he had become a courageous and successful general.

The life of Alexander the Great comes to us from five surviving histories. All of them were written 300 years or more after Alexander's death but were based on older accounts of his life drawn from contemporary sources, including those of two of his generals and a historian who accompanied him on his campaigns. From this we know that the great conqueror was not physically imposing. He was of less than average height and rather stocky. He may have had an inherited physical deformity of the neck and spine that made him keep his head unnaturally high forcing him to look upwards and to one side. It seems too that he had different coloured eyes – one blue, one brown. These titbits of information make Alexander all the more intriguing. He was not some colossal lion of a man. Like many great conquerors his power came from within, from a belief, perhaps, in his own destiny that rode relentlessly across all hindrances in its path. He knew how to act decisively.

Two years after the victory at Chaeronea, Philip II was murdered by his bodyguard during the wedding of one of his daughters. Alexander was immediately proclaimed his successor, but his position was precarious. He promptly had the nearest rivals to the throne murdered – his own cousin among them – and quashed the revolts that sprang up on the news of his father's death. The league of city-states that Philip had managed to put together began to fall apart as its members realised that its creator was dead. Alexander, brushing aside advice that he should pursue diplomacy, rallied his army and forced the surrender of Thessaly, the country directly south of Macedon. The other Greek states surrendered and acknowledged Alexander

He had relentless physical energy but enjoyed long nights of drunkenness.

as their leader, but when the tribes of Thrace to the north of Macedon also rebelled, the Greeks took the opportunity to rise up once more. Alexander's vengeance was terrible. The city of Thebes was demolished and its people sold into slavery. Athens took the hint and surrendered. Demosthenes, who had urged the Athenians to rebel because, he said, the Macedonians 'treat our city with contempt', was saved from the life of exile that Alexander demanded. The new leader of Greece had more important matters to concern him. He would carry out the task that that had been denied to his murdered father – the conquest of the Persian Empire.

For the next twelve years, from the age of twenty until he died at the age of thirty-two, Alexander the Great carried out an epic campaign of conquest. In 334 BC he led his army out of Greece, crossing the Hellespont (later know as the Dardanelles) into Asia Minor to attack the Persian Empire under the rule of Darius III. He defeated a force sent by the Emperor to challenge him at the

Grancius River, not far from the site of Troy, and then continued to march down the Ionian coast capturing naval bases in order to weaken the Persian fleet. He then turned inland. At the city of Gordium he is said to have solved the problem of the Gordian Knot, a tangle of bark that tied an ox cart to a post in the palace of the former kings of Phrygia, a country that had become a vassal state of the Persian Empire. Alexander, having failed to untie the knot by conventional methods, is supposed to have cut through it with his sword – a resolution that prompted the prophecy that he would become ruler of Asia.

Darius had avoided meeting Alexander in battle, but in 333 BC he decided to confront him at Issus in southern Turkey. The Persian leader was defeated and fled, opening up the way for Alexander to take Syria and then Egypt. Alexander's invasion of the Middle East was delayed at the port of Tyre, on the Mediterranean coast, which held out against his advancing army for seven months. It capitulated after a long siege. Alexander, enraged by this long defence, is said to have sold 30,000 of its population into slavery. In 331 BC he advanced once again into the heart of Persian territory to face Darius at Gaugamela near Mosul in northern Iraq. Once again the Persian Emperor was defeated and turned and fled. 'The result of this battle,' the historian Plutarch said later, 'was the complete destruction of the Persian Empire.' Alexander pursued Darius but the Persian leader was killed by conspirators who proclaimed Bessus, the Governor of Bactria in Central Asia, as his successor. In 329 BC, Alexander's army forced the conspirators to surrender Bessus who was then executed. As the Gordian prophecy foretold, Alexander proclaimed himself King of Asia with his capital at Babylon.

Alexander gave the culture of classical Greece to the rest of the world.

Alexander's campaign of conquest was not finished. With the treasure of Persia to support him, he travelled even further east, to the fringes of the known world and the Indian subcontinent. Between 327 and 326 BC he fought fierce battles with the tribes of what is now north-west Pakistan and was wounded twice. He soldiered on, crossed the Indus River and fought a pitched battle against the ruler of the Punjab, King Porus, at the Hydaspes River. Porus was a tough opponent. Alexander's victory was so narrow that he returned Porus's kingdom to him and the Indian ruler became his ally in the next phase of his military operation. But Alexander's army was growing mutinous. Years of heavy fighting had taken their toll and they could not be sure where the endless campaigning would take them. One of his most trusted commanders, Coenus, made a speech in which he said that the majority of Greeks and Macedonians who had followed Alexander at the start of his campaign had now perished. 'Few are left out of many,' he went on, 'and these few are no longer equally vigorous in body; while in spirit they are much more exhausted. All those whose parents still survive feel a great yearning to see them once more; they feel a yearning after their wives and children; and a yearning for their native land itself.' Alexander reluctantly ordered the army's return to Persia. In 323 BC, he died in Babylon.

He tore through the world before him like a violent wind. When the wind died everything had changed.

His march of conquest was one of history's most extraordinary military achievements. Rather like Frederick the Great of Prussia in the eighteenth century, Alexander seems to have been a conflicting mixture of sensitivity and brutality. He could be very kind but also hideously cruel; he had a quick temper but sometimes displayed kindness and gentleness; he was remorseless but knew how to listen to advice; he had relentless physical energy but enjoyed long nights of drunkenness. His character has been picked over and analysed ever since his early death, but his genius is still cloaked with mystery. In the end, however, it is not his character but his legacy that matters.

Alexander the Great gave the culture of classical Greece to a wider world. The ancient structure of the Greek city-states was dealt its death blow by him and his father, but Alexander's mission of conquest allowed it to grow new roots in the lands to the east of its birthplace. Most conquerors tend to leave behind the footprints of their own civilisation, even if territory and treasure, rather than art and learning, are their primary concerns. In this Alexander was no different. The empire he built in a few years did not survive in any physical form for long. That is hardly surprising: it was created with such speed, and was so dependent on its creator, that it was bound to wither under successors of less spirit. It was divided into four areas ruled by dynasties founded by Alexander's former generals – Macedon itself, the Pergamon Empire in Asia Minor, the Seleucid Empire further east and the Kingdom of Egypt. All of them were eventually absorbed into the burgeoning Roman Empire, but not before they had enjoyed long years of power in which Greek culture and ideas grew to dominate the whole of the Near and Middle East. Cities like Alexandria in Egypt and Antioch in what is now Syria were world centres where vigorous commerce went hand in hand with intellectual achievement. Many of the ideas that shaped Rome and, after that, the modern world, were first nursed in the new towns and cities of Alexander the Great's hastily erected empire. He was a tornado; he tore through the world before him like a violent wind. And when the wind died everything had changed.

The Return to Amsterdam of the Second Expedition to the East Indies on 19th July 1599 by Andries van Eertvelt (1590–1652). The provinces of the Netherlands each had their own fleets before the formation of the Dutch East India Company in 1602.

This picture by John Trumbull (1756–1843) shows the five men who drafted the Declaration of Independence presenting their work to Congress on 28 June 1776. It is housed in the rotunda of the United States Capitol in Washington DC. The man who became the country's third president, Thomas Jefferson, stands at the front holding the draft itself.

Sikh officers from Hodson's Horse, an irregular cavalry regiment raised by Brevet Major William Hodson to help suppress the rebellions of 1857. Many Sikhs from the Punjab remained loyal to the British during the Indian Mutiny.

'This is how traitors are punished.' A crowd carry the heads of the guillotined, an example of French revolutionary propaganda.

C'est ainsi que l'on Punit les Traîtres.

The signing of the Treaty of Versailles in the Hall of Mirrors of the Versailles Palace in 1919. The French Prime Minister, Georges Clemenceau, sits in the middle with the President of the United States, Woodrow Wilson, on his right and the British Prime Minister, David Lloyd George, on his left.

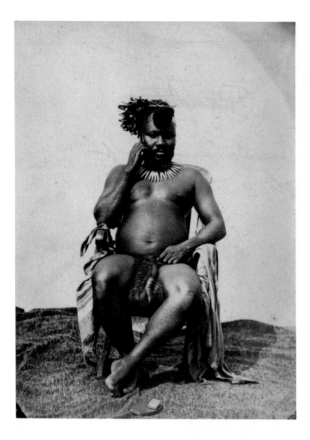

Cetshwayo, the last king of the independent Zulu nation, photographed around 1880.

Gone but not forgotten. A Chinese paramilitary policeman stands in front of the huge portrait of the former Chinese leader, Mao Zedong, at the Tiananmen Gate, Beijing in April 2010.

Not Hollywood but Leeds. The world's first moving pictures were taken by a Frenchman, Louis Le Prince, who used paper film and a single-lens camera to record these scenes of traffic on Leeds Bridge.
Le Prince disappeared after boarding a train from Dijon to Paris in 1890 and was never seen again. It was left to others to claim the credit for an invention that would change the way man looked at the world.

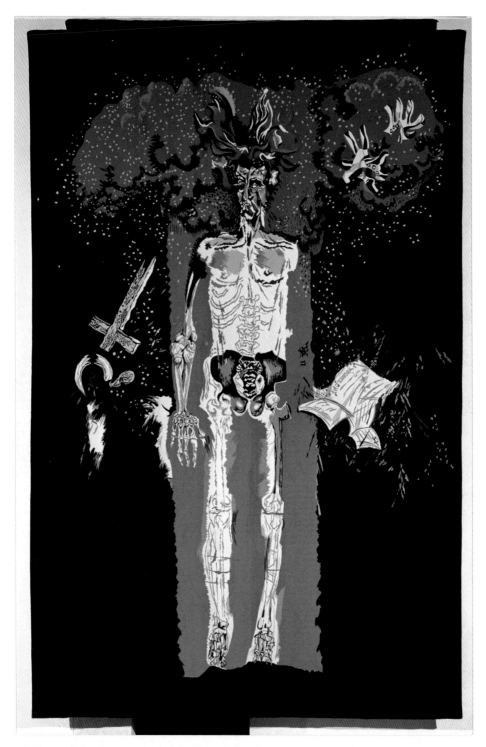

L'Homme d'Hiroshima, a panel from *Le Chant du Monde* (*The Song of the World*), a series of ten monumental tapestries created by Jean Lurcat between 1957 and 1965. Lurcat was inspired by the largest tapestry in the world, *The Apocalypse*, made in Angers in north-west France in the fourteenth century.

The first men to land on the moon. Neil Armstrong (right) and Buzz Aldrin (left), with their third crew member, Michael Collins (centre), meet President Richard Nixon, while still in quarantine following their safe return to earth.

It's all over now. East German border guards simply stand and wait before the demolition of the Berlin Wall begins in November 1989.

Hail to the new South Africa! Nelson Mandela greets residents from the Phola Park squatter camp during his tour of South African townships in September 1990.

An electronic display board in Tokyo makes grim reading as the financial markets plummet following the collapse of Lehman Brothers, the American investment bank, in September 2008.

CHAPTER 3

The Sack of Rome

410 AD

> 'At the beginning of the fifth century AD, Visigoths invaded Rome and ransacked its great monuments. It was a symbolic moment in the decline and fall of the Roman Empire.'

History has passed a derisive judgment on the reputation of the Roman Emperor Honorius. He became ruler of the Western Roman Empire in 395 AD at the age of ten. The lands of Italy were under constant threat of barbarian invasion and Honorius moved his capital from Milan to Ravenna on the east coast, where the sea and marshland provided better protection. But while he and his court enjoyed greater safety, the empire he ruled, particularly its historic capital of Rome, was left exposed to enemy threats. In 408 AD the leader of the Visigoths, Alaric, invaded Italy, laid siege to Rome and extorted a hefty ransom from its occupants. Honorius simply watched from the sidelines. Only when Alaric joined forces with a usurper to the imperial throne did he try to save the situation. Although he persuaded the Visigoth leader to abandon his new ally, he failed to secure a lasting agreement with him. In 410 AD Alaric and the Visigoths returned to Rome and sacked it.

Honorius had a great love for poultry birds, which he kept as pets. On hearing the news that Rome had fallen he is reported to have assumed the messenger was referring to the death of one of his pet hens called 'Roma' and cried out in anguish: 'But it has only just eaten from my own hands!' The story is probably apocryphal but it provides a picture of how the last rulers of the Roman Empire have tended to be regarded by historians. In his *Decline and Fall of the Roman Empire*, the eighteenth-century historian Edward Gibbon observed that 'the amusement of feeding poultry became the serious and daily care of the monarch of the West'. Honorius, he added, 'passed the slumber of his life, a captive in his palace, a stranger in his country, and the patient, almost the indifferent, spectator of the ruin of the Western Empire'. An emperor more concerned about the safety of a hen than the security of a great city is an image that radiates through history. Rome, corrupt and careless, fell to the barbarians through idleness and self-indulgence, a tired rump no longer capable of, or interested in, defending itself. But the Roman Empire did not just suddenly collapse. As the problems surrounding the maintenance of its vast territory increased, its strength slowly deteriorated. No empires last forever: their decline often begins at the peak of their power. Rome, the greatest empire of world history, was no different.

Rome, corrupt and careless, fell to the barbarians through idleness and self-indulgence.

In the century or so before the accession of Constantine in 306 AD there were thirty-five Roman emperors. The first, Pertinax, succeeded to the title in 193 AD; the last, Severus ruled briefly in the period of war prior to Constantine's final victory. Of the thirty-five, nineteen were murdered or executed. Five died in battle; one committed suicide; and another either killed himself or was murdered. One died in captivity after he was captured. The remaining eight died of natural causes, although one of these may have in fact been assassinated. With one exception their names are largely forgotten and in most cases their reigns were alarmingly brief. Only Diocletian, who came to power in 284 AD and died peacefully in retirement during the reign of Constantine after abdicating in 305 AD, brought stability to the management of the Roman Empire. Diocletian's achievement was considerable. He devolved imperial power, appointing a co-emperor, Maximian, to run the western half of the Empire while he retained control of the east. He and Maximian each took the title of 'Augustus' and both of them devolved the responsibility for governing half of their lands to two 'Caesars' who were also their heirs apparent. Diocletian's hope was that this would not only make government more efficient but also ensure a smooth succession.

Called the 'tetrarchy', this was a system that divided the Empire into four quarters, reinforcing it with a large bureaucracy and a greatly strengthened army. Diocletian moved among his people like a deity, a remote and absolute figure trying, after years of dissension and misrule, to resurrect the majesty of imperial office. But the Empire had moved far beyond the ideas that had sustained it when Augustus, the first emperor, was granted his title by the Senate in 27 BC. In his rise to power Augustus displayed appalling ruthlessness, but he also created a system in which the virtues of the old republic lingered on in the Senate and other institutions of Roman life. By the time Diocletian took office any pretension to political representation in the government of the Empire had disappeared. It was a military dictatorship. Half a million men were under arms, deployed across its frontiers from Hadrian's Wall in northern Britain to the foothills of the Atlas Mountains in Africa. Diocletian introduced conscription and changed the way the army operated. It was divided into two with a frontier force that guarded the Empire's boundaries and reserves that could be marched as quickly as possible to trouble spots. Expensive to run, difficult to control and under constant threat of incursion from those it subjected, the Roman Empire had swung slowly from an offensive to a defensive entity. Diocletian restored some of its grandeur but he could not rescue its vitality.

Diocletian's carefully manufactured plans dissolved when he abdicated. The members of the tetrarchy fought among themselves. The ultimate victor, in 324 AD, was Constantine the Great. He rose to be sole Emperor from the position of Caesar and then Augustus in the west, a journey that took him from the city of York, where the army first acknowledged his claim to power, to victories over the Germanic tribes of the Rhineland and after that to great triumphs over his main rivals to the throne, Maxentius and Licinius. History would remember Constantine for his military prowess alone, but his most important contributions to the Roman Empire were more enduring than any success on the battlefield. These were his conversion to Christianity and his building of Constantinople. Christianity was, by the beginning of the third century AD, a powerful force. Generally tolerated and sometimes persecuted, its existence was never, before the age of Constantine, condoned by the authorities. Christianity seemed to them to be un-Roman, a superstition that undermined the civic code and social order that they admired. Societies often look for scapegoats when they suffer and, as the management of the Empire ran into difficulties during the second century AD, Christians became an increasing focus of Roman concern. Diocletian persecuted them mercilessly, so did his immediate successors.

Christians became an increasing focus of Roman concern.

Constantine's own devotion to the Christian idea cannot be certain. While co-emperor with Licinius in 313 AD, he issued the Edict of Milan granting toleration of worship to all Christians, but this could have been the act of a pragmatic politician as much as a convinced believer. As Christianity proliferated, Europe grew used to rulers capable of harnessing religion to their political needs. Whatever his true motives, he took the enormous step during his reign of declaring himself a Christian and supporting the activities of the Orthodox Christian Church – even going so far as to lead an army against a group of dissenting Christians, the Donatists, in North Africa. Although he continued to indulge in some forms of pagan ritual, his acceptance of the main principles of Christian teaching fundamentally changed the nature of the Roman Empire. The Christian Church was still in the very early stages of organisation: its beliefs were a fervent mission and would remain so for centuries to come. Its members were Christians first and Romans second. As their power and influence grew, the idea of what it meant to be 'Roman' began to disappear. This process was exacerbated by the way the Empire, as it aged, amalgamated people from the countries that it ruled into the Roman way of life – it practised multiculturalism long before anywhere else – many of whom absorbed Christianity's ideas as one of its essential features.

The building of Constantinople represented the final rejection of the city where the Roman Empire began. Rome had been in decline for many years. Diocletian, who preferred to stay in the eastern half of the Empire and announced his abdication in Nicodemia, not far from where Constantinople was later built, moved the western capital from Rome to Milan in 293 AD. The Senate was reduced to an institution with municipal rather than imperial responsibilities, but its real power had declined anyway as Diocletian and Constantine tried to control affairs by assuming more power to themselves and their armies. At the same time status replaced responsibility as a reason for office. Sons followed fathers into military, bureaucratic or governmental jobs. Large private estates began to dominate the countryside and the wealthy landlords who owned them became the power brokers of the Roman provinces. The process of

The Roman Empire twisted itself out of shape.

decline was very long. The reign of Constantine the Great was only one of the turning points in a sequence of events leading to the Sack of Rome in 410 AD. Even this was not the final point of collapse. The Empire lost Britain at about the same time that Alaric rampaged through its former capital, but the date of its final end is normally given as 476 AD when a German prince, Odoacer, proclaimed himself King of Italy. Gaul did not technically separate from it until ten years later when its last Roman governor was defeated by Clovis at the Battle of Soissons in 486 AD. In between, Rome was forced to fight on many fronts but it was not involved in a siege where its people and culture were fighting a last-ditch battle for survival. The Roman Empire was so big and its population made up of so many different elements that it would be quite wrong to think of it as a homogenous entity shrinking under the pressure of outside forces. It shifted and turned, absorbed and rejected until it had twisted itself out of shape and was no longer visible as the force it had once been.

Constantinople was made the official capital of the Roman Empire in 330 AD. From that moment on it turned to face the sun as the warm lands of Asia Minor and the Eastern Mediterranean became its preferred sphere of influence. Once the Western Empire finally disintegrated in the second half of the fifth century AD, Constantinople became the heart of a new one,

Byzantium, that lasted for more than a thousand years. By the middle of the seventh century it had shaken off many of its Roman trappings. Oriental in flavour, Greek in language and religion, it enjoyed a rich culture drawn from the many ethnic groups within its boundaries. The history of the west was very different. It too was Christian with the head of its Church stationed in the ancient seat of empire, Rome. But as Roman authority collapsed it fell prey to a great migration of peoples who poured out of the east and the north to feast on the remains of the Empire. Jutes, Angles and Saxons emigrated from the North German lands to overrun Britain; the Franks moved out of territory further south to cross the Rhine into France; and the Visigoths emerged from areas north of the Black Sea to penetrate Italy and Spain. The meticulous, urban pattern of Roman affairs was swept away by a tide of humanity hungry for new land on which to raise their cattle, grow their crops and feed their families. The destruction, according to some, was terrible. The Celtic monk, Gildas, writing in the sixth century AD, described the Anglo-Saxon invasion of Britain: 'In the middle of the streets lay the tops of lofty towers, tumbled to the ground, stones of high walls, holy altars, fragments of human bodies, covered with livid clots of coagulated blood, looking as if they had been squeezed together in a press …'. Some people, Gildas wrote, 'were murdered in great numbers; others, constrained by famine, came and yielded themselves to be slaves forever to their foes.' This image of wanton desecration earned the period between the fall of the Roman Empire in the west and the thin beginnings of a new social order around 800 AD the name 'the Dark Ages' – a time of benighted turmoil in which civilisation became lost.

The long, slow emergence of a Christian continent – Europe – had begun.

The confusion that surrounded the end of the Roman west disguised the birth of a new and ultimately equally powerful creation. Christianity may have contributed to the sapping of the pagan empire in which it was born, but it proved to possess the strength and resources needed for its own survival. It worked its way through the invading peoples with missionary determination: many of their leaders were converted to its beliefs. The Bishop of Rome, abandoned by the empire that had first installed him, set about the construction of his own, based on the Christian message. The Sack of Rome and the events that followed it seemed to leave the former Empire in the west without direction and without hope, while the east, based at Constantinople, was resurrected in a new form. Gradually, however, the balance was restored. The long, slow emergence of the nations of a Christian continent – Europe – had begun.

CHAPTER 4

The Coronation of Charlemagne

800 AD

Charlemagne was a king of the Franks whose conquests greatly extended the territory he ruled. In Rome in 800 AD he was crowned 'Emperor of the Romans' by the Pope, acknowledging his leadership of the Christian countries of Western Europe.

The coronation of Charlemagne in 800 AD is one of history's most intriguing riddles. On Christmas Day the King of the Franks, who had come to Rome to protect the Pope from attacks from the local nobility, entered St Peter's Basilica for a holy service. The building, begun on the orders of the Emperor Constantine in about 330 AD, had grown in importance since its foundation and had become a significant centre of the Christian Church. Very different from the St Peter's of today, it had five aisles, each divided by twenty-one marble columns. Designed in the shape of a Latin cross it had a gabled wooden roof about a hundred feet high. At its entrance was a large atrium known as the 'Garden of Paradise'. It was one of the great architectural glories of the last days of the Roman Empire, a surviving reminder of its ancient splendour.

The congregation cried out: 'To Charles, most pious Augustus, crowned by God.'

Charlemagne may have felt this sense of history as he joined the Pope, Leo XIII, in worship. During the service Leo placed a crown on the King's head and the congregation cried out: 'To Charles, most pious Augustus, crowned by God, great and peace-loving Emperor, life and victory.' This invocation was repeated twice and then, according to a contemporary account, 'after the laudation he was adored by the Pope in the manner of the ancient princes and ... he was called Emperor and Augustus.'

It was clearly a magnificent occasion, but what did it all mean? One of his biographers claimed later that Charlemagne said he would not have entered the church had he known what the Pope intended to do. This may be nothing more than a version of events in which Charlemagne chose judicious self-deprecation in order to cover his tracks. But questions lingered. Of what exactly had he been made emperor? And why? One thing is certain: the coronation of Charlemagne was an event of supreme importance in the history of early medieval Europe.

The Franks were a group of tribes from what is now western Germany who flooded into Gaul (essentially modern France) as the Roman Empire collapsed. Their first great leader was Clovis, who defeated a Roman army at the Battle of Soissons in 486 AD and became the King of the Franks. Clovis was baptised in the Christian faith during a coronation ceremony near Rheims, in whose later cathedral all French kings would be crowned. He left the government of his kingdom to be divided among his four sons and this became the pattern of succession thereafter. Although they regarded their country as one entity, the Franks were governed by different princes belonging to the Merovingian dynasty that Clovis founded. Inevitably they quarrelled among themselves and in some cases lost their power to an important new official called 'the Mayor of the Palace'. The mayor was the person who ran things while the King confined himself to purely ceremonial functions. One of the most successful mayors was Charles Martel who defeated the invading Moors at the Battle of Poitiers (also known as the Battle of Tours) in 732 AD and unified and strengthened the Frankish kingdom. He never took the title of King, happy to preserve the fiction that the monarch was the ruler when in fact all the power was concentrated in his hands. His son, Pepin III, took a different view. After succeeding his father as mayor he sent two emissaries to Rome in 759 AD to ask for the Pope's opinion on who had the rightful authority to govern the Franks. The Pope responded that he thought the right to rule lay with the ability to wield power rather than the entitlement of office. Pepin took this to mean that he could assume the kingship and despatched his hapless monarch, Childeric III, to a monastery, having first shaved off his hair to signify his reduction in status from ruler to monk.

The Pope had an ulterior motive in supporting Pepin's claims. He needed an ally against the Lombards, another Germanic tribe that had conquered large parts of Italy in the sixth century. The Lombards were Arian Christians whose beliefs the Catholic Church regarded as heretical, and therefore brought them into conflict with the papacy. Pepin's assumption of power strengthened the Frankish kings' relationship with Rome. In 754 AD, Pope Stephen II travelled to Paris and anointed Pepin as King, naming him as a protector of the Church at the same time. Pepin died in 768 AD. As was the custom, he divided his lands between his two sons, Carloman and Charles. The two brothers were not close and this separation of power might have set the Frankish kingdom on a course of conflict. But in 771 AD, Carloman died and Charles became the one and only king.

Charlemagne was above all else a warrior. Tall – his skeleton suggested a height of about six feet three inches when his tomb was opened in 1861 – with long white hair and a thick neck, he seems to have enjoyed rude good health. We are told that he liked eating roast meat, which was against the advice of his doctors who urged him to try it boiled. Although he dressed up for big events he preferred to wear the simple costume of the Franks – a linen shirt and breeches covered by a tunic fringed with silk. In winter a coat of animal skins protected him from the cold. In a reign of more than forty years he instigated or led a ceaseless series of campaigns creating an empire that covered the whole of Western and Central Europe, with the exception of the British Isles, southern Italy, Iberia and Scandinavia.

He began his conquests in Lombardy. A year before he succeeded to the throne, Charlemagne, encouraged by his mother, repudiated his wife and married the daughter of the King of Lombardy, Desiderius. A year later he repudiated her too. Desiderius refused to return territory belonging to the papacy which he had captured and, angry at Charlemagne's treatment of his daughter, paid no attention to the Frankish King's requests to do so. Charlemagne crossed the Alps to confront him, laid siege to his capital in Pavia and once he had secured victory, returned the land to the Pope and had himself crowned as King of the Lombards. At the same time he turned his attention to the lands north and east of his kingdom where the Saxons, who were pagans, were resisting him and his attempts to convert them to Christianity. Charlemagne waged war against them for more than thirty years. He defeated their chief, Widukind, in 779 AD, but the Saxons rose up again and in 782 AD Charlemagne suppressed their rebellion with grisly ferocity. He killed about 4,500 and then deported many others, giving their land to loyal Slavic tribes. He also rampaged through country further south, subduing the Duke of Bavaria in 788 AD. After that he moved east to confront the Avars, a people who had migrated from territory south of the Black Sea to build a kingdom in what is today Austria and Hungary. In 795 AD, Charlemagne's son, Pepin, inflicted a final defeat on them and captured all their treasure. It was not only a defeat of the Avar people, but of the Avar race too: from this time on they began to disappear as a separate ethnic group on the European continent.

The only door Charlemagne could not force open was that of the Moors.

The only door that Charlemagne could not force open was that which led to Iberia and the land of the Moors. He was encouraged to cross the Pyrenees by a local Arab ruler who promised him that he could expect strong support were he to attack the Emir of Córdoba, whose Muslim government controlled most of the country. The support was not forthcoming and Charlemagne was forced to retreat. In the Roncesvalles Pass through the Pyrenees his army was ambushed and his nephew, Roland, killed in a desperate rearguard action. The story of his death is enshrined in the eleventh-century *Song of Roland*, one of the oldest works in French literature, in which Roland and his great friend Oliver fight to the bitter end for the glory of their country and their great Emperor.

We in the field have won so many fights,
Combating through so many regions wide
That Charles holds, whose beard is hoary white!
Be you not his who turns from any in flight!
A good vassal has held you this long time;
Never shall France the Free behold his like.

The image of Charlemagne as a great and noble ruler has been preserved in history in the account of his life written in Latin by one of his courtiers, Einhard. Although a work of hero worship, Einhard's *Life of Charlemagne* provides many details about how the Frankish government operated. In particular, Einhard describes how the treasure captured from the Avars was used to pay for Charlemagne's extensive building programme. He tells us that the Franks seized all the wealth and treasure amassed by the Avars over many years. 'No one,' he wrote, 'can recall any war against the Franks that left them richer or better stocked with resources.' Charlemagne used this wealth to build himself a palace in his capital at Aachen (in French Aix-la-Chapelle) and to endow monasteries and churches throughout his kingdom. The Palatine Chapel in Aachen, where Charlemagne's throne can still be seen, is a fine example of the architectural style of his reign. He and his architects borrowed from the past, but added their own refinements in order to build something that was unique to a new imperial age. This was the other side of the relentless warrior: though Charlemagne was a man of rudimentary education, he developed a love of learning and recognised its importance. He invited an English monk, Alcuin of York, to start a school at his court. It became a vigorous cultural center, where a standard script was developed – the 'Carolingian miniscule' – which enabled the Latin alphabet to be understood by all literate people across the Empire. Using simple but revolutionary innovations, such as regular use of capital letters and clear spacing between words, its letters remained the principal form of writing in Europe for 400 years after Charlemagne's death. 'The multitude of learned men is the safety of the world,' said Alcuin, who no doubt observed the Emperor himself struggling to master the art of writing. 'He also tried to write,' said his biographer, Einhard, 'and used to keep tablets and blanks in bed under his pillow that at leisure hours he might accustom his hand to form the letters.' But he had started too late in life to learn such things and 'they met with little success'. Charlemagne's scholars also collected a large collection of Latin and vernacular texts that became the most valuable European library of the period.

The Frankish Empire lacked an administrative infrastructure and the orderly pyramid of control operated by the Romans disappeared as their empire evaporated. Charlemagne, like his father and grandfather before him, had to improvise in order to ensure he could be an effective governor. He adapted a system, first introduced by Charles Martel and continued under Pepin III, of using court officials as imperial legates to make regular visits to designated regions and enforce the Emperor's will. They had responsibility for both secular and religious matters, but finding loyal and competent recruits for this sort of work proved difficult and the system began to falter after Charlemagne's death. His empire, like many others before and after it in world history, was a personal achievement and did not survive politically for long once he was gone. Observing custom he divided his empire between his three sons, but only one of them, Louis, survived and became sole emperor in 814 AD. Three years later his life was saved in an incident in which a wooden bridge collapsed and Louis, seeing this as an omen, decided to share power with his three sons and his nephew. They quarreled among themselves and although Louis managed to preserve unity until his death in 840 AD, civil war continued after that. In 843 AD his three sons met at Verdun on the River Meuse in north-eastern France and carved up all their territory. One of them, Louis, took all the land to the east of the Rhine – Germany; another, Charles, the land to the west – France; and the third, Lothair, the middle portion – the Low Countries, Alsace and Lorraine and Italy. The Empire that Charlemagne created could never be restored as a physical entity. Its legacy lay in the ideas and culture it had invented and protected.

His empire was a personal achievement and did not survive politically for long once he was gone.

Charlemagne's coronation was an event more important for what it symbolised than for what it achieved. He had been to Rome three times before. Perhaps he was aware, as he struggled to read and write and to build a court of learning and the arts around him, that he controlled an empire overshadowed by something grander and more sophisticated than he had managed to build. Or perhaps he thought he could build it. The Roman Empire in the west had collapsed more than 300 years before the Pope called Charlemagne a great and peace-loving emperor and placed the iron crown of Lombardy on his head. Since the fall of Rome, the responsibility for defending the Christian Church had passed to the Empire in the east, based at Constantinople. But in the chaos that followed the invasion of Italy and Gaul by the Germanic tribes, the task of protecting the Church fell naturally to the city of Constantine, the home of the first Christian Roman Emperor. At first it was vigorous in its task. The Emperor Justinian, who reigned from 525 AD to 565 AD, sent his general, Belisarius, to attack the Ostrogoths in Italy and succeeded in briefly recovering Rome itself in 536 AD. Gradually, however, these efforts ebbed away. By the time of his death, Justinian's hope of restoring the Empire had faded completely, and the countries he governed began the final process of separation from its Roman links. Charlemagne, the last and most successful in a line of three powerful Frankish rulers, had brought order to the Europe of the west; and as he did so, long-forgotten ideas of empire were resurrected. This was Charlemagne's achievement. He gave shape and hope to a continent emerging from a long period of disarray. It was upon that shape that it would eventually build its future.

CHAPTER 5

Chinggis Khan Becomes Sole Ruler of the Mongol People

1206

Chinggis Khan – *Chinggis* is now the preferred spelling of Genghis – united all the tribes of the Mongol plains under his leadership in 1206. He went on to build the largest territorial empire the world had ever seen, exerting a lasting influence over the peoples of Eastern Europe, Central Asia and the Far East.

In 1995 *The Washington Post* chose Chinggis Khan as the most important person in world history out of the past thousand years. Dismissing Leonardo da Vinci, Christopher Columbus, Thomas Jefferson and Martin Luther, among others, it opted for the great Mongol leader, arguing: 'As an apostle of the extremes of the last thousand years there exists no better candidate than Chinggis Khan who embodied the half-civilised, half-savage duality of the human race.'

The choice of a conqueror whose historical reputation has tended to be one of brutal savagery was no doubt designed to cause a flutter of surprise among the newspaper's readers. But it was prompted by more than just sensationalism. Chinggis Khan built an empire that stretched from the shores of the Caspian Sea to the Sea of Japan. His successors founded dynasties that ruled China and the whole of Russia and Central Asia for more than 200 years after his death. They opened up trade routes between Europe and the Far East and introduced important innovations, such as printing and firearms, that had a profound effect on the societies they governed.

Chinggis Khan was born in about 1162. Raised near the banks of the Onon River in eastern Mongolia, a region of the world remote even today, Chinggis Khan was a primitive tribesman whose furious energy and sense of destiny turned him into the greatest world leader of the Middle Ages. The main source for information on his life is the *Secret History of the Mongols*, written for the Mongol royal family some time after his death. Part folklore and part fact it was written in the Mongol language and handed down orally through succeeding generations. The original version became lost and was only preserved in a few rare Chinese translations. The work reached the West in the nineteenth century, when the leader of the Russian Orthodox mission to Beijing, Pallady Kafarov, discovered it.

The *Secret History* tells us that Chinggis Khan was born with the name 'Temüjin' and that he emerged from the womb with a clot of blood the size of a knuckle bone grasped in his fist, a sign in folklore that he was destined to become a great leader. His father had just returned from a raid in which he had captured a Tatar called Temüjin and, following a tradition that said that a baby's name should commemorate the most important event at the time of birth, called his son after his prize. Temüjin's grandfather succeeded in uniting the different tribes of the steppe, but on a visit to the Chinese Emperor's court his rough manners led him to tweak the Emperor's beard with disastrous consequences. Thereafter the Chinese attacked the Mongolian tribes, destroying their unity. 'The whole nation was in strife,' the *Secret History* records.

'I am the flail of God,' he told one of his enemies.

By the time Temüjin was born, the tribes of the steppe were a nomadic people who lived off the land and formed alliances with each other as they needed. It was a raw, unstable way of life. Warfare, acts of revenge, raids on others' property and thieving were all commonplace. The people were shamanists: natural events, they believed, were guided by spirits whose activities could only be controlled through the intercession of a shaman, a sort of priest who had the power to communicate with the world of magic beyond human understanding. At the age of eight, Temüjin was betrothed to a girl called Börte from a neighbouring tribe with whom he was left. But his father died soon afterwards and he returned home. His mother, Hoelun, had no means of support and, abandoned by relatives and fellow tribesman, survived as best she could, hunting to feed herself and her children. After seven years of a hand-to-mouth existence, Temüjin was returned to Börte's people and the two young people were married.

Temüjin set about trying to draw the different people of the steppe into one confederation. He was attacked by the Merkit tribe who managed to kidnap Börte. She was given to the brother of the tribal leader as a trophy of war. Temüjin gathered together a large force and succeeded in routing the Merkits and recovering his wife, but she became pregnant as she returned. The paternity of Temüjin's eldest son, Jochi, always remained a matter of doubt as a result. Temüjin's campaigns against other rivals continued. In a final assault he defeated the Naiman tribe, led by a childhood friend of his, and was proclaimed the leader of all the Mongols. In 1206, at a council of chiefs, he was acknowledged as the 'khan', or emperor, of the newly consolidated tribes. A white standard, decorated with a falcon and mounted with a gold trident from which hung four white horse tails, was paraded before the assembled tribesmen. Around the falcon, Temüjin's symbol, were nine points representing their new unity. The horse tails told of their dependence on cavalry and their abiding belief in the power of the horse. Temüjin took the title of 'Chinggis Khan', the universal emperor. A leading shaman declared that he was 'the eternal blue sky', the supreme god of the Mongols. 'I am the flail of God,' he told one of his enemies. 'If you had not committed great sins God would have not sent a punishment like me upon you.' A terrifying force had risen up from the Mongolian steppe, but one that relied on more than pure brutality and violence. Chinggis Khan did not depend only on family ties; he rewarded merit as well. Those who joined him were promised a share in the spoils of future victories and the tribes he conquered were absorbed into his organisation. He even encouraged his mother to look after enemy orphans. His

Those who joined him were promised a share in the spoils of future victories.

harsh upbringing, it seems, taught him how to manage peace as well as how to wage war.

Once unified, the Mongols prepared to look beyond the steppe. Their first target lay to the south where the Tangut people maintained a state in what is today north-western China. Chinggis Khan knew that the Jin dynasty that controlled the rest of northern China would not come to the Tanguts' assistance and after a series of raids in 1205 and 1206 decided to launch a ferocious assault that would destroy them completely. He marched his army 650 miles across desert and over mountains to lay siege to their capital city of Yinchuan. The city and state fell into Mongol hands. The Mongol Emperor then turned his attention to the Jins whose lands ran all along his south-eastern border, across the north of what is today Korea to the Sea of Japan. Chinggis Khan's hordes advanced across a huge area. Their different divisions were sometimes hundreds of miles apart but they kept in touch with each other through scouts and messengers. Capturing such a diffused territory was a complicated task, but in 1211 they overwhelmed the Jin army at the Battle of Badger Pass. The Mongols killed thousands. No one knows how many Jin died – perhaps as many as half a million – but a priest passing through the area ten years later reported that the bones of the victims were still visible on the slopes of the hillside where the battle was fought. The Mongols allowed nothing to stand in their way. They laid siege to towns with catapults, used captives as human shields as they advanced in battle, and flew birds into enemy lines with incendiary devices attached. In 1215 the Mongols captured Beijing: northern China was theirs.

Chinggis Khan then turned west. He absorbed the territory on his south-western front, where the leader of his old tribal enemy, the Naiman, had taken refuge, and then invaded the Khwarez-mian Empire (straddling what is today Iran and Iraq), beyond it. This was an attack of immense importance. It opened up the valu-able silk routes to Mongol control and brought them face to face with the Arab states of Islam. Chinggis Khan led one contingent of his army through northern India and Afghanistan; the other pushed into Armenia and Azerbaijan. He captured Samarkand

and once the Khwarezmian Empire had fallen gave permission to two of his best generals, Subutai and Jebe, to continue their campaign. The two men overran Georgia with astonishing speed and at the Battle of the Kalka River in 1223 defeated a Russian army. When the Russian generals sued for peace they were put to death in a particularly brutal way: six of them were crushed to death under a wooden platform on which Subutai liked to dine. Carrying everything before them the generals encircled the Caspian Sea and made their way back to their Emperor in Mongolia, although Jebe died during the journey. Chinggis Khan's success depended on such unswerving loyalty. 'As felt protects from the wind,' Subatai is supposed to have told him, 'so I will ward off your enemies.'

To this day, on the hour, a bugle call is played from the tower of St Mary's church in Kraków, Poland. The melody is never completed. Each time the call stops abruptly, signifying the moment in 1241 when a bugler tried to warn the city of the approach of the Mongols but was shot in the throat by one of their archers as he sounded the alarm. It is an eerie reminder of what living within the range of a Mongol incursion must have been like. A contemporary Persian historian described how towns were taken unawares by the arrival of Chinggis Khan's armies. 'Suddenly they beheld a small group of horsemen who arrived like a puff of smoke before the gates of the town,' he wrote. Soon the puff of smoke was transformed into a murderous cyclone of hell. In one town, he said, 'no male was spared who stood higher than the butt of a whip and more than 30,000 were counted among the slain; while their small children ... were reduced to slavery'. The walls of the town were reduced to dust and all the remaining inhabitants driven out into the fields.

In one town, he said, 'no male was spared who stood higher than the butt of a whip'.

The Mongols developed a reputation for invincibility, an unstoppable force that tolerated no opposition to its all-consuming advance. But behind their savagery lay strict discipline and a rudimentary political structure. The Mongols had pulled

Chinese Imperial Dynasties

Qing dynasty 221–206 BC

Qin Shi Huangdi, the 'first sovereign emperor of China', founded the first Chinese Empire by uniting several competing kingdoms. The building of the Great Wall began and a central administrative system was established. Unity came at a price. This was a regime renowned for its brutality. When he died, Qin's tomb was guarded by more than 8,000 life-size terracotta warriors. His actual body is buried in a pyramid believed to be laid out as a model of the Chinese world, complete with palaces and a mercury river.

Han dynasty 206 BC–220 AD

This was a time of cultural and technological development, territorial consolidation and cultural and intellectual growth. The Silk Road began to increase trade with the outside world, Confucianism became the state philosophy and Buddhism was first introduced to China.

Three Kingdoms and Six Dynasties Period 220–80 AD; the Jin dynasty 265–420 AD; and the Sixteen Kingdoms 304–439 AD

The collapse of the Han dynasty led to a long period of disunity and loss of central power as the kingdoms of the Wei, Shu and Wu fought against one another. The Sima family tried to unite the country under the Jin dynasty but its divisions led to the War of the Eight Princes. The Eastern Jin fled south and founded a new court near modern Nanjing. Inner China was then governed by a succession of rulers from nomadic tribes in the north who called themselves 'Emperor' or 'King'. After the Eastern Jin collapsed in 420 AD, civil war broke out between the Wei dynasty in the north and the Liu Song dynasty to the south. Despite these divisions, China's art and culture continued to develop and there were advances in science, medicine and mathematics.

Sui dynasty 589–618

The Sui reunified the country and attempted costly expansionist military campaigns. They constructed the 1,500km-long Grand Canal linking the Yellow and Yangzi Rivers, which is still the longest canal in the world. Essential for the country's communications system it became an important feature in its economic development.

Tang dynasty 618–906

Seen as a golden age in Chinese History, the Tang Empire became the most powerful in the world with Chang'an as the world's largest city. China became open to foreign ideas and culture and the arts, particularly poetry, were allowed to flourish. The Tang dynasty is distinguished by having the only female Empress, Wu Zetian. In 756 a military commander called An Lushan led a rebellion against the Emperor and once more power began to ebb slowly away from central government.

Five Dynasties and Ten Kingdoms Period 907–60

The shift of power from the centre to the outer regions continued after the collapse of the Tang and China again became divided among warring kingdoms. The north witnessed the rapid succession of five dynasties and twelve independent states were established, mainly in the south.

Song dynasty 960–1279

The Song dynasty united inner China once again but lost control of northern China in 1127. It was the first government in the world to issue paper money – Europe did not have such a thing until the seventeenth century – and also turned to shipbuilding and sea trade, using compasses for the first time. A new type of rice was cultivated to help feed the growing population in expanding cities.

Yuan dynasty 1279–1368

The successful conquests of the Mongol Khans established rule over China with Beijing as the new capital. The Mongols were nomads from the steppes of Asia but once they conquered China they took on the trappings of an imperial dynasty. Marco Polo visited their court at the end of the thirteenth century. One of the greatest classical works in Chinese literature, *The Romance of the Three Kingdoms*, is thought to date from towards the end of their period in power. Published in twenty-four volumes and 800,000 words long, it tells the story of the turbulent times before China was reunited under the Jin dynasty and extols the Confucian values of loyalty to one's family, friends and superiors.

Ming dynasty 1368–1644

The Ming – the word means 'brilliant' in Chinese – was founded by a former peasant who overthrew the Yuan. To begin with the capital was based in Nanjing, but in 1403 moved back to Beijing where work on the Forbidden City, the largest palace complex in the world, began. This was a time of economic growth, commercialisation and urbanisation accompanied by a flowering of literature and art. Chinese porcelain was exported to Europe in huge quantities. Under the Ming, China sought to extend its control across the Indian Ocean and organised a series of large maritime expeditions under the command of its admiral, a Muslim eunuch called Zheng He. Trade with countries such as Spain, Portugal and Holland developed strongly but by the beginning of the seventeenth century, China's supply of silver, its principal medium of exchange, began to dry up because of wars among the European powers.

Qing dynasty 1644–1911

The last ruling dynasty of China was founded by the Manchus, an ethnic minority from present-day north-east China. The Qing forced all Chinese men to wear their hair as they did, in a pigtail, as a symbol of Manchu control over the country's other ethnic groups. The eighteenth century was a high point in China's development. Its borders reached their widest extent and the country was run by a highly efficient centralised bureaucracy. In the nineteenth century, the Qing began to lose control of the country following the Opium Wars, threats from Japan and internal rebellion. The Republic of China was created when the last Emperor was deposed in 1911.

themselves out of a nomadic, anarchic past in one extraordinary surge. Their acts of conquest were due as much to their management skills as their natural brutality. Once subordinated, people lived under a '*pax Mongolica*', a code of laws that kept the peace. Blood feuds, adultery and theft were forbidden. A degree of religious toleration was allowed, essential in an empire that embraced Muslim, Buddhist and Christian beliefs. After Chinggis Khan's death, a Christian missionary, William of Rubruck, was told by Möngke, Great Khan of the Mongolian Empire, that just as God had created different fingers on a single hand, so had he given people different beliefs and customs. William of Rubruck's accounts of his time with the Mongols persuaded the thirteenth-century English philosopher and scientist, Roger Bacon, to conclude that they were a people who had 'succeeded by science'. Although warlike, their success was due to their devoting 'their leisure to the principles of philosophy'.

The conquests of Chinggis Khan were continued by his successors. His eldest son, Jochi, died before him, relieving his father of deciding on the tricky issue of his legitimacy and therefore entitlement to part of the Empire. Ögedei, his third son, inherited his father's title and the lands of eastern Asia, including China. Beneath him were two of Jochi's sons, Batu and Orda, who came into possession of the Empire's western section, later known as the Golden Horde, an area that covered the territory north-west of the Black and Caspian Seas and which eventually stretched into Poland and Hungary. Chagatai, Chinggis Khan's second son, became the ruler of Central Asia and northern Iran while his youngest, Tolui, received the Mongol homeland, essentially present-day Mongolia. Ögedei was thought to be his father's favourite. He had the character and ability to pursue Chinggis Khan's ambitions, consolidating Mongol victories over the Tanguts of northern China and extending the Empire's boundaries into Persia and Eastern Europe. He also turned against the dynasty ruling the rest of China, the Song, starting a war that would see Kublai Khan, Chinggis Khan's grandson, become the founder of the Yuan dynasty and the Mongol Emperor of all China in 1279.

Chinggis Khan died in 1227. His death was kept secret to allow time for his heirs to prepare for their new responsibilities. Legend has it that his funeral escort killed anyone who crossed its path: only its members knew the location of the unmarked grave in which the great conqueror was interred. It is believed that it lies somewhere near his birthplace close to the Onon

River, but no one knows for sure. When he was little it was said there was 'fire in his eyes and light in his face'. He lived a wild, fierce life in which he and his brothers complained that 'apart from our shadows we have no friends'. But when he grew up he changed the shape of his world. When he lived he was all-powerful; but in death he retreated to the anonymity from which he once so frighteningly emerged.

CHAPTER 6

The Fall of Constantinople

1453

On Tuesday 29th May 1453, the city of Constantinople was captured by the Muslim army of the Ottoman Empire. The city had stood as an important Christian capital ever since it was founded by the Roman Emperor Constantine more than a thousand years before.

Apologising for acts of history has become a fashionable part of modern political life. Britain, Australia, Canada, Japan and Germany have all apologised, or expressed sorrow, for activities in their past. On the whole these regrets cover comparatively recent history – the slave trade, the Holocaust, the mistreatment of indigenous people by expanding colonial powers. In the religious world, however, expressions of remorse reach further back. On a journey to Greece and the Eastern Mediterranean in May 2001, Pope John Paul II told the Archbishop of Athens that 'some events' had left 'deep wounds in the minds and hearts of people to this day'. He was thinking, he said, 'of the disastrous sack of Constantinople', and he entrusted 'the heavy burden of the past' to God's endless mercy.

The event to which Pope John Paul referred took place in 1204. Crusaders from France and Italy bound for the Holy Land diverted instead to Constantinople and overran the city. The Christian soldiers of the west looted the Christian capital of the east, murdering and terrorising its population. Their barbarous behaviour appalled many European onlookers, not least because its mindless savagery revealed the fragility of Christendom's historic bastion. The city of Constantine the Great, from which the Roman Empire had first proclaimed the Christian message, was unable to defend itself from fellow-believers. Ultimately it would surrender altogether and fall to the forces of Islam.

The fall of Rome in 410 AD and the subsequent disintegration of the Western Roman Empire had handed the legacy of maintaining the Roman achievement to Constantinople. Standing at a strategic crossroads between Europe and Asia, the city and Empire found themselves under constant threat. During his long reign in the sixth century AD, the Emperor Justinian had managed to recover much of the Empire's lost territory and extend its power across Asia Minor into North Africa to the east, and through the Balkans to the banks of the Danube in the west. But after that the jurisdiction of Constantinople began to shrink. As Europe fell prey to invading Germanic tribes, and Arabs fired by the message of Mohammed conquered the Middle East, what had once been the mighty Roman Empire of the east shrank to what is now Greece and Turkey. This was Byzantium, a name derived from the ancient Greek name for Constantinople, 'Byzantion'.

The city would surrender altogether and fall to the forces of Islam.

To contemporaries it remained a crucially important centre, a reminder of the greatness of Rome and the triumph of Christianity. Its economy was strong and supported by an efficient network of trading routes. The Emperor was the sole and absolute ruler, drawing his authority from God, and managing the government through a large and well-ordered bureaucracy. The culture was a mixture of Greek and oriental influences, dominated by the interpretation of the Christian religion. The painting and manufacture of icons became a principal source of art, but their veneration resulted in fierce controversy during the eighth and ninth centuries. Iconoclasts believed that worshipping physical representations of the Holy Family was heresy and should not be reproduced or encouraged by 'the evil art of painters'. But controversy was not enough to assuage creativity: Constantinople was the world's link to a glorious classical heritage and its citizens saw themselves as the intellectual heirs of Greece and Rome.

The fortunes of Byzantium revolved around the ability of its leaders to maintain or expand its territory. Basil II, Emperor between 976 and 1025, concentrated on trying to regain its

Balkan lands from the Bulgars. In 1014 he defeated them at the Battle of Kleidon in what is now south-west Bulgaria. Having captured 15,000 prisoners it is said that he ordered ninety-nine out of a hundred to be blinded, leaving one in each group with the sight of a single eye to lead the rest home. When the Bulgarian Emperor, Samuel, saw the distressed remnants of his army he suffered a heart attack and died. For almost exactly a hundred years between 1081 and 1180 Byzantium was ruled by three emperors of the Komnenos dynasty who were successful in restoring much of the Empire's power, both militarily and economically. Once again it was able to dominate the Balkans and the Eastern Mediterranean, withholding advances from the Turks who were already beginning to threaten its eastern frontier. Its art and culture flourished. It enjoyed a network of alliances with European powers. But one thing it had lost forever: its right to be regarded as the leader of the Christian Church. In 1054 ecclesiastical bickering on matters of theology between the papacy and the Patriarchate of Constantinople came to

Its citizens saw themselves as the intellectual heirs of Greece and Rome.

a head. The Pope's legates insisted that the patriarch, Michael Cerularius, accept that Rome was the Head of the Church, but he refused. The cardinal leading the Roman delegation promptly excommunicated the patriarch, who then excommunicated him in return.

This division, known as 'The Great Schism', was serious. It opened an unhealable wound and provoked tensions between the Orthodox east and the Catholic west that spilled over into the commercial life of the city. Constantinople began to rely on the trading strengths of the Italian city-states, such as Venice, Genoa and Pisa. Their merchants used their financial muscle to snub imperial authority and they began to fight among themselves. In 1182 popular resentment at their behaviour turned to violence and a mob massacred thousands of Latin inhabitants of Constantinople. The clergy was a particular target of its anger. The Pope's representative was executed and his head dragged through the streets tied to the tail of a dog. Constantinople came to be viewed with deep suspicion by its Western European neighbours. When in 1202 the army of the Fourth Crusade found itself stuck in Venice unable to pay its debts, the Venetian authorities decided to turn the situation to their advantage. Venice had agreed to fund the cost of the Crusade, which sought to conquer Jerusalem by mounting an invasion through Egypt. But the number of knights recruited for the expedition was far fewer than expected and they were unable to afford the huge fleet the Venetians had assembled on their behalf. Venice would not let the Crusaders leave until they had paid their debts. They struck a deal in which the religious mission was temporarily sacrificed in favour of political and military objectives. In return for the money owed, the Crusaders would agree to capture the city of Zara (now 'Zadar') on the Dalmatian coast, which had declared independence and removed itself from Venetian influence. Some Crusaders demurred and left the expedition; the rest carried out the plan.

Having secured Zara the Crusaders went one step further. A Byzantine prince, Alexius Angelus, promised them money and men if they would help him topple the reigning Emperor in Constantinople, who had succeeded to the throne after deposing his brother. It was an offer too good to refuse: in 1204 the Crusaders sailed to the ancient Christian capital and sacked it. A contemporary historian described the appalling scenes. 'In the alleys, in the streets, in the temples, complaints, weeping lamentations, grief, the groanings of men, the shrieks of women, wounds, rape, captivity, the separation of those most closely united. Nobles wandered about ignominiously, those of venerable age in tears, the rich in poverty ... All places everywhere were filled full of all kinds of crime. Oh, immortal God, how great the afflictions of men, how great the distress!'

The Crusaders' attack on Constantinople was a blow from which the Empire of Byzantium never recovered, although it survived in a fragmented form for another 250 years. Venice, having contributed to the attack on the city, helped itself to three eighths of the Byzantine Empire. The rest became a feudal Crusader kingdom. The Roman Catholic Church was restored and one of the leaders of the Crusade, Count Baldwin of Flanders, was crowned

Emperor. This clumsy arrangement, resented by the population and attacked by Bulgaria in the west, collapsed in 1261 when the exiled Byzantine nobility recaptured Constantinople from its base in Nicaea in Asia Minor. But Byzantium was no longer a cohesive whole. Surrounded by enemies and, by the 1340s, devastated by a civil war, it became increasingly isolated. Ultimately it was encircled by a new world power – the Empire of the Ottoman Turks.

The founder of the Ottoman Empire was Osman, from which the name Ottoman is derived. He was the leader of a group of Turks who had fled westward into Anatolia to escape the Mongol invasions of the early thirteenth century. He succeeded his father in 1281 and by the time of his death in 1326 had given his people an important toehold on the fringes of Europe, with a capital at Bursa on the borders of the Sea of Marmara. Like the Mongols from whom they had originally fled, the Turks were fierce fighters and in 1346 they helped the Byzantine Emperor, John VI, secure the imperial throne at the end of the civil war. Asked to intervene again in 1352, the Ottoman armies moved further west and by 1365 had established their capital at Adrianople (modern Edirne) on what is today the Greek-Turkish border. Constantinople was completely surrounded. From their new capital the Turks waged war against the Balkan states to the north. At the Battle of Kosovo in 1389 they defeated the army of the Serbs; at Nicopolis in 1396 they defeated a Christian force made up of soldiers belonging to Hungary, France and Venice. They suffered a disastrous defeat at the hands of Tamerlane, the Mongol conqueror, at Ankara in 1402, when their sultan was captured and imprisoned, but twenty years later had revived sufficiently to be on the march once more. At the second battle of Kosovo in 1448 they won another important victory after a series of long and bloody campaigns against the Christian west led by the Hungarian general, John Hunyadi. When Sultan Mehmed II succeeded to the Ottoman throne in 1451 the capture of Constantinople became his priority. While it stood as a Christian city it remained an obstacle to the consolidation of Ottoman power, a symbol of defiance and a cause for Crusaders to unite against the Muslim world.

Constantinople collapsed, as it had been built, with a ruler called Constantine at its head. He watched helplessly as the Turks began to construct forts along the Dardanelles and a castle on the Bosphorous to control all shipping in and out of the Black Sea. The story goes that he rejected the offer from a Hungarian engineer to build him enormous cannon so their inventor sold his services to the Turks instead. The machines were transported to the battlefield by 70 oxen and 10,000 men. The Byzantines built a boom across the Golden Horn, the estuary that flowed beneath the city walls, but the Turks dragged their ships around it across wooden logs laid out on its opposite shore. Constantine XI, aware that an attack was imminent, appealed for help to the Christian rulers of the west, but none was forthcoming. For fifty-five days the Turks kept up a bombardment. On the morning of the 29th May, believing that a relief force of Hungarians might be approaching, Mehmed II ordered a full assault. The last Constantine was killed defending the city that the first emperor of that name had raised to glory 1100 years before. 'This was surely,' said one contemporary historian, 'the most grievous catastrophe known to history, and the complete destruction of the Greeks matches the fall of Troy.' The Western powers were largely to blame for what happened. Rivalry among themselves, combined with a dislike of the independent Orthodox Church, prevented them from defending the one thing they prized above all else: Saint Sophia, the great monument of Christianity in the East, became a mosque.

The last Constantine was killed defending the city that the first emperor of that name had raised to glory 1,100 years before.

The Turkish victory was a decisive moment in the history of Europe and the world. Originally the Turks were, like the Franks and Mongols, a nomadic people displaced by invasion and divided into tribal loyalties who learned to unite. In capturing Constantinople, which they renamed Istanbul, they laid the foundations of an empire effectively the same in size as the Eastern Roman Empire. They displayed strong governmental and military skills: their infantry, called 'janissaries', became a feared fighting force. But they understood the common sense of toleration. Greek culture inevitably began to die out slowly under Turkish rule, but

Christianity and other religions were allowed to survive under the 'millet' system which permitted separate beliefs to flourish as long as their followers were loyal to the Empire. Although Christianity enjoyed some measure of protection, Christian Europe did not. The Ottoman Empire did not turn from its ambition to capture territory in the west until the end of the seventeenth century. By the end of the fifteenth they had taken Bosnia and Herzegovina; in the first quarter of the sixteenth they conquered Serbia and Hungary. They captured Cyprus and Crete and battered frequently at the gates of Vienna, mounting their last attack on the Austrian capital in 1683 when they besieged it for two months.

Until the Ottomans took Constantinople in 1453, Europe and the Near East were connected, not by ethnicity, but by religion. Christianity's Nicene Creed, setting out the fundamental principles of its belief, was adopted at Nicaea, east of Constantinople in 325 AD. Many of the early fathers who shaped Christian doctrine, like Augustine, Ignatius, Origen and Polycarp – came from the towns and cities of the Middle East and North Africa. The birthplace of Christianity was lost to Islam in the seventh century AD, but its ideas and traditions continued to flourish as the dominant force in Asia Minor: Byzantium was always as strongly Christian as Italy, England or France. The Ottoman Empire changed all that. It brought the religious frontier between Europe and the Orient a thousand miles westwards, opening a gulf between East and West that has widened with the passing of time.

Today Turkey, as an ally of Western Europe and the United States, is seeking to join the European Union but some existing members object to its application on the grounds that it is not a European country. A former President of France, Valéry Giscard d'Estaing, said that if Turkey were allowed to join it would, in his opinion, be 'the end of Europe'. Six hundred and fifty years ago there were many in Europe who ached to see the capital of the Turkish Empire united in common cause with the West. Perhaps those long-forgotten ambitions will eventually be resurrected, not by the zeal of religion, but by the more practical benefits of commerce.

The Crusades

For nearly 200 years, Christian Europe was engaged in a series of military campaigns aimed at restoring Christian control over the Holy Land. They never achieved their aim, but the impact of the wars they fought was far reaching.

The eleventh century saw a flourishing of intense Christian piety coupled with growing hostility towards Muslims. In 1095 the Byzantine Emperor, Alexius I, appealed to Pope Urban II for help to resist Muslim attacks on his territory in the Byzantine Empire. The Pope saw the advantages of a Christian 'just war' which might reunite a Christian world divided since the Great Schism of 1054 which had divided Constantinople and Rome. He also saw it as an opportunity to bolster the power of the papacy. He exhorted all Christians to join the war against the Turks, promising those who did that they would receive immediate remission of their sins. Soon, though, Crusaders identified a bigger prize – the recapture of the Holy Land itself.

Within four years, Crusaders besieged Antioch and Jerusalem where they massacred large numbers of Muslims and Jews. 'The slaughter was so great that our men waded in blood up to their ankles,' wrote one Frankish observer. Four Crusader states, including the Kingdom of Jerusalem, were created. In reality these 'kingdoms' were little more than a group of towns along the Mediterranean coast crippled by isolation from Europe and the unwillingness of European countries to send large-scale reinforcements. As the twelfth century progressed, Muslim forces captured Antioch in 1149 and Damascus in 1154. A Second Crusade was launched in 1147 to defend Jerusalem but enjoyed no lasting success. Jerusalem was lost to the Islamic leader Saladin in 1187 and all the remaining Crusader strongholds were recaptured by 1291.

The story of the Crusades after 1187 is the story of the repeated failure to reconquer the Holy Land. The Crusaders, even though they were supported by the might of Europe and the papacy, never achieved what they were after. The Third Crusade, led by Richard I of England – the 'Lionheart' – managed to recapture Acre and Jaffa but stopped short of Jerusalem. Pope Innocent III then called for a Fourth Crusade, hoping to take advantage of the civil war raging in Egypt after Saladin, Egypt's ruler, died. Lacking funds for their fleet, the Crusaders made a detour to Constantinople where they sacked the Eastern capital of Christianity. They never made it to the Holy Land. Several other Crusades followed in the early thirteenth century. The Sixth Crusade managed to retake Jerusalem, Nazareth and Bethlehem between 1228–29. But it was not to last; Muslims regained control in 1244. Once again, European leaders rallied to the cause, organising a further three Crusades all of which failed.

The Crusades gave Christianity a bad name and widened the gulf between it and Islam. But they opened up the lands of the Eastern Mediterranean to trade and commerce and contributed to the profitable development of the Italian city-states such as Venice and Genoa. Christianity suffered greatly as knights and their retinues brawled and murdered their way from West to East, but the secular activities of merchants and traders often prospered in their wake.

CHAPTER 7

The Conquest of Mexico

1521

In 1521, after a two-year campaign, a Spanish force under the command of Hernán Cortés defeated the Aztec people of Mexico. Just over ten years later, Francisco Pizarro conquered the Incas of Peru. These victories changed the continent of South America forever.

On 19th January 1927, Europe's last colonial link with Mexico, Princess Charlotte of Belgium, died quietly at the Castle of Bouchot at Meise near Brussels. As the Empress Carlota she had sat as consort to her husband, Maximilian, when he occupied the Mexican throne for a brief period in the middle of the nineteenth century. The Empress lost her mind, driven into a state of mental collapse by the extraordinary events of their reign together.

In 1821 Mexico gained its independence from Spain, exactly 300 years after Cortés and his soldiers first conquered it. Independence, as often happens, brought neither peace nor liberty. It was a big country. Its territory stretched into what is today a large corner of the southern United States and included all of Texas, California, New Mexico, Nevada, Arizona and Utah. Spanish settlers first occupied the area around San Francisco in 1776, the same year as the Declaration of Independence. In the main the people were divided between a landowning elite, descended from Spanish colonial families and the mixed-race population who represented the majority. Divided in government it also began to lose its northern states to America. Texas declared its independence in 1836 and joined the United States ten years later. By 1848 the frontier between Mexico and its northern neighbour had shrunk to the line of the Rio Grande.

A civil war in Mexico between 1858 and 1861 resulted in the victory of a liberal reformer, Benito Juárez, but he came to power in a country that was sadly reduced. Furthermore he had no money to repay foreign creditors in France, Britain and Spain from whom the Mexican government had first borrowed money on achieving independence. When he suspended interest payments on the debt, the European nations decided to send a fleet to try to get their money back by force. The British and Spanish withdrew when they realised that the French ambition was not simply to collect debt, but to conquer the country. Napoleon III, the French Emperor, backed by a group of Mexican conservatives, offered the throne of Mexico to Archduke Ferdinand Maximilian of Austria, which he accepted. In 1864 he installed himself with his wife in Mexico City, but his position was hopeless. The liberals refused to recognise him; the conservatives became suspicious when he supported policies of reform; and the French, realising that conquering a South American country was no longer an easy matter, withdrew. Maximilian chose not to go with them. His wife then left the country to try to enlist help from European rulers, while Maximilian's sense of duty kept him in Mexico. In 1867 he was captured by the army of Benito Juárez and executed. His death and the sad decline of his widow, Charlotte, is an operatic story, a hardly credible cameo in the turbulent history of the Americas.

Like the Holy Roman Emperor, Charles V, who occupied the Spanish throne when the first forces landed in Mexico in 1519, Maximilian was a Habsburg. But he made a mistake that his ancestor would not have done. All experiments designed to regenerate European royalty in the territories of the colonial world ultimately ended in failure. On the whole kings and queens left the management of empire to the people who knew it best – buccaneering soldiers, sailors, mercenaries and merchants, and in the New World, conquistadors.

To those living in Christian Europe during the second half of the fifteenth century, the frontiers of the continent seemed to be shrinking. The fall of Constantinople in 1453 had finally put paid to the fiction of an Eastern Roman Empire: the Ottoman Empire was now the greatest power in south-east Europe and the Eastern Mediterranean. The last of the Moors were driven out of the Iberian Peninsula in 1492, the same year that Christopher Columbus reached the Americas; but this was the final act of a long, drawn-out process that hardly compensated for the loss of so much influence elsewhere. Spain's trade routes with Asia were severely disrupted by the Ottoman advance. It was hardly surprising, therefore, that the country's settlers fell upon the newly discovered islands of the Caribbean with such speed and purpose. Supported by a papal bull commanding them to conquer the pagan inhabitants and convert them to Christianity, adventurers began to arrive in considerable numbers within a few years of Columbus's discovery. Among them was Hernan Cortés, an ambitious and restless Castilian who rose to become the mayor of Cuba's capital township, Santiago, after fifteen years. In 1519 he was commissioned by the Governor of Cuba, Diego Velázquez, to lead an expedition to explore and conquer the Mexican interior, but this was revoked at the last minute because of disagreeable relations between the two men. Cortés, hungry for such an opportunity, ignored his governor's orders and set sail anyway. It was a typically rash act of a man whose motives were often personal. The subjugation of the Aztecs was in no small measure due to the vanity of Hernan Cortés.

The subjugation of the Aztecs was in no small measure due to the vanity of Hernan Cortés.

The Aztecs – or Mexicas – were a nomadic tribe that had settled in the central valley of Mexico from about the middle of the twelfth century. By the time the Spaniards arrived at the beginning of the sixteenth century, the Aztecs had expanded to become the dominant power, forming alliances with some tribes in order to conquer the rest which then became vassal states. It was a process not dissimilar from that which had seen the great powers of Asia and Europe, the Franks, Mongols and Turks, achieve their positions of supremacy. The Aztec capital, Tenochtitlan (from 1585, part of 'Mexico City'), was built on a lake, Lake Texcoco, and connected to the neighbouring city of Tlatelolco by a series of canals and causeways. It was big, with a bustling market and fresh water brought by an aqueduct from springs nearby: the Spaniards were impressed by the cleanliness of its citizens who liked to bath more frequently than they did. The population ran into tens, possibly hundreds, of thousands – certainly bigger than most European cities of the time. 'I do not know how to describe it,' wrote one conquistador, long after he had returned to Spain, 'seeing things as we did that had never been heard of or seen before, not even dreamed about.' This extraordinary place, full of temples and palaces, was also the capital of the Aztec religion. They believed in gods and demons, many of whom originated from the sun and whose humours had to be appeased by human sacrifice. The Aztecs were warriors: they needed to be, in order to capture prisoners to sacrifice for their religious beliefs.

Cortés landed on the Mexican coast on the site of the modern city of Vera Cruz. Aware that he had disobeyed the orders of the Governor by setting off on his voyage, he scuttled the ships of his little fleet to prevent any of his men from going back to Cuba. He formed an alliance with the Tlax-calans, a tribe who resented the influence of the Aztecs and, accompanied by a native woman who had become his mistress, marched inland. At Cholula, the second biggest city after Tenochtitlan, he massacred thousands of Mexicans when he suspected that they were about to turn against him.

Accompanied by a native woman who had become his mistress, Cortés marched inland.

After three months he reached the capital of the Aztecs where he was met by their leader, Moctezuma. Cortés wanted three things: the cessation of the Aztecs' pagan rituals, their conversion to Christianity and their gold. He took Moctezuma hostage to enforce his demands. Events then took an extraordinary turn. Cortés learned that the Governor of Cuba had sent another force to Mexico to take charge of the expedition and arrest him. Leaving some men behind in Tenochtitlan, he took the rest of his band back towards the coast, surprised his pursuers and overcame them. He then persuaded them to come with him back to the Aztec capital which, he explained, was full of gold. They complied, but when they reached Tenochtitlan they discovered matters had slipped out of control: the troops Cortés had left behind had murdered some of the Aztecs because they feared an attack and Moctezuma had lost the confidence of his people. At this point, Moctezuma died, perhaps killed on the orders of Cortés and the Spaniards decided they had no choice but to flee. Grabbing as much gold as they could they tried to make their escape, but many of them were killed and their looted treasure lost. Cortés was desperate. His only chance of retrieving the situation lay in persuading the Tlaxcalans to join the Spaniards in an attack on Tenochtitlan and in 1521 their combined forces laid siege to the city. It was captured and razed to the ground. The first Europeans to see the city in all its splendour were the last.

The conquest of Peru followed a similar pattern to that of Mexico. From the end of the thirteenth century the Inca people began to establish an empire that eventually extended through much of the western side of the South American continent. At its centre stood the mountain range of the Andes with its lakes, rivers and fertile valleys. Its capital was the town of Cuzco, 11,000 feet high, in what is today modern Peru. But Inca influence also stretched north as far as the modern border between Ecuador and Colombia and, by the time the Spanish arrived, as far south as Chile and parts of Argentina. Here too the people worshipped a sun god and sometimes carried out human sacrifice. They were tough and well organised: their lands were divided into four sections under the supreme authority of their ruler, the 'Sapa Inca'. They were industrious builders. The city of Machu Picchu, for long lost to Western eyes and only rediscovered at the beginning of the twentieth century, is one of the most famous archaeological sites in the world, a magnificent example of the Incas' astonishing architectural talents.

This civilisation was destroyed by a gang of Spanish soldiers under the command of another adventurer, Francisco Pizarro, a second cousin of Cortés. He had made a number of unsuccessful journeys along the western coast of South America but had discovered enough to convince himself that great treasure lay inland. In 1529 he received a licence from Isabella of Portugal, the wife of Charles V, to 'continue for us and in our name and in the name of the royal crown of Castile, the said discovery, conquest and colonisation of the said province of Peru'. Three years later, with only 160 men rather than the 250 men his instructions stipulated, Pizarro arrived on the Peruvian coast. The Incas were embroiled in a civil war in which one of their leaders, Atahualpa, had defeated his half-brother, Huáscar. The Spaniards marched to Cajamarca in the north of the country where Atahualpa was encamped. After a meeting between the two sides, Pizarro's troops killed the Inca leader's bodyguard and took him prisoner. He offered his captors gold in return for his life. The Spaniards took both: Pizarro put Atahualpa on trial on a charge of plotting against him and had him executed. When the Incas rose up against him he crushed their rebellion and in 1533 entered their capital in Cuzco.

The Spanish conquest of South America was based, essentially, on two things: language and religion. The Spaniards taught the indigenous people their own tongue and inculcated them with Roman Catholicism. The Inquisition was established soon after the arrival of the first settlers. As with other colonising powers in Europe, the Spanish regarded their overseas territories as extensions of their domestic realms, with the monarch's representatives operating from its principal centres in Mexico, which they called New Spain, and Peru. The areas they valued most were Mexico, which had good agriculture; the Caribbean islands, which produced sugar; and Peru, which had silver mines. Peruvian treasure kept the Spanish Empire well supplied from the moment of Pizarro's conquest and helped pay for ambitious expeditions including the Spanish Armada and the war in the Netherlands. The Spanish introduced a system in which settlers were given *encomiendas*, or small estates: they exercised feudal control over a collection of villages, subjecting their populations to a form of serfdom. As the estates grew, particularly in the Caribbean, another form of forced labour, African slavery, was introduced to the mix. But although there was a clear distinction between the European overlords and their native 'inferiors', this did not extend to matters of sex and human relationships. Unlike the French and the British, the Spanish (and in Brazil, the

Portuguese) interbred, creating a class that came to resent the wealth and status of its European 'superiors'.

Some of the clergy had the courage to criticise the injustices meted out to these native populations. Bartolomé de las Casas, who first visited South America as a settler but later became a Dominican friar, tried to persuade the Spanish government that its treatment of the indigenous people of the colonies was unjust. In 1542 he published a book called *The Destruction of the Indies* in which he condemned his countrymen for their 'ambition and avarice'. They had assaulted 'innocent sheep ... like most cruel tigers, wolves and lions hunger starved, studying nothing for the space of forty years after their first landing but the massacres of these wretches'. His appeal for a more humanitarian approach to colonisation was not entirely ignored but he could do little to divert the course of events. Spain's territories in the New World remained, in Spanish eyes, an extension of the European homeland. This attempt to smother an indigenous civilisation with an imported one had repercussions that many parts of South America feel to this day.

Hernan Cortés died in Spain in 1547. Following his victory over the Aztecs he was made Governor and Captain-General of New Spain. However his lordly manner irritated his compatriots and he was forced to return home in 1528 to secure royal support. He returned in 1530 with a grand title, Marquis of the Oaxaca Valley, but no real power and retired to his estates from which he organised further voyages of exploration. He went back to Spain in 1541 where he died six years later, grumbling about the treatment he had received from the Spanish Crown. Pizarro, meanwhile, was also made a marquis and installed as the Governor of Peru in its new capital at Lima. He quarrelled with one of his fellow adventurers, Diego de Amlagro, who claimed that Pizarro had promised him the city of Cuzco in the division of the spoils. Pizarro had him killed. Three years later Pizarro himself was assassinated when Amalgro's supporters stormed his palace in Lima. The men who conquered South America died as they had lived, wealthy and ennobled, squabbling and fighting, but still hungry for more.

Kings, Queens and Colonies: the Portuguese Monarchy in Brazil

European countries regarded their colonies as a useful addition to the homeland, not as a replacement for it. But in early-nineteenth-century Portugal, that is what the colony of Brazil became. On 29th November 1807, one day before their capital Lisbon was attacked and taken by Napoleon's invading army, the Portuguese royal family and about 15,000 courtiers, politicians and soldiers fled to Brazil. The two countries reversed roles. In March 1808, Rio de Janeiro was declared the new Portuguese capital. The ruler of the country was Prince John, acting as regent for his mother who was mentally ill. When she died in 1816 he became King of Portugal, but chose to remain in Rio even though his country had been liberated from French occupation two years previously thanks to the efforts of the Duke of Wellington.

The Portuguese administration and royal court stayed in Brazil until 1821 when John was forced to return home and accept his new position as a constitutional monarch. He left his son, Pedro, behind. Pedro sided with the independence movement in Brazil and in 1822 was proclaimed Emperor. After his father died in 1826 he was accused by nationalists of hankering after the Portuguese Crown and in 1831 abdicated, returning to his native land as he had first arrived, accompanied by a British warship. His five-year-old son then became Emperor and ruled Brazil until 1889 when the country became a republic, following the abolition of slavery the year before. These events provide a curious episode in European colonial history. By running away to Brazil, the Portuguese royal family helped fuel liberal independence movements in both their home country and overseas territories which contributed to the eventual extinction of their position as rulers. The Portuguese monarchy was finally abolished in 1910.

CHAPTER 8

The Exile of Napoleon Bonaparte to St Helena

1815

Napoleon Bonaparte was exiled to St Helena, a British island in the South Atlantic, after his defeat at the Battle of Waterloo in 1815. As First Consul of France and then as Emperor he had almost succeeded in conquering the whole continent of Europe.

In 1949 the Dutch historian, Pieter Geyl, published a book called *Napoleon For and Against*. Geyl had spent most of the Second World War as a German prisoner, including thirteen months at Buchenwald concentration camp. With the example of Hitler in mind he embarked on an examination of how French writers and historians had made judgments about the Emperor Napoleon, from the moment he fell from power to the middle of the twentieth century.

Napoleon stands across the path of modern French history like a mountain that has to be climbed. There is no way round: until you have reached the summit you cannot have a complete view of what it is like. He rescued France after the earthquake of the French Revolution, restoring its authority and covering it with glory. But he was vainglorious, dictatorial and careless of human life: hundreds of thousands of French soldiers died in his wars of conquest. He seems to have had some of the same qualities, and present some of the same problems, as Oliver Cromwell in British history. Both were outsiders, men on their own; both were brilliant generals; and both changed the course of their countries' histories. The nineteenth-century writer Thomas Carlyle made a comparison between the two men in his book

On Heroes, Hero-Worship and the Heroic in History published in 1841. Cromwell, he said, 'grappled like a giant, face to face, heart to heart, with the naked truth of things', while Napoleon had 'a certain instinctive ineradicable feeling for reality'. Comparisons like these never lose their fascination. The history of the world is sometimes about nothing more or less than the achievements of astonishing individuals.

The essence of Napoleon's time in power is nowhere better captured than in the events that ended his career. The fifteen months between his unconditional abdication as Emperor of the French on 6th April 1814 and his departure for St Helena in the South Atlantic on 8th August the following year were breathtakingly dramatic. Following his defeat at the Battle of Leipzig in October 1813, the Emperor withdrew to the Palace of Fontainebleau, his favourite residence, south-east of Paris. Although he had subsequently managed to win some victories, the armies of the allies were advancing into France. Paris was surrounded by Austrian, Russian and Prussian troops while the British general, the Duke of Wellington, had finally pushed the French army out of the Iberian Peninsula and was marching north. Right up until the last moment Napoleon was hoping to mount a counterattack. Its success depended on Marshal Marmont, the Duke of Ragusa, who with 20,000 men was stationed several miles west of Fontainebleau. The duke defected to the enemy (the word *raguser* came to mean betray as a result) and the Emperor's plans were dashed. 'Marmont,' he declared, 'has dealt me the final blow.' After Napoleon had abdicated his Imperial Guard took their leave. The Polish contingent led by Baron Jan Kozietulski, who had personally saved Napoleon's life during a battle in the invasion of Russia, were the last to go, utterly loyal to their emperor until the end. A few days later Napoleon tried to kill himself, but the poison he used was old and had lost its potency, and after a night of dreadful stomach pains he recovered. The following month he set off for Elba, the

The little island off the Tuscan coast was supposed to be his home for the rest of his life.

little island off the Tuscan coast that the victorious allies had decided was to be his home for the rest of his life.

Bonaparte had other ideas. While the great powers of Europe gathered in Vienna to discuss the best way of putting the Continent back to what it had been before the Revolution, the man who was the cause of their congress escaped. He had been in captivity for nine months. Landing at Golf Juan, between Cannes and Antibes, on 1st March 1815, he issued a proclamation to the French people. It reminded them of Marmont's desertion to the allies and announced: 'Frenchmen, in my exile I heard your complaints and wishes ... You were blaming me for my long sleep ... I crossed the seas amid all sorts of dangers; I arrived among you to regain my rights, which are yours.'

'I crossed the seas amid all sorts of dangers; I arrived among you to regain my rights, which are yours.'

In less than three weeks he was once again back in Paris. His brilliant gamble seemed to have paid off. He had arrived on the coast of France with a force of less than a thousand men and entered the capital with an army at his back. On his journey north the whole adventure nearly came to an end when outside the city of Grenoble he was confronted by a regiment of infantry blocking the road. He stood alone before them in his grey overcoat and having ordered his own men to lay down their arms, asked them. 'Would you kill your Emperor?' They would not and rushed towards him with cries of support. 'Before Grenoble,' he said later, 'I was an adventurer; at Grenoble I was a reigning prince.'

The Bourbon King, Louis XVIII, fled from the throne to which he had recently been restored and went into exile in Ghent. Marshal Ney – 'the bravest of the brave' according to Napoleon – was sent to capture the returning Emperor. He had turned against him the previous year, telling him it was time to abdicate, but on meeting his former commander again he handed him his sword and rode with him into Paris. Napoleon knew he had little time: he had to attack the allies one by one before they regrouped and came in strength against him. By June he was on the battlefield again, winning what would be the last victory of his career against the Prussians at Ligny. Two days later, on 18th June, he fought his final battle at Waterloo. The general in charge of the coalition forces, the Duke of Wellington, had fought many battles against the French in Spain, Portugal and southern France, but had never met the Emperor Napoleon face to face. The twentieth-century French historian, Georges Lefebvre, compared the two men. Describing Wellington's aristocratic *hauteur* he wrote that 'pride of race tied him fast to his caste and to the country of which it was in his eyes the lawful proprietor. He never had a thought but to save it, his dry soul, bare of imagination and affection, preserving him from the romantic individualism which ruined Napoleon, while lending to his genius an imperishable attraction.' The tough, resilient soldier defeated the passionate, quixotic emperor, who was forced to abdicate once more. In a proclamation profound in its understatement he told the French people: 'Circumstances seem to me to have changed.' This time the allies made certain of his imprisonment and he was sent to the remote British island of St Helena in the South Atlantic. Here he ruminated on his vivid career. He knew that the loyalty he commanded was fragile, a self-earned commodity unbound by any sense of tradition and easily dissipated by circumstance. 'I had risen from the masses too suddenly,' he said. 'I felt my isolation.' He died on the island in 1821.

This time the allies made certain of his imprisonment.

Napoleon was born in Corsica in 1769. He was educated in France, attended the Ecole Militaire in Paris and prospered during the Revolution, not least because emigration and the guillotine reduced the number of young men capable of military duty. He was lucky too. He became a close confidant of Augustin Robespierre, brother of the revolutionary leader Maximilien, and a fanatical supporter of his ideas. Augustin was guillotined on the same day as Maximilien – 'I share his virtues, I want to share his fate' he exclaimed – and Napoleon was arrested on suspicion of collaboration. Released soon afterwards he became close friends with the Vicomte de Barras who rose to power as the leading member of the Directory that governed France after the fall of Robespierre and the Terror. France was fighting on all fronts. The European powers had united against it in a coalition determined to turn back the tide of the Revolution. At the age of twenty-six, Napoleon was given command of the French Army of Italy and in 1796 prepared to fight against the allied forces of Piedmont-Sardinia and Austria.

Napoleon proved to be a military genius. He read and enjoyed strategy, planning each encounter carefully and executing it according to the requirements of the moment. 'I have fought sixty battles,' he later reflected on St Helena, 'and I learned nothing which I did not know at the beginning.' In Italy between April 1796 and October 1797 he fought and won more than a dozen victories, campaigning across the north of the country and eventually crossing into Austria. His success turned him into a national hero and he attempted to build on his reputation by persuading the Directory to let him invade and conquer Egypt. This egotistical expedition was not such a conspicuous success and he returned to France in 1799 still popular with the people but regarded with suspicion by the authorities. But the Directory was corrupt and incompetent. Napoleon, in collusion with some of its members and its foreign minister, Talleyrand, organised a coup d'état. It was another Napoleonic gamble, but it came off. He became First Consul of France, in theory sharing power with two others but out-manoeuvring his fellow conspirators to become the person in real control. He consolidated his position by mounting another attack against the Austrians who had been allowed to rebuild their strength in Italy in the four years since his previous campaign. In 1800 he led the French army in a daring crossing of the Alps and defeated his enemy at the Battle of Marengo. It was a narrow victory but an important one. Napoleon was saved by the return of one of his marshals, Louis Desaix, whom he had dispatched to block what he expected to be an Austrian retreat. Sensing that his commander was in difficulties, Desaix returned to the battlefield. After remarking to the First Consul that this battle seemed to be lost but there was still time to win another one, he threw his forces against the Austrians. Desaix was killed, the Austrians fled and Napoleon lived to become the master of Europe.

In 1802, France and Britain agreed the Treaty of Amiens. Britain was one of the countries in the coalition against France but both sides recognised that British victories at sea and French victories on land had created a situation in which hostilities could end. Under the terms of the treaty, Britain recognised the new French republic, thereby formally abandoning its opposition to the revolutionary cause. Napoleon's reputation played a large part in this. He seemed to many people to have brought stability and common sense to a country that had been in turmoil since the outbreak of the Revolution in 1789. The British politician George Canning said that while he was no 'panegyrist' of Napoleon, he could not close his eyes to the 'superiority of his talent, the dazzling ascendancy of his genius'. But underlying suspicions between the two countries could not be signed away in a peace treaty: a year later they were at war again. From this moment on, Napoleon showed his true colours, being crowned 'Emperor of the French' by the Pope in Paris in 1804; a year later a coronation in Milan made him 'King of Italy'. In 1806 he made his elder brother, Joseph, King of Naples and Sicily, and in 1808, King of Spain, replacing him in his previous role with one of his marshals, Murat. Another brother, Louis, became King of Holland in 1806. In 1807 he gave his youngest brother, Jerome, the title of King of Wesphalia, in Germany.

The transformation of the Bonaparte family into manu-factured European royalty was the result of Napoleon's wars of conquest in which he tried to make France the heart of a great empire. This grand design was brought to an end by his disas-trous invasion of Russia in 1812 and the terrible retreat of his broken army. He pushed on to Moscow against his marshals' advice and had to turn back through the Russian winter when the city was burned before him. The exact number of men that he lost in the campaign is hard to judge. Most estimates assume that he crossed into Russia with an army at least half-a-million strong but that only about a tenth came back. From this point on, the Napoleonic Empire started to unravel. The Emperor told his people that defeat had been due to the 'premature rigour of the

Bolívar

Napoleon's invasion of Spain in 1808, overthrowing the Spanish Bourbon dynasty, triggered independence movements among its South American colonies. Their resentment had been brewing for a long time, not least because of the introduction of Enlightenment ideas of political reform. By 1810 many regions had achieved de facto independence, although few gave it that name. Conflicts and civil wars embroiled much of the region until well into the 1820s.

A Spanish royalist counterattack in 1815, comprising the largest force ever sent to Latin America, threatened to undo the colonies' victories. Two men led the second, decisive phase of the independence struggle: the Venezuelan Simón Bolívar (1783–1830) and the Argentine general José de San Martín (1778–1850). Both were wealthy and aristocratic (Bolívar's father was a distant relative of the Castilian King, Fernando III, in Spain) and both as young men spent time in Europe. Their combined activities in the late 1810s and the early 1820s, which inadvertently amounted to a 'pincer' movement from both ends of the continent, resulted in the liberation of most of Spanish South America.

When San Martín returned from Europe in 1812 he joined the independence force in Argentina and subsequently led an army over the Andes. In 1817 he took Chile and was proclaimed its governor. Full independence was declared the following year. Next he turned his attention to Peru, sending a 'manifesto' to its people in September 1820 which argued that 'the outcome of victory will make Peru's capital see for the first time their sons united, freely choosing their government and emerging into the face of earth among the rank of nations'. Provisional independence was declared in 1821, and San Martín was named 'Protector of Peruvian Freedom'. One of his first acts was to

season', but they began to realise that it was due to his impossible ambition.

Napoleon was more than just a conqueror. He always claimed that he wanted to bring the greatest ideals of the French Revolution – liberty and equality – to the rest of Europe. His introduction of the Civil Code in 1804 was a monumental establish a library in Lima, which he saw as 'of the most efficient means to spread our intellectual values'.

Bolívar, meanwhile, led rather a short-lived invasion into Venezuela in 1813 but in 1819 and with Haitian reinforcements, he was able to retake it as part of a much larger invasion strategy which included New Granada (today called Colombia). On 7th September 1821, Gran Colombia (comprising modern Venezuela, Colombia, Panama, and Ecuador) was created with Bolívar as president. San Martín and Bolívar then met in July 1822 to plan their strategy for Latin America. The meeting was held in secret, and has been the subject of intense debate ever since. It is possible that San Martín simply yielded to Bolívar's ambition. Alternatively Bolivar refused to allow San Martín to share military command of their combined forces. Whatever happened, the result was that San Martín withdrew. He resettled as a farmer in Mendoza, Argentina, while Bolívar took over the task of fully liberating Peru. He was named 'dictator' in 1824, and decisive success against the Spanish followed later that year. In August 1825, the Congress of Upper Peru voted to form the Republic of Bolivia, named after its liberator.

Bolívar wanted to see an American-style federation for Gran Colombia's component republics, bound together with himself as a life-long president. While claiming to be a believer in Jeffersonian federal democracy, he doubted whether such liberal freedom was possible under what he called the 'triple yoke of ignorance, tyranny, and vice' in South America. He survived an assassination attempt in 1828 and died two years later after a bout of tuberculosis. His reported last words were that, 'All who have served the Revolution have ploughed the sea.' He is revered as a national hero throughout Latin America.

achievement, providing his country with an entirely new system of law based on the rights of individual citizens that became an example to the whole world. He created the basis of France's administrative and legal structure that is still in use today. He worked ceaselessly. His personal habits were frugal and he wrote and spoke with a frankness and charm that was difficult to dislike. These are the qualities that make him such an absorbing character. He and Adolf Hitler are the last two individual conquerors in European history – men who could perhaps be compared to Julius Caesar or Charlemagne in what they tried to achieve. But the clear difference is that Hitler is only to be vilified and condemned. His whole career was founded on a philosophy of evil that was executed with pitiless cruelty. Napoleon's career, on the other hand, was full of achievements that both contemporaries and subsequent observers have admired. Talleyrand, who served him as foreign minister but broke with him as he saw his ambition advance, remarked that his career was 'the most extraordinary that had existed for a thousand years'. The last judgement, however, should be Napoleon's own: 'What a romance my life has been.'

'What a romance my life has been.'

CHAPTER 9

The Indian Mutiny

1857

In 1857 Indian soldiers – sepoys – defied their commanders in the army of the British East India Company. Their mutiny spread to became a civilian rebellion. These events, sometimes called India's First War of Independence, exemplified Britain's approach to empire.

Britain's history is inseparable from that of its empire. The British Empire, combined with the Industrial Revolution that fed it, earned Britain its place on the world stage. Britain's sense of nationhood grew strongly during the seventeenth century and was enshrined in the Act of Union of 1707 that joined England and Scotland together with a new official name – Great Britain. The country might have felt great but it had yet to prove that it deserved such an epithet. In the century that followed, in no small part due to the activities of Scottish men and women who had become its citizens, it transformed itself into a great maritime power with foreign possessions in every quarter of the world.

In 1815, the year of Waterloo, Britain had valuable footholds in India, South Africa, Canada and Australia. By the end of the nineteenth century these mainly coastal possessions had expanded, consolidating British rule over enormous territorial areas. Britain not only ruled the waves but the lands they washed as well. The process by which it achieved such power was complicated and contradictory. The Empire was never ruled by a monarch with a religious mission like Philip II of Spain; it never submitted to the glamour of a great conqueror like Napoleon in France; and it was never manipulated by a wily empire-builder like Germany's

Bismarck. Yet religion, conquest and wiliness all played their part in constructing the British Empire. It evolved out of the British themselves, a worldwide reflection of their aptitude for commerce, their innate preference for toleration, and, as success strengthened them, their firm belief in their racial superiority.

In 1883, the historian Sir John Seeley wrote an essay called 'The Expansion of England' in which he remarked that Britain seemed 'to have conquered and peopled half the world in a fit of absence of mind'. Such a languid view of Britain's imperial destiny appealed to many Victorians. They had not built their empire: it had simply grown up around them, the natural fruit of a country's efforts. Its existence, however, imposed certain 'obligations', what Seeley referred to as 'Greater Britain', that is: the extension of British ideas and British values overseas. Britain stood between two gigantic land powers, Russia and America. Thanks to the Industrial Revolution, whose inventions had helped reduce the difficulties of time and space, Britain could think of itself and its empire as an entity in the same way. Between these neighbours, said Seeley, 'equally vast but not continuous, with the ocean flowing through it in every direction, lies, like a world-Venice, with the sea for streets, Greater Britain.' This idea of the Empire as 'Greater Britain' emerged during the last phase of the nation's imperial growth – a far cry from the buccaneering exploits of Sir Francis Drake in South America, the dangerous voyage of the Pilgrim Fathers to New England, or the unscrupulous conniving of Robert Clive in India. Trade and religion, greed and piety, humanity and cruelty all played their part in building the British Empire and many aspects of its long, uneven history can be seen in the Indian Mutiny of 1857.

Britain's defeat at the hands of the thirteen American colonies in the War of Independence in 1781 felt to many Englishmen like a death blow. 'We shall moulder piecemeal into our insignificant islandhood,' wrote Horace Walpole; 'the term Great Britain will be a jest.' His was a view shared by many of his contemporaries and by observers from abroad. Britain's badly handled and arrogant attempt to coerce the colonists had ended in disaster and reduced the nation forever. In fact, however, Britain simply swung her gaze from west to east. The loss of America became an important motive for the development of its Indian possessions where Britain had gained the upper hand from France after the Battle of Plassey in 1757. Following the battle the wealthy province of Bengal fell into its hands providing it with the resources it needed to strengthen its position.

The administration of India, however, was completely different from that which had operated in America. From the moment the British arrived on the coast of western India in the early sixteenth century, to the moment nearly two hundred years later when it became the principal focus of its colonial attention, British interests there were run, not by the state, but by a company. Robert Clive, the victor of Plassey, was an employee of the East India Company. His army was made up of company troops. His motives were always primarily commercial and he made sure he profited as much as his shareholders did from his intrepid adventures. Public opinion at home grew critical of the way he had grown rich and he had to withstand a parliamentary enquiry before he died by committing suicide in 1774. Meanwhile the East India Company had got into financial difficulties and was unable to meet the annual payments it made to the British government in order to preserve its trading monopoly. The government moved to protect its interests and appointed a Governor-General to act as the local regulator of the company's affairs: political and commercial interests became inextricable from one another.

The curious nature of the East India Company from the end of the eighteenth century to the middle of the nineteenth epitomised Britain's approach to imperial expansion. It was the company that increased Britain's Indian possessions, taking direct control of Delhi, Sindh and Punjab and administering other areas, such as Jaipur and Hyderabad, through local Indian princes. But the state also increased its hold over the continent's affairs. As it did so it awakened public interest in a part of the world that was beginning to be seen as more than just a source of wealth. British administrators delved into Indian languages and culture, missionaries worked to convert Hindus to Christianity and liberals began to criticise the military authoritarianism with which the East India Company liked to maintain order. These different trends coalesced between 1846 and 1856 under

Lord Dalhousie, the Governor-General, who more than any other before him tried to turn India into an Asian version of the British way of life. He connected the country with a railway system, opened universities, reformed the country's administration and military and encouraged wherever possible a Western European approach to all aspects of its society and government. It was in its way a prototype of a 'Greater Britain'.

British administrators delved into Indian languages and culture; missionaries worked to convert Hindus to Christianity.

The furious pace of change in India was disrupted by the Indian Mutiny. The army in India had four times as many Indian soldiers as it did British. In Bengal, where the rebellion began, many of these sepoys were from the higher castes of Indian society. They became concerned that privileges they enjoyed – such as avoiding flogging – would be removed as the British took more control of Indian affairs and imposed its own fierce military discipline. In 1853 the army introduced into service a new Enfield Rifle. Rumours began that its cartridges, which the sepoys had to bite open before using, were greased with pork or beef fat, an act that offended Muslims and Hindus respectively. British officers tried to quash the rumours, but in March 1857, on a parade ground near Calcutta, a young sepoy rebelled. The Indian commander of the quarter guard was ordered to arrest him, but he refused. Both men were court-martialled and hanged. The following May a detachment of Indian troops broke into open revolt after a British officer, unsympathetic to their concerns about the rifle cartridges, ordered them to perform firing drills. They killed a number of British soldiers and civilians, freed their imprisoned colleagues and then marched on Delhi.

From this moment the unrest developed into a series of widespread but disjointed rebellions involving not only soldiers but Indian landlords, peasants and merchants as well. Although mainly contained within Bengal it represented a wide cross-section of Indian society. It was not just a mutiny against military discipline, but against the whole British way of life. The revolt spread across north-west India with enormous speed as mutinous troops, assisted by angry civilians, attacked and killed Europeans in the cities of Delhi, Benares (modern Varanasi), Cawnpore (modern Kanpur) and Allahabad. Cawnpore was besieged for three weeks but the centre of the uprising, the place that came to represent in British minds what it was all about, was Lucknow.

Sir Henry Montgomery Lawrence was a typical Victorian man of India. He was born in Ceylon (today Sri Lanka), educated in England and left for India at the age of sixteen where, apart from two short return visits home, he spent the rest of his life. His health was undermined by an early attack of malaria and dysentery, but Lawrence soldiered on, serving in a number of important military and civil service posts and distinguishing himself in the wars between the East India Company and the Sikhs of the Punjab in the late 1840s. He disagreed with Lord Dalhousie about the British decision to annex the Punjab following the Sikhs' defeat and in 1857 found himself in Lucknow as the chief commissioner and agent to the Governor-General of the province of Oudh. Realising that the city was likely to come under attack from Indian rebels he set about preparing for its defence but at the end of June found himself outnumbered. He retreated to his residency with a large number of unarmed men, women and children supported by a force of about 1,600 European and loyal Indian troops. Within a week he was dead, killed by shrapnel wounds he received while surveying his position from a room at the top of the residency building. He asked that his epitaph should be: 'Here lies Henry Lawrence who tried to do his duty.'

Rumours began that the rifles' cartridges were greased with pork or beef fat.

The defenders struggled on for another three months before relief came. 'God knows what the end will be,' wrote one woman, Mrs Harris, in her journal, 'or if the lives of any English in the country will be spared.' Many of them died, but Sir Henry Lawrence's determination to be seen to do his duty helped save the lives of many more. Alfred, Lord Tennyson, who had become poet laureate seven years earlier, seized the moment in his 'Defence of Lucknow' with the refrain: 'And ever upon the topmost roof our banner of England blew'.

> *Handful of men as we were, we were English in*
> *heart and limb,*
> *Strong with the strength of the race to command, to*
> *obey, to endure,*
> *Each of us fought as if hope for the garrison hung*
> *but on him;*
> *Still – could we watch at all points? We were every*
> *day fewer and fewer …*

The British crushed the Indian Mutiny mercilessly; their treatment of the rebels was often no more than bloodthirsty revenge. Once the bloodletting was over, however, the British set about restoring imperial control in a different manner. The East India Company was disbanded and India became governed by a Secretary of State in London and a Governor-General, later the Viceroy, in Delhi. In 1876 the Prime Minister, Benjamin Disraeli, persuaded Queen Victoria to take the title of Empress of India. The Indian Civil Service was created. The British Raj had begun: for nearly another hundred years a few thousand Englishmen would guide and control the destinies of millions.

The government of India today refers to the mutiny of 1857 as 'The First War of Indian Independence'. In many ways that is what it was, although unlike the war fought by the American colonists more than eighty years previously, the rebels were not closely organised and possessed no strategy *It was a mutiny* for a new nation of their own. But just as *against the whole* in 1776 the British government believed the American colonies were an extension *British way of life.* of Britain, so in 1857 it had the same attitude towards India. In America it decided to fight a war it was almost certainly bound to lose, but in India superiority of arms ensured that it was able to suppress revolt. The people it was dealing with were not emigrants from its own country but an indigenous population to whom the British felt, as Tennyson's poem expressed, innately superior. In the same year as the Indian Mutiny, a determined Christian missionary called David Livingstone was describing his extraordinary discoveries in the heart of Africa to excited audiences in London. Christianity and commerce, he maintained, were the twin engines that would drive the British advance through these new lands. It was a message that those who heard him received with enthusiasm. To conquer through Christianity while enriching the nation through commerce was an imperial doctrine they understood. It had worked in India: it could now work in the rest of the world as well.

CHAPTER 10

Hiroshima

1945

In August 1945, the United States dropped two atomic bombs on the Japanese cities of Hiroshima and Nagasaki. About two hundred thousand people were killed immediately. Many more died subsequently. The Second World War had come to an obliterating end.

On 14th August 1945, Emperor Hirohito of Japan made a radio broadcast to his people. Many of his subjects had never heard him speak before and were surprised at the high, rather squeaky voice in which he addressed them as well as the traditional courtly language he used. Japan, he said, had 'declared war on America and Britain out of our sincere desire to ensure Japan's self-preservation'. Territorial aggrandisement, he went on, had never been part of Japanese intentions and, employing masterly understatement, added: 'the war situation has developed not necessarily to Japan's advantage, while the general trends of the world have all turned against her interest'. He then referred to the dropping of atomic bombs. 'Moreover, the enemy has begun to employ a new and most cruel bomb … Should we continue to fight it would not only result in an ultimate collapse and obliteration of the Japanese nation, but it would also lead to the total extinction of human civilisation.' With such equivocation did the most destructive war in the history of the world come to its final end.

It was a far cry from the speech made by Japan's prime minister and army commander, Hideki Tojo, to the country's parliament three years before. Japan, he announced, was in total control of the all the nations throughout the Pacific. Burma had been freed from British rule to enjoy independence under Japan's guidance. India would be next. Australia should think seriously about where its interests lay. 'Imperial Japan,' he concluded, 'has firm confidence in the attainment of ultimate victory in this sacred war and our military operations, which are magnificent and unparalleled in this world, are being expanded.'

The Japanese leadership presented itself as the natural defender of historic Asian values in a region that had become polluted by Western decadence, but national self-interest played the larger part in its aggressive tactics. In 1931 it invaded Manchuria, a Chinese province on the border between Russia and China, establishing a puppet regime to prevent interference from the Soviet Union that it felt was damaging to its interests. In 1937 it invaded the rest of China and held and defended the whole of the eastern part of the country throughout the Second World War. In 1941 it attacked the naval base at Pearl Harbor in Hawaii to prevent the American fleet from operating against it as it sought to expand its control throughout Southeast Asia. In the ten years before the outbreak of the Second World War, Japan gradually surrendered all political affairs to the military. War and conquest became the solution to its problems, the foundation necessary for future success. In that respect it was not that different from its European ally, Nazi Germany.

Japan signed an alliance with Germany and Italy in September 1940. Although the ideologies of the three powers were different – Japan never adopted anti-Semitism, for instance – they were bound together, not only by the need to support each other with goods and armaments, but by a ruthless militaristic approach as well. The Germans pursued their Final Solution with the Holocaust; the Japanese with the mass murder of the peoples they conquered, and the use of slave camps and enforced prostitution. Adolf Hitler sounded not unlike Prime Minister Tojo when he told the members of the Reichstag in Berlin in May 1941: 'I can assure you that I look into the future with perfect tranquility and great confidence. The German Reich represents power, military, economic and, above all in moral respects, is superior to any possible coalition in the world.'

Aggression cloaked with moral fervour, but always supported by immense firepower, was the method by which Germany and

Japan brought the world to total war. History provided them with plenty of examples: the moral idea of empire was often the product of the battlefield. In 1871, when the new German Empire was founded after the Prussian victory in the Franco-Prussian War, many of its new citizens believed morality and warfare to be natural comrades in arms. 'The dreadful work of the battlefields served a higher ethical purpose,' wrote the dramatist Gustav Freytag, who described Germany's imperial birth as 'the poetry of the historical process'. In France there were some writers who looked back with longing to the days of Napoleon, who had declared himself Emperor in 1804 in a coronation ceremony modelled on that of an even earlier ruler, Charlemagne; his military exploits had saved his country, and they could do with him again. He was, said Frederic Masson, 'the most admirable specimen of the human race'. Hankering after glory is a useful tendency for politicians to exploit. In the Second World War millions of people in Germany, Italy and Japan were seduced by the idea that military triumph was a worthwhile achievement in itself.

Adolf Hitler committed suicide in Berlin in April 1945 as the Allies closed in on Berlin. The leader of Italy, Benito Mussolini, was captured and shot by Communist partisans a few days earlier on the shores of Lake Como while trying to escape to Switzerland. The rapidly approaching end of the war in Europe, however, did not at first deter the Japanese. The people knew that it was coming to an end. Prime Minister Tojo resigned in July 1944. He later tried to shoot himself but recovered, and was put on trial as a war criminal and executed. A new military government took power as the Americans drew closer to Japan. In June 1945 they captured the island of Okinawa where a quarter of a million Japanese soldiers were killed. Even this terrible battle brought no surrender. On 26th July 1945, the Allies, meeting in Potsdam outside Berlin, issued Japan with an ultimatum saying that unless it surrendered unconditionally they would mount an attack resulting in 'the inevitable and complete destruction of the Japanese armed forces and just as inevitably the utter devastation of the Japanese homeland'. The Prime Minister of Japan rejected the ultimatum. His country was suffering appalling bombing raids in which tens of thousand people were dying but he hoped that the Soviet Union might be able to negotiate a peace agreement that would prevent an Allied occupation and preserve the institutional apparatus of the Emperor.

In August this last dream faded as the Russians declared war. Later that month the first and only nuclear bombs used in the history of warfare were dropped on Hiroshima and Nagasaki. 'I felt the city of Hiroshima had disappeared all of a sudden,' recalled one survivor who was fourteen at the time. 'Then I looked at myself and found my clothes had turned to rags as a result of the heat ... I saw a man whose skin had completely peeled off from the upper half of his body and a woman whose eyeballs were sticking out.' There are many similar accounts, descriptions of horrific injuries, of the fierce, constant heat and the loss, confusion and fear that the bombs, nicknamed 'Little Boy' and 'Fat Man', had brought to Hiroshima and Nagasaki. Illness and sickness dogged thousands of survivors. The bombing persuaded Emperor Hirohito to break ranks with his military advisors and sue for peace. Although the attack ended the war, it prolonged human suffering for years afterwards.

'Little Boy' and 'Fat Man' brought fear and confusion to Hiroshima and Nagasaki.

The atomic bombing of Japan was the last military act in the world's most recent global war. Only one other, the conflict of 1914 to 1918, is commonly given the title of a 'world war', though some earlier wars were fought on a global scale. The campaigns of Alexander the Great, the conquests of Chinggis Khan, and the Seven Years' War between the principal European powers in the eighteenth century, covered enormous, if not all, areas of the planet. The Second World War was also the last great war of conquest in which powers in possession of military strength sought to overcome and subvert their smaller, weaker neighbours. It was fought because in Europe, Germany and Italy, and in Asia, Japan, wanted to extend their boundaries for reasons of national glorification. The total collapse of their ambitions transformed the nature of their countries. Under pressure from the forces that had defeated them, but also from a self-developed realisation of the futility of what they had attempted, they converted themselves from highly militaristic states into determinedly democratic civilian ones. In Japan, under the energetic supervision of the Supreme Commander of the Allied Powers, General Douglas MacArthur, the country was driven towards the removal of its military culture and the introduction of democracy. Emperor Hirohito was kept in position, eventually becoming acceptable enough to be invited on diplomatic visits round the world.

By 1951, MacArthur told the American Congress: 'The Japanese people since the war have undergone the greatest reformation recorded in modern history.' In Germany and Italy the story was similar, although in Italy the people did not require the same external pressure to enforce change. Fascism had lost its glamour and most of them were only too glad to return to representative government. In Germany, divided into East and West by the Allies, the problem was more acute. The German Nazi Party had enjoyed a membership of 8 million people: ensuring that the country's new government was cleansed of these influences was a painstaking, and not always successful, task. Those leaders who had not escaped or committed suicide were put on trial. In 1960, one of the last key surviving Nazis and chief architect of the Holocaust, Adolf Eichmann, was captured in Argentina, brought back to Israel, found guilty and hanged in 1962.

The A-bomb attack ended the war but prolonged human suffering for years afterwards.

The greatest movement for a different future, however, came not from military tribunals but from the establishment of the European Coal and Steel Community in 1951 under whose auspices West Germany, France, Italy and the Benelux countries of Belgium, Luxembourg and the Netherlands agreed to create a common market for their coal and steel production. Its purpose was both economic and political. In the words of its founder, Robert Schuman, 'it would make war not only unthinkable, but materially impossible'. Today's European Community grew directly from that first institution.

Today, in 2010, the West has survived sixty-five years of comparative peace, one of the longest interludes without a large, destructive conflict in its history. After the defeat of Napoleon in 1815, the European powers put in place a structure they hoped would preserve peace for many years. At the Congress of Vienna they resurrected and reinforced authoritarian monarchical government, balancing all their interests to prevent further warfare. To a large extent it worked. Revolution flared up, particularly in 1848, when several European governments found themselves challenged by libertarian movements that sought to overthrow the old order, but on the whole they survived. The solution the European powers found at Vienna allowed the wealthy and privileged to continue the domination of government for more than fifty years after Napoleon's defeat. The Franco-Prussian War of 1870 changed all that. It brought a new power, Germany, into the world and finally overthrew royalist rule in France. The German Empire developed a stern militaristic approach which contributed considerably to the outbreak of the First World War. Germany was defeated, but because the victors failed to address properly the concerns of their defeated enemy, they laid the foundations of a second, even bigger war, between 1939 and 1945. This killed more than 60 million people and made the world realise that it needed a resilient method of preventing international warfare more urgently than it had ever been before. To begin with the division between the Communist East and the democratic West seemed to undermine the possibility of ever finding one. But the collapse of the Soviet Union and the reunification of Germany in 1990 ended the so-called 'Cold War' between the two sides and that, combined with the expansion of the European Union, seemed to provide the framework for peace.

Historically war has been the preferred method by which man achieves change. He continues to employ it: the war in Iraq is a good recent example. After the Second World War the victorious powers tried to avoid the need for future conflict by investing in reconstruction and developing different institutional structures from those that had operated before. These changes were embraced willingly by the people whom they had defeated: victors and vanquished agreed on a common approach for the future. Today, when threats to world peace appear not to come from within Europe, or the Far East, but from the resentment felt by the Muslim world towards Western capitalism, the countries involved are struggling, but have not yet been successful, in developing new structures and new ways of doing things. Peace will not come without them. As Emperor Hirohito said as he concluded his remarks to the nation his government had devastated in a long and savage war: 'Keep pace with the progress of the world.'

5 Discovery

Introduction

The genius of man lies in his curiosity. His intelligence in solving the problems of everyday life is the main reason for his survival. From the discovery of fire to the invention of the wheel; from the development of writing to the invention of printing; and from an understanding of the planets of the universe to landing on the moon, man has always stretched to the limit his desire to enquire. The discovery of one age raises the curtain on the discoveries of the next. Nothing can stop this process. Man will continue to discover until he invents himself out of existence or, more probably, adapts himself to the different world he has helped create. 'The more we really look at man as an animal,' said G. K. Chesterton, 'the less he will look like one.' Writing in 1925 he was setting out the argument for Christianity, approaching the history of mankind from a spiritual point of view. He believed that to relegate man to nothing more than another point on the road of evolution was to reduce him. 'Every sane sort of history,' he said, 'must begin with man as man, a thing standing absolute and alone … This creature was truly different from all other creatures; because he was a creator as well as a creature.'

This optimistic belief in man's special qualities is not confined to the religiously-minded like Chesterton. In the generation before him, the Victorian poet Algernon Charles Swinburne celebrated the greatness of man from an entirely opposite point of view. Chesterton and Swinburne were not only very different in their thinking, but in their style and attitudes too. Chesterton was physically large, thoughtful, witty and a convinced Christian. Swinburne was tiny, fiery, radical and passionate. But in his poem, 'Hymn of Man', written in 1871, he used atheism to celebrate man's achievements:

By thy name that in hell-fire was written, and
  burned at the point of thy sword,
Thou art smitten, thou God, thou art smitten; thy
  death is upon thee, O Lord.
And the love-song of earth as thou diest resounds
  through the wind of her wings –
Glory to Man in the highest! For Man is the master
  of things.

Whether you are religious or an avowed atheist, any discussion of man's creative genius brings with it many problems. Knowledge is power and man has often enjoyed using his new discoveries unscrupulously: one man's brilliant invention can be another's curse. We are saddled with our own cleverness. In the words of the twentieth-century German philosopher, Ernst Cassirer: 'Man cannot escape from his own achievement.' Furthermore this achievement seems to gather pace as time advances. From the conquests of Alexander the Great to the outbreak of the First World War, a period of 2,300 years, man's principal method of transport on land was horse power. Within the space of twenty-five years he discarded this for the motor car. I am writing this on a laptop. I will email it to my publishers when I have finished. Thirty years ago, perhaps less, I would have been forced to peck it out on a typewriter, or write it by hand and then ask someone else to type it, before putting it in the post. Both transformations, from the horse to the car and from physical to virtual communication, have had profound effects on human civilisation, changing our world beyond recognition with startling speed. The idea that man will stop inventing and discovering is absurd. He will continue for as long as he has a place in the universe, delighting in his extraordinary gifts – until they come to haunt him. At the end of the Second World War, despite the destruction caused by six years of mechanised warfare and the nuclear bombing of Japan, people did not think of the world's environment as a problem. It was still there to be conquered, to be improved with faster communication on land, sea and air with bigger, better, housing at every destination. Today we sometimes wring our hands at the outcome. How could we have been so stupid, so short-sighted? But were we? Perhaps we were just clever, and this cleverness has led us determinedly towards a better future.

This chapter is about man's belief in a better future. It starts in Syracuse in Sicily in the second century BC, where Archimedes mused on the infinite possibilities of numbers. He worked out a way of establishing the density of solid objects after lying in his bath and is supposed to have run naked through the city shouting 'Eureka!'. More significantly he is also said to have remarked: 'Rise above yourself and grasp the world.'

Our journey of discovery takes us next to China and the invention of printing in the late seventh century. It would be another 600 years before the ability to print and circulate reading matter reached Europe. In China it fed the needs of a cultural elite. In Europe it gave voice to the dispossessed. The invention of printing was one of the engines of the Renaissance. As the world turned from the medieval to the modern, Leonardo da Vinci threw open artistic and scientific windows to let in new light: he saw a vision of the future clearer and more powerful than anything that had gone before. Leonardo lived at a time when the world was there for the taking and a man who grasped it eagerly was the Portuguese sailor Vasco da Gama. Clever and ruthless, his ambitions were less refined, representing the more mercenary aspects of the Age of Discovery

The growth of scientific knowledge followed hard on the heels of the world's expansion. Voyages of discovery taught man to adapt to the planet on which he lived: Isaac Newton's discovery of gravity at the end of the seventeenth century helped him learn about the universe beyond. But the discovery of earthly things was not finished. Towards the end of the eighteenth century, as the American colonists proclaimed their independence, one still hidden part of the world fell under European control – Australia. In the nineteenth century the industrial revolution transformed the basis of man's wealth and at the end of it the first flickering images of the cinema helped him forget some of its more stressful aspects. By changing the way in which people enjoyed themselves, the invention of film, and then television, had a profound effect on human civilisation.

The discovery of DNA prised open man's unique physical structure and led him on the road to understanding the genetic secrets of his life. Finally the invention of the worldwide web created a system of human communication that is still growing and expanding, shrinking the gap between different peoples across the world while constantly widening their horizons.

From ancient Syracuse to last night's TV schedule, from the splendour of the Renaissance to Google, man's cleverness and creativity has not deserted him.

CHAPTER 1

Archimedes of Syracuse
287–212 BC

Archimedes was one of history's greatest mathematicians. He invented machines that were useful in war and peace, but his most important contribution to human knowledge was in the area of geometry and theoretical mathematics.

I suspect that most people do not understand pure mathematics and I should confess that I am one of them. We recognise the importance of arithmetic because it is something we use in our everyday lives; and we understand the value of mathematics when it provides calculations applied to scientific inventions. But the infinite and mysterious world of numbers for their own sake is something many of us may appreciate but cannot comprehend. The English mathematician, G. H. Hardy, wrote about this in an essay he published in 1940 called 'A Mathematician's Apology'. He was sixty-three and felt his creative powers were declining. 'I have never done anything 'useful', he claimed. 'No discovery of mine has made, or is likely to make ... the least difference to the amenity of the world.' This, however, did not make his life's work unimportant – far from it. History proved, he said, that 'mathematical achievement, whatever its intrinsic worth, is the most enduring of all'. And he had special praise for the Greeks. 'Greek mathematics,' he said, 'is the real thing ... Greek mathematics is "permanent", more permanent even than Greek literature. Archimedes will be remembered when Aeschylus is forgotten, because languages die and mathematical ideas do not.' Hardy felt that the beauty of mathematics was under-appreciated because most people did not need to use any form of science on a regular basis: the gas burner on the kitchen cooker worked automatically, the broken car went straight to the garage, and so on. This idea was taken up and developed by another Cambridge professor, C. P. Snow, who, in a lecture in 1959, lamented the division between the 'two cultures' – science and the arts – in modern life.

More than 2,000 years ago things were rather different. Intellectual men like Archimedes, working in the Greek-dominated culture of the Mediterranean basin, enjoyed a refined cultural existence in which the boundaries between the arts and sciences were less distinct. Their world had developed through the conquests of Alexander the Great whose ideas of government were influenced by his tutor, Aristotle, a man as much at home with science as he was with philosophy and politics. Before he died in 323 BC, Alexander founded the *museion* at Alexandria in which scribes copied out and stored scientific works covering subjects such as navigation, geography and astronomy. When he was a young man Archimedes may have been sent to Alexandria to study. Some of his works were addressed to fellow mathematicians who worked there. He lived at a time when today's academic boundaries did not exist: intellectual enquiry flourished for its own sake.

The boundaries between the arts and the sciences were less distinct.

The rapid conquests of Alexander the Great were starting to disintegrate by the time Archimedes was working in Syracuse. A new power, the Republic of Rome, was emerging in southern Europe. As it extended its influence it came into conflict with the Carthaginian Empire based in modern Tunis in North Africa. Rome gained control of most of Sicily in its first war against the Carthaginians between 264 and 241 BC. One of its allies was the separate city-state of Syracuse in the south-east of the island, ruled by King Hiero. In 219 BC another war between Rome and Carthage began. The Carthaginian general, Hannibal, invaded Italy from the north, crossing the Alps with a cavalry of elephants and defeating the Romans in a series of battles as he made his way down the length of the peninsula. At the Battle of Cannae in 216 BC he inflicted one of the worst defeats on the army of Rome in the whole history of its republic and empire. In that year King

Hiero of Syracuse died to be succeeded by his grandson Hieronymus, a fifteen-year-old who succumbed to the advice of those
who told him that it was time for the city to switch sides and
support the new masters of the region – Carthage. Hieronymus
was assassinated just over a year later but the Romans, anxious
to ensure that Sicily did not slip out of their grasp, sent a force
under the command of General Marcellus to lay siege to Syracuse. The siege began in 214 BC and lasted for about two years.

We know very little about the life of Archimedes, but there is
more than one story about how he died. Archimedes was in his
mid- to late-seventies when the Romans decided to try to capture
Syracuse. He was well known for having
invented a number of mechanical devices,
in particular a screw for drawing water out
of low-lying areas. The machine is still used
today for transferring water from canals to
other areas in need of irrigation. The screw
sits inside a cylinder and as it turns draws
the water upwards through its concentric
layers. Archimedes was also asked by King
Hiero to ascertain whether a crown he had

He regarded
'as ignoble
and sordid the
business of
mechanics'.

been given was pure gold or mixed with lead. He discovered how
to calculate its specific density while lying in his bath, prompting
him to run naked through the city streets shouting 'Eureka!' The
story may be apocryphal but the facts of Aristotle's discovery are
not. In his *On Floating Bodies* he stated, without any reference to
his bath, that: 'Any floating object displaces its own weight of
fluid.' In another work, *On The Equilibrium of Planes*, he explained
the way in which levers could be used to lift weights, a discovery
that, according to a later Greek mathematician, caused him to
remark: 'Give me a place to stand on, and I will move the earth.'
Despite his inventiveness he was, according to the historian
Plutarch, always happier when pondering the beauty of numbers
and regarded 'as ignoble and sordid the business of mechanics
and every sort of art which is directed to use and profit'.

But Archimedes was prepared to allow his practical
inventiveness to be pressed into service for the defence of his
city. Syracuse was well protected, the pre-eminent city in 'Magna

Graecia' or 'Greater Greece' – the name given to a string of important Greek towns along the coastline of southern Italy. It was encircled by walls more than fifteen miles long with the huge fortress of Euryalos standing at its western end. The Roman

The Roman ships were lifted out of the water and shaken or capsized by an iron hook.

fleet was made up of quinqueremes, ships they had copied from the Carthaginans, but equipped with a plank that could be dropped and hooked onto an enemy vessel to allow the Romans to board and fight hand to hand – the method of engagement they preferred. They were built for speed rather than stability and were not suited to the manoeuvring procedures needed for a siege. Lashed together they provided a platform on which the Romans could

stand, scaling ladders to try to climb Syracuse's formidable walls. This was a risky process in any circumstances. At Syracuse the Romans also had to withstand an onslaught from catapults which, though not new in basic design, had been modified by Archimedes to allow them to hurl missiles at different distances. Then, once they reached the walls, they were confronted by something entirely new in naval warfare – Archimedes's 'iron claw'. Later historians of the siege describe how the Roman ships were lifted out of the water and shaken or capsized by an iron hook lowered by pulley from the top of the city walls. Marcellus, the Roman commander, is supposed to have cried as he watched his ships being scattered by this devilish apparatus: 'Can we not put paid to this geometrical Briareus [the Greek god of sea storms] playing pitch and toss with our ships!' But they could not. The Romans became too frightened, and retreated at the first sight of anything unusual appearing above the parapets of the city. Other stories tell of Archimedes inventing 'burning glasses', big mirrors that deflected the sun's rays onto attacking ships' sails causing them to catch alight. Eventually the Romans had to withdraw in order to plan a different method of capturing Syracuse. They first took the outer city by breaking in at night and then fought their way into the centre. During the attack Archimedes was killed.

Most accounts of Archimedes's death agree that he was engaged in mathematical contemplation moments before the end. General Marcellus had given licence to his troops to loot the city but had asked them to ensure that the life of the elderly mathematician was spared. One account says that Archimedes was looking intently at figures he had drawn in the dust and, in the chaos following the Roman victory, was killed by a soldier who did not know who he was. Another has Archimedes walking through the town carrying a selection of geometrical instruments when a group of soldiers found him and decided to kill him because they thought the instruments were gold. A third, the most colourful, tells the story that a soldier found him hunched over a problem and asked him to follow him to Marcellus. Archimedes, absorbed in thought and concerned that the Roman would spoil his work, told him to stand away from some diagrams he had drawn. The soldier, enraged, murdered him.

We cannot know whether any of these stories are true but the fact that later Roman historians felt the need to tell them demonstrates the reverence in which Archimedes was held. He was a thinker of supreme originality. He covered a wide field – he wrote and experimented in astronomy, geography, arithmetic, mechanics and hydrostatics – but he did not repeat or compile the work of his predecessors. He often referred to previous thinkers in generous terms, but in each case he took their work and extended it, coming up with ideas and solutions that were entirely his own. His introduction to his treatise *On the Sphere and Cylinder* is a good example, charming in the straightforwardness of its language even if, to the layman, the mathematical calculations that follow later are difficult to understand. Writing to his colleague Dositheus in Alexandria he first sets out his new findings: 'Certain theorems not hitherto demonstrated have occurred to me,' he says, 'and I have worked out the proofs of them.' He then goes on to explain these, for instance: 'the surface of any sphere is four times its greatest circle'. Having summarised his findings

He was engaged in mathematical contemplation moments before his end.

he says he would have liked to have seen them published when the astronomer Conon, who died in Alexandria in 220 BC, was still alive. 'But as I judge it well to communicate them to those who are conversant with mathematics, I send them to you with the proofs written out, which it will be open to mathematicians to examine. Farewell.' This chatty letter to a fellow intellectual is one of the last examples of the marriage of science and philosophy in the ancient world. The new conquerors, the Romans, had little interest in mathematics for its own sake. Marcellus wanted Archimedes alive so he could learn from him how to build engines of war, not to be instructed by a brilliant mind.

There were some Romans who understood the importance of men like Archimedes. Cicero, one of the greatest politicians and writers of Republican Rome, appreciated Greek culture and did much to introduce it to his fellow countrymen. When he was serving as *quaestor* – a fiscal administrator working for central government – in the province of Sicily, he asked to see Archimedes's grave. The Syracusans denied all knowledge of it, but Cicero had a good look round the graves near the city gate and spotted it. He knew that Archimedes had asked for a model of a cylinder encircling a sphere to be placed on top of his grave, with the ratio of the former to the latter inscribed beneath it, and hidden in the undergrowth he found what he was looking for. He had the area cleared and the lasting resting place of Archimedes, who had died nearly 140 years before, was revealed.

It is a touching story – but then the life of Archimedes has the quality to touch succeeding ages. William Wordsworth in his longest poem 'The Excursion', published in 1814, attempted to describe 'how exquisitely the individual mind to the external world is fitted' and referred with passion to the Greek mathematician's respect for the immaterial. 'Call Archimedes from his buried tomb/ Upon the plain of vanished Syracuse,' he wrote, 'And feelingly the Sage shall make report/ How insecure, how baseless in itself,/ Is the Philosophy, whose sway depends/ On mere material instruments ...'. Archimedes was the perfect intellectual, a man who rejoiced quietly and modestly in the distillation of different ideas. Asked to defend the city he loved he carried out his task with supreme ability and died in the bloody mayhem of its overthrow. But his greatest achievement long outlived the clever devices he put at the disposal of his fellow citizens. His mathematical ideas were some of the last gifts of the Greek mind to a world that was about to yield to Roman supremacy in which the genius of organisation would replace the refinements of philosophical contemplation.

CHAPTER 2

The Chinese Invention of Printing

seventh century AD

Woodblock printing allowed the Chinese to enjoy a flourishing literary culture long before Europe. Even the invention of the more efficient mechanical movable type by Johannes Gutenberg in the fifteenth century did not deter them from using it.

In his book *Ruins of Desert Cathay*, published in 1912, the explorer Sir Aurel Stein described the circumstances of one of the most exciting archaeological finds of the twentieth century. Stein was dedicated to the East. Small, physically strong and utterly uninterested in the material trappings of life – he never married, or owned his own home – he spent most of his life uncovering its secrets. In 1907 he travelled to the 'Cave of a Thousand Buddhas' in Dunhuang in north-west China, a famous site of ancient Buddhist art that had been discovered by Europeans in the late nineteenth century. Stein heard that behind the walled-up entrance to a recess in the complex of caves was a collection of manuscripts hidden from public view for centuries. To get to them he had to earn the trust of a local priest who had become the documents' self-appointed guardian. Worried that the 'timorous priest, swayed by his worldly fears and possible spiritual scruples' might be moved 'to close down his shell before I had been able to extract any of the pearls', Stein suggested to him that they shared a common patron saint, the monk Xyanzang who in the seventh century BC travelled through China and India spreading the message of Buddhism. The whole negotiation required 'very careful handling and our suavest manners to obviate anything like a breach'. This approach, and a bribe of 500 Rupees, did the trick. The recess was broken open and its treasures revealed.

Perfectly preserved in the dry cavernous air was a huge pile of precious manuscripts many of which Stein and his team smuggled out under cover of darkness over a period of seven nights. Stein did not read Chinese so could not be sure of the importance of what he had found. But one thing he knew. 'Here was conclusive evidence,' he wrote 'that the art of printing books from wooden blocks was practised long before the conventionally assumed time of its invention.' In fact his discovery was even richer than that. Among the printed scrolls that he packed up carefully and sent back

Once prepared the block could print a thousand copies a day.

to London for further investigation was a printed copy of an important Buddhist text – the Diamond Sutra. This work, which today resides in the British Library in London, is the oldest surviving copy of a printed book in the world. It is dated 11th May 868 and inscribed with the words: 'Reverently made for universal distribution by Wang Jie on behalf of his two parents.' Each one of its seven sections was written on thin paper and then pasted onto a wooden block. A carver then used the paper as a trace with which to score the text into the wood following the reversed shapes of the characters. Once prepared the block could print a thousand copies a day.

Buddhism helped drive the proliferation of printing in China. Its ideas took root in northern India where its followers believed that relics were the continued presence of the Buddha in a different form. They counted texts among these. This explained why the Diamond Sutra, and the many other printed documents that were found by Aurel Stein, had been carefully kept in secret. Texts had a practical religious function and were often written for the purpose of generating good karma – the actions of an individual that provide the foundations of happiness – for those who had recently died. Once written they were burned, drowned or hidden, giving them the eternal properties they needed to fulfil their mission. The long survival of the Diamond Sutra in a cave in north-west China was a permanent reminder of the Buddha's message of the impermanence of existence:

Thus shall you think of this fleeting world:
A star at dawn, a bubble in a stream,
A flash of lightning in a summer cloud,
A flickering lamp, a phantom and a dream.

The development of printing was the natural heir to the proliferation of Buddhism in China, which became the state-sponsored religion towards the end of the sixth century AD. When the country was unified under the Emperor Wen of Sui, the production of manuscripts and the distribution of relics, including texts, accelerated. More than 900,000 scrolls were produced between 604 and 618 AD. Printing emerged in the early seventh century and the technology spread to Korea and Japan. But it was not until the middle of the tenth century that Chinese printing began to have a widespread cultural effect. Between 932 and 953 AD the government printed the 'Five Classics of Confucianism' in 130 volumes using movable wooden blocks. This undertaking was the idea of the Prime Minister, Feng Dao, who wanted Confucian ideas to reach readers in the same way as Buddhism. The publication of many standard literary works followed: China became a reading nation. But those who read were the educated classes, the scholars and officials who organised and ran the Empire. Their books were printed using woodblock techniques: in China systems of movable type never supplanted the traditional methods. In 1040 AD a man called Bi Sheng devised a way of printing using movable type made out of clay, but his fragile pieces were unsuitable for mass production and it was never widely used.

Metal type, of the kind used by Johannes Gutenberg in the fifteenth century, reached Korea in the last quarter of the fourteenth. As in China, however, the techniques were prohibited from straying far from the royal court whose foundry cast the type for the process. Reading matter remained the prerogative of the ruling class. In China woodblock printing was still in use when Sir John Barrow visited the country as part of the failed British mission to persuade the Chinese to open up their trade with Britain in the late eighteenth century. 'As to the art of printing,' he wrote, 'there can be little doubt of its antiquity in China, yet they have never proceeded beyond a wooden block.' He thought the reason was probably due to the nature of the Chinese alphabet. 'The difficulty of putting them together upon the frame, into the multitude of forms of which they are capable, is not be surmounted.' In fact the opposite is true. Chinese ideograms are of a manageable size and recur at infrequent intervals. This makes them easier to deal with mechanically than the Western alphabet where small figures are repeated all the time. Carving the script into wood was therefore a much simpler process than it was in Europe and met the needs of the Chinese perfectly adequately.

Barrow had to admit that the Chinese enjoyed plenty to read and observed that newspapers circulated freely in the city. 'It is a singular phenomenon in the history of nations, how the government of an empire of such vast magnitude as that of China should have preserved its stability without any material change for 2,000 years,' he said. This idea of China as a place that never changed was the general European view for centuries, and there was some truth in it. But no situation lasts forever. In the late nineteenth century, as China was forced to open its doors to foreign trade following the Opium Wars, lithographic printing became established in the ports of Shanghai and Hong Kong. Missionaries and merchants seized the opportunity to disseminate information and China's old scribal culture and its ancient printing techniques were submerged beneath the excited distribution of religious tracts and popular fiction.

China and the West were very different in the way they managed the invention and distribution of the printed word, but in both places it was belief and the hunger for knowledge of spiritual ideas that prompted the need for a method by which words could reach people quickly and easily. In the East, Buddhism and then Confucianism drove the process. In the

West, the Catholic Church and its opponents were the forces of change. In about 1439 a German goldsmith called Johannes Gutenberg invented a printing system using movable type made from metal. The most distinctive fruit of this discovery were copies of the Latin Bible that he printed in the 1450s. The Gutenberg Bible was a beautiful piece of work using high-quality paper imported from Italy and oil-based ink that stuck better to the typeface. Gutenberg calculated carefully how to get the right amount of print on each page so that the final work was even and easy to read. The result was the '42 line Bible', a book of 1,282 pages with spaces left for coloured decoration by hand. It is an object as important to the culture of the West as the text of the Diamond Sutra is to the East.

From Gutenberg's Bible, and the other books that he produced, sprang an industry that by the end of the century had transformed the way people behaved. It is estimated that by 1500 about 35,000 separate editions of different books had been published – a total of somewhere between fifteen and twenty million copies. Gutenberg's Bible was produced in Latin, but editions in German and other European languages soon began to appear, galvanising people's desire for information and undermining the power of the Catholic Church. In 1501, Pope Alexander VI issued a bull forbidding the printing of any books in Germany without Church authority and ordered three archbishops to control publication. It was perhaps an early-sixteenth-century version of the tussle that is being fought today between the owners of the internet search engine, Google, and the Chinese government. The Chinese want to control access to information on the worldwide web which Google provides. The papacy had the same fears about the growth of printing.

The development of printing contributed to many changes that were beginning to affect the development of Europe at the end of the fifteenth and beginning of the sixteenth centuries. Increased knowledge of the arts and sciences, the discovery of new territories in the Indies and Americas, and the assault on the long-standing dominance of the Catholic Church combined to make for an era of turmoil, the hinges that swung open the doorway between the medieval and modern worlds. There were many effects of these changes, but the principal one was a considerable broadening of the sort of people who began to be involved in the business of government. The power of the state in Europe had begun to depend on men and women outside the immediate confines of the nobility for some time before the ideas of the Renaissance and Reformation took hold, but these events quickened things. Power relied on commerce. A new nobility began to emerge whose members were recruited from promoted adventurers returning from abroad, or canny businessmen prepared to lend their profits to impecunious monarchs.

This enlarging of the state did not happen in Imperial China whose civilisation was scholarly and grand and enjoyed heights of learning equal to, if not better than, that of the West. The Chinese were not only the first people to have the use of printing, but gunpowder too; they also had the compass and maps before European sailors. Their use of these enhancements, however, was very different. The Chinese regarded the qualities of care and refinement above all else – hardly the primary virtues of a cannonading conquistador or puritan pamphleteer. They were content to contain their knowledge within the boundaries of an existence they felt to be superior to the barbarity of the world beyond. In Europe new technology was unleashed: in China it was kept on a lead held firmly by the scholars and officials who dictated the pace of life. The copy of the Diamond Sutra found by Sir Aurel Stein and the Gutenberg Bible provide a good example of the antithesis between the genius of East and West. In one the art of invention was far older but its power and uses were not seen as necessary to service anything beyond certain precisely defined needs. In the other it was younger, but youth gave it the vigour to change things well beyond its original conception.

CHAPTER 3

Leonardo da Vinci

1452–1519

Leonardo da Vinci was a supreme genius of the Renaissance.

Is it possible to say anything new about Leonardo da Vinci? Revered in his lifetime, his reputation for brilliance has grown with the years; no man in the history of the Western world has been so utterly admired. He lived at an extraordinary time, the great flowering of art, science and thought that became known as the Renaissance, and his work is regarded as its perfect representation. In one sense he *is* the Renaissance: the embodiment of man's knowledge and talents at a unique moment in his history. His stature is enhanced by our ignorance of many of the details of his life. Aspects of Leonardo's character are a matter of speculation rather than fact, and we tend to build our own picture of the man using his work and the things we know about his life as our raw material. In this way he becomes a symbol, a reflection of our ideas about art and humanity. There is no need to say anything new about him because he is one of the few historical figures whose achievements mean that he stands for all time.

Leonardo was born in the village of Anchiano near the town of Vinci west of Florence in 1452. He became an apprentice to the sculptor and painter, Andrea del Verrocchio, with whom he stayed for ten years. In 1476 he was accused of sodomy, a charge that was later dropped. In 1482 he went to work for Ludovico Sforza, the Duke of Milan, where he painted *The Last Supper*. When the duke fell from power, Leonardo spent a brief period in Venice before returning to Florence in 1500. In 1502 he was briefly employed as an architect and engineer for Cesare Borgia, brother of Lucrezia, and the son of the Pope, Alexander VI. In

1503 he was commissioned to paint the *Mona Lisa* by a Florentine family, the Gherardinis. Between 1513 and 1516 he spent time in Rome. In 1516 he entered the service of the King of France, Francis I, who gave him the use of a manor house, Clos Lucé, near the royal chateau in Amboise in the Loire Valley. Leonardo died there in 1519.

Leonardo da Vinci seems to have become a man whom everyone wanted to know, even possess. He began his life in humble circumstances in a Tuscan village. He ended them as the prize of the King of France, the cultural trophy *par excellence*, living proof of his patron's exquisite taste. He had not been dead long before his reputation began to be built. The painter, Giorgio Vasari, wrote about many of the artists of the period. His life of Leonardo began as follows: 'The greatest gifts are often seen, in the course of nature, rained by celestial influences on human creatures; and sometimes, in supernatural fashion, beauty, grace and talent are united beyond measure in one single person ... so great was his genius and such its growth, that to whatever difficulties he turned his mind, he solved them with ease.' Leonardo was 'truly marvellous and celestial'. European historians and writers of the nineteenth century were equally overwhelmed. The German, Jacob Burckhardt, who published one of the most important books on the Renaissance in 1860, said that: 'The colossal outlines of Leonardo's nature can never be more than dimly and distantly conceived.' The French historian, Jules Michelet, who coined the modern term 'Renaissance', called him 'this Italian brother of Faust'; to the French critic, Hippolyte Taine, he was 'the precocious originator of all modern ideas ... a subtle and universal genius'. The English writer, Walter Pater, in a famous essay about Leonardo written in 1869, said that he 'seemed to his contemporaries to be the possessor of some unsanctified and secret wisdom'. He wrote of the artist's most famous painting, the *Mona Lisa*: 'perhaps of all ancient pictures time has chilled it least'.

These hymns to Leonardo's brilliance have not quietened in our own time. He remains a figure of global reverence and his drawing of *Vitruvian Man*, displaying the precise proportions of the human body, can be seen on tourist t-shirts in every city of the world. Men and women achieve historical greatness because their talents seem to represent perfectly, or nearly perfectly, the general aspirations of the age in which they lived. Such a man was Leonardo da Vinci.

All contemporary accounts describe Leonardo as a man of striking physical beauty. He impressed with his looks almost as much as with his skills. The charge of sodomy suggests that he was homosexual – apparently common in early sixteenth-century Florence although not condoned – but after the case was dropped he does not appear to have had a close relationship with anyone of either sex. He was a vegetarian and left-handed. He wrote most of his personal notes in mirror writing so that they could only be read if reflected in a glass. We have little pictorial evidence of what he actually looked like, but some of his pictures are thought to contain characters that may be self-portraits. A drawing in red chalk of the head of a man with flowing hair and a beard, made towards the end of his life, has come to be seen as a picture of him because it seems to depict the idea of 'Renaissance Man', but we cannot be sure that even this is really him. To understand him we have to rely on his work.

Most of his personal notes were written in mirror writing.

The exact period of the Renaissance is hard to define. There is no precise historical border crossing between the medieval and modern worlds: the Renaissance was a cultural movement that accompanied other trends that began to transform Western Europe during the fifteenth century. It was the means by which men gave expression to a changed feeling about the continuity of their existence. The medieval world of Christendom was dominated above all by an unswerving belief in divine direction. Humans lived according to God's plan. In one of the most influential works of the Middle Ages, *Of The City of God,* written shortly after the Sack of Rome in 410 AD, St Augustine of Hippo explained how the world was God-given and God-directed and that Rome had fallen because of its paganism and immorality. This view contributed to the way people thought and wrote. The greatest work of medieval literature, Dante's *Divine Comedy,* was a brilliant allegory about the journey of the soul after death, poetic fiction rooted in Christian theology. During the Renaissance the unrelenting hold of religion began to be loosened by ideas drawn from elsewhere. Classical antiquity and the ideas of Greece and Rome, removed from the context of an entirely Christian view of the world, started to be appreciated for their intrinsic value. Figurative painting and the beauty of classical design and proportion began to be seen as a valuable foundation for art.

The career of the Florentine philosopher, Marsilio Ficino, summed up this new approach. In 1462 he was asked by the ruler of Florence, Cosimo de' Medici, to take charge of a new academy, founded on the principles of Plato in Athens. Under Ficino's guidance, the Academy became the intellectual home of many of the greatest artists and thinkers of the time. He himself translated the works of Plato into Latin, the common language of the educated classes, but he was also a priest and a Christian scholar. He believed strongly in the value of painting which he believed was capable of explaining, through the use of visual imagery, the relationship between man in the world and his divine soul. He never left the area around Florence, but he wrote to like-minded thinkers all over Europe. His knowledge of classical literature combined with his deep faith gave him a flexible approach to understanding God's requirements of man. The Christian religion was unalterable, but it did allow for variety in the way in which it was observed. The world of Greece and Rome was not a pagan past to be ignored, but a time of beauty to be restored. In a letter of 1492 he wrote: 'This century like a golden age has restored to light the liberal arts that were almost extinct ... Achieving what was honoured among the ancients, but almost forgotten since.' From Italy, men like Ficino started a movement that spread well beyond its borders. By the middle of the sixteenth century, its influence was felt in all parts of the Continent, embracing ideas that seeped into every branch of human existence including politics. Machiavelli's *The Prince*, with its practical, ruthless recommendations on the art of successful government is, in its recognition of the realities of life, also a product of the Renaissance. European artists, writers and intellectuals in the period between 1450 and 1550 began to enjoy a new strength and rely on resources they had previously ignored. But they did not leave an old world behind. Its ideas came too, albeit refreshed and repolished for the time ahead.

The extraordinary depth of one Renaissance mind is concealed in Leonardo da Vinci's notebooks. When he died in France he left behind thousands of pages of manuscript that were collected by his assistant, Francesco Melzi, and taken back to Italy. When Melzi died his family sold them and they became scattered. Some were lost altogether, others were gathered up and bound together. The biggest collection, *The Codex Atlanticus* – the name 'Atlanticus' is used to indicate the breadth of subjects covered – has twelve volumes of nearly 1,200 pages containing drawings and writings on mathematics, botany, weapons, flight and musical instruments. Another, *The Codex Arundel* – so-called because it belonged to the Earl of Arundel in the seventeenth century – includes, among other things, Leonardo's observations on hydraulics and mechanics. There are other manuscripts too, including a small unfinished *Treatise on Painting*. These fantastic pages reveal Leonardo to have been a man who ranged over the whole field of human knowledge: nothing was a barrier to his curiosity. In one fifty-page section of *The Codex Atlanticus*, he wrote about the tides of the Black and Caspian Seas; the distance of the earth from the sun; the increase in the size of a pupil in an owl's eye; the evaporation of water in the Mediterranean; deliberations on the laws of gravity; sketches and a study for a flying machine; architectural drawings; a study of the angle of incidence and the law of refraction as well as innumerable mathematical calculations and diagrams – all written in his own mirror language as if he never wanted them to leave his presence. As he wrote in one of his notebooks: 'If you are alone you belong entirely to yourself.'

In the end, however, it is Leonardo da Vinci's paintings that remind us of his contribution to our history. He was a notorious procrastinator, laying aside works before they were

He ranged over the whole field of human knowledge; nothing was beyond his curiosity.

completed and never finishing others at all. But in the small collection of pictures he left behind, as well as his drawings, he revealed himself to be a great master. In his *Treatise on Painting*, he explained the 'three branches' of perspective – linear perspective, the perspective of colour and the perspective of disappearance. 'Perspective,' he said, is 'no more than a scientific demonstration in which experience shows us that every object sends its image to the eye by a pyramid of lines and which shows that bodies of equal size will create a pyramid of smaller or larger size according to their distance.' Basic principles such as this, said Leonardo, give a painter technique. Perspective is essential to good drawing and painting but the artist who only relies on 'practice and the eye' is no better than 'a mirror which copies slavishly everything placed in front of it and has no consciousness of the existence of these things'. A painter must use his intellect. Then 'the universe can be completely reproduced and rearranged in its entire vastness!'.

That description of an artist's job is not a bad description of what the whole Renaissance was about. Leonardo, like the other painters, writers and scholars of the age, wanted to reproduce the universe, placing mankind not just in an artistic but also a historical perspective. In *The Last Supper*, the picture he painted on the walls of the refectory in a Milanese convent, he demonstrated these intentions perfectly. He arranged Jesus and his disciples with careful symmetry, but the action and drama he created within this framework radiates life and intensity. Leonardo's *Last Supper* is a real occasion, not simply a symbolic depiction of an important religious event. In the *Mona Lisa* he painted what is probably the most famous picture in the world. Seized on by nineteenth-century romantic writers as symbol of eternal femininity, the painting has grown in popularity ever since. Its subject looks towards the viewer in a welcoming but reserved manner. She sits, perhaps at a window, in front of a great landscape stretching far into the distance, a human link between the world in which we live, the one we have left behind and the one that is yet to come. It impresses as much with its modernity as by its age and in that sense is the embodiment of the Renaissance.

Five Renaissance Men

Michelangelo

Michelangelo di Lodovico Buonarroti Simoni (1475–1564) was
a painter, sculptor and architect of genius. At thirteen he was
apprenticed to the painter Ghirlandaio who recommended him
to Lorenzo de' Medici for his humanist academy in Florence.
His most celebrated works of sculpture, the *Pietà* (1499) and
David (1504), were created soon afterwards, before he turned
thirty. Between 1508 and 1514 he painted the ceiling of the
Sistine Chapel in Rome. The section showing the hand of God
imparting life to Adam is one of the most famous in all of art.
He painted *The Last Judgment*, behind the chapel's altar, twenty
years later. Contemporaries called him *Il Divino* ('the Divine
One').

Van Eyck

Jan van Eyck (*c.*1395–1441) was a leading Renaissance painter
who came from Bruges. He is considered one of the greatest
Northern European painters of his day, and is sometimes
called 'the father of oil painting' because he was one of the
first Flemish painters to use oil-based paints. In 1425 van Eyck
secured the patronage of Duke Philip the Good of Burgundy,
for whom he went on several journeys as an envoy and artist.
These left him exceptionally well paid, but he supplemented
his income with private commissions. Among these the Ghent
Altarpiece (*c.*1426–32) is a particularly fine example.

Machiavelli

Niccolò di Bernardo dei Machiavelli (1469–1527) was a
Renaissance philosopher. He began his career as a civil servant
and diplomat in the Florentine Republic, the regime which
deposed the Medici family in 1494. In 1512 the republic was
in turn overthrown by the Medicis and he was arrested and
tortured. On his release he retired to his estate where he
wrote political treatises. He is best known for his short work

The Prince, written in 1513 and circulated privately during his lifetime. It is one of the earliest works of modern philosophy in which Machiavelli describes the pragmatic methods a prince should use to acquire and maintain power, giving rise to the phrase 'Machiavellian'.

Erasmus

Known as the 'Prince of the Humanists', Desiderius Erasmus Roterodamus (1466/69–1536) was a Dutch Renaissance philosopher and Catholic theologian. Born Gerrit Gerritszoon, he was given a privileged monastic education and went on to study at the University of Paris, a great centre of reformist theology. As a classical scholar Erasmus worked in several European countries, including England where he was Professor of Divinity at Cambridge University. Some of his most important work was the preparation of Latin and Greek editions of the New Testament which paved the way for the Protestant Reformation. To the disappointment of many Protestants, including Martin Luther, Erasmus remained committed to reforming the Catholic Church from within.

Francis I

Francis I was King of France from 1515 to 1547, and an exact contemporary of Henry VIII. He was an important patron of artists of the Renaissance, particularly Andrea del Sarto and Leonardo da Vinci. He hired agents to buy works of art in Italy, and paintings by masters like Michelangelo and Titian formed the basis of the collection that can be seen in the Louvre in Paris today. Like all good humanist kings, Francis wrote poetry and read avidly, building an impressive library. Militarily and politically, he was less successful. He tried to defeat his longstanding enemy, the Holy Roman Emperor, Charles V, whom he wanted to replace and, despite his humanist views, embarked on policies of Protestant persecution.

CHAPTER 4

Vasco da Gama Discovers a Sea Route to India

1498

In May 1498 the Portuguese sailor, Vasco da Gama, arrived at the port of Calicut on the west coast of southern India. His voyage opened up a trade route to the East and began the struggle for the European domination of India.

The church of St Francis at Kochi, formerly Cochin, in south India does not have any particular architectural merit but it has profound historical significance. It is the first European church to have been built in India. Originally constructed of wood it was founded by Franciscan friars who accompanied a Portuguese voyage in 1500. In 1516 it was rebuilt with stone and given a tiled roof. In 1524 it became the first burial place of the Portuguese viceroy, Vasco da Gama. Facing west with a bell tower surmounting a gabled front, the church is a small, somewhat battered, reminder of the history of European colonisation in Asia.

When Vasco da Gama set out on his first journey to India in 1497 he believed that he would find multitudes of Christians when he got there. Europeans had long been fascinated by stories of Prester John, the Christian king who ruled an empire lost among the pagan lands of the East. This fable was a concoction of muddled information about the travels of early missionaries fortified by European ignorance of geography. They thought Africa, China and India were all one – the Indies. There is strong historical evidence to support the fact that the apostle Thomas – 'doubting Thomas' – arrived in India not far from Cochin in 52 AD and began converting the local population. Others followed at various times throughout the intervening years, but by the time Vasco da Gama landed, the few Christians living there were, in the eyes of the Roman Catholic Church, actually heretics. They were Nestorian Christians and believed in a distinct separation between the human and divine qualities of Jesus. As in the Spanish conquest of South America, the Portuguese set up the Inquisition not long after their arrival, but by the middle of the seventeenth century their power in India began to subside. In 1663 the church of St Francis in Cochin fell under the control of the Dutch Protestants and remained in their possession until the end of the eighteenth century when it was surrendered to Anglicanism, the established religion of India's new masters, the British. It is a little church with a big story to tell – the story of the capture of much of Asia by the European powers and the domination of one form of civilisation by another.

The Portuguese began the business of serious exploration in the first half of the fifteenth century. Their inspiration was religious as much as it was commercial. Henry, a prince of the Kingdom of Portugal, and known as 'The Navigator', organised and paid for a number of expeditions to explore the Atlantic Ocean. At his castle in Sagres on the country's southernmost tip, he gathered around him mapmakers and mathematicians to help him in his task. His purpose was to skirt the flank of Islam, entrenched throughout North Africa and the Middle East and still occupying the Iberian kingdom of Granada, and carry the message of Christianity to the Indies. Helped by the revenues of the Order of Christ, of which he was the Grand Master, he wanted to look beyond the confines of the Mediterranean to ensure the survival and spread of the true religion. He won important papal support. In 1452, Pope Nicholas V granted to the King of Portugal, Alfonso V, the right to capture and enslave Saracens and pagans wherever they were found, following this up with the bull of 1454 which gave Portugal the right to conquer and control 'all the Orient' in perpetuity. Henry died in 1460, but the work he had begun prospered. During the reign of King John II (1481–95), the Portuguese established a trading post on the shores of what is today Ghana, explored the area along the coast of Angola, discovered the River Congo and began a settlement on the islands off the coast of Guinea from which it traded slaves and imported gold. In 1488 Bartholomew Diaz discovered the Cape of Good Hope and with it the prospect of lands beyond the Indian Ocean. Ten years later the Portuguese king who succeeded John, Manuel I, decided that a new, big expedition was called for.

Vasco da Gama came from a well-connected family. He was brought up in the southern Portuguese province of Alentejo, where presumably he learned maritime skills. In looking for someone to lead the expedition of 1497, King Manuel's eyes fell first on da Gama's father, Estevao, but he died and Vasco was chosen as his successor. The King needed someone tough. Bartholomew Diaz had been forced to return home from his voyage after his crew mutinied. On 8th July 1497, Vasco da Gama set sail from the port of Belem on the mouth of the River Tagus in Lisbon. He had four ships. He commanded the flagship, with twenty guns and a flag with a large cross of Christ flying from its mast; his brother, Paulo, commanded another vessel which had been built by Bartholomew Diaz. Da Gama followed Diaz's route to southern Africa, passed the place where he had turned back and reached the east coast of southern Africa by Christmas, giving the land that he could see the name of Natal – the 'birth of Christ'. But it was not a voyage without incident. Men died of fever and scurvy and one ship was abandoned after being damaged in a storm. The expedition met an unfriendly reception in Mozambique and further north in Mombasa, but was welcomed in Malindi where da Gama hired a pilot who knew the trade winds of the Indian Ocean and guided the fleet to its eventual landfall at Calicut. The whole journey took less than a year, but created a sea route that would last for centuries. It did not penetrate lands and oceans that were completely unknown: Arab and Indian traders had worked the route between India and Africa for many years before – one reason why da Gama had been able to find an experienced navigator. India, too, was known to some Europeans, such as Marco Polo, who travelled across land to reach the East during the

The journey took less than a year, but created a sea route that would last for centuries.

Middle Ages. But no one before had travelled from Europe with the same sense of purpose as the four Portuguese ships that left Lisbon in the summer of 1497. They were the advance party, not just of an age of discovery, but of an age of the many changes discovery would bring; and the cannon they carried beneath the fluttering cross of Christ was an indication of the turmoil to come.

Vasco da Gama did not find a multitude of Christians when he landed in southwest India, but instead many of the people he was hoping to circumvent, the Muslims of North Africa whose trade with India was centuries old. Furthermore they were highly sophisticated and uninterested in the trinkets that he had been given with which to try to trade. He returned to Portugal empty-handed, but with the news that India had plentiful riches ripe for exploitation. In 1500 the Portuguese sent a far bigger fleet – thirteen ships and 1,500 men – to force the ruler of Calicut to give them the religious jurisdiction and trading monopolies they required. When this expedition did not succeed, da Gama was dispatched in 1502 on his second voyage to see if he could establish the domination that the Portuguese sought. The Flemish merchants of Antwerp, recognising the commercial possibilities of what was happening, had begun to invest and their cash helped keep the Portuguese project going. Da Gama's second voyage demonstrated the piratical nature of global exploration at the beginning of the sixteenth century. As he approached the Indian coast he captured an Arab ship

As he approached the Indian coast he captured an Arab ship carrying Muslim merchants and their families.

carrying Muslim merchants and their families. Having looted it he sealed the passengers inside and burned it, killing hundreds of men, women and children. 'The Moors were left swimming,' says one contemporary account, 'and the [Portuguese] boats plied about killing them with lances.' He then called on the ruler, the Zamorin of Calicut, to kill all the Muslim traders in his city. When the Zamorin tried to negotiate de Gama captured local fishermen whom he mutilated by cutting off their hands and

An Empire by Accident: the Voyages of Christopher Columbus

In 1492, Christopher Columbus (1451–1506) set off on a haphazard mission across the Atlantic that would change the world. He became, quite by chance, the first European to colonise the Americas.

By the end of the fifteenth century the lucrative overland trade routes to India and China that brought silks and spices into Europe had become disrupted as the Ottoman Empire of the Turks dominated the lands through which these routes passed. Columbus, who came from the city-state of Genoa in Italy, devised a plan to reach the Indies by sailing west across the Atlantic. Throughout the 1480s he approached several European royal monarchs for patronage but all of them rejected his ideas because expert advice told them his calculations were wrong. They were, indeed, wrong. Although Columbus did not believe that the world was flat, he did considerably underestimate the circumference of the earth. He thought it was possible to sail all the way to Asia in one journey.

After several years of negotiation, the Spanish monarchs Ferdinand and Isabella finally agreed to give him their backing. Portugal had discovered a sea route round the Horn of Africa

feet. The Muslim traders started to flee the area and the Zamorin, realising he was confronted with a new and brutal power, gave way.

Vasco da Gama's savage behaviour heralded a new age. The discoveries of the sailors at the end of the fifteenth and sixteenth centuries created what became known as the 'New World'. At the same time as the Portuguese were navigating the coasts of Africa and striking at the heart of India, the Spanish were sailing westwards, finding the beginnings of a continent that no one knew existed before – America. In 1522 a Portuguese captain called Ferdinand Magellan attempted a complete circumnavigation of the globe. He was murdered in the Philippines, but his crew completed the journey. Where Portugal and Spain began, England, France and Holland followed. In 1494 a treaty between Spain and Portugal tried to rationalise the papal decrees that and they were keen to establish a competitive route. Columbus departed on 3rd August 1492 and on 12th October sighted land. He believed he was in the East Indies: in fact he was in the Bahamas – although nobody quite knows where. Over the following months, Columbus explored Cuba and Hispaniola before returning to Spain, where he announced he had reached an island off the Chinese coast. He presented his trophies – including a handful of natives, gold, tobacco and turkeys – to an astonished court. He then set sail once again for the Americas, and in his three further expeditions discovered other Caribbean islands and the Central and South American mainland.

Columbus insisted on being made governor of the places he had discovered but he was a poor administrator and his men accused him of being tyrannical and corrupt. Recalled to Spain, he was briefly imprisoned and, like many of his intrepid contemporaries, spent the last years of his life a disappointed man. He is one of the most important figures in world history. His four voyages of exploration, which started with a lucky accident, began the process of European colonisation of the Americas and changed both the Old and the New Worlds forever.

gave both countries the right to carve up the discoveries of the New World between them. It awarded newly-discovered lands to the east of the Cape Verde Islands to Portugal, those to the west to Spain. Other European powers, anxious not to be excluded from new opportunities, began to muscle in. In 1496, Henry VII of England granted an Italian sailor whose anglicised name was John Cabot the rights to explore a northern passage across the Atlantic Ocean. In one small ship, *The Matthew*, he reached the coast of Canada in the summer of 1497. These were extraordinary developments, providing European nations with treasure beyond their wildest dreams. No longer needing to draw their resources from their own lands (or through protracted warfare from their neighbours), they turned to places they had either only vaguely heard about before, or had never known existed. They seized this opportunity with determination – a measure of their growing confidence in their ability to manage their affairs in a unified fashion. Europe conquered the world. From the fall of Rome to the fall of Constantinople, Europe had been largely in retreat, forced to accept limitations to most of its boundaries as it fell back against the advance of Islam. The Age of Discovery changed that, and the nations of Europe began to move forward confidently once again.

Following his second voyage, Vasco da Gama did not return to India for another twenty years. But his reputation as a reliable man in a crisis could not escape him and in 1524, having become the first Portuguese man not of royal blood to be ennobled with the title of count, was asked by the King to take up the position of Viceroy of India. He died of malaria within three weeks of his arrival. In the church at Cochin there is a contemporary account of his funeral: 'It pleased the Lord to give this man so strong a spirit, that without any human fear he passed through so many perils during the discovery of India ... all for the love of the Lord, for the great increase of his Catholic faith, and for the great honour and glory and ennobling of Portugal.' His remains were returned to Portugal fifteen years after his death. He had grown rich in the service of his country, but many of his countrymen, and the people of other countries too, would grow as rich as a result of what he achieved.

Da Gama's brutality heralded a new age.

The little church at Calicut was only one of the destinations that now fell under European eyes. People's perception of where the centre of the world lay had begun to move. Finding it would still be an uncertain process: the art of cartography was still in its infancy and the task of developing a chronometer accurate enough to keep time on a long voyage would take another 200 years. But the journey had begun. Vasco da Gama, full of human brutality and Christian confidence, was one of those who pointed out the way.

CHAPTER 5

Sir Isaac Newton Publishes the *Principia*

1687

In 1687, Sir Isaac Newton published his *Philosophiae Naturalis Principia Mathematica*, or 'The Mathematical Principles of Natural Philosophy' – the *Principia*. It was the most important mathematical and scientific work written since the days of ancient Greece, and laid the foundation for the study of physics for a further two centuries.

In the same year that he was to publish the book that would revolutionise the study of science, Isaac Newton was called to appear before one of the most fearsome men of the age. The Lord Chancellor of England, George Jeffreys, had been asked by the King, James II, to interrogate the vice chancellor of Cambridge University, John Peachell, and senior fellows including Newton, about why they would not agree to admit a Benedictine monk, Alban Francis, as a Master of Arts. Any officer of the university was required to swear the oath of supremacy, recognising the monarch as head of the Church, but the King had ordered that Francis be excused. To the vice chancellor and his colleagues this seemed another case of their Catholic King trying to unpick their Protestant freedoms and they appealed. Jeffreys had been elevated to Lord Chancellor following his successful prosecution of the rebels in the Duke of Monmouth's army two years previously, hanging them in public after their defeat at the Battle of Sedgemoor. He heard the academics' arguments in council at Westminster, but was in no mood to listen. The vice chancellor, Peachell, was browbeaten mercilessly by Jeffreys and removed from office. 'As for you,' he said, turning to Isaac Newton and his colleagues, 'go your way and sin no more, lest a worse thing happen to you.'

The incident gives us a glimpse of the turbulent times in which Isaac Newton lived. He was born in 1642, the year of the first battle of the English Civil War. He was a child so sickly, as he later told a colleague, that when two women were sent to neighbours to fetch something for him 'they sate down on a stile by the way and said there was no occasion for making haste for they were sure the child would be dead before they could get back'. His father died shortly before he was born and his mother left him to be brought up by her parents when she remarried and started another family. She returned to the original family house in 1653, the year Oliver Cromwell became Lord Protector, and in

His life coincided with the events that put the finishing touches to the modern British state. He represented the spirit of its genius.

1654 Newton was sent to the local grammar school in Grantham, Lincolnshire. In 1661, the year after the restoration of Charles II to the English throne, he entered Trinity College, Cambridge. Here he remained as an undergraduate, a fellow and then a professor until appointed warden, and later master, of the Royal Mint in 1696 when he left the university and settled in London. Following the Glorious Revolution that unseated James II in 1688, he served as an MP in the Convention Parliament that offered the throne to William III and Mary, based on their agreement to the Bill of

Rights. He lived to see the Union of England and Scotland in 1707, the War of the Spanish Succession against France and the accession of the Hanoverian monarchy under George I in 1714. He lost money in the South Sea Bubble in 1720 and died, aged eighty-five, in 1727. The life of Isaac Newton coincided with the hectic events that put the finishing touches to the modern British state: he represented the spirit of its genius.

Judge Jeffreys would not have known that one of the quiet university deputies arguing their rights under the law was the greatest scientific mind that England had so far in its history produced. Isaac Newton entered Cambridge as a 'sizar' – a lowly position for a man who came from prosperous country stock. He had failed to take over the management of the family estate and his mother may have resented the fact that her oldest boy preferred study to farming. He was well versed in Latin and began to read the prescribed texts of the classical philosophers such as Plato and Aristotle. He worked alone – he was an introverted student – and as he did so his mind took him out of the classical world and into the one in which he was living. He discovered that he preferred the works of Galileo, who had died at the same time as he was born, and Descartes, the man whose philosophy encouraged people to discover what they knew rather than rely on what they believed. These were revolutionary ideas in the middle of the seventeenth century, investing men with the power of scientific enquiry while still preserving a framework of strong religious belief. Within four years, working outside the prescribed curriculum, he had begun to discover the mathematical principles of calculus and the scientific theory of gravity. He developed some of these ideas while he worked at home in Lincolnshire, to which he had retreated in order to avoid the plague in Cambridge. His famous story of understanding the law of gravity as he watched an apple drop from a tree in the orchard happened at this time. On his return to the university he became the Lucasian Professor of Mathematics, a post with few onerous duties thus allowing him to pursue his research. He worked in optics and in 1669 constructed the world's first reflecting telescope, correcting the weaknesses of the refracting telescope that distorted the image under observation. His discovery was displayed at the Royal Society in London, which promptly made Newton a fellow.

The Royal Society was founded in 1660. It began as an informal gathering of like-minded intellectuals who met to discuss their experiments and ideas. The new King, Charles II, approved of their work and gave them a Royal Charter. The men who made

Within four years he had begun to discover the mathematical principles of calculus and the scientific theory of gravity.

up its membership were some of the finest scientific minds in Britain, including the astronomer and architect, Christopher Wren and the chemist, Robert Boyle. They could look back on a long period of scientific enquiry that had begun in the first days of the Renaissance and continued since then, constantly probing the boundaries between religious belief and analytical research. In 1543, the year he died, the German-Polish astronomer Nicolaus Copernicus published a book in which he stated unequivocally that: 'All the spheres revolve round the sun at their mid-point, and therefore the sun is the centre of the universe.' His findings were condemned by the Catholic Church, but Protestantism was more forgiving, and in 1596 Johannes Kepler, a teacher from Graz in Austria, published a work that took the Copernican theory of heliocentrism (the sun as the centre of the planetary system) as its core proposition. Other supporters of this idea were not so fortunate. In Italy in 1642, Galileo died having been held for ten years under house arrest for his heliocentric views.

But the forces of religion could not stem the tide of science. In England in 1627 a book written by Francis Bacon called *The New Atlantis* was published by his literary executor. Written in the years before his death, it set out a vision for a Utopia, one of whose principal features was the unfettered pursuit of scientific enquiry. The king in Bacon's Utopia created a society called 'Salomon's House', whose members were instructed to sail the world in order 'to give us knowledge of the affairs and state of those countries to which they were designed, and especially of the sciences, arts, manufactures, and inventions of all the world; and withal to bring unto us books, instruments, and patterns in every kind.' It sounded not unlike the purposes of the Royal Society. By the middle of the seventeenth century men had developed an overwhelming desire to examine the natural construction of the world. Most of them did not think that their discoveries contradicted the idea of a universe created by God. Kepler thought his discovery of the way planets moved elliptically round the sun was God's geometrical plan: in the scientific revolution of the seventeenth century there

> *The forces of religion could not stem the tide of science.*

were many great minds who believed that through the study of 'natural philosophy' (the understanding of the mechanical structure of God's universe) they would reveal the mathematical and physical ingenuity of the Almighty.

The *Principia* reached the world by a happy accident. In 1684 Newton was visited in Cambridge by an energetic young scientist called Edmond Halley, whose fame today rests on his accurate prediction of the occasional reappearance of one of the comets of the solar system. He and members of the Royal Society had been discussing the inverse square law of attraction, which they were convinced implied that planets circled elliptically, but they could not prove it. Halley asked Newton during their conversation what he thought the orbit of the planets would be if their distance from the sun was subject to this law. 'Sir Isaac replied immediately that it would be an Ellipsis,' we are told, and 'the Doctor struck with joy and amazement asked him how he knew it, why saith he I have calculated it, whereupon Dr Halley asked him for his calculation without any farther delay,

'From these forces,' he wrote, 'we deduce the motion of the planets, the comets, the moon and the sea.'

Sir Isaac Newton looked among his papers but could not find it, but he promised him to renew it; and then send it to him.' The picture of Newton rummaging about to find a set of calculations that had the ability to transform human understanding of the universe is an endearing one. Under Halley's guidance, and with the help of his money, Newton's findings were gathered and published: Halley was, in his own words, 'the Ulysses who produced this Achilles'. The work itself, written in Latin, was a sensation. Using mathematical principles that he called 'fluxions', but which today we refer to as calculus, Newton set out his three laws of motion and his universal law of gravitation. 'From these forces,' he wrote in the preface to the first edition, 'by other propositions which are also mathematical, we deduce the motion of the planets, the comets, the moon and the sea.' In clear and economic language he presented the world with a revolution in knowledge.

Isaac Newton remained a man of deep religious faith throughout his life. Unlike Halley, whose known scepticism prevented him at first from getting the academic positions he deserved, Newton never wavered in his beliefs. 'When I wrote my treatise about our System,' he wrote in later life, 'I had an eye upon such Principles as might work with considering men for the belief of a Deity and nothing can rejoice me more than to find it useful for that purpose.' He spent as much time examining theological concepts of creation as he did the physical evidence for the structure of the universe. These enquiries led him to believe in Arianism, a form of ancient Christianity that questioned the eternal nature of Jesus. Arians believed that Jesus was created by God and therefore inferior to him, not part of the Holy Trinity that put him on an equal footing. This interpretation of the Scriptures was the most serious heresy to afflict the Christian Church before the advent of the Reformation in the sixteenth century and was something that neither Catholics nor Protestants accepted. Revealing his beliefs would have jeopardised Newton's position as a Cambridge professor. Subscription to orthodox religion was axiomatic for a university don. He kept his opinions secret – perhaps not difficult for the self-contained personality that had not thought to come forward with the mathematical calculations the world needed to prove the physical movements of the planetary system.

Today, in an age in which scientific evidence is often taken as the final proof of the non-existence of God, it is interesting to consider how a man like Newton, who knew so much about reality, could have expended intellectual energy exploring the unknowable. He also dabbled in alchemy: for Newton mystical ideas were as worthy of forensic examination as physical ones. At the end of the seventeenth century, the differences between natural philosophy and theology, or the earthly interpretation of God's commands, were very fine. Knowing how the world worked did not mean that God had not created it. His memorial in Westminster Abbey tells us that he had a strength of mind 'almost divine' and that he 'vindicated by his philosophy the majesty of God mighty and good'. Isaac Newton, the greatest scientist the world had produced for nearly two thousand years, was always a man of his time.

CHAPTER 6

Australia's First Colony
1788

In 1788 a fleet of eleven British ships carrying 1,300 people, more than half of whom were convicts, arrived on the coast of east Australia. Under the command of Captain Arthur Phillip they established the colony of New South Wales – a penal settlement that grew into a great country.

The village of Gruline on the Isle of Mull off the north-west coast of Scotland is about 11,000 miles away from the coast of eastern Australia, but one of its buildings provides a link between them. Enclosed within a low grey wall stands the mausoleum of Major General Lachlan Macquarie. It is a simple stone building, but then Lachlan Macquarie was a simple, stony sort of man, one of many resolute, hard-working Scots who built and guided the fortunes of the British Empire. He died in London and his remains were brought back to his birthplace for final interment. The inscription on his tomb reads: 'The high estimation in which both his character and government were held rendered him truly deserving the appellation by which he has been distinguished the Father of Australia.' It is a modest resting place for a man called the father of a nation and says a great deal about the way Britain regarded the territory he had administered on its behalf.

On New Year's Eve 1809, Macquarie arrived in Australia to replace William Bligh in the post of Governor-General. Bligh was a man whose fundamental sense of decency always seemed to land him in trouble. Having sailed with Captain Cook on his last fateful voyage, served under Nelson at the Battle of Copenhagen, and lost his ship, HMS *Bounty*, to mutineers, he was forced from office in Australia by a rebellion of officers who objected to his attempts to stifle their lucrative rum trade. Macquarie inherited a prison camp that was struggling to become a civilised society. It was run by military officers who formed the social elite and relied for much of its labour on the convicts who had been transported there as punishment. Since labour was scarce, convicts could earn their liberty and become emancipated workers. Some became accepted members of this unusual community, but others remained unreformed, adding a debauched and rather dangerous air to its activities. Macquarie ruled with a rod of iron – the autocratic powers of Britain's rulers of its remote dribbles of territory were immense – building roads, churches, schools and public offices, as the population trebled to nearly 40,000 people. He also gave his fiefdom identity. He believed prisoners who had served their sentences should be treated as free and equal citizens, a sensible as well as humanitarian policy in a place teeming with social uncertainty. At heart he was always a straightforward soldier, but he used his time in a faraway corner of the British Empire to lay the foundations of a new country. The 'Father of Australia' was not much thanked for his efforts. By the time he left office in 1821 the British government had commissioned a report recommending that the cost of its penal settlement in Australia should be reduced. Perhaps Australia was just too far away; perhaps the lessons of America left scars that made the British suspicious of colonial ambition. Whatever the reason, the vast continent Britain had recently uncovered was never much cherished in its infancy.

Australia was the last habitable continent in the world to be settled by people from Europe. Until the last quarter of the eighteenth century it remained the unknown land of the south, 'Terra Australis', a vague, vast continent covering the whole southern quarter of the earth. It was ignored by the inhabitants of Asia as well. In the early fourteenth century a Chinese map maker called Chu-SSu-Pen confessed that he could not include this part of the world. 'Regarding the foreign countries of the barbarians south-east of the South Seas,' he wrote, 'there is no means of investigating them because of their great distance ... Those who speak of them are unable to say anything definite while those who say something definite cannot be trusted.' In the first years of the seventeenth century, a Portuguese expedition reached the islands of what are now called the New Hebrides and charted the southern coastline of New Guinea but failed to realise its dream of establishing a Christian outpost called Nova Jerusalem. In 1642 a Dutch sailor, Abel Tasman, was dispatched from the Dutch East India Company's headquarters in Java, then called Batavia, to look for gold in the uncharted southern continent. He landed in Tasmania, which he named Van Diemen's Land after the Governor-General of the Dutch East Indies, and sailed along the coast of New Zealand. In a second voyage he mapped part of Australia's north coast, but failed to discover the fabulous wealth of which he and his colleagues dreamed. The Dutch, having called their discoveries 'New Holland', turned their attention elsewhere. In 1691 an English buccaneer, William Dampier, turned up in London with observations and stories about his adventures in New Holland that so excited the Admiralty that he was asked to lead an expedition in 1699 to charter the waters between New Guinea and the Australian mainland. His scientific observations and ideas about navigation proved invaluable to later explorers but for the most part the unknown land of the south continued to keep its secrets.

Captain James Cook was the most important sailor and navigator in European history after Christopher Columbus. He had many advantages over his great predecessor. For a start he knew roughly where he was going, and he had the inventions of the intervening years to support him. Columbus belonged to the age of discovery – wild and adventurous; Cook lived in the age of enlightenment – thoughtful and precise. He used the resources at his disposal carefully and was able, over the course of three momentous voyages, to establish beyond further doubt the existence of the Australian continent. The son of a Yorkshire labourer he learned his seamanship on coal ships in the North Sea, difficult and dangerous work that gave him an ideal grounding for his career in the Royal Navy. He was a skilled navigator – his charts and sailing directions were published – and when the Royal Society asked the Navy to provide them with a ship to sail to the South Pacific to make observations that could be used to calculate the distance of the earth from the sun, the Navy insisted that Lieutenant Cook take command. It also gave him secret instructions. Once he had carried out the Royal Society's requirement of observing the transit of Venus across the face of the sun from Tahiti he was to sail south in search of the great undiscovered continent: 'taking care before you leave the Vessel to demand from the Officers and Petty Officers the Log Books and Journals they may have Kept, and to seal them up for our inspection and enjoyning them, and the whole Crew, not to divulge where they have been until they have Permission to do so'. Between 1768 and 1771 Cook did as he was ordered; in two further voyages (1772–75 and 1776–79) he proved that 'Terra Australis' did not exist, outlined the territories of Australia and New Zealand, charted the islands of the South Pacific and became the first European to explore the coastline of northwest America around Vancouver Sound. On his last voyage he was killed in a skirmish with natives on Hawaii, but by that time he had discovered most of what was left to be discovered of the world in which he lived.

Cook named the south-east part of Australia 'New South Wales', and the place where he landed 'Botany Bay'. Nearly twenty years after these discoveries the British came again in a voyage almost as skilful but with a purpose rather more menacing. Captain Arthur Phillip led his fleet – two warships, six transports and three store ships – from Britain, round the coast of Africa to the coast of Australia. The last leg of the journey, from Cape Town to Botany Bay, took three months, all of it entirely at sea. All eleven ships arrived safely and at the same time. Only forty-eight people out of a total of more than 1,300 died during the voyage. It was a remarkable achievement, particularly since more than half of those on board were convicts with no experience of sea travel and little interest in their destination. Getting to Australia safely was only the beginning of Arthur

More than half of those on board were convicts with no experience of sea travel and little interest in their destination.

Phillip's arduous task. Having arrived he found that Botany Bay, although it had impressed James Cook, was unsuitable as a place to found a colony and after a few days moved the whole enterprise to Port Jackson about twelve miles to the north. He struggled against colossal odds to keep things together. Some of the convicts refused to work, and some of the marines refused to supervise them, believing guard duty to be below their status. People got drunk. The weather was unpredictable. But Arthur Phillip managed these matters with unremitting determination. By the time he left to return home in 1792 the little colony had become established.

Some of the convicts refused to work, and some of the marines refused to supervise them.

The story of the foundation of Australia is one of the most extraordinary in all of colonial history. In the corner of a continent 11,000 miles away, the British government entrusted to a succession of loyal sailors and soldiers the business of establishing a settlement using as its workforce men and women whom it no longer had use for at home. Despite the successful voyages of Captain Cook, it knew very little about the people or the environment to which it was consigning those whom it sent there. Thanks largely to the human aptitude for survival, coupled with the remarkable discipline of the eighteenth century Royal Navy, the project took root and prospered. In the first quarter of the nineteenth century, ordinary emigrants joined the flow of people seeking to settle in the new colony and Australia took shape as a dominion of the British Empire.

Australia remained as it had been created, a microcosm of Britain in an alien environment, throughout the nineteenth century. But eventually people from Asia, who had never ventured to explore the South Pacific, and had thus allowed it to pass into European hands, began to be attracted to the new country. Worried that this would undermine its economy and destroy the labour market, the newly-formed Federation of Australia approved a 'White Australia' policy in 1901 that prevented the immigration of Africans, Asians and Polynesians. 'The doctrine of the equality of man,' argued Australia's new Prime Minister,

New Zealand: A Very Brief History

The first settlers in New Zealand, the Māoris, came
from Eastern Polynesia in around 1280. By the end of the
fifteenth century they had hunted New Zealand's abundant
big game almost to extinction and began to lead a sedentary,
horticultural way of life. The first European to reach New
Zealand was the Dutchman Abel Tasman in 1642. He sighted
South Island, and believing that it was linked to Staten Island
off Argentina, named it 'Staten Landt'. Dutch cartographers later
changed the name to Nieuw Zeeland, after the Dutch province
of Zeeland.

Dutch interest in the islands was never particularly strong
and it was not until 1769 that the next European, Captain
James Cook, visited New Zealand, and changed its name to
the anglicised form. European and American traders and
missionaries began to settle in the country but they were
notoriously lawless and behaved aggressively towards the
Māori inhabitants. In 1839 the British, anxious to control the
settlers and forestall intervention by other European powers,
moved to annex New Zealand and persuade the Māoris to cede
sovereignty. About forty chiefs signed the Treaty of Waitangi
a year later, but it divided Māori opinion and created lasting
bitterness. After 1840 European settlement increased rapidly.
For the Māoris, land represented an important part of their

Edward Barton, 'was never intended to apply to the equality of
the Englishman and the Chinaman'. Another politician, Alfred
Deakin, said rather more forgivingly, if rather ingenuously,
that it was the Asians' good qualities rather than their bad ones
that made them dangerous to Australians. Their 'inexhaustible
energy' and 'power of applying themselves to new tasks' made
them dangerous competitors, he said.

The hard-won victory of prising the Australian continent out
of obscurity and into a condition that made it habitable for Europeans was not one to be sacrificed easily. The people who settled
there had learned by hard experience that the only part of their
huge territory that was fit for development was its seaboard: they
planned to cling on to it as firmly as they could. After the Second

cultural identity and the pressure on them to sell it created tensions that erupted into a series of Land Wars in the 1860s and 70s. Colonial troops invaded Māori regions and confiscated property and the Māori population almost halved in the century after Cook's voyage.

At the end of the nineteenth century, the New Zealand government, which had a measure of autonomy from the British Crown, established a welfare state and in 1893 was the first country in the world to give women the vote. In 1907 it became a separate 'dominion' rather than joining the Commonwealth of Australia. Its economy remained closely aligned with Britain's, and New Zealand was hit hard by the Great Depression: in the early 1930s, average farm incomes dipped briefly below zero. In the years preceding the outbreak of the Second World War, the Māori politician, Apirana Ngata, emerged as a champion of economic recovery and Māori rights. In the 1960s a Māori protest movement led to the establishment of the Waitangi Tribunal to investigate unresolved Māori grievances. Politics became more liberal in the 1980s, with the deregulation of the economy, a relaxation on immigration policy and decriminalisation of homosexuality. New Zealand has debated whether it should become a republic but the British monarch remains the official head of state.

World War the policy changed and Australia started to move towards the vigorously mixed community it has since become. Its geographical position reinforced this trend. Its raw materials were imported increasingly from Japan and its economy began to look, not towards the distant 'motherland' of Great Britain, but to the fast developing Asian nations on the other side of the Pacific Rim. Separation from Britain has today reached the point where there are many Australians who support the idea of their country becoming a republic and severing all ties with the British monarchy.

Such notions would have appalled James Cook, Arthur Phillip and Lachlan Macquarie. They were, above all, loyal servants of the Crown, tough military men sent off to the other side of the world to do their country's bidding. James Tuckey, a Navy lieutenant whose ship carried convicts to New South Wales in 1802, summed up his feelings as he stood at last on the faraway shore to which he had come. 'I beheld a second Rome rising from a coalition of *banditti*. I beheld it giving laws to the world, and superlative in arms and in arts, looking down with proud superiority upon the barbarous nation, of the northern hemisphere; thus running over the airy visions of empire, wealth and glory, I wandered amidst the delusions of imagination.' With such soldierly dreams did Europe embrace the last outpost of the discovered world.

> *'I beheld a second Rome rising from a coalition of* banditti.'

CHAPTER 7

John Logie Baird Demonstrates the First Moving Television Images

1926

In 1926, John Logie Baird, a Scottish engineer, gave the first public demonstration of how television images could be transmitted into people's homes. The flickering pictures were the beginning of a worldwide cultural revolution.

It was Auntie Nellie who was responsible for introducing me to the pleasures of television. When she died in the mid-1950s she left her 'television set' to my mother. It was a beautiful thing. It looked like an expensive piece of furniture. Its small screen was set within a cabinet of highly polished wood, creating the effect of something that was more decorative than functional. My father viewed its arrival with suspicion. He believed that television was bound to distract us all from the more important things in life and decreed that it should be installed in one of the least frequented parts of the house. It was despatched to the frigid isolation (we had no central heating) of the front room. Bit by bit, however, it became an object of ever-increasing pilgrimages. When the weather was very cold we would put on our coats and scarves so we could go and watch it. 'There's no point in lighting a fire,' my father would say. 'We're only going to be half an hour.' But as the half hours turned into hours, and as my father himself became more interested in the programmes it was showing, the fire was lit and we began to enjoy cosy evenings in front of the telly. For the first ten or eleven years of my life I never watched television. By the time I was thirteen or fourteen I was steeped in it, part of the post-war generation that grew up under the spreading shadow of its enormous influence. For millions of people today television is a commodity, as essential a feature of their everyday lives as water or electric light. But unusually it is a commodity that does not simply offer a service, but has the power to deliver ideas as well. For this reason it created one of the greatest cultural transformations in the history of the world.

Scientists had been hunting for a method of sending moving images across distances for nearly half a century before John Logie Baird's first public demonstration. In the early 1870s an English telegraph engineer, Willoughby Smith, discovered that the element selenium had properties that allowed it to conduct electricity more easily in the light than in the dark. A decade later, the German scientist Paul Nipkow used selenium in his model of how images could be transmitted using a scanning rotating disc. The word 'television' came into use in the first years of the twentieth century as further experiments brought the idea towards fruition. Baird gave two demonstrations of his system before he achieved a scanning rate high enough to provide a recognisable moving image. 'It has yet to be seen to what extent further developments will carry Mr Baird's system towards practical use,' reported *The Times,* acknowledging his success in constructing light sensitive cells that could work at the high speed required, adding: 'Trials of the system may shortly be made.' But the Baird system was not the one that eventually formed the basis of the new television service. In America, telephone companies using the electronic technology of the cathode ray tube began their own experiments. They formed a partnership with a British firm to create a rival to Baird's and when both were given permission to start broadcasting on an experimental basis in London at the end of 1936, it was clear that the Anglo-American partnership, operated by Marconi-EMI, had the better system. The following year it began broadcasting. The age of television had begun.

It created one of the greatest cultural transformations in the history of the world.

Gone With the Wind

Released in 1939, and winning ten Academy Awards, *Gone With the Wind* is the apotheosis of Hollywood's 'golden age', and one of the world's most popular films. Based on the 1936 novel by Margaret Mitchell, it tells the story of southern beauty, Scarlett O'Hara (Vivien Leigh); her romance with profiteer Rhett Butler (Clark Gable); and her love for Ashley Wilkes (Leslie Howard), a gentleman who loves the South but not necessarily the Confederacy. Set against the backdrop of the American Civil War the action revolves around the burning of Atlanta by Union troops and its aftermath.

It cost nearly $4 million to make and took $4 billion worldwide at the box office, setting a record that it held for thirty-five years. *Gone With the Wind* was the archetypal Hollywood blockbuster and provided an early formula for mass market success. Its secret was to turn its release into a major event. The premiere was held in Atlanta and was preceded by three days of festivities when thousands of people flocked the streets to watch a parade of limousines carrying stars from the film. After that, its star performances, memorable dialogue and striking use of Technicolor ensured cinematic immortality.

People in Europe and America were well used to watching moving images on screen long before television entered their homes. In 1910 the film director D. W. Griffith made a movie called *In Old California*, which he shot in a place called Hollywood. The area developed rapidly as the centre of the American film industry, where rivalrous studios engaged in melodramatic activities as vivid as the plots of their movies. The tycoons who ran companies like Warner Brothers, MGM, Paramount and Twentieth-Century Fox built a commercial empire described by one screenwriter as being like 'Venice under the Doges'. To begin with their films, such as *Ben Hur, The Gold Rush* and *The Four Horsemen of the Apocalypse*, were all silent. They made international stars out of names such as Lillian Gish, Mary Pickford and Charlie Chaplin. In 1927 the first 'talkie', *The Jazz Singer*, appeared. Produced by Warner Brothers it made $2.6 million in America and internationally – a huge amount of money for the time. A few years afterwards the silent film had died. Colour came in the early 1930s: in 1939 MGM released David O. Selznick's *Gone With the Wind*, starring Vivien Leigh and Clark Gable, to became one of the most popular films of all time. Europe, too, produced popular cinema entertainment. In England, Alfred Hitchcock began his career as a director of thrillers before moving to Hollywood; Alexander Korda travelled in the opposite direction, moving from America to London; and the Ealing Studios stayed firmly British, producing comedies tethered in a very insular sense of humour. The first half of the twentieth century was a period of enormous consumer growth in the Western world, during which many different appliances, from cars to washing machines, became commonplace. Mass entertainment was an important by-product of this process: cinema fed the dream of the easy life.

The Second World War interrupted the development of television, but once it was over its real growth began. It was, however, a very different proposition from cinema because it reached people in their homes. In Britain the idea of entertainment and information being broadcast freely as a domestic service had troubled the authorities since radio first arrived in the mid-

Unlike cinema, it reached people in their homes.

1920s. The government created a regulatory structure where a public body answerable to Parliament, the British Broadcasting Corporation, was given an exclusive right to provide services paid for out of a licence fee levied on every home that owned a radio set. It simply extended this arrangement to cover television as well endorsing, as the historian A. J. P. Taylor remarked, 'the moral case for monopoly'. The BBC was given a commercial competitor, ITV, in 1955, but television in Britain remained carefully regulated, overseen by government-appointed bodies that supervised the activities of the broadcasters. Countries in the rest of Europe, as they began to recover from the effects of Nazi occupation, moved gingerly towards establishing television networks that were for the most part largely under political control. In both France and Germany, television remained part of the political structure until the end of the twentieth century.

Its enormous popularity was, for many in government, its most alarming feature. Between 1951 and 1958 the number of television licences issued to British homes rose from 750,000 to 9 million. Such immense influence, ran the argument, required disciplines that only 'the great and the good' could provide. In 1962 a report commissioned by the British government said that it had looked at the growth of television to see what effect it would have 'on the character of society' with an eye to ensuring that the medium's potential was used 'to give people the chance of enlarging worthwhile experience'. The word 'worthwhile' said it all.

The British determination to make television 'worthwhile' was driven to a large extent by concerns that certain American programmes, particularly westerns and crime series, were becoming too popular with viewers in the United Kingdom. The reason for this was that television in the United States had been built on completely different foundations from those in Europe. As soon as it began it was left in the hands, as cinema was before it, of commercial expertise. The powerful Hollywood Studios were joined by new, equally powerful national television networks, funded entirely by advertising and putting the popularity of their programmes before everything else. These new arrivals had their roots in radio and possessed unerring judgment about what was meant by 'mass entertainment'. Quiz shows, situation comedies and dramas were pumped into people's homes. The networks began to form alliances with the studios which began to allow their old films to be shown on television and also used Hollywood expertise to make their television dramas and comedies. The high production values of the cinema began to appear on the small screen. Television companies like CBS (the Columbia Broadcasting System), NBC (the National Broadcasting Company) and ABC (the American Broadcasting Company) dominated the daily lives of millions of Americans. In the 1960s they moved into the area of politics when they staged a series of presidential debates between Richard Nixon and John F. Kennedy. Nixon was the front-runner. He had served for eight years as vice-President to the popular Dwight D. Eisenhower and with this experience behind him seemed to tower over his rival. But the television cameras preferred a youthful Kennedy to an old (and sometimes perspiring) Nixon and this contributed enormously to his ultimate victory. In 1980 the American networks were joined by a rival that many thought could never succeed – CNN. The Cable News Network was devoted entirely to covering news events, bringing them live to the screen wherever possible. In 1991 it followed the First Gulf War when America and its European allies drove Iraq out of the occupation of Kuwait. War became a live television event.

In February 1941 the American publisher, Henry Luce, wrote an article for *Life* magazine in which he described the twentieth century as 'The American Century'. America, he said, was 'the Good Samaritan, really believing again that it is more blessed to give than to receive'. Its economic power, combined with its ideals of freedom, would bring international benefits to the world. Among these were 'movie men' and 'makers of entertainment'. Luce's self-confident American vision made uncomfortable reading for many people and his article has often since been derided. But he was accurate in his description of the colossal strength of the United States in the middle of the twentieth century – a strength that was bound to exert great influence over the rest of the world. At the end of the First World War in 1918 the American President, Woodrow Wilson, had failed to sell his concept of a League of Nations to his own people. The Senate refused to accept American membership of an international organisation joining together to safeguard world peace. But once the world was engulfed in a Second World War, attitudes changed. The United States was finally ready to take on an international role. Its attention was mainly concentrated on its economic, military and political involvement, but Henry Luce's movie men and makers of entertainment also played a leading part. They supported America's more overt activities, providing an image of a life to which poorer nations eagerly aspired.

Today, the worldwide influence of television is for the most part an American phenomenon. Once it was let loose to grow commercially it was unstoppable. Unrestrained by the niceties of cultural regulation it operated mainly on the basis of giving people what they wanted. Not everything it did was simply populist, but most of it was, and it provided the networks with the

Soap Operas

Soap operas derive their name from pre-war radio serials in America which were sponsored by soap manufacturers. They told vivid stories about family life and personal relationships and always included sudden plot twists and last-minute revelations leaving each episode on a cliffhanger. The first soap was *Clara, Lu, and Em*, which began broadcasting in 1930 and was sponsored by Colgate-Palmolive. Radio soap operas thrived in the 1930s and 40s, before making the transition to television in the 1950s. The longest running soap, the American drama *Guiding Light*, started as a radio drama in 1937 and was seen or heard nearly every weekday until it was cancelled in 2009.

British and Australian soaps tend to be rather different from their counterparts around the world. *EastEnders*, *Coronation Street* and *Neighbours* like to portray life as naturalistic and unglamorous and draw their characters from working-class communities. They are shown at primetime and are (in theory at least) indefinite. In other parts of the world *telenovelas*, with their melodramatic, simple plots, have become extremely popular – and can prove influential too. In Brazil the role models provided by the independent-minded women of the dramas produced by the television station, Globo, have, according to research by an international bank, contributed to the national reduction in the birth rate, from an average of 6.3 children per woman in 1960 to 1.8 in 2006. In 2008 the Turkish soap *Noor* was shown across the Muslim world, challenging taboos such as gender equality, pre-marital sex and abortion. A record 85 million viewers tuned into the final episode but the religious authorities, including the Saudi Grand Mufti, issued a fatwa against it.

wealth and strength to sell their programmes abroad. On the whole this was one-way traffic: America exported its television and the rest of the world imported it; there was virtually no trade the other way round. While the programmes produced by national broadcasting systems remained very popular in their own countries, they rarely succeeded in finding an extensive market elsewhere. The BBC, which enjoyed a reputation as a reliable producer of quality, had some success, particularly in the area of documentary and natural history programmes, but global television was, and remains, essentially an American business. There is a view that the expansion of the economies of Asia may mean that the American century is coming to an end, but we should be cautious before making predictions of this kind. A quick look at this week's television schedules in Britain reveals that a programme from the NBC network is 'pick of the week', a film from the Paramount studio is 'film of the week', that most other movies to be seen for the next seven days come from Hollywoood, and that one whole channel belonging to the British broadcaster 'Five' is devoted to American shows. We may or may not live in an American century any more, but on television it is still very much an American week.

CHAPTER 8

The Discovery of the Structure of the DNA Helix

1953

In 1953 two British scientists, James Watson and Francis Crick, discovered the structure of the DNA helix, the molecule that contains genetic information and passes it from one generation to another. It was the most important biological discovery of the twentieth century.

In 1843 a young man called Gregor Mendel entered the monastery of St Thomas in Old Brno in what is today the Czech Republic. He was from a local peasant family. Career opportunities for a twenty-one-year-old like him were limited and a life in the Church offered not only security but possibilities for study and research. He started as a novice, was ordained priest in 1847 and then attended the University of Vienna. Between 1854 to the time he became Abbott in 1868 he carried out a series of experiments on plants in the monastery garden. These fourteen years were some of the most significant in the history of science. Using pea plants he studied the nature of heredity, trying to determine the factors that passed characteristics from one generation of the same species to the next. By cross-fertilising the plants, and analysing the different colours of flower they produced, he established two basic principles. Firstly he said that the factors which determine the characteristics to be passed from one generation to the next are separate and inherited randomly. This was his 'Law of Segregation'. Secondly he said that inherited traits are derived from the previous generation independently from one another. This was his 'Law of Independent Assortment'. Hidden within these two laws was the basis of modern genetics, a term that Mendel did not use. He was simply interested in the nature of heredity.

In the middle of the nineteenth century a whole new branch of science was beginning to develop, strongly influenced by the work of Charles Darwin whose *On the Origin of Species* had appeared in 1859. Darwin's theory of evolution assumed that one generation inherited its characteristics from another through a blending process; children were a mixture of their parents' features. Mendel demonstrated that these features came from individual roots by chance depending on the strength of the factor that transmitted them in the first place. In any individual's particular trait there were two 'factors', one from each parent. A factor (called an allele, one variant of a gene) could be either 'dominant' or 'recessive'. A dominant factor (say for a red flower) will hide a recessive factor (say for a white flower) making the flower in question appear red, even though it has inherited the genetic coding for a white flower from one of its parents. The way in which inherited features blend together therefore depends on distinct types.

He delivered his findings in a paper that he read to Brno's Natural History Society in 1865, and it was published a year later. After that it was largely ignored, until in 1900, two botanists, a German called Carl Correns, and a Dutchman, Hugo de Vries, both independently started to come to the same conclusions as Mendel and included his findings in their published research. They realised that when an organism produces a sperm or an egg, the resulting sperm or egg contains half the genetic material of a full cell. This in turn is a random combination of genetic material inherited from that organism's parents and is made up of recessive and dominant factors. Mendel's findings have always been controversial. Some scientists today believe that his results were too good to be true – even if he drew the right conclusions from them. We may never know the truth. Mendel's papers were destroyed at some point, perhaps by himself. He stopped all his research during the last years of his life as he became embroiled in the opposition to the special tax imposed on religious houses by the Austrian imperial authorities. Mendel resisted the plan strongly and by the time of his death was the last abbot in the Empire still doing so. The government eventually repealed the tax but only after its money-raising idea had imposed a final curfew on a rare and important piece of scientific exploration.

The publication of Darwin's book gave rise to a burst of interest in the biological principles of heredity and their power over the development of man. In 1869, Francis Galton, a distant relation of Darwin's, published a book called *Hereditary Genius* in which he explored the scientific basis of human intellectual and moral ability. In 1883 he invented the term 'eugenics' to describe the idea of using scientific knowledge about heredity to improve human behaviour by improving the gene pool. Galton wanted to define the characteristics that were bred through *There was a darker side to this new science.* 'nature', and those that were the result of 'nurture', in other words the effects of the environment in which people were brought up. He hoped it would be possible to selectively breed clever people and proposed that couples with the right qualifications should be given incentives to have children. Eugenics became a fashionable philosophy.

There was a darker side to this new science. In Britain the writer H. G. Wells, who had started life as a convinced Christian but abandoned his faith in the face of the onward march of Darwinism, became one of its strongest supporters. In 1902 he published a book called *Anticipations of the Reaction of Mechanical and Scientific Progress upon Human Life and Thought*. In one chapter he looked at how science might influence faith, morals and public policy. 'The ethical system which will dominate the world state,' he said, 'will be shaped primarily to favour the procreation of what is fine and efficient and beautiful in humanity – beautiful and strong bodies, clear and powerful minds, and a growing body of knowledge – and to check the procreation of base and servile types, of fear-driven and cowardly souls, of all that is mean and ugly and bestial in the souls, bodies, or habits of men.' He anticipated, he went on, that in this new world the small minority of people afflicted with transmissible diseases or mental disorders would only be tolerated on the grounds that they did not breed. 'I do not foresee any reason to suppose that they will hesitate to kill when that sufferance is abused.'

Wells imagined that as religion weakened, science would take its place, building its own ethical structures out of its power to shape the destiny of man. It was a vision closer to reality than he may have realised. In 1907 the State of Indiana in America passed a compulsory sterilisation law under which people defined as 'confirmed criminals', 'idiots', 'imbeciles' or 'rapists' were given operations to prevent them from having children. In the two years the law was enforced – it was scrapped by the governor who took office in 1909 – nearly 2,500 men and women were forcibly sterilised, most of them from an institution called the 'State School for Feeble-Minded Youth'. The sterilisations – vasectomies for men, tubal ligations for women – still allowed the victims to participate in society but without the ability to pass on the degenerate germplasm the scientists believed they carried.

H. G. Wells softened his stance on eugenics as the twentieth century advanced. He was aware that in the wrong hands it could be reduced to nothing better than totalitarian murder. Science meanwhile continued to probe the mysteries of heredity. Mendel's laws and Darwin's theory of evolution ran on parallel tracks, with some scientists preferring the monk's principles of heredity to the other's idea of natural selection. In the 1920s an American embryologist, Thomas Hunt Morgan, discovered the importance of the role of the gene. *Today DNA is used to identify the activities of human beings everywhere.* Through studying the fruit fly – he chose it because of its short lifecycle and because it was inexpensive to keep – he was able to demonstrate that genes are the physical basis for heredity and are carried by chromosomes. But it was an Englishman, Ronald Fisher, who brought the two branches of genetic science together. In 1930 he published *The Genetical Theory of Natural Selection*, a book he dedicated to Charles Darwin's son, Leonard, and in which he proved that Mendel's ideas were not only mathematically compatible with the theory of natural selection, but were its vital missing piece. Fisher applied mathematical and statistical concepts to ideas of evolution. Mendel had demonstrated how heredity was passed from generation to generation within individual species; Darwin had proposed something more general – that all life on earth was subject to a process of natural selection. Fisher took Mendel's laws and examined how they would affect populations as a whole. Crucially he demonstrated that larger populations had a better a chance of survival because they carried more genetic variation. This meant, in very broad terms, that Darwin's natural selection took place through the process of heredity that Mendel had identified: the science of genetics had been given a unified approach.

The importance of DNA – deoxyribonucleic acid – emerged in 1944 when an American, Oswald Avery, discovered that this was the substance from which genes and chromosomes were made. His work completed a cycle of research that stretched back to the nineteenth century when a Swiss biologist, Friedrich Miescher, published findings which identified chemicals that he called *nuclein* in white blood cells. What Miescher had found was in fact DNA, the molecules that Avery, working seventy-five years later, proved to be the carriers of genetic information. The pieces were now all in place. The principles of heredity were understood; genes and chromosomes had been proved to be the carriers of biological information from one generation to another; and DNA had been identified as the molecule from which these genes and chromosomes were made. One question was left: how did DNA work? The answer to that lay in its structure.

In 1951 an American biologist, James Watson, joined forces with an English physicist, Francis Crick, to see if they could establish how DNA did its extraordinary work. They were building on the discoveries of others and already knew that a DNA molecule was made up of four different bases stacked on top of each other in a helical structure – a bit like a coiled spring or a spiral staircase. In January 1953, Watson was shown an X-Ray diffraction photograph of a DNA crystal taken by a fellow scientist, Rosalind Franklin. 'The instant I saw the picture,' he wrote later, 'my mouth fell open and my pulse began to race.' The photograph revealed a fuzzy X shape in the middle of the molecule and convinced Watson that its structure had to be in the shape of a double helix – two congruent helical shapes with the same axis. Together he and Crick began to build a stick and ball model of how it might hold together. At first the two scientists could not get it to work but they eventually realised that the bases always joined up in the same pairs. Their final model stood more than six feet high, but they were sure that it contained the secrets of life's continuity. They published their findings in the British journal *Nature*, remarking, with elegant restraint, that their structure 'has novel features of considerable biological interest'. They added: 'It has not escaped our notice that the specific pairing we have postulated immediately suggests a possible copying mechanism for the genetic material.' With this reserved announcement scientific history was made. Watson and Crick had revealed how genetic material passes from one generation to another. They had broken the code of DNA, the molecule of heredity and the engine of evolution.

'The instant I saw the picture my mouth fell open and my pulse began to race.'

The history of genetics and the discovery of DNA is one of the most absorbing in all science. It spanned a century, beginning with the momentous, well-publicised findings of Charles Darwin and the hidden researches of Gregor Mendel. It involved the work, not only of scientists, but of philosophers and writers from all over the world during the second half of the nineteenth century and the first half of the twentieth. It embraced all of human life before finishing in the laboratory of a great university in 1953. Except, of course, that it has not finished. Today DNA is used to identify the activities of human beings everywhere. The unique structure of their eyes and their fingerprints are used to track their movements; particles from other parts of their bodies can be stored as evidence

The history of the discovery of DNA is one of the most absorbing in all science.

of their whereabouts and used in criminal trials. Information relating to every living person's characteristics is now available to anyone with the ability to know where to look. Man's increasing knowledge of his own biology is both his friend and his enemy. It is being used, as H. G. Wells predicted, to shape the future of his race.

CHAPTER 9

Apollo 11 Lands on the Moon 1969

On 20th July 1969 two American astronauts, Neil Armstrong and Buzz Aldrin, became the first human beings to walk on the surface of the moon. Watched on television by millions of people all over the world, Armstrong said as he left his spacecraft: 'That's one small step for man, one giant leap for mankind.'

The moon has always fascinated us. In early times it was a subject of fantasy, unknown but visible, a celestial body around which writers could invent stories peopled by imaginary creatures of all shapes and sizes. Later it became a useful place for creating contrasts, good and bad, with the earth, a distant mirror of happiness or despair. One of the first writers to refer to the moon was a Greek, Lucian of Samosata, living in the Roman Empire during the second century AD. In *The True History* he described how a ship and its crew were scooped up to the moon in a violent whirlwind where they experienced strange adventures. It was a series of fantastic lies concocted by Lucian purely to amuse his readers. 'Everything which I met with in the moon was new and extraordinary,' he wrote. He went on to describe how the people of the moon preferred baldness to hair; how their bodies had no livers or intestines but opened like doors to provide shelter for their children; and how their clothes were made of soft glass.

Ariosto's *Orlando Furioso*, an Italian epic poem of love and death published in 1532, contains a passage where an English knight flies to the moon to discover things that have been lost on earth. 'A place wherein is wonderfully stored/ Whatever on our earth below we lose./ Collected there are all things whatso'er/ Lost through time, chance, or our own folly, here.' What is probably the world's first work of proper science fiction, however, was written, appropriately enough, by a scientist. In 1634, four years after his death, a work called *Somnium* – Latin for 'The Dream' – by the German astronomer and mathematician, Johannes Kepler, was published by his son. Kepler was part of the radical scientific community of the seventeenth century who understood, like Galileo, that the earth moved round the sun. In his story a mother and son are transported to the moon by a supernatural spirit, but Kepler adds information about their journey which demonstrates his understanding of planetary activity. The travellers are put to sleep to help them survive the anti-gravitational force of their journey; they experience something rather similar to the weightlessness of later astronauts; and they are shielded from the full force of solar power.

But the growth of scientific knowledge encouraged writers to use the moon and other planets as a warning to mankind, rather than a cause of celebration. In a story called *Micromégas*, published in 1752, the French writer Voltaire used a conversation between creatures from distant planets to reflect on the fragility of human existence. Monsieur Micromégas is from the star Sirius. 'We are always complaining about how short life is,' he tells a companion from Saturn. 'It must be one of the universal laws of nature.' To which his companion replies: 'We live for only five hundred complete revolutions of the sun ... As you can see, that means dying almost as soon as one is born.'

'We live for only five hundred complete revolutions of the sun.'

From the beginning of the nineteenth century, stories about moon adventures began to become very popular. In 1835, an American newspaper, *The New York Sun*, ran a series of hoax articles claiming that life had been discovered on the moon. Its stories of semi-human creatures with bat-like wings improved its circulation enormously. Later authors like Jules Verne and H. G. Wells enjoyed great success with their novels, which began to make a real landing on the moon sound like a distinct possibility. In *Around the Moon*, published in 1870, Verne described the lunar atmosphere. 'Without an instant's warning the temperature falls from 212 degrees Fahrenheit to the icy winter of interstellar space. The surface is all dazzling glare or pitchy gloom.' By the middle of the twentieth century, fiction drew even closer to reality. In 1952 the American magazine, *Collier's*, ran a series of illustrated articles about the possibility of manned space flight entitled 'Man Will Conquer Space Soon'. One of the authors was Wernher von Braun, the German engineer who had designed the V2 rocket for the Nazis in the Second World War and who, in a secret operation, had been taken to America with his design team once the war was over. The articles, accompanied by detailed illustrations, bore a strong resemblance to what man's eventual journey into space would look like.

Man can only leave the earth's gravity with the aid of a rocket. Rocket technology developed out of cannon and gunpowder, but although devices grew more sophisticated they did not have the necessary power to propel themselves into space until the first half of the twentieth century. On a bitterly cold day in March 1926, an American engineer, Robert Goddard, launched a rocket from a farm in Massachusetts that was propelled by liquid fuel, a mixture of liquid oxygen and petrol. It rose 41 feet, flew for two and a half seconds, and travelled a distance of 184 feet before landing in a cabbage patch. It proved that liquid fuels could work. With private funding from the Guggenheim family, Goddard went on to develop bigger rockets from a base in Roswell, New Mexico, but none of them reached a height of more than 9,000 feet, lower than the height at which passenger jets fly.

The space race became a natural accompaniment to the arms race.

It had been the urge to build weapons during the Second World War that brought crucial advances to rocket technology. The German V2 rocket could send warheads a distance of 170 miles using liquid oxygen and alcohol for fuel. The detonation of the atom bombs over Hiroshima and Nagasaki drove the USSR and America into competing for the most effective method of unleashing nuclear weapons on one another. The space race became a natural accompaniment to the arms race: the potential destruction of the earth went hand in hand with the possible conquest of the universe. To many people's surprise, the Russians drew ahead, launching the first man-made satellite to orbit Earth, *Sputnik 1*, in 1957. The following year the Americans successfully launched their version, *Explorer*. They also formed the National Aeronautics and Space Administration (NASA). The two nations then leap-frogged into space. In April 1961, a Russian cosmonaut, Yuri Gagarin, became the first man to orbit earth. During his re-entry his spacecraft did not completely separate from the equipment module and parts of it caught fire. Gagarin was forced to eject and landed separately from his vehicle, although at the time the Russians insisted that they had finished the journey together. His flight lasted 108 minutes. In February 1962, an American, John Glenn, followed where Gagarin had led.

The American President, John F. Kennedy, told the United States Congress in 1961 that he believed that America should commit itself before the end of the decade to the goal 'of landing a man on the moon and returning him safely to earth'. A moon landing fitted his aspirations for his nation. As the Cold War intensified he felt that beating the Russians to the moon would help secure America's position as leader of the free world. In a speech a year later he expanded on this theme. 'Space science, like nuclear science and all technology, has no conscience of its own. Whether it becomes a force for good or ill depends on man, and only if the United States occupies a position of pre-eminence can we decide whether this new ocean will be a sea of peace or a new terrifying theatre of war.' NASA, plentifully funded in order to fulfil this lunar dream, began to develop plans. The mission's spacecraft would have two components: a command module and a landing vehicle. While the command module stayed in orbit around the moon, the landing vehicle, or lunar module, would descend to the surface. The astronauts inside would take a walk and then travel in their vehicle back to the command module for the return journey to earth. To prepare for this historic event,

Beating the Russians to the moon would help secure America's position as leader of the free world.

NASA sent a series of unmanned spacecraft to take samples of the moon's soil while others took photographs and mapped its entire surface. It did not have the field to itself. The Russians also carried out a series of successful space missions. In 1965, Alexei Leonov became the first human being to carry out a space walk. From the end of a tether nearly six yards long he spent twelve minutes floating separately from the craft that had carried him into orbit. But the Russians did not have the money and resources to match NASA's efforts, and the Americans drew ahead. In July 1969 two of its astronauts, Neil Armstrong and Buzz Aldrin, landed safely on the surface of the moon. Man had conquered space.

It is sometimes hard to believe that the achievement of one of mankind's greatest ambitions, his 'giant leap', took place more than forty years ago. Journeys of exploration are expensive. The Portuguese, Spanish and Dutch knew this when they began to open up the world in which they lived in the sixteenth century. They saw immediate returns for their efforts and rapidly accumulated both treasure and territory. Four hundred years later the material advantages of space exploration were not so clear. Not least, the cost of building spacecraft that were destroyed as soon as their journeys were over proved an unsustainable financial burden. To overcome these difficulties NASA introduced the space shuttle – a manned transport system that allowed crews to orbit in space on observational missions while their craft returned to earth in one piece. The end of the Cold War at the end of the 1980s replaced competition with collaboration between the United States and Russia. Since Neil Armstrong uttered his famous phrase innumerable exploratory missions have recorded information about life in space and what man might need to exist in it. The Hubble Space Telescope, launched in 1990 as a collaboration between NASA and the European Space Agency, has made a number of discoveries about planets and stars, most of which lie beyond earth's solar system. Recently the American government turned its attention to exploration beyond the moon. In a speech at NASA's headquarters in April 2010, President Barack Obama said that he believed that further voyages to the moon were not a priority. By the mid-2030s he wanted to see

NASA carry out an expedition to Mars, in which a human would orbit and land on the planet and return safely from it.

For man, space remains a vast laboratory rather than a tempting destination. He will continue to explore it and extend his knowledge of what it contains. But he will also question what value lies in the cost of constant journeys into space. There are many aspects of human life that have derived benefits from them – in medicine, manufacturing and everyday technology. But the great prize, of the kind that once drove men to the unknown places of their own planet, remains elusive. In his speech, President Obama said that the moon landing of forty years ago 'was one of the greatest achievements in human history'. He added: 'And the question for us now is whether that was the beginning of something or the end of something.' He chose, he said, to believe that it was the only beginning – and it is hard to imagine that such an enormous achievement has not laid the foundations of something enormous for the future. The question is: what will that be?

CHAPTER 10

The Creation of the Worldwide Web

1990

In 1990 a British scientist called Tim Berners-Lee built a worldwide web, a network of computer links capable of providing access to information available anywhere in the world.

In 1867 the British author Anthony Trollope resigned from his position with the Post Office. He had worked there for thirty-three years, a period during which, as he said in his auto-biography, he had given more attention to his organisational duties than he had his literary efforts. He had been concerned to ensure: 'That the public in little villages should be enabled to buy postage stamps; that they should have their letters delivered free and at an early hour; that pillar letter boxes should be put up for them ...'. He had also taken great pleasure in writing his official reports, hoping that he had made them pleasant to read and allowing them to leave his desk with 'their original blots and erasures'. Trollope believed that a person's handwriting formed an essential part of his ability to communicate: 'the writer of a letter, if he wishes his words to prevail with the reader, should send them out as written by himself, by his own hand, with his own marks, his own punctuation, correct or incorrect, with the evidence upon them that they have come out of his own mind'.

Trollope's office was situated in the headquarters of the General Post Office in St Martin's le Grand in the City of London, a neo-classical building completed in 1829, the magnificent centre of a postal system that fed the nation its daily supply of precious mail through a network of fast horse-drawn coaches.

Three years after Anthony Trollope's resignation in 1870, it began a telegraph service. In 1912 it introduced the national telephone system. As the twentieth century advanced it became increasingly sophisticated, reaching homes by every possible means from bicycle to van and train. In 1936 the Post Office's film unit produced a documentary about the night-mail train from London to Scotland. A poem by W. H. Auden was used for its commentary:

> *Letters of thanks, letters from banks,*
> *Letters of joy from girl and boy,*
> *Receipted bills and invitations,*
> *To inspect new stock or to visit relations,*
> *And applications for situations*
> *And timid lovers' declarations,*
> *And gossip, gossip, from all the nations,*
> *News circumstantial, news financial,*
> *Letters with holiday snaps to enlarge in,*
> *Letters with faces scrawled on the margin,*
> *Letters from uncles, cousins and aunts,*
> *Letters to Scotland from the South of France ...*

With a beat that changed rhythm to match the varying speed of a steam train Auden's poem celebrated an essential piece of British life. I can remember watching the film, *Night Mail*, and hearing the poem when I was at school, and it seemed to me to represent perfectly a part of the world in which I lived. It was the modern manifestation of the organisation that Anthony Trollope had dutifully worked to create, in which handwriting and letters, the arrival of the morning post and the pile of paper in the office in-tray were the physical features of human communication. Today that world has not entirely disappeared, but it is receding fast. The Royal Mail, once the proud backbone of a connected country, is struggling to compete against email and all other forms of virtual communication. We no longer write but go online, encouraged to do so by institutions that find it easier and cheaper to deal with us through a computer screen than by post. Trollope's smudged letters and Auden's night mail are pieces of history, whisked away from us with terrifying speed by the internet. We have willingly surrendered to the embrace of the worldwide web.

The internet grew out of military needs. Up until the early 1960s communication between two points was achieved through a method known as 'circuit switching' where a single link was used to make a connection between different terminals, and remained completely occupied during the process of communication. This was the basis of the telephone system and all other methods of data transmission. In 1969 a division of the United States' Defence Department developed a communications system called 'packet switching' that allowed data to be transmitted from one computer terminal to several others along a single link. Called ARPANET (after the Advanced Research Projects Agency that developed it) it built a network connecting four American universities. Other universities joined and as the system grew methods of standardisation – or 'protocols' – were introduced to ensure that the same information could be transmitted to differently designed computers. In 1971 it invented the email; by 1985 it had grown into the internet – a new technology that provided services to various communities of developers and researchers in military, governmental and academic positions. This group of users widened all the time. During the second half of the 1980s the number of hosts connected to the system grew to 200,000: computers became smaller and cheaper. But this growth, though rapid, was still confined. The invention that opened it to huge popular use came with three letters: www.

Tim Berners-Lee was working at the 'European Organisation for Nuclear Research' (CERN) when he came up with the idea for the worldwide web. Once the idea had been formulated it was built and developed, like many other aspects of the internet, with remarkable speed. Berners-Lee recognised that hypertext, a method of linking and accessing information of different kinds,

It became the one-click passport to an ever-unfolding world of data and information easily reached by anyone who wanted it.

Google

Google is proof of the human desire to search. Its search
engine processes over a billion requests every day, making it
the internet's most visited website. To 'Google' has become an
accepted verb in the English language, recognised in the Oxford
English Dictionary. Google was first created as a research
project in America by two Stanford University postgraduate
students in 1996. Larry Page and Sergey Brin invented a search
engine that was quite different from any others because it
ranked its results according to the number and importance of a
website's pages rather than by the number of times it used the
search words entered to find it. They named their system named
'Google', derived from the word *googol* which means the number
1 followed by 100 zeros. They said their mission was 'to organise
the world's information and make it universally accessible and
useful'. In this they have been remarkably successful.

could be used to build a web through which users could browse
at will to find what they wanted. In the proposal he prepared for
his colleagues at CERN he said: 'There is a potential large benefit
from the integration of a variety of systems in a way which allows
a user to follow links pointing from one piece of information
to another one.' History is often made by understatement. The
proposal continued: 'A programme which provides access to
the hypertext world we call a browser ... The texts are linked
together in a way that one can go from one concept to another
to find the information one wants. The network of links is
called a web ... a small number of links is usually sufficient for
getting from anywhere to anywhere else in a small number of
hops.' This simple explanation, accompanied by an undertaking
that the necessary work could be completed in six months and
arguing that it should be provided free to all users, turned the
internet from an important but quite small operation into a
global phenomenon. The web browser, or search engine, became
the agent of change, the one-click passport to an ever-unfolding
world of data and information easily reached by anyone who
wanted it. Barely twenty years ago none of this existed. Today

it is a staple of life all over the world, as necessary to human existence as the electric light or running water.

The power of the internet is an obvious feature of modern life. Online shopping is now commonplace, an increasingly important part of the developed world's economy. The downloading of books, music and video content is a normal activity for millions of people. The travel industry relies on the internet for booking hotels and transport. At the same time it gives rise to many different problems. Children can be lured into danger by unscrupulous people who use social messaging sites; valuable content can be stolen through file-sharing; and private information can be detected by sophisticated and intrusive technology. As much as the internet improves our lives, making them easier and providing us with education and information never previously available, so it damages them, introducing elements that we did not predict and some of which we regret. In this, of course, it is no different from other twentieth-century inventions such as the car or the aeroplane, both of which brought mankind huge benefits while at the same time causing problems never foreseen. But nevertheless the worldwide web has qualities that other inventions do not possess, and it is this that sets it apart.

The worldwide web provides individuals with route maps to a virtual world of their own choosing, taking them on journeys that are comparatively unregulated. They can go where they like, watch what they want and talk to whomever they meet. There are very few, if any, other inventions in the history of the world that have given them such freedom. Printing brought people intellectual liberty through the proliferation of books. But books can be censored or burned, and often were. The car brought them freedom of travel, but as its numbers increased so did the restrictions on driving them. Television brought entertainment into their homes, but only in a way that was controlled either by the broadcasters or by government authorities. The internet is entirely driven by its users and many of its

Very few inventions in the history of the world have given us such freedom.

most popular sites are created out of material devised and generated by them. All of this takes place in a 'virtual' world which
prevents physical travel and the sensation of touching or being
in the presence of other people. Everything else, however, can
be reached, seen or heard – people, places, voices and ideas. The
worldwide web is home to millions of human aspirations, from
political protest to scientific discovery. Nothing like this has
existed in the world before. Its pace of development has been
fast, and seems to increase its speed as it grows. It is impossible to predict how it will end, but it has already transformed
the lives of millions. Marshall McLuhan, who died in 1980,
well before the internet came of age, was a Canadian academic
who coined telling phrases about the media and the way people
communicate with one another. He referred in particular to the
'global village' in which the world began to share a similarity of
outlook and customs thanks to the influence of ubiquitous electronic communication. He had in mind the power of television,
but the worldwide web may prove to be a better example of what
he predicted.

In his autobiography Trollope told the story of how he first
entered the Post Office. In 1834 he applied to become a clerk and
as a test of his ability was asked to copy out some lines from *The
Times* with an old quill pen, 'and at once made a series of blots
and false spellings'. He was allowed to go home and practice and
'under the surveillance of my elder brother made a beautiful
transcript of four or five pages of Gibbon'. When he returned the
next day he was immediately found a seat and told to start work.
'Nobody,' he remarked ruefully, 'even condescended to look at my
beautiful *penmanship.*' Trollope's description of his entry into the
work of the Post Office is a gentle literary echo of a world that has
been completely obliterated by modern technology. He was about
to begin a career in the greatest communications organisation of
the most powerful nation in the world where an ability to wield
an old quill pen was considered a useful qualification. And so it
remained until well in to the twentieth century – even if the quill
was replaced by more efficient writing implements such as the
fountain pen and the biro. I learned handwriting at school more
than fifty years ago, splodging and blotting like a young Trollope;

but many children do not any more. The computer keyboard is today's writing tool of choice. This is a colossal change. As we enter the second decade of the twenty-first century one of the greatest influences on how our world develops will come from the fathomless virtual universe that sits behind the screens of our computers.

Index

Picture acknowledgements

Credits are by page number in order from left to right and top to bottom:

1 – Dinodia/The Bridgeman Art Library; The Stapleton Collection/The Bridgeman Art Library; 2 – Tang Chhin Sothy/AFP/Getty Images; Giraudon/The Bridgeman Art Library; 3 – The Bridgeman Art Library; APIC/Getty Images; 4 – The Bridgeman Art Library; 5 – The Bridgeman Art Library; Imagno/Getty Images; 6 – Archives Charmet/The Bridgeman Art Library; 7 – The Bridgeman Art Library; © DHM/The Bridgeman Art Library; 8 – De Agostini/Getty Images; 9 – The Bridgeman Art Library; Photo © Boltin Picture Library/The Bridgeman Art Library; 10 – Felice Beato/Getty Images; Archives Charmet/The Bridgeman Art Library; 11 – The Bridgeman Art Library; 12 – Henry Guttmann/Getty Images; Tomohiro Ohsumi/Bloomberg via Getty Images; 13 – SSPL via Getty Images; 14 – © ADAGP, Paris and DACS, London 2010/Giraudon/The Bridgeman Art Library; 15 – SSPL via Getty Images; Tom Stoddart/Getty Images; 16 – Trevor Samson/AFP/Getty Images; Kiyoshi Ota/Getty Images.